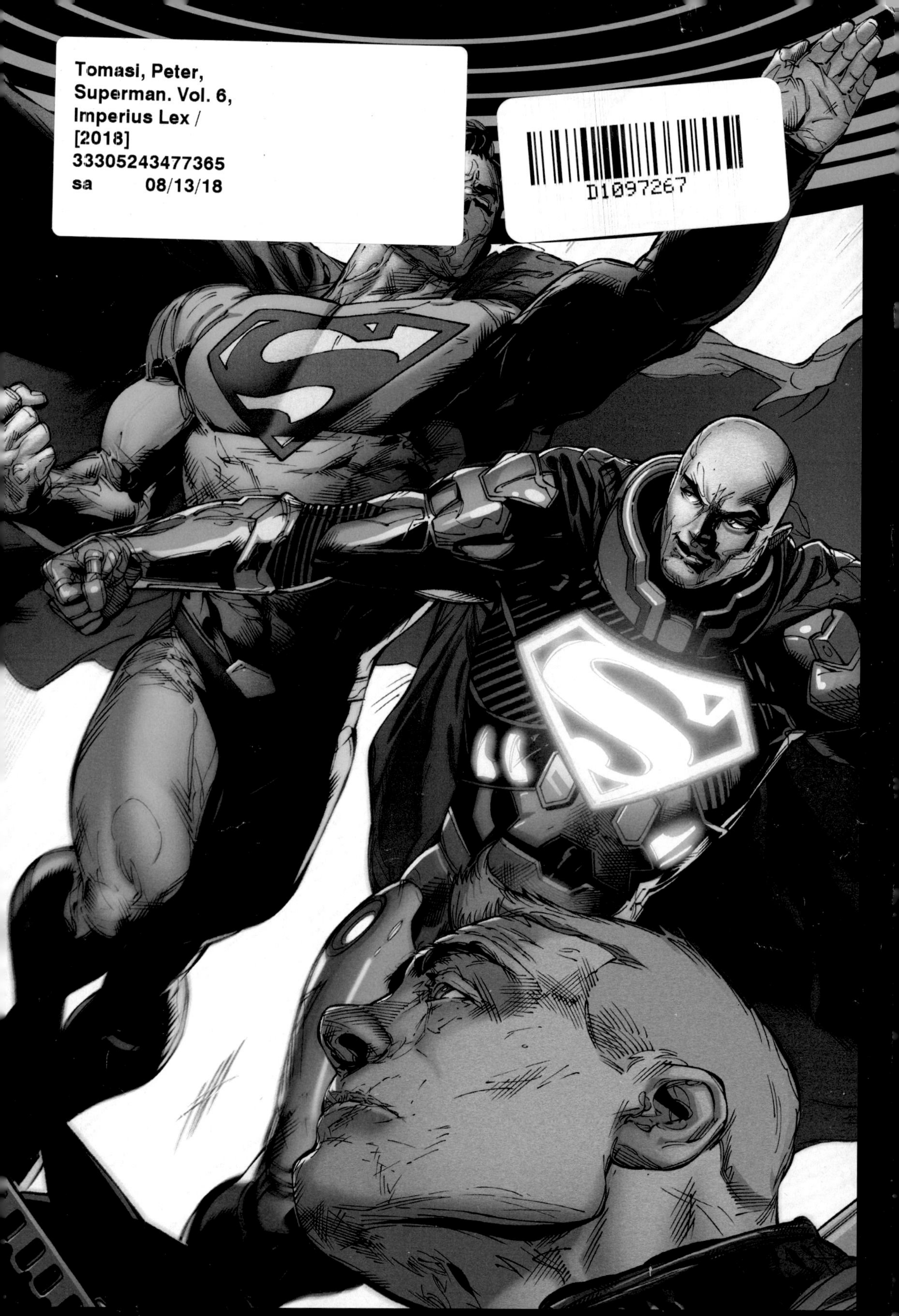

SUPERMAN
VOL.6 IMPERIUS LEX

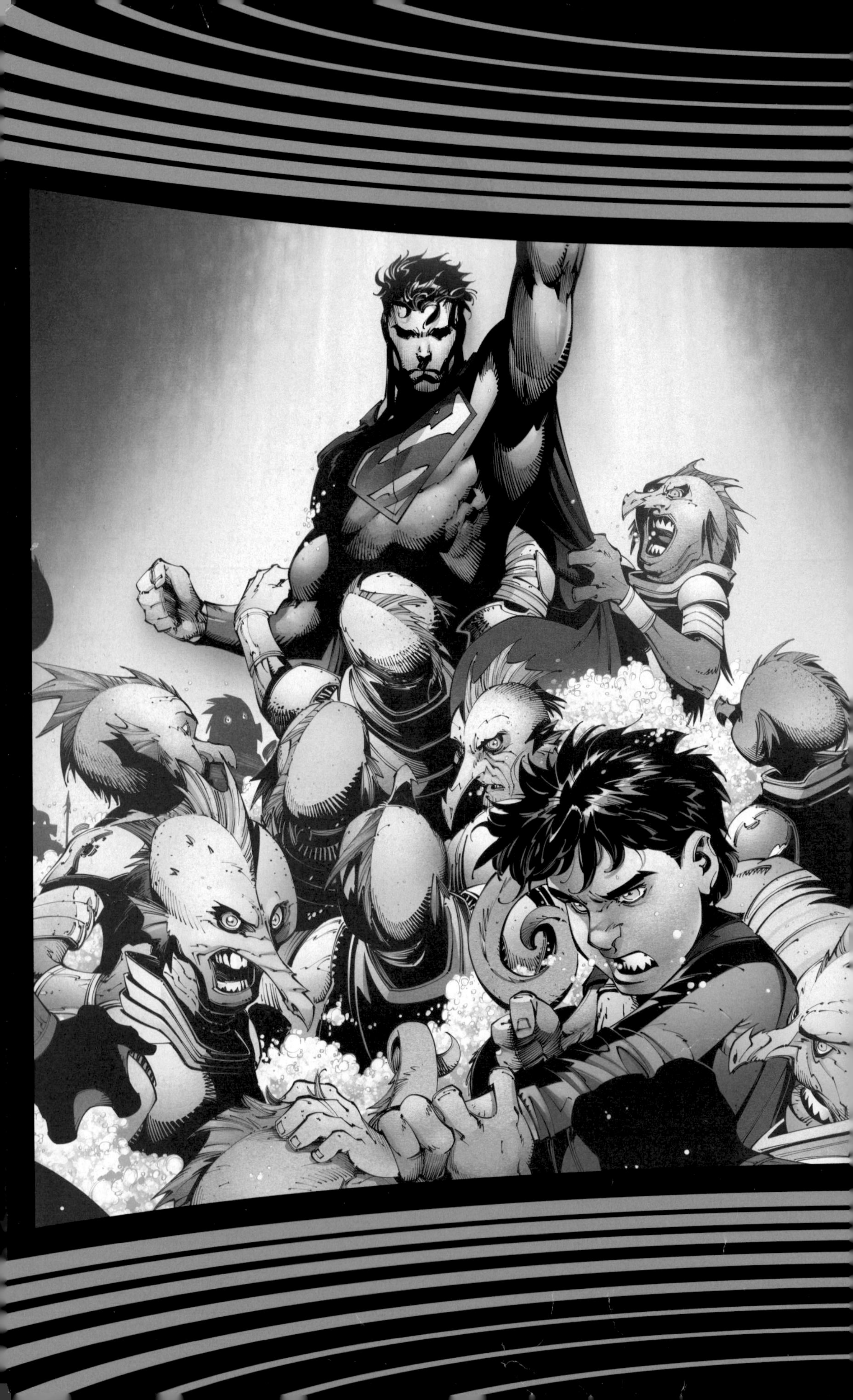

SUPERMAN
VOL.6 IMPERIUS LEX

PETER J. TOMASI * **PATRICK GLEASON** * **JAMES ROBINSON**
writers

DOUG MAHNKE * **JAIME MENDOZA** * **ED BENES**
JACK HERBERT * **TRAVIS MOORE** * **STEPHEN SEGOVIA**
ART THIBERT * **BARRY KITSON** * **SCOTT HANNA**
artists

WIL QUINTANA * **DINEI RIBEIRO** * **GABE ELTAEB**
colorists

ROB LEIGH
letterer

RYAN SOOK
collection cover artist

PATRICK GLEASON and **DEAN WHITE**
CHRIS BURNHAM and **NATHAN FAIRBAIRN**
VIKTOR BOGDANOVIC and **MIKE SPICER**
original series covers

SUPERMAN created by **JERRY SIEGEL** and **JOE SHUSTER**
SUPERBOY created by **JERRY SIEGEL**
By special arrangement with the Jerry Siegel family

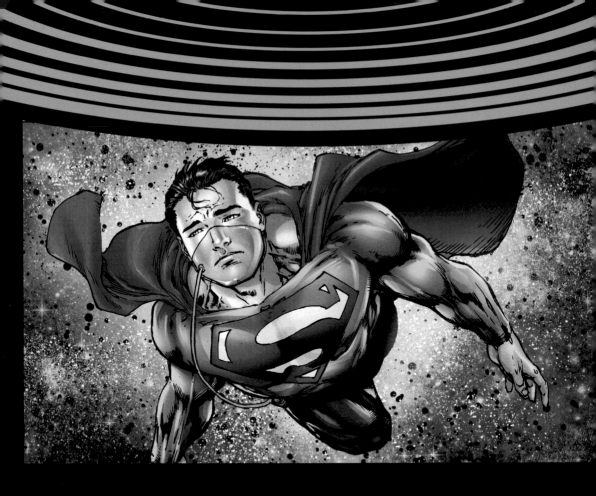

PAUL KAMINSKI EDDIE BERGANZA Editors - Original Series * **JESSICA CHEN** Associate Editor - Original Series
JEB WOODARD Group Editor - Collected Editions * **ROBIN WILDMAN** Editor - Collected Edition
STEVE COOK Design Director - Books * **MONIQUE NARBONETA** Publication Design

BOB HARRAS Senior VP - Editor-in-Chief, DC Comics
PAT McCALLUM Executive Editor, DC Comics

DIANE NELSON President * **DAN DiDIO** Publisher * **JIM LEE** Publisher * **GEOFF JOHNS** President & Chief Creative Officer
AMIT DESAI Executive VP - Business & Marketing Strategy, Direct to Consumer & Global Franchise Management
SAM ADES Senior VP & General Manager, Digital Services * **BOBBIE CHASE** VP & Executive Editor, Young Reader & Talent Development
MARK CHIARELLO Senior VP - Art, Design & Collected Editions * **JOHN CUNNINGHAM** Senior VP - Sales & Trade Marketing
ANNE DePIES Senior VP - Business Strategy, Finance & Administration * **DON FALLETTI** VP - Manufacturing Operations
LAWRENCE GANEM VP - Editorial Administration & Talent Relations * **ALISON GILL** Senior VP - Manufacturing & Operations
HANK KANALZ Senior VP - Editorial Strategy & Administration * **JAY KOGAN** VP - Legal Affairs * **JACK MAHAN** VP - Business Affairs
NICK J. NAPOLITANO VP - Manufacturing Administration * **EDDIE SCANNELL** VP - Consumer Marketing
COURTNEY SIMMONS Senior VP - Publicity & Communications * **JIM (SKI) SOKOLOWSKI** VP - Comic Book Specialty Sales & Trade Marketing
NANCY SPEARS VP - Mass, Book, Digital Sales & Trade Marketing * **MICHELE R. WELLS** VP - Content Strategy

SUPERMAN VOL. 6: IMPERIUS LEX

DC Comics, 2900 West Alameda Ave., Burbank, CA 91505
Printed by LSC Communications, Kendallville, IN, USA. 6/29/18. First Printing.
ISBN: 978-1-4012-8123-6

Library of Congress Cataloging-in-Publication Data is available.

PEFC Certified
Printed on paper from sustainably managed forests, controlled sources
PEFC
PEFC/29-31-337
www.pefc.org

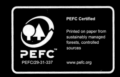

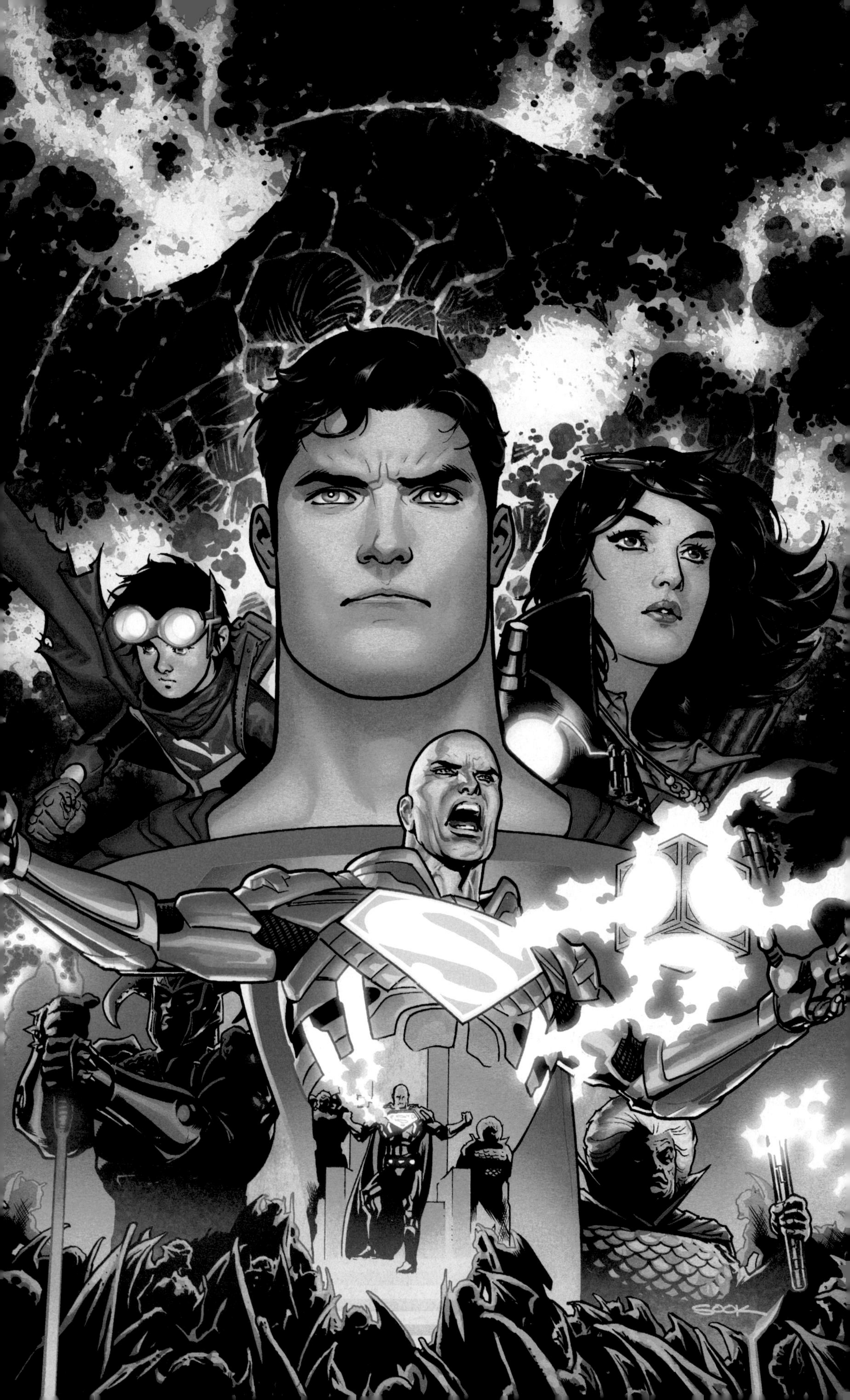

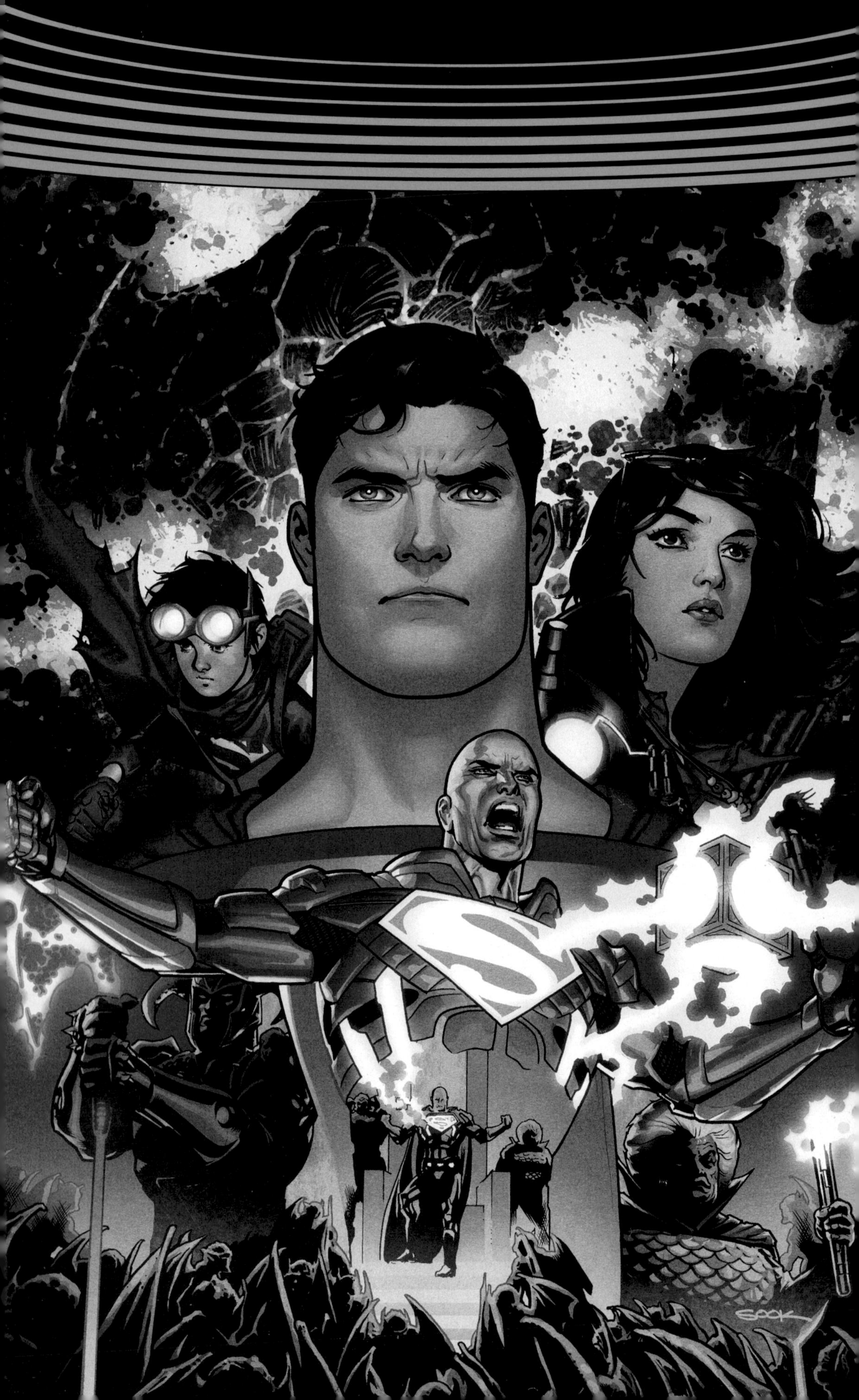
SOOK

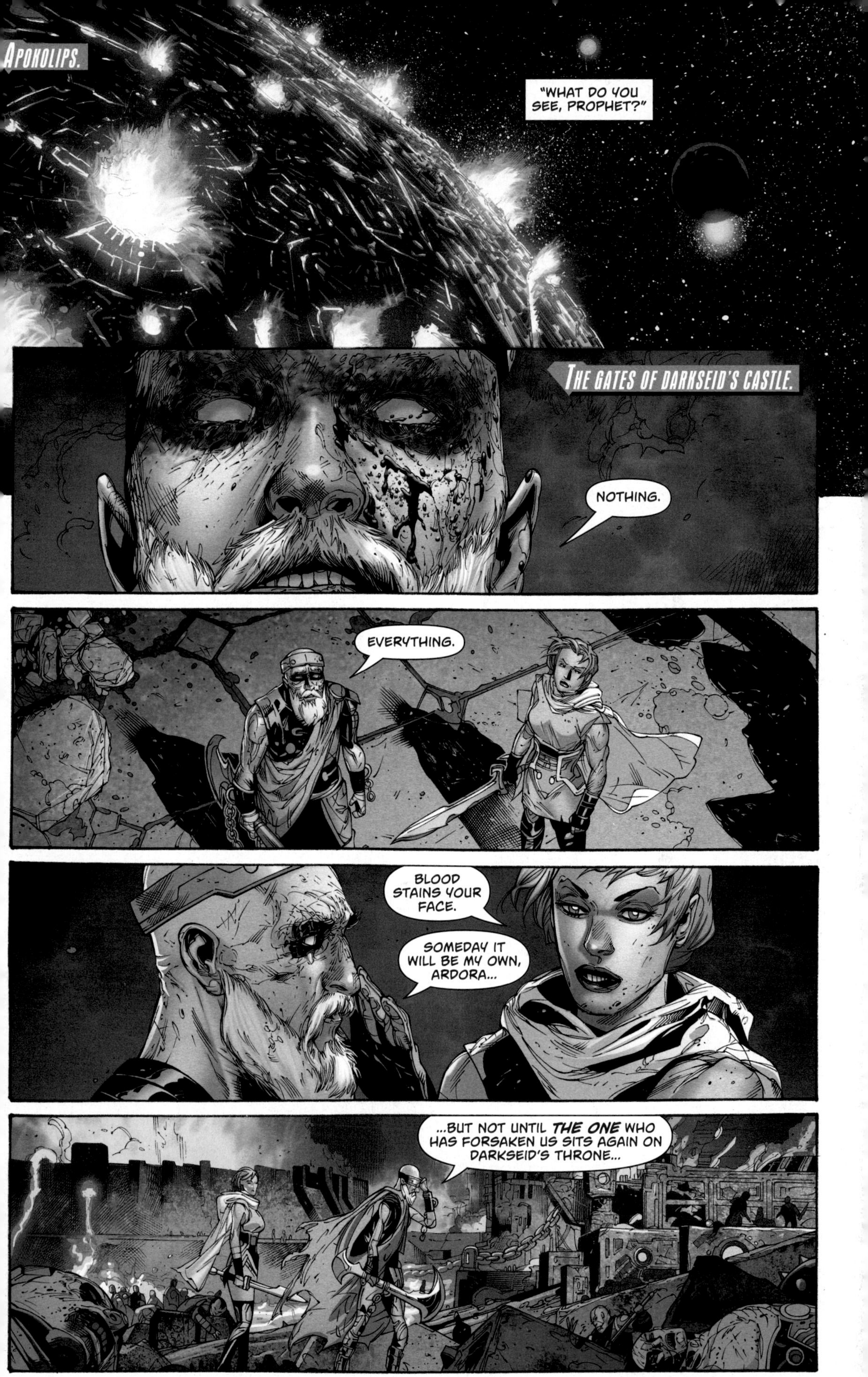
APOKOLIPS.
"WHAT DO YOU SEE, PROPHET?"
THE GATES OF DARKSEID'S CASTLE.
NOTHING.
EVERYTHING.
BLOOD STAINS YOUR FACE.
SOMEDAY IT WILL BE MY OWN, ARDORA...
...BUT NOT UNTIL *THE ONE* WHO HAS FORSAKEN US SITS AGAIN ON DARKSEID'S THRONE...

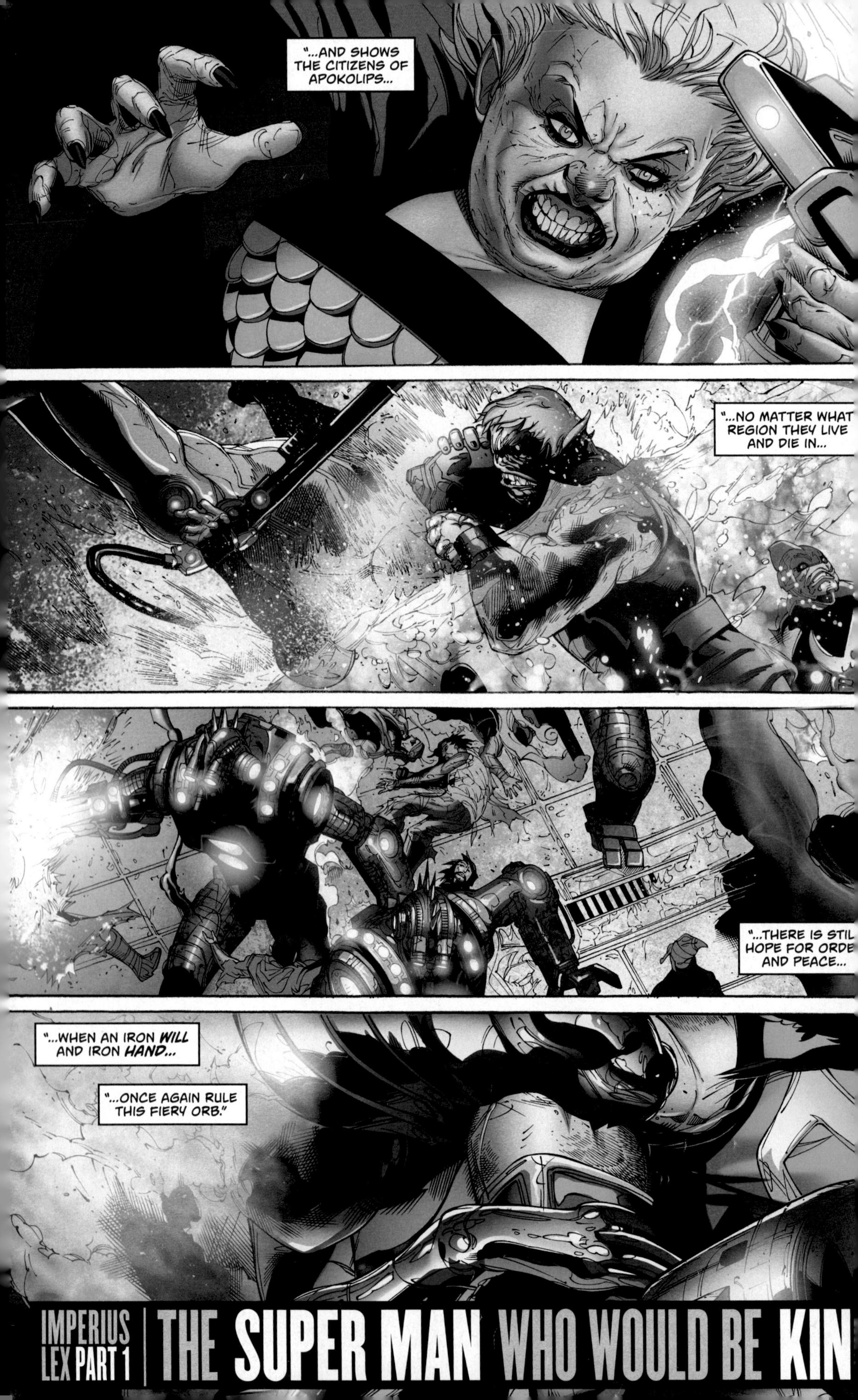
"...AND SHOWS THE CITIZENS OF APOKOLIPS...
"...NO MATTER WHAT REGION THEY LIVE AND DIE IN...
"...THERE IS STIL HOPE FOR ORDE AND PEACE...
"...WHEN AN IRON WILL AND IRON HAND...
"...ONCE AGAIN RULE THIS FIERY ORB."
IMPERIUS LEX PART 1
THE SUPER MAN WHO WOULD BE KIN

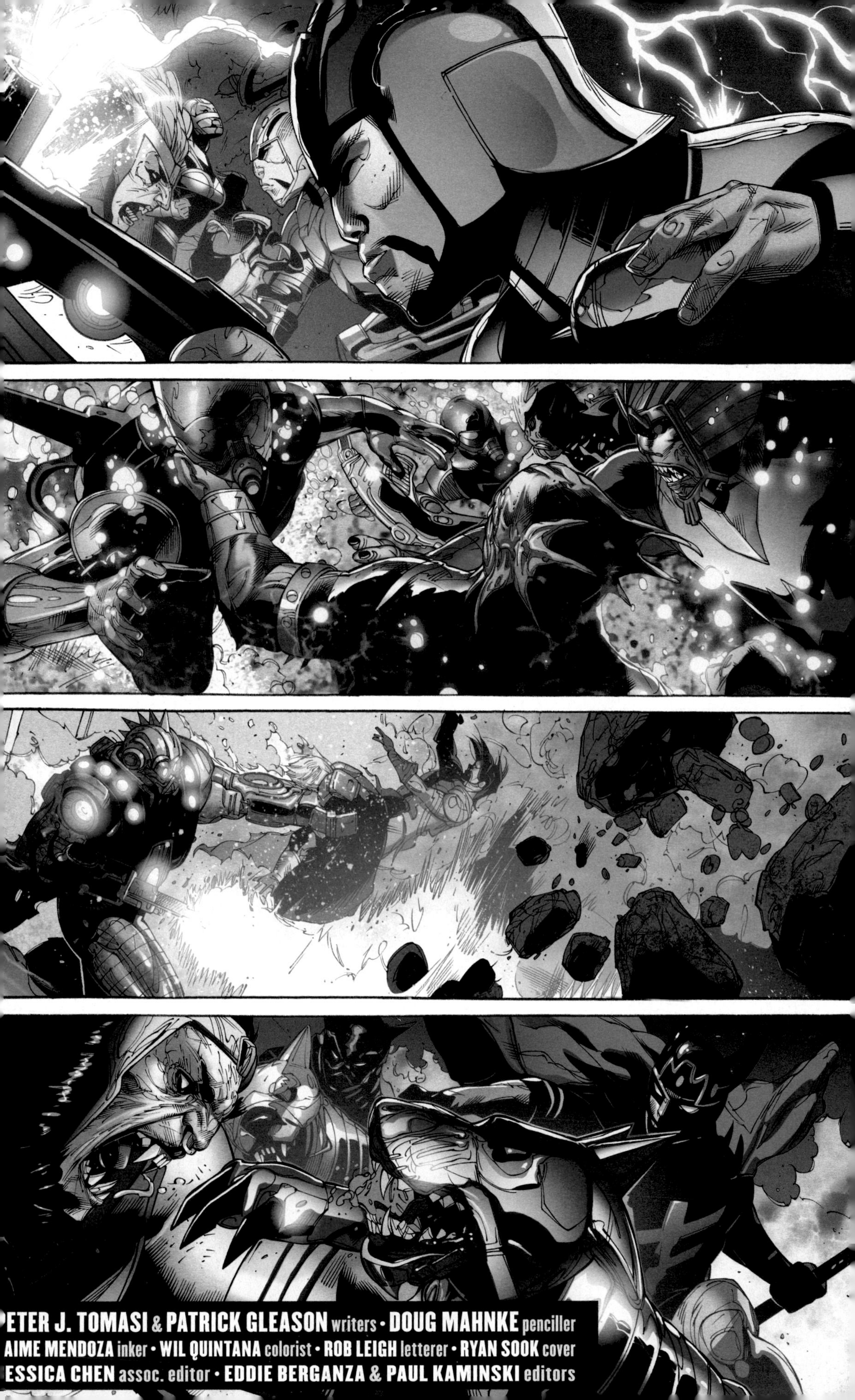

ETER J. TOMASI & PATRICK GLEASON writers • DOUG MAHNKE penciller
AIME MENDOZA inker • WIL QUINTANA colorist • ROB LEIGH letterer • RYAN SOOK cover
ESSICA CHEN assoc. editor • EDDIE BERGANZA & PAUL KAMINSKI editors

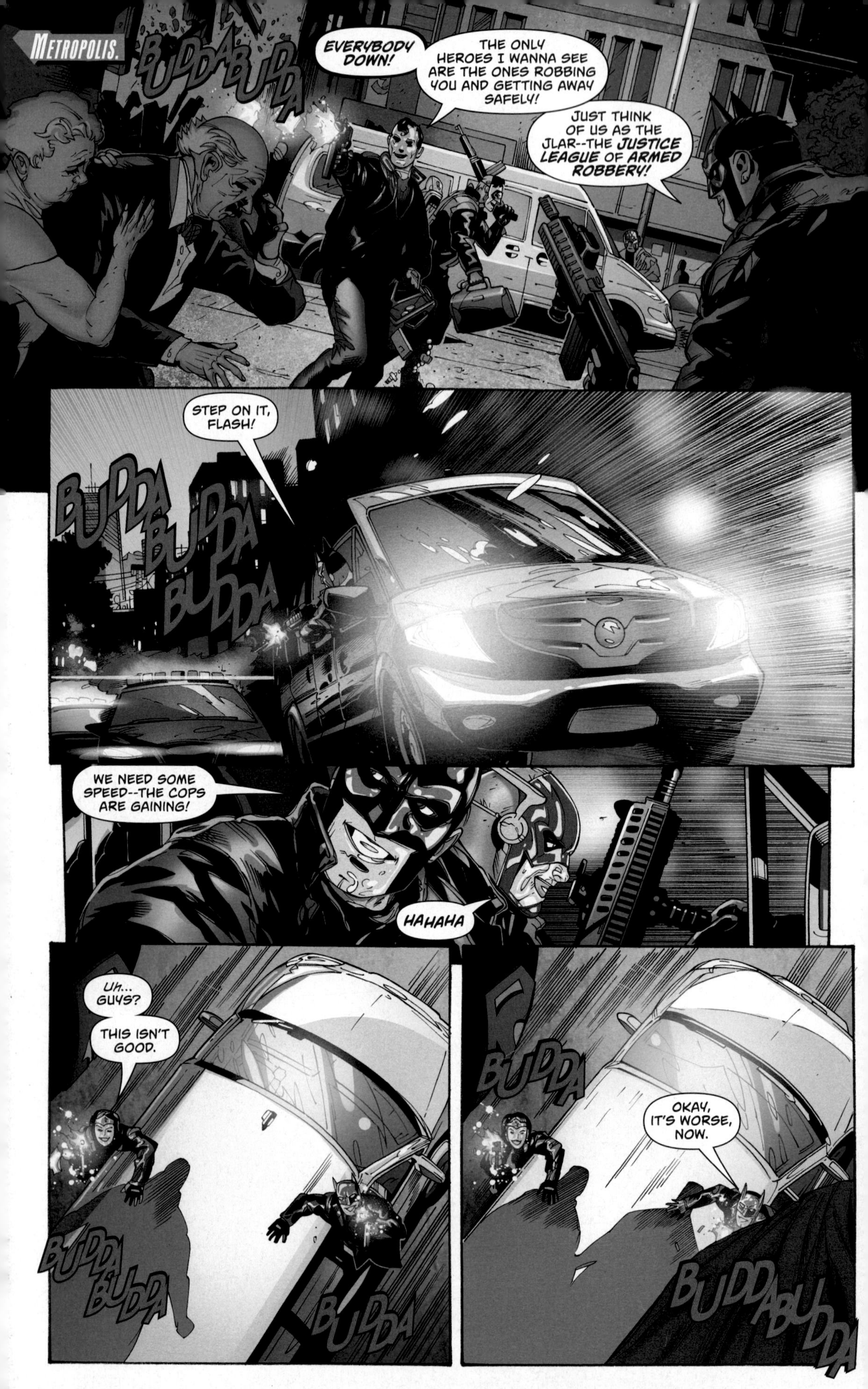
METROPOLIS.
BUDDABUDDA
EVERYBODY DOWN!
THE ONLY HEROES I WANNA SEE ARE THE ONES ROBBING YOU AND GETTING AWAY SAFELY!
JUST THINK OF US AS THE JLAR--THE JUSTICE LEAGUE OF ARMED ROBBERY!
STEP ON IT, FLASH!
BUDDA BUDDA BUDDA
WE NEED SOME SPEED--THE COPS ARE GAINING!
HAHAHA
Uh... GUYS?
THIS ISN'T GOOD.
BUDDA BUDDA
BUDDA
BUDDA
OKAY, IT'S WORSE, NOW.
BUDDABUDDA

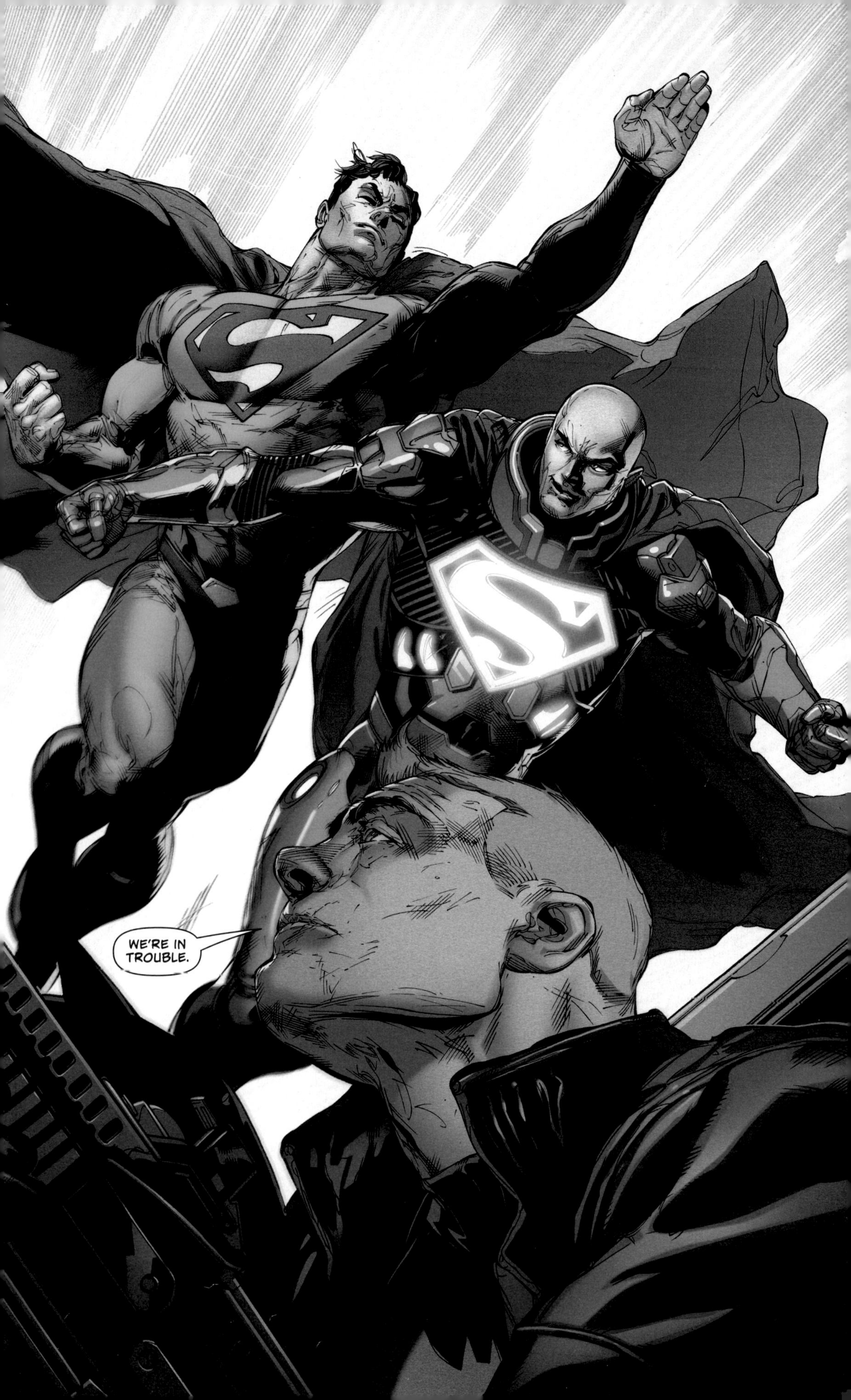
WE'RE IN TROUBLE.

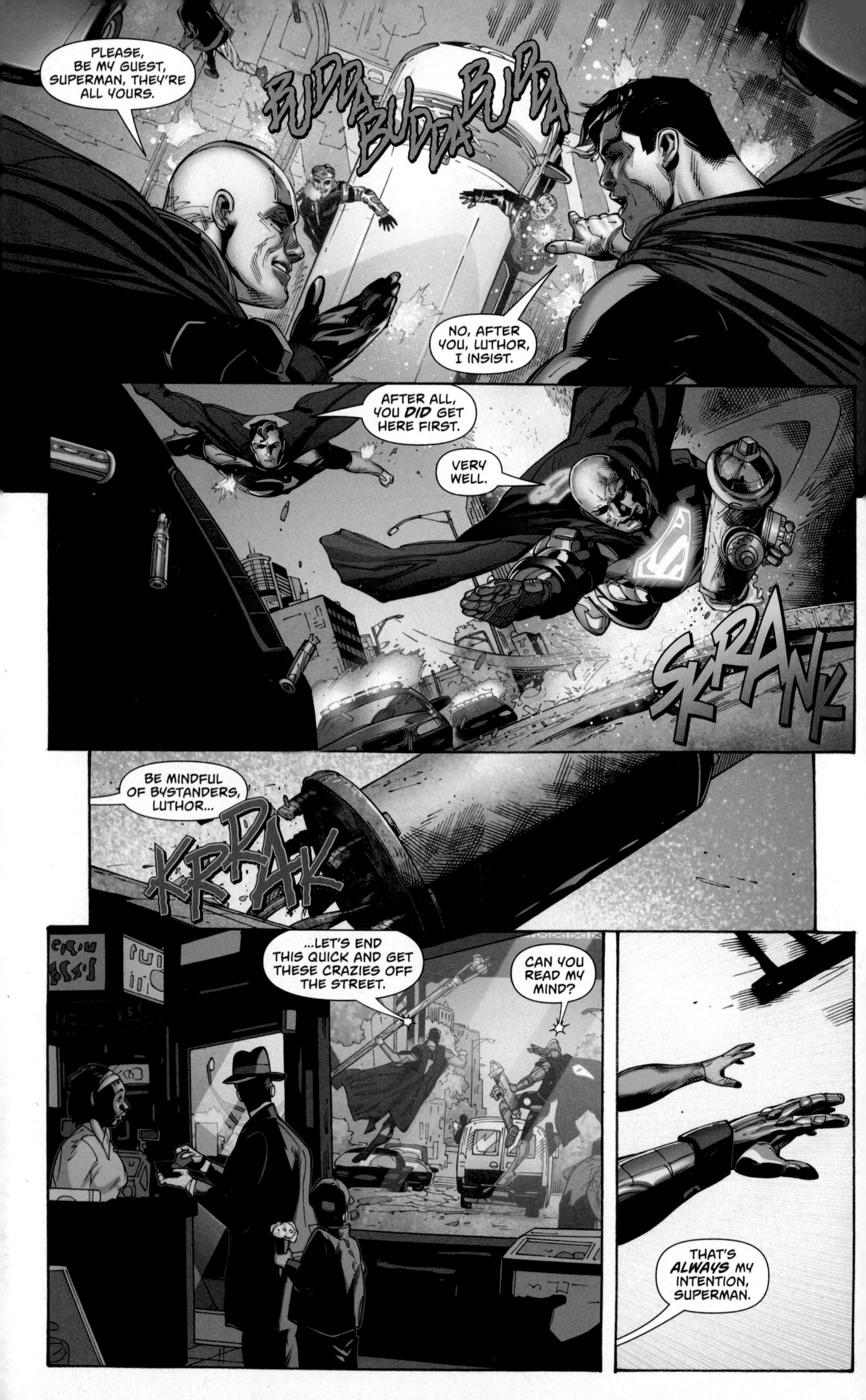

PLEASE, BE MY GUEST, SUPERMAN, THEY'RE ALL YOURS.
BUDDA BUDDA BUDDA
NO, AFTER YOU, LUTHOR, I INSIST.
AFTER ALL, YOU **DID** GET HERE FIRST.
VERY WELL.
SKRANK
BE MINDFUL OF BYSTANDERS, LUTHOR...
KRRAK
...LET'S END THIS QUICK AND GET THESE CRAZIES OFF THE STREET.
CAN YOU READ MY MIND?
THAT'S **ALWAYS** MY INTENTION, SUPERMAN.

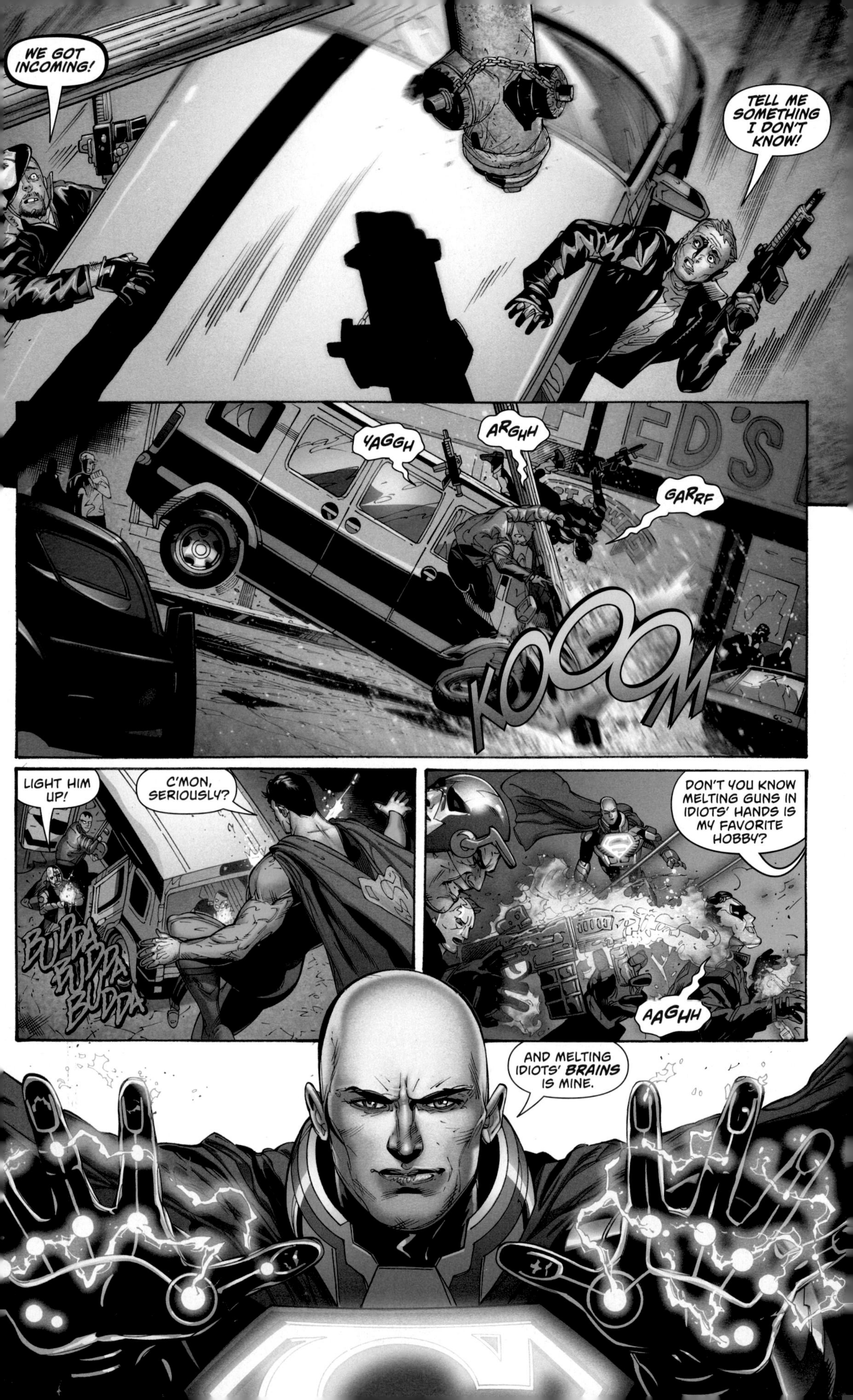
WE GOT INCOMING!
TELL ME SOMETHING I DON'T KNOW!
YAGGH
ARGHH
GARRF
KOOOM
LIGHT HIM UP!
C'MON, SERIOUSLY?
BUDDA BUDDA BUDDA
DON'T YOU KNOW MELTING GUNS IN IDIOTS' HANDS IS MY FAVORITE HOBBY?
AAGHH
AND MELTING IDIOTS' BRAINS IS MINE.

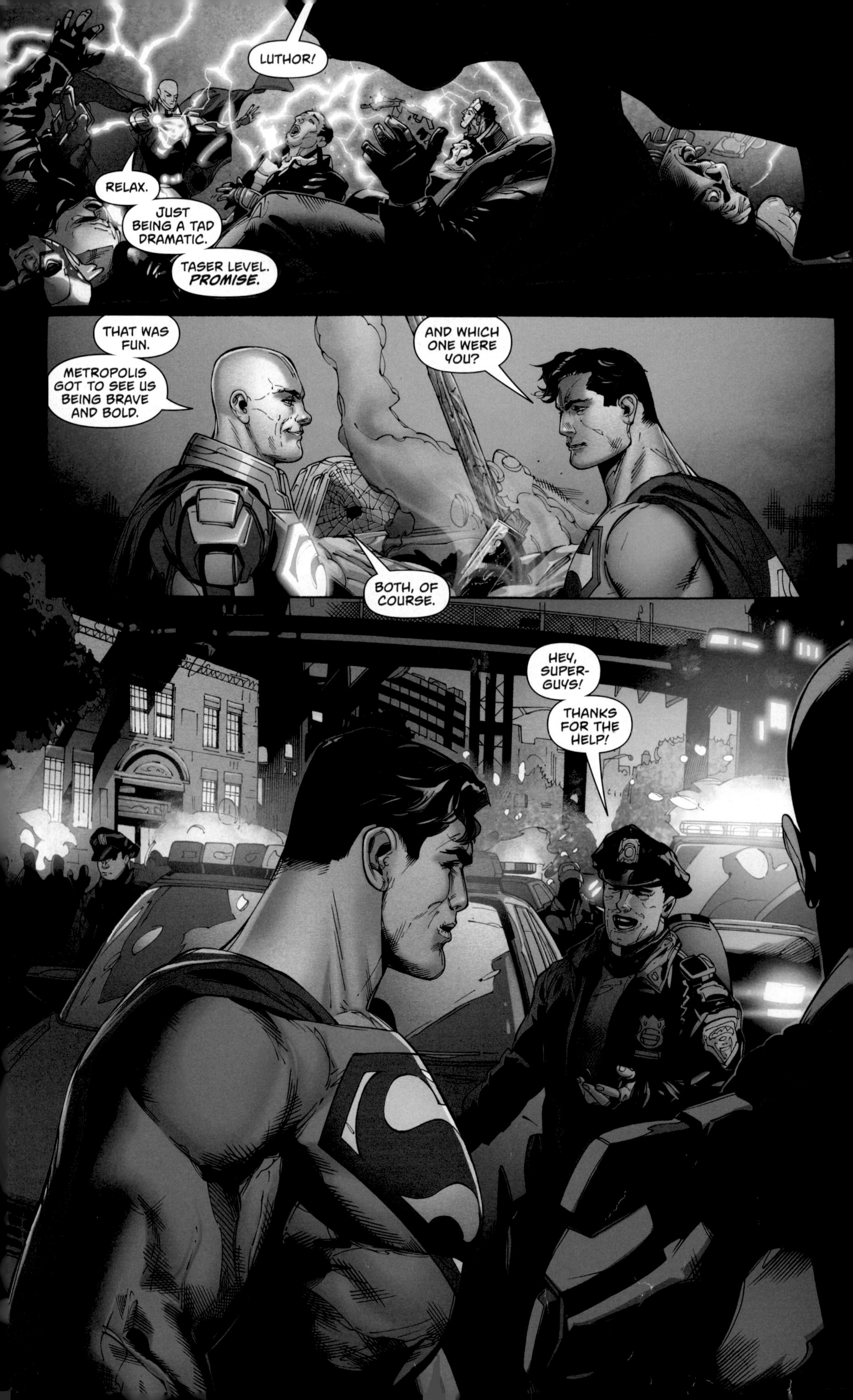
LUTHOR!
RELAX.
JUST BEING A TAD DRAMATIC.
TASER LEVEL. PROMISE.
THAT WAS FUN.
METROPOLIS GOT TO SEE US BEING BRAVE AND BOLD.
AND WHICH ONE WERE YOU?
BOTH, OF COURSE.
HEY, SUPER-GUYS!
THANKS FOR THE HELP!

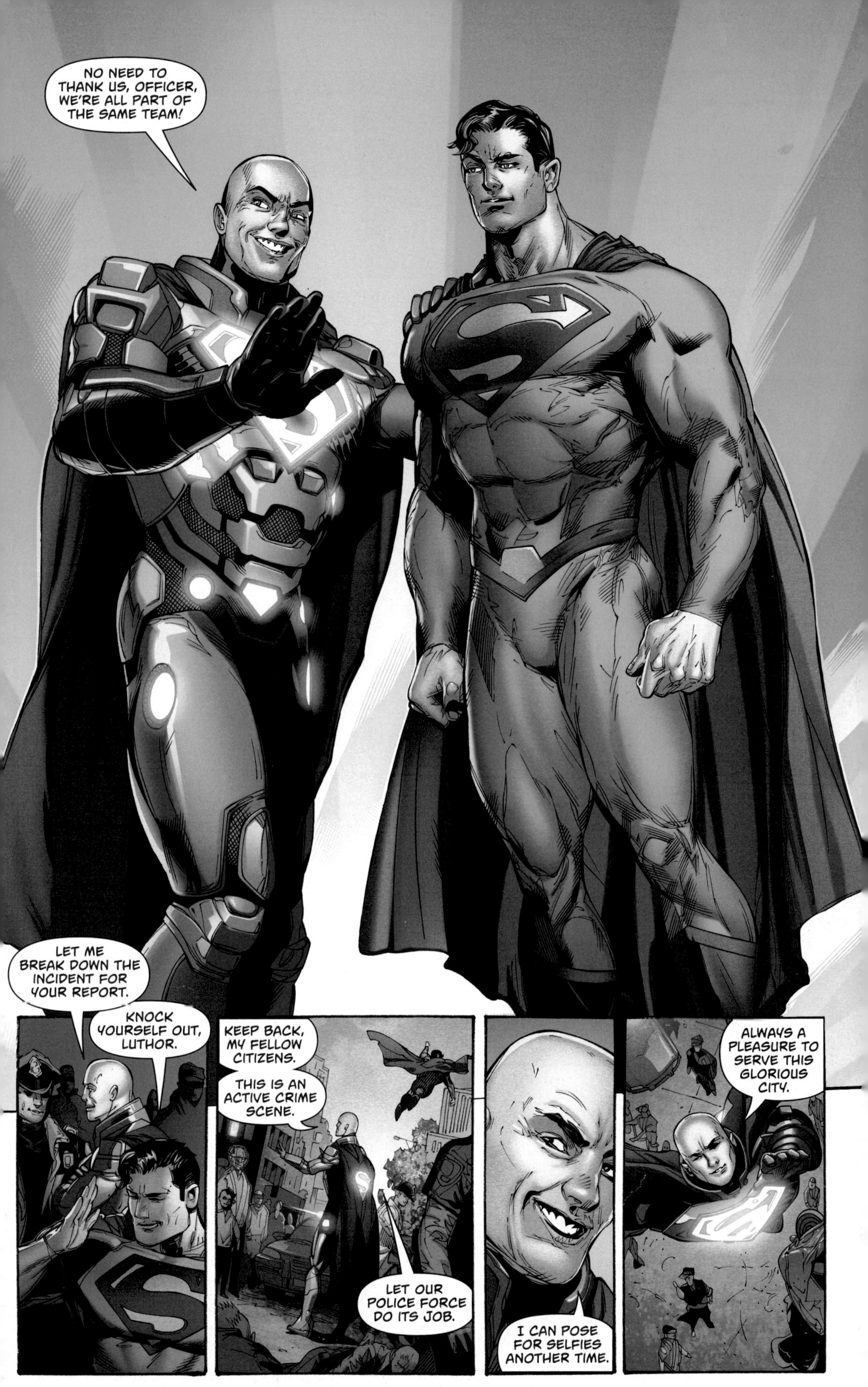
NO NEED TO THANK US, OFFICER, WE'RE ALL PART OF THE SAME TEAM!
LET ME BREAK DOWN THE INCIDENT FOR YOUR REPORT.
KNOCK YOURSELF OUT, LUTHOR.
KEEP BACK, MY FELLOW CITIZENS.
THIS IS AN ACTIVE CRIME SCENE.
LET OUR POLICE FORCE DO ITS JOB.
I CAN POSE FOR SELFIES ANOTHER TIME.
ALWAYS A PLEASURE TO SERVE THIS GLORIOUS CITY.

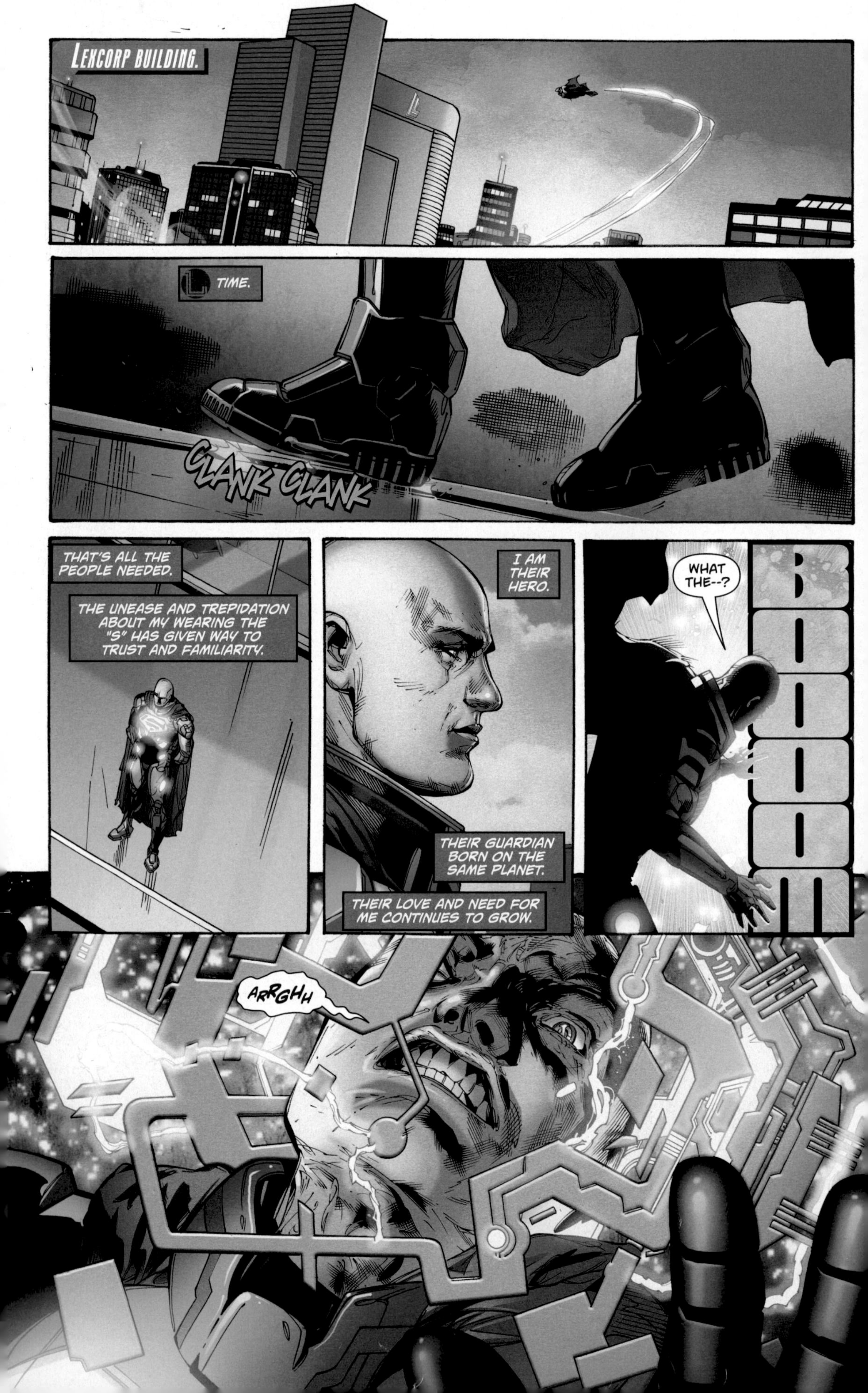
LEXCORP BUILDING.
TIME.
CLANK CLANK
THAT'S ALL THE PEOPLE NEEDED.
THE UNEASE AND TREPIDATION ABOUT MY WEARING THE "S" HAS GIVEN WAY TO TRUST AND FAMILIARITY.
I AM THEIR HERO.
THEIR GUARDIAN BORN ON THE SAME PLANET.
THEIR LOVE AND NEED FOR ME CONTINUES TO GROW.
WHAT THE--?
BOOOOOM
ARRGHH

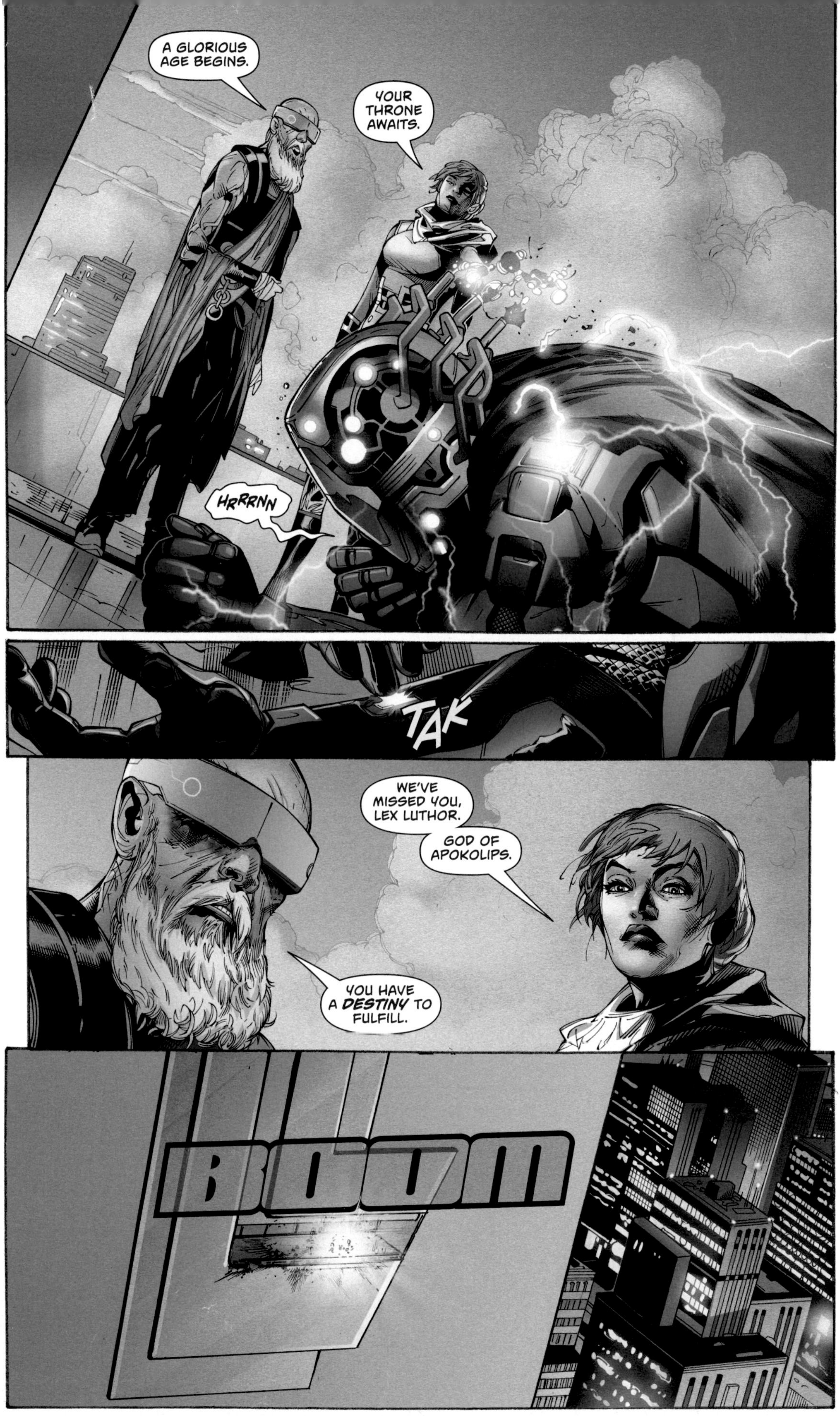
A GLORIOUS AGE BEGINS.
YOUR THRONE AWAITS.
HRRRNN
TAK
WE'VE MISSED YOU, LEX LUTHOR.
GOD OF APOKOLIPS.
YOU HAVE A DESTINY TO FULFILL.
BOOM

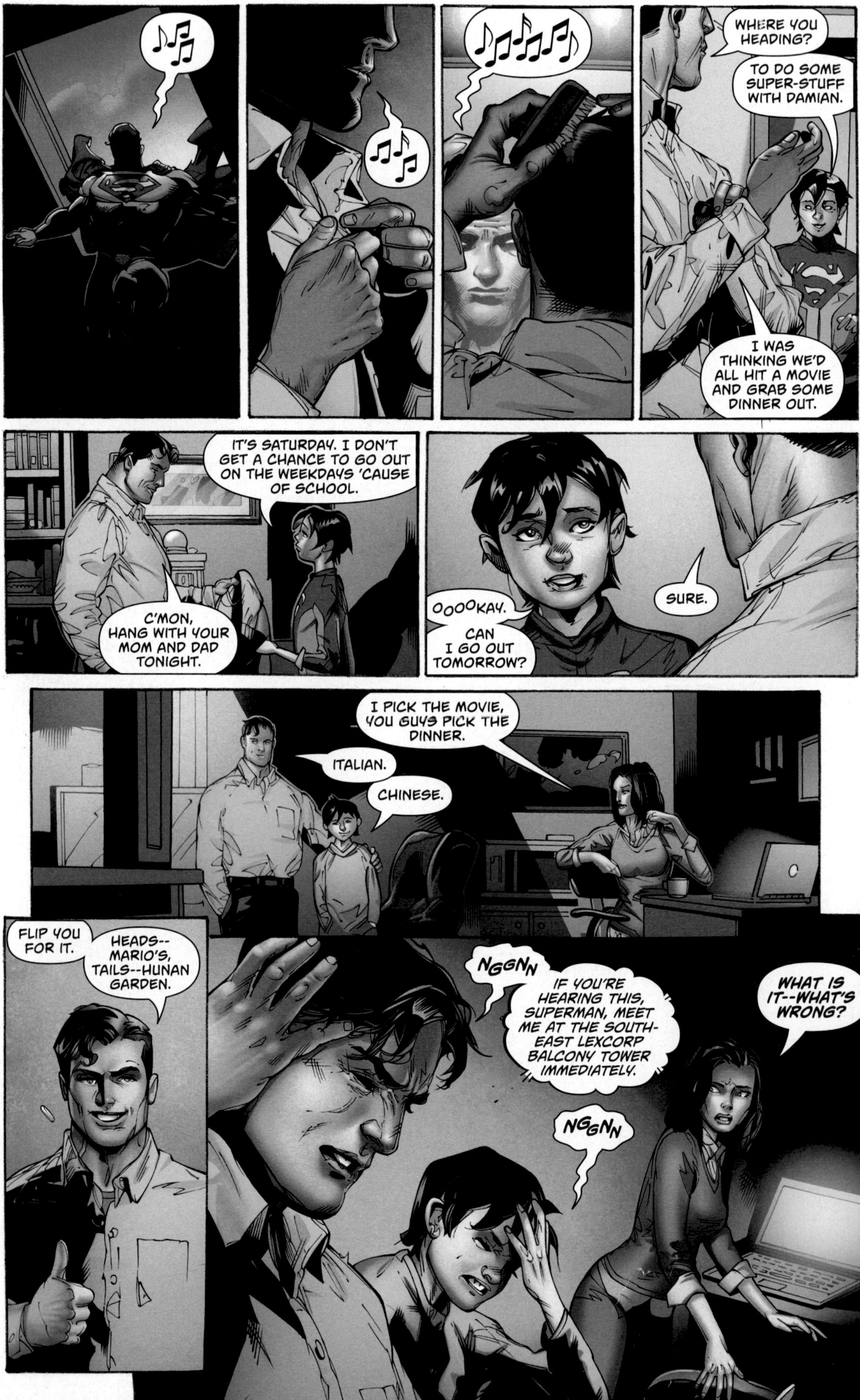
WHERE YOU HEADING?
TO DO SOME SUPER-STUFF WITH DAMIAN.
I WAS THINKING WE'D ALL HIT A MOVIE AND GRAB SOME DINNER OUT.
IT'S SATURDAY. I DON'T GET A CHANCE TO GO OUT ON THE WEEKDAYS 'CAUSE OF SCHOOL.
C'MON, HANG WITH YOUR MOM AND DAD TONIGHT.
OOOOKAY.
CAN I GO OUT TOMORROW?
SURE.
I PICK THE MOVIE, YOU GUYS PICK THE DINNER.
ITALIAN.
CHINESE.
FLIP YOU FOR IT.
HEADS--MARIO'S, TAILS--HUNAN GARDEN.
NGGNN
IF YOU'RE HEARING THIS, SUPERMAN, MEET ME AT THE SOUTH-EAST LEXCORP BALCONY TOWER IMMEDIATELY.
WHAT IS IT--WHAT'S WRONG?
NGGNN

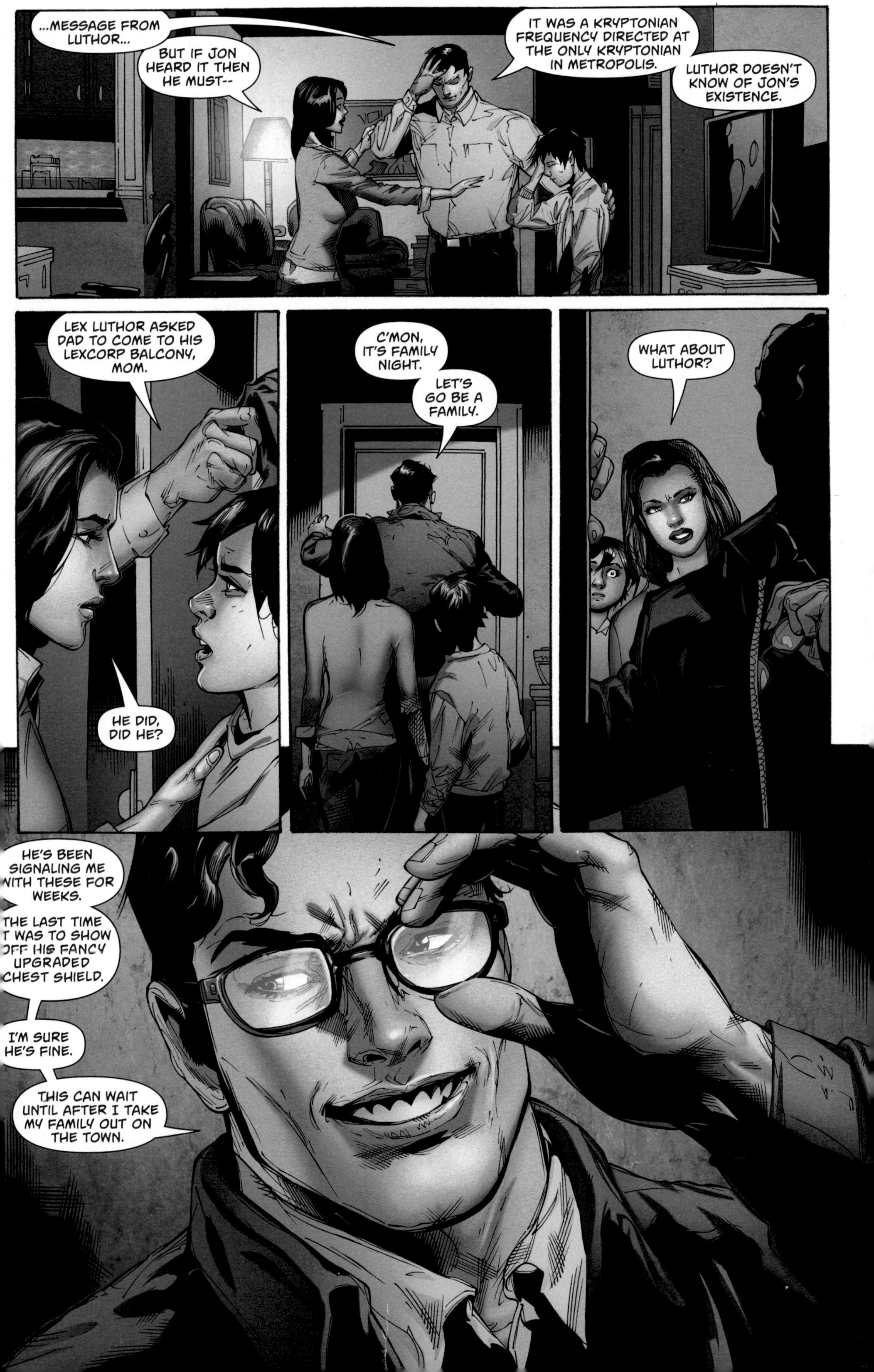
...MESSAGE FROM LUTHOR...
BUT IF JON HEARD IT THEN HE MUST--
IT WAS A KRYPTONIAN FREQUENCY DIRECTED AT THE ONLY KRYPTONIAN IN METROPOLIS.
LUTHOR DOESN'T KNOW OF JON'S EXISTENCE.
LEX LUTHOR ASKED DAD TO COME TO HIS LEXCORP BALCONY, MOM.
HE DID, DID HE?
C'MON, IT'S FAMILY NIGHT.
LET'S GO BE A FAMILY.
WHAT ABOUT LUTHOR?
HE'S BEEN SIGNALING ME WITH THESE FOR WEEKS.
THE LAST TIME IT WAS TO SHOW OFF HIS FANCY UPGRADED CHEST SHIELD.
I'M SURE HE'S FINE.
THIS CAN WAIT UNTIL AFTER I TAKE MY FAMILY OUT ON THE TOWN.

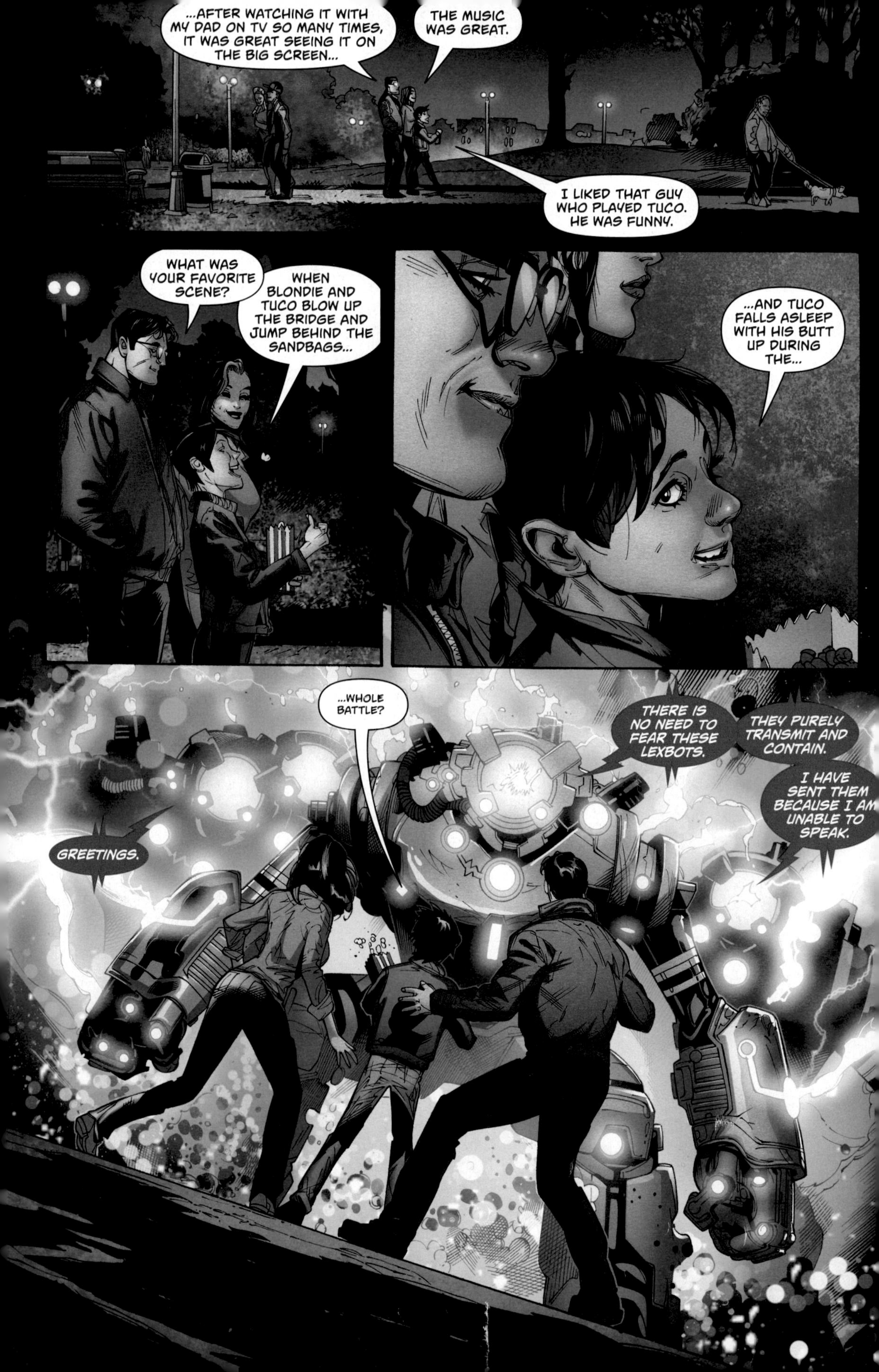
...AFTER WATCHING IT WITH MY DAD ON TV SO MANY TIMES, IT WAS GREAT SEEING IT ON THE BIG SCREEN...
THE MUSIC WAS GREAT.
I LIKED THAT GUY WHO PLAYED TUCO. HE WAS FUNNY.
WHAT WAS YOUR FAVORITE SCENE?
WHEN BLONDIE AND TUCO BLOW UP THE BRIDGE AND JUMP BEHIND THE SANDBAGS...
...AND TUCO FALLS ASLEEP WITH HIS BUTT UP DURING THE...
...WHOLE BATTLE?
GREETINGS.
THERE IS NO NEED TO FEAR THESE LEXBOTS.
THEY PURELY TRANSMIT AND CONTAIN.
I HAVE SENT THEM BECAUSE I AM UNABLE TO SPEAK.

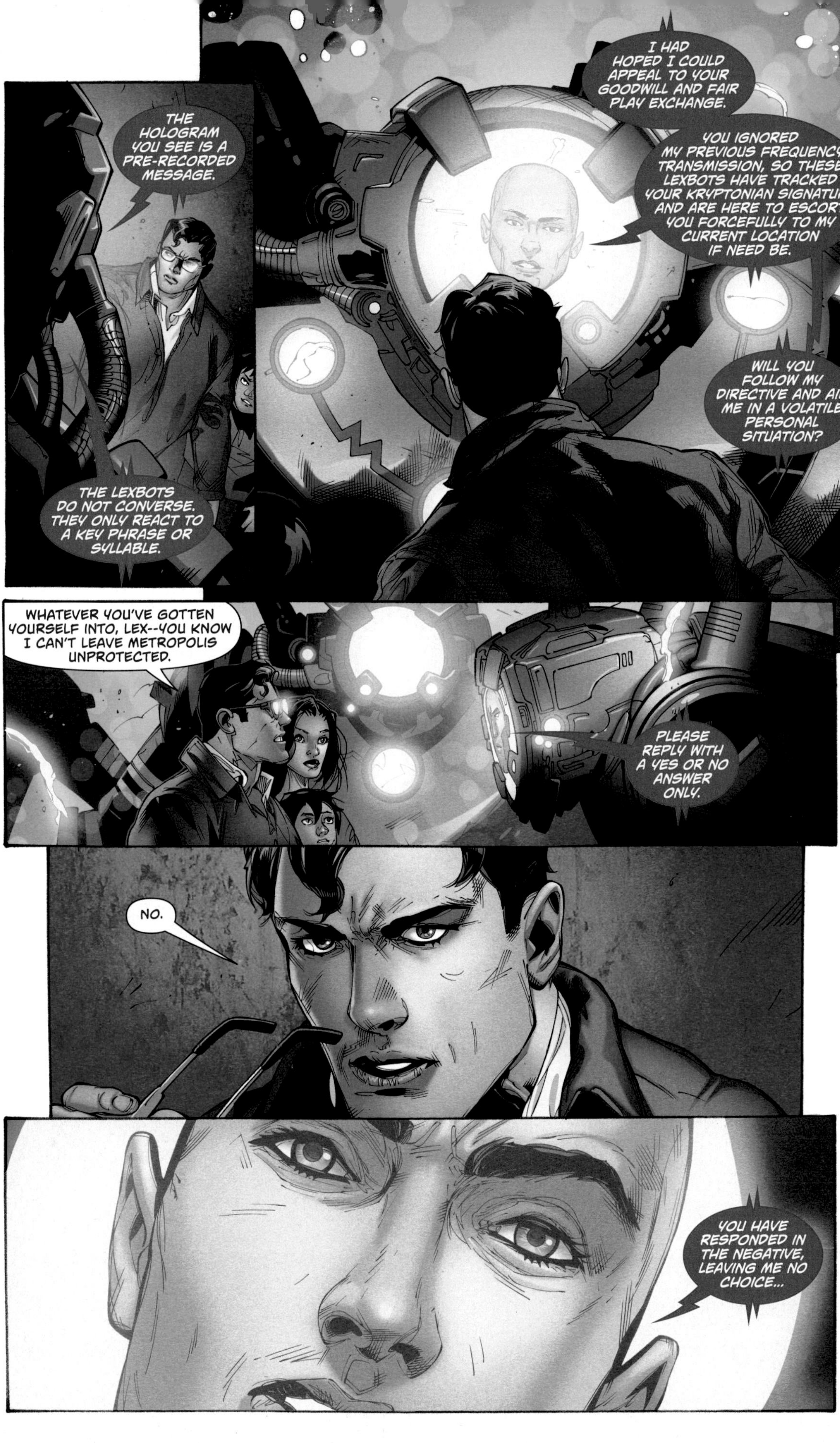
THE HOLOGRAM YOU SEE IS A PRE-RECORDED MESSAGE.
THE LEXBOTS DO NOT CONVERSE. THEY ONLY REACT TO A KEY PHRASE OR SYLLABLE.
I HAD HOPED I COULD APPEAL TO YOUR GOODWILL AND FAIR PLAY EXCHANGE.
YOU IGNORED MY PREVIOUS FREQUENCY TRANSMISSION, SO THESE LEXBOTS HAVE TRACKED YOUR KRYPTONIAN SIGNATURE AND ARE HERE TO ESCORT YOU FORCEFULLY TO MY CURRENT LOCATION IF NEED BE.
WILL YOU FOLLOW MY DIRECTIVE AND AID ME IN A VOLATILE PERSONAL SITUATION?
WHATEVER YOU'VE GOTTEN YOURSELF INTO, LEX--YOU KNOW I CAN'T LEAVE METROPOLIS UNPROTECTED.
PLEASE REPLY WITH A YES OR NO ANSWER ONLY.
NO.
YOU HAVE RESPONDED IN THE NEGATIVE, LEAVING ME NO CHOICE...

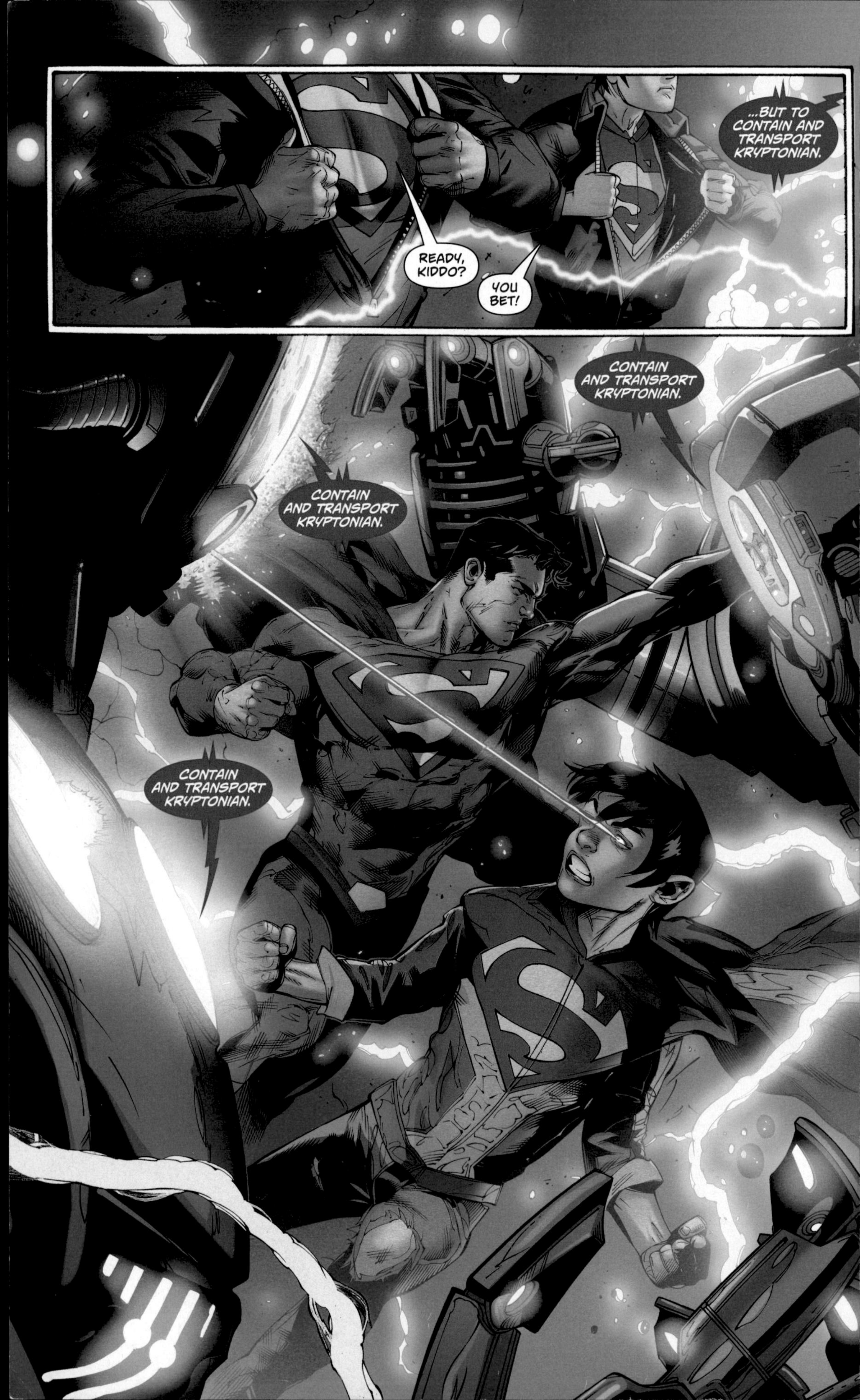
...BUT TO CONTAIN AND TRANSPORT KRYPTONIAN.
READY, KIDDO?
YOU BET!
CONTAIN AND TRANSPORT KRYPTONIAN.
CONTAIN AND TRANSPORT KRYPTONIAN.
CONTAIN AND TRANSPORT KRYPTONIAN.

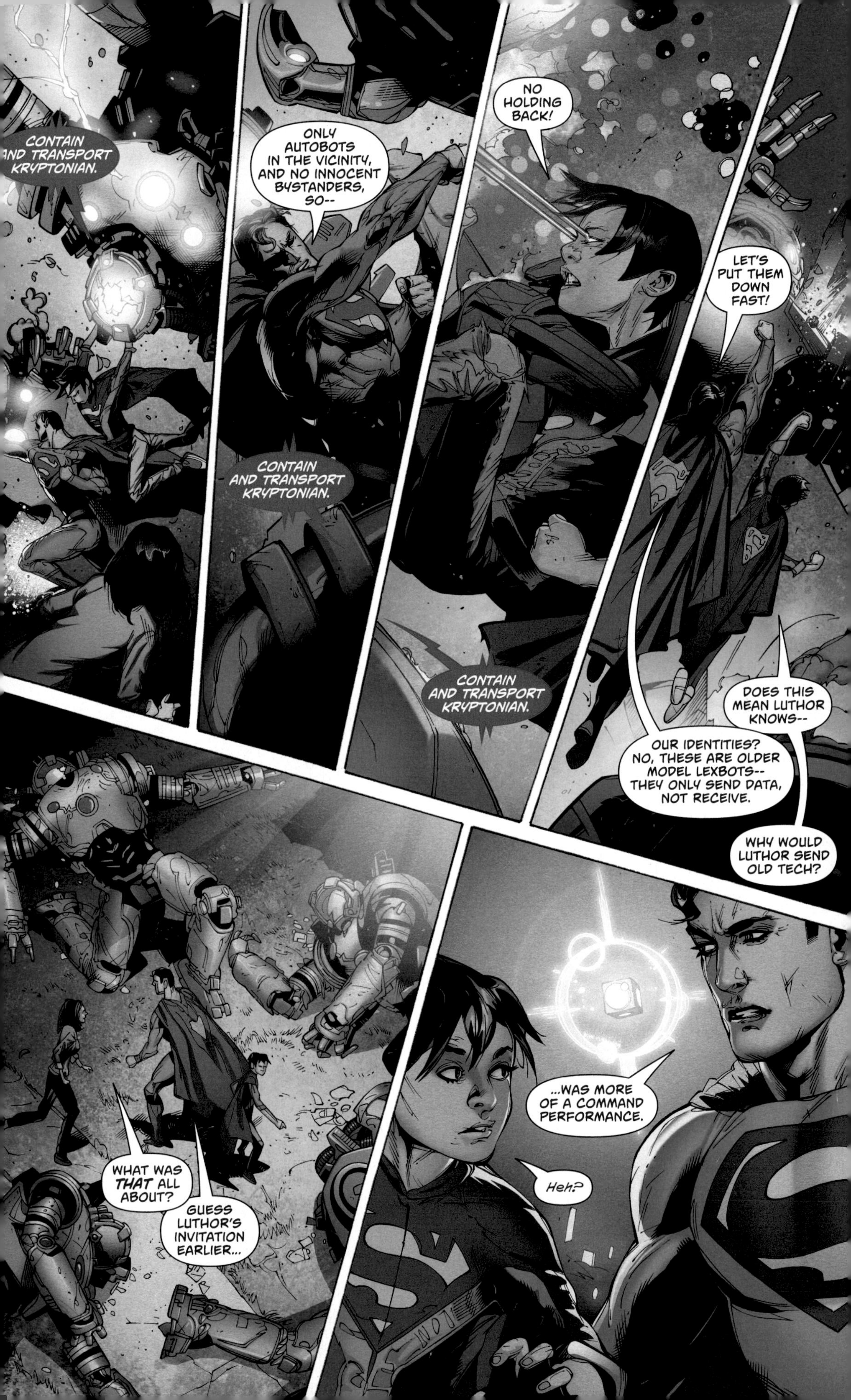
CONTAIN AND TRANSPORT KRYPTONIAN.
ONLY AUTOBOTS IN THE VICINITY, AND NO INNOCENT BYSTANDERS, SO--
CONTAIN AND TRANSPORT KRYPTONIAN.
NO HOLDING BACK!
CONTAIN AND TRANSPORT KRYPTONIAN.
LET'S PUT THEM DOWN FAST!
DOES THIS MEAN LUTHOR KNOWS--
OUR IDENTITIES? NO, THESE ARE OLDER MODEL LEXBOTS-- THEY ONLY SEND DATA, NOT RECEIVE.
WHY WOULD LUTHOR SEND OLD TECH?
WHAT WAS THAT ALL ABOUT?
GUESS LUTHOR'S INVITATION EARLIER...
...WAS MORE OF A COMMAND PERFORMANCE.
Heh?

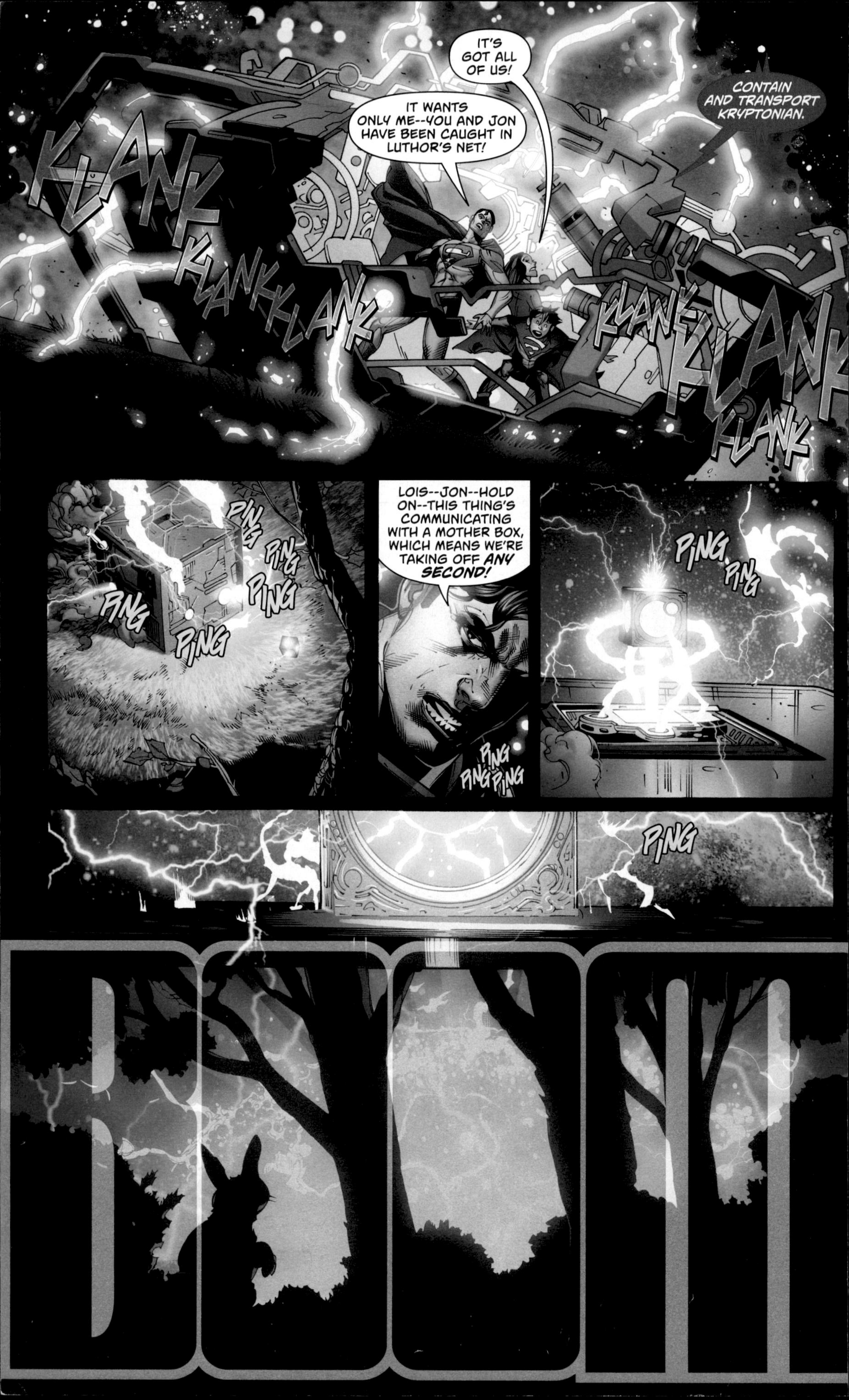
KLANK
KLANK KLANK KLANK
IT'S GOT ALL OF US!
IT WANTS ONLY ME--YOU AND JON HAVE BEEN CAUGHT IN LUTHOR'S NET!
CONTAIN AND TRANSPORT KRYPTONIAN.
KLANK KLANK
KLANK
PING PING PING PING PING PING
LOIS--JON--HOLD ON--THIS THING'S COMMUNICATING WITH A MOTHER BOX, WHICH MEANS WE'RE TAKING OFF *ANY SECOND!*
PING PING PING
PING PING
PING
BOOM

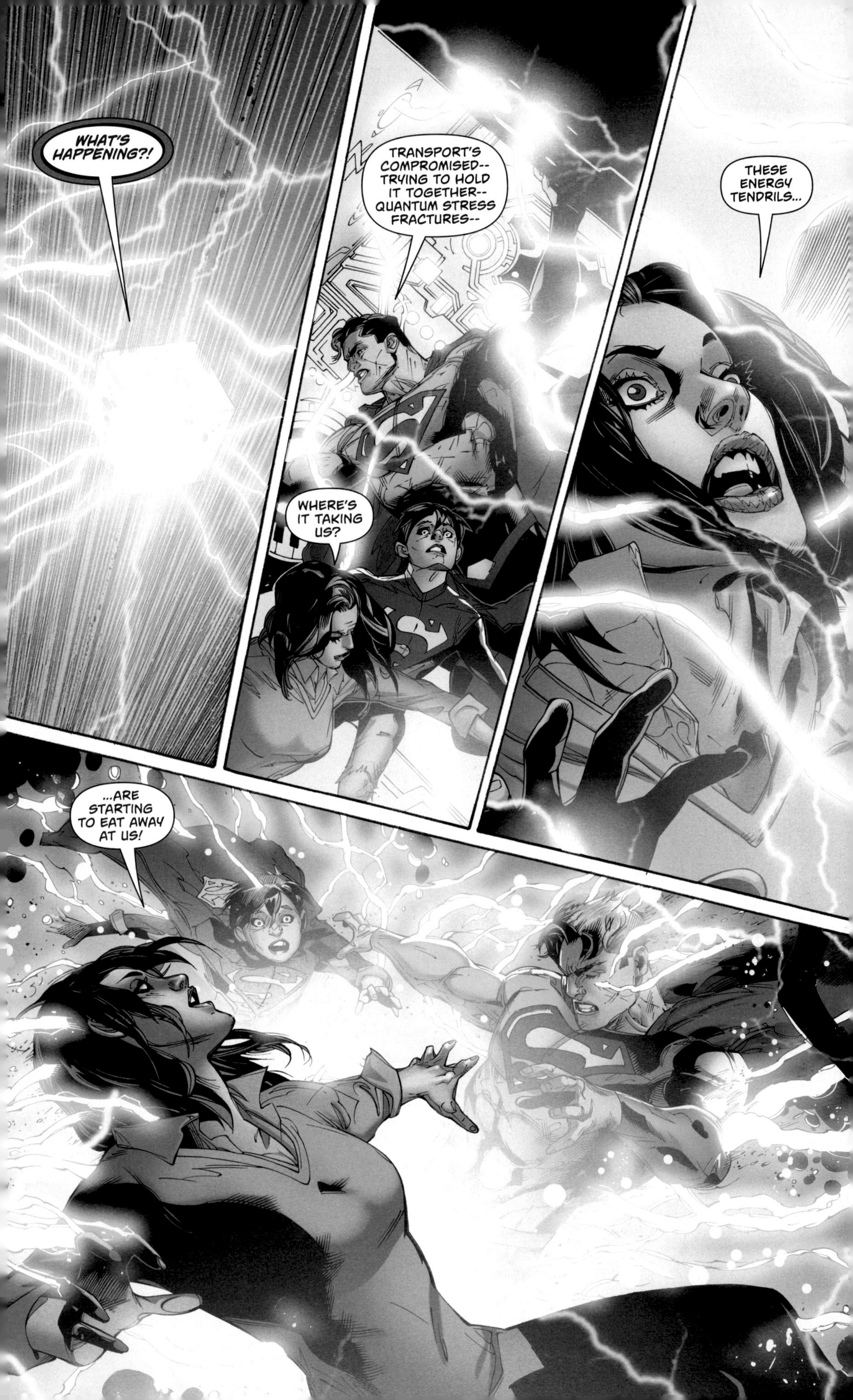
WHAT'S HAPPENING?!
TRANSPORT'S COMPROMISED-- TRYING TO HOLD IT TOGETHER-- QUANTUM STRESS FRACTURES--
WHERE'S IT TAKING US?
THESE ENERGY TENDRILS...
...ARE STARTING TO EAT AWAY AT US!

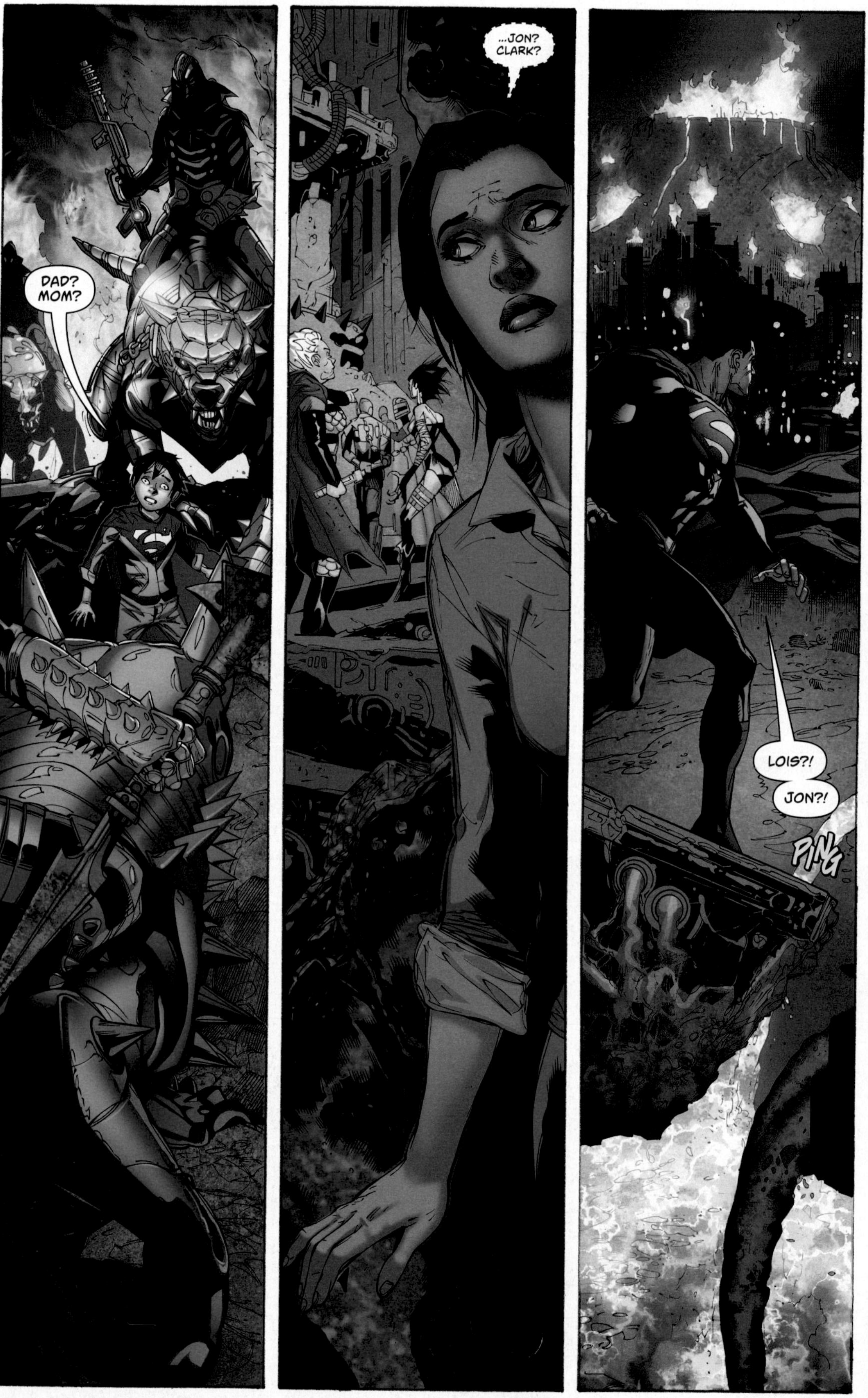
DAD? MOM?
...JON? CLARK?
LOIS?!
JON?!
PING

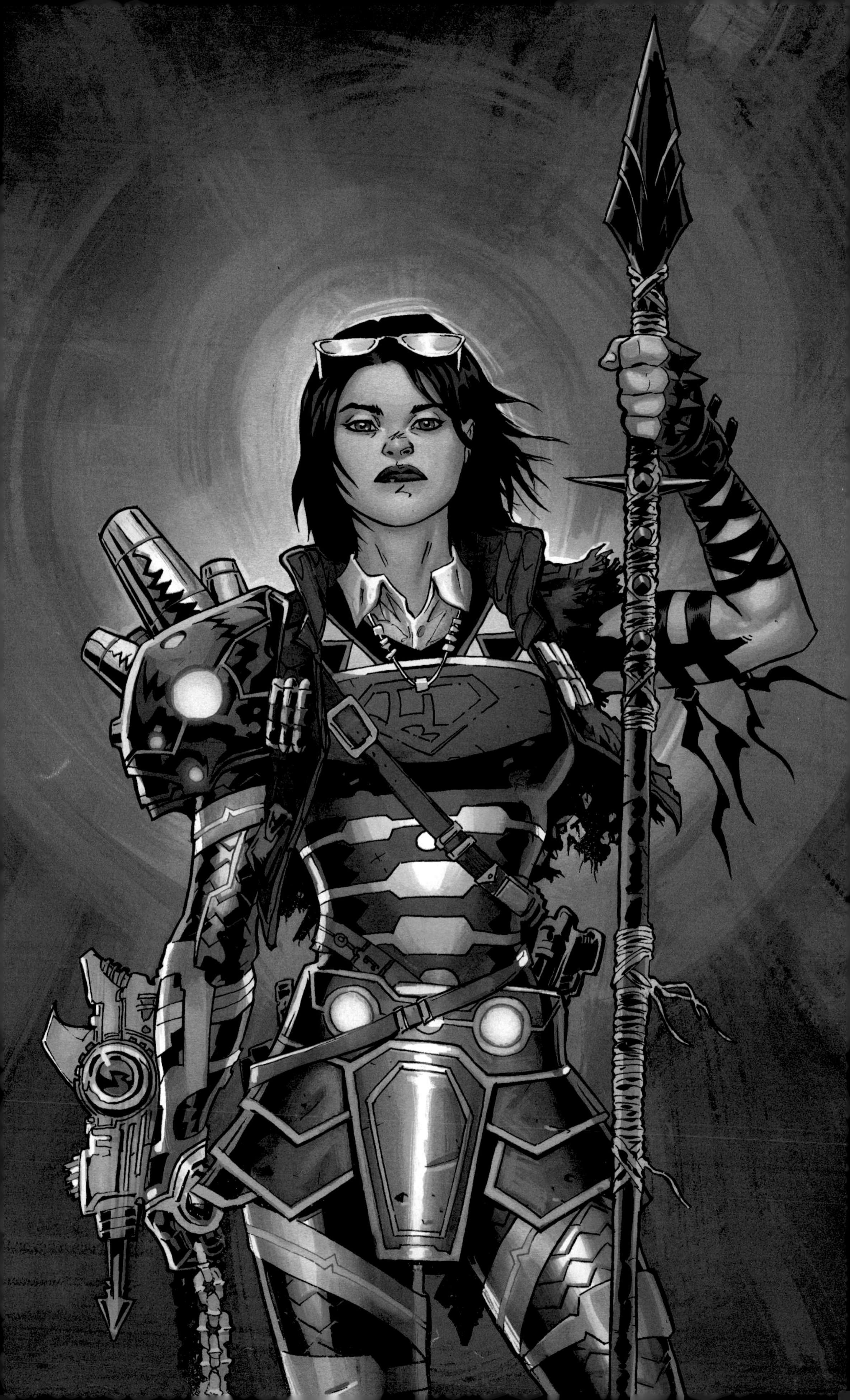

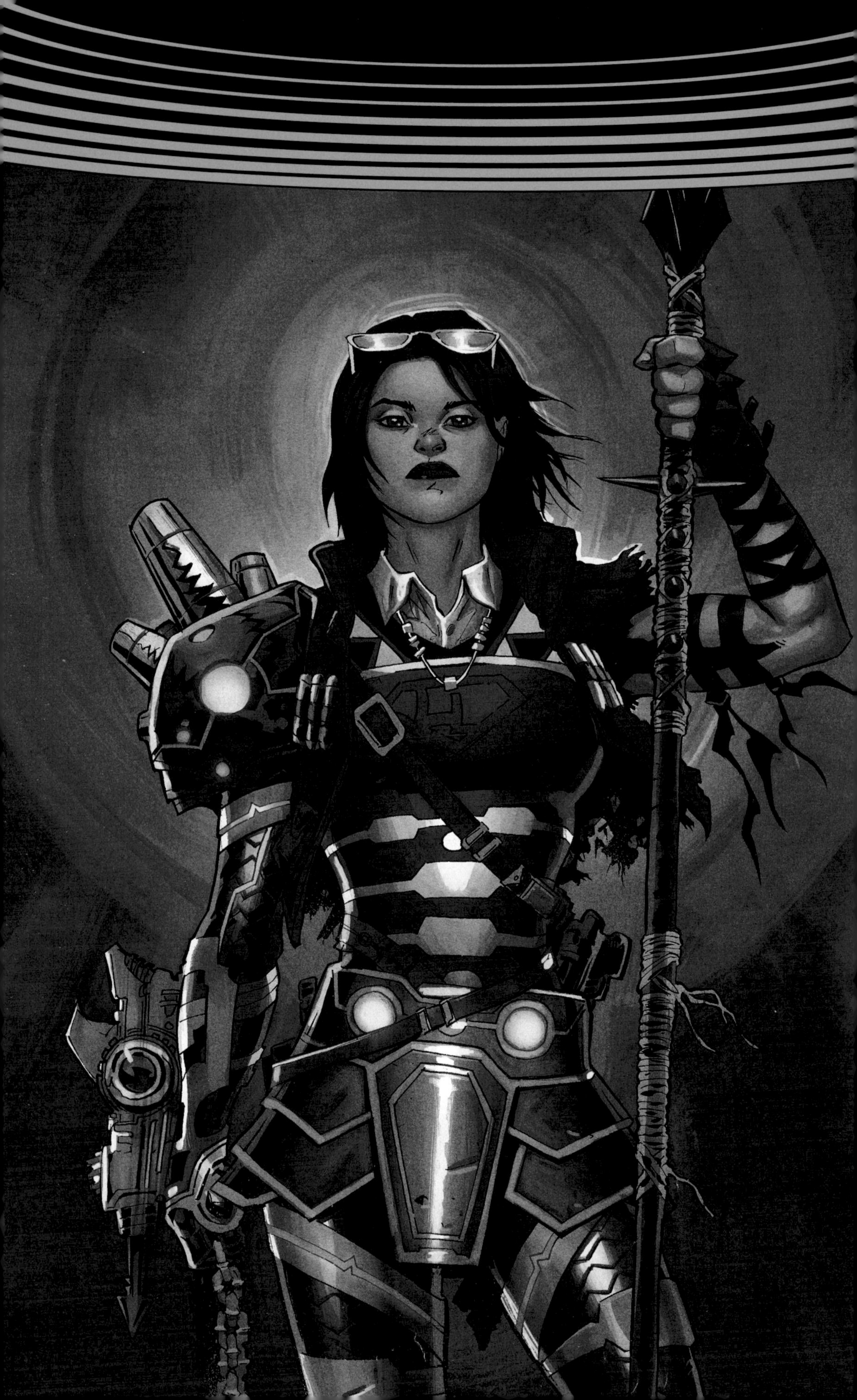

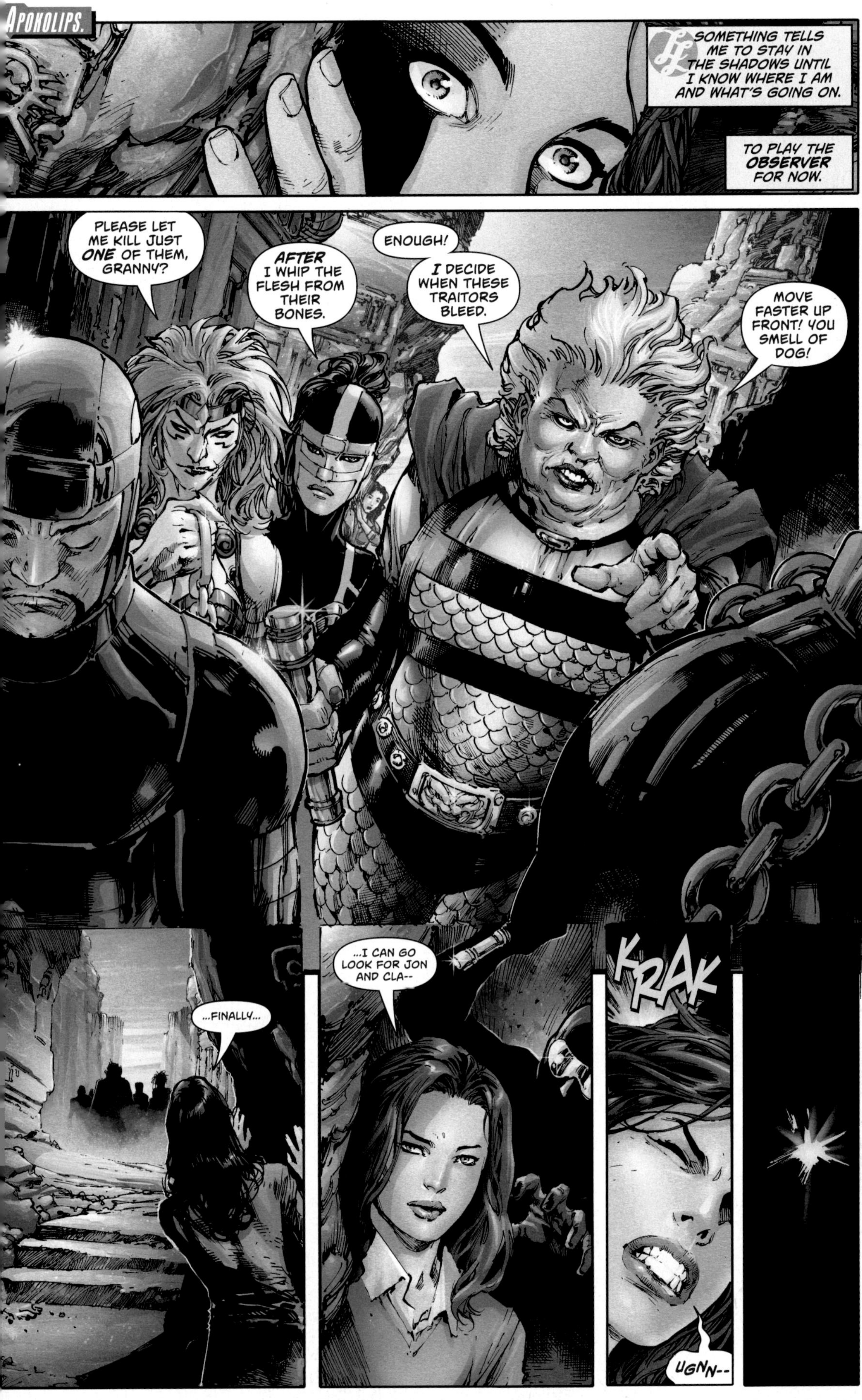

APOKOLIPS.
SOMETHING TELLS ME TO STAY IN THE SHADOWS UNTIL I KNOW WHERE I AM AND WHAT'S GOING ON.
TO PLAY THE OBSERVER FOR NOW.
PLEASE LET ME KILL JUST ONE OF THEM, GRANNY?
AFTER I WHIP THE FLESH FROM THEIR BONES.
ENOUGH!
I DECIDE WHEN THESE TRAITORS BLEED.
MOVE FASTER UP FRONT! YOU SMELL OF DOG!
...FINALLY...
...I CAN GO LOOK FOR JON AND CLA--
KRAK
UGNN--

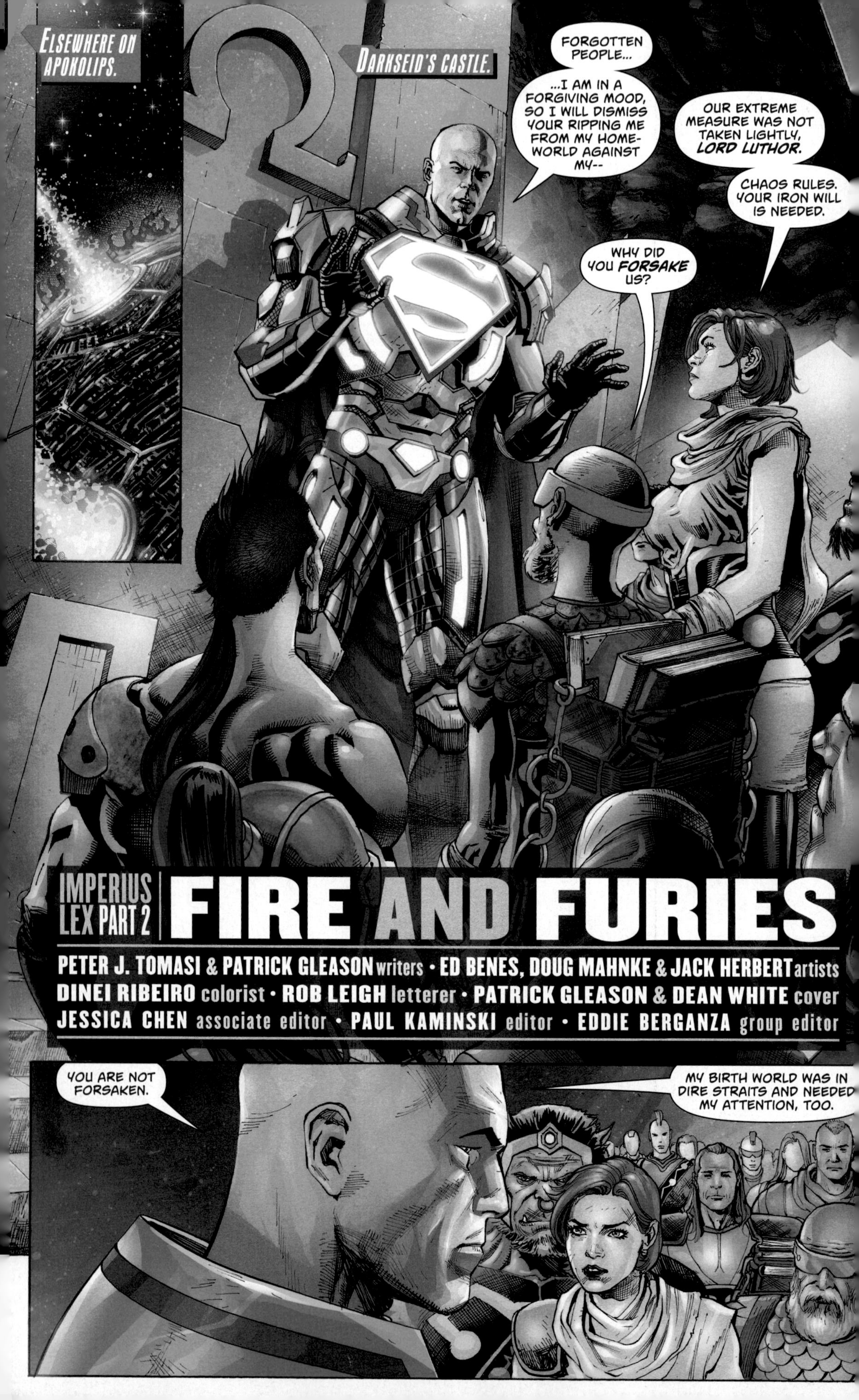
Elsewhere on Apokolips.
Darkseid's castle.
FORGOTTEN PEOPLE...
...I AM IN A FORGIVING MOOD, SO I WILL DISMISS YOUR RIPPING ME FROM MY HOME-WORLD AGAINST MY--
OUR EXTREME MEASURE WAS NOT TAKEN LIGHTLY, LORD LUTHOR.
CHAOS RULES. YOUR IRON WILL IS NEEDED.
WHY DID YOU FORSAKE US?
IMPERIUS LEX PART 2
FIRE AND FURIES
PETER J. TOMASI & PATRICK GLEASON writers • ED BENES, DOUG MAHNKE & JACK HERBERT artists
DINEI RIBEIRO colorist • ROB LEIGH letterer • PATRICK GLEASON & DEAN WHITE cover
JESSICA CHEN associate editor • PAUL KAMINSKI editor • EDDIE BERGANZA group editor
YOU ARE NOT FORSAKEN.
MY BIRTH WORLD WAS IN DIRE STRAITS AND NEEDED MY ATTENTION, TOO.

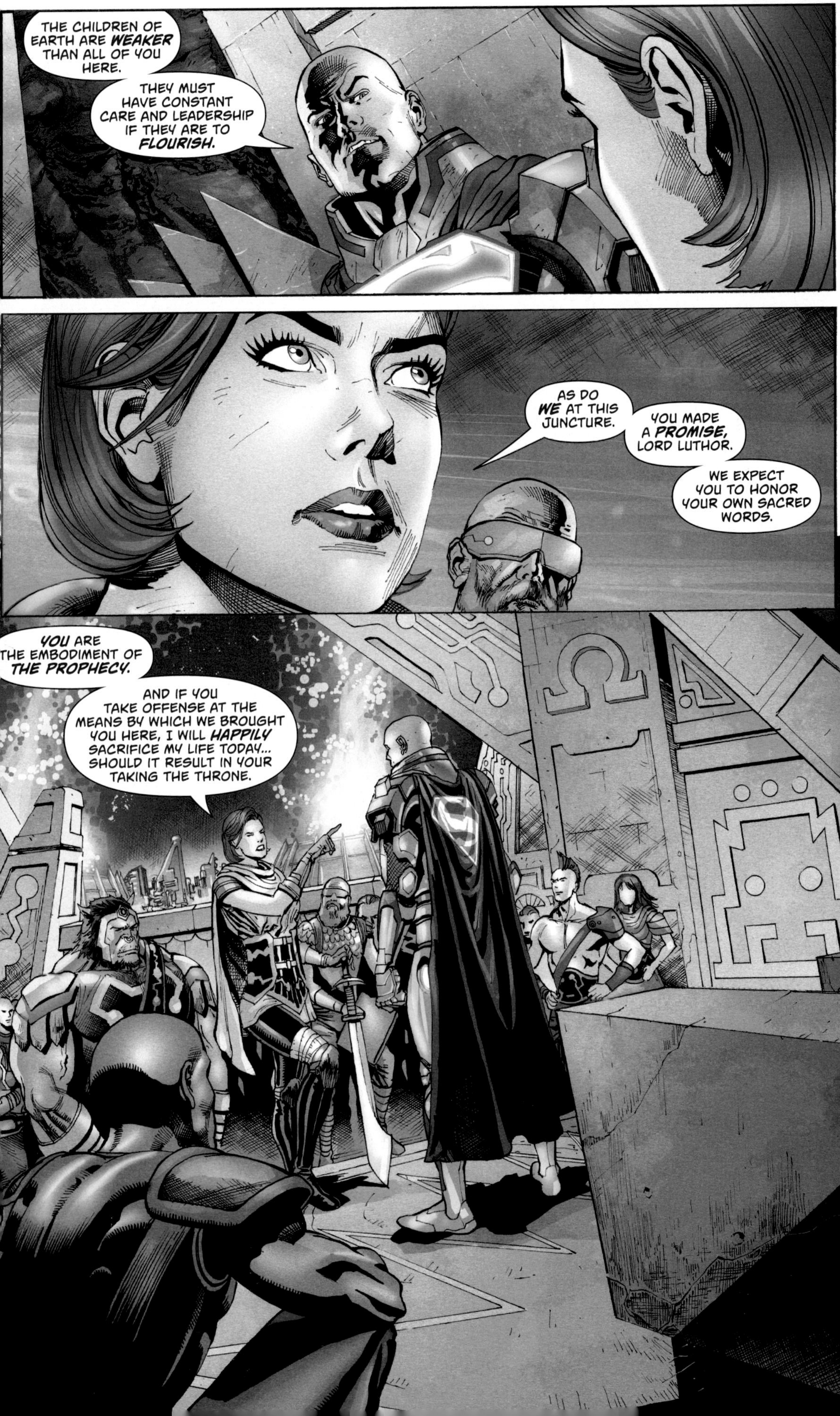

THE CHILDREN OF EARTH ARE WEAKER THAN ALL OF YOU HERE.
THEY MUST HAVE CONSTANT CARE AND LEADERSHIP IF THEY ARE TO FLOURISH.
AS DO WE AT THIS JUNCTURE.
YOU MADE A PROMISE, LORD LUTHOR.
WE EXPECT YOU TO HONOR YOUR OWN SACRED WORDS.
YOU ARE THE EMBODIMENT OF THE PROPHECY.
AND IF YOU TAKE OFFENSE AT THE MEANS BY WHICH WE BROUGHT YOU HERE, I WILL HAPPILY SACRIFICE MY LIFE TODAY... SHOULD IT RESULT IN YOUR TAKING THE THRONE.

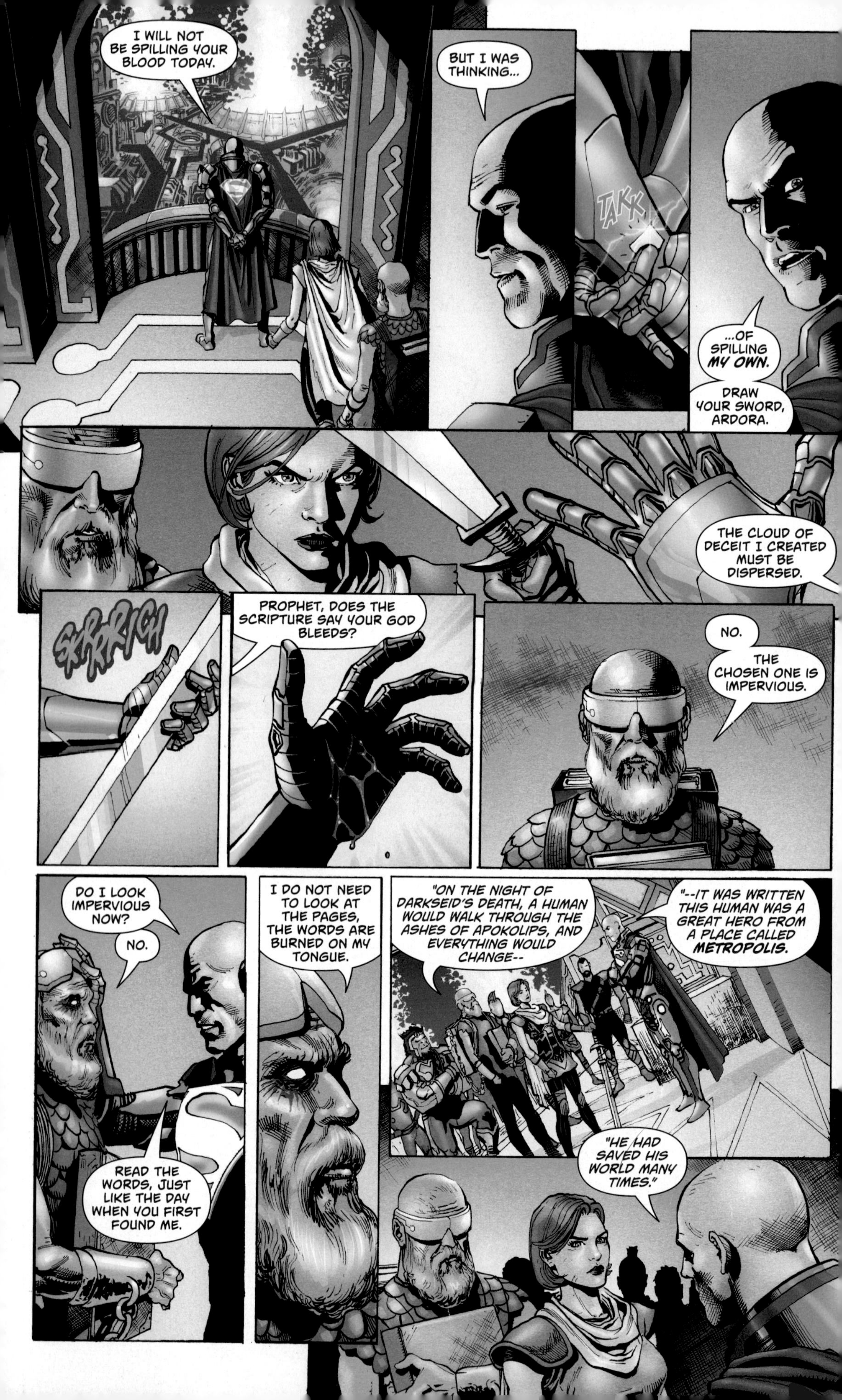
I WILL NOT BE SPILLING YOUR BLOOD TODAY.
BUT I WAS THINKING...
TAKK
...OF SPILLING MY OWN.
DRAW YOUR SWORD, ARDORA.
THE CLOUD OF DECEIT I CREATED MUST BE DISPERSED.
SKRRRICH
PROPHET, DOES THE SCRIPTURE SAY YOUR GOD BLEEDS?
NO.
THE CHOSEN ONE IS IMPERVIOUS.
DO I LOOK IMPERVIOUS NOW?
NO.
READ THE WORDS, JUST LIKE THE DAY WHEN YOU FIRST FOUND ME.
I DO NOT NEED TO LOOK AT THE PAGES, THE WORDS ARE BURNED ON MY TONGUE.
"ON THE NIGHT OF DARKSEID'S DEATH, A HUMAN WOULD WALK THROUGH THE ASHES OF APOKOLIPS, AND EVERYTHING WOULD CHANGE--
"--IT WAS WRITTEN THIS HUMAN WAS A GREAT HERO FROM A PLACE CALLED METROPOLIS.
"HE HAD SAVED HIS WORLD MANY TIMES."

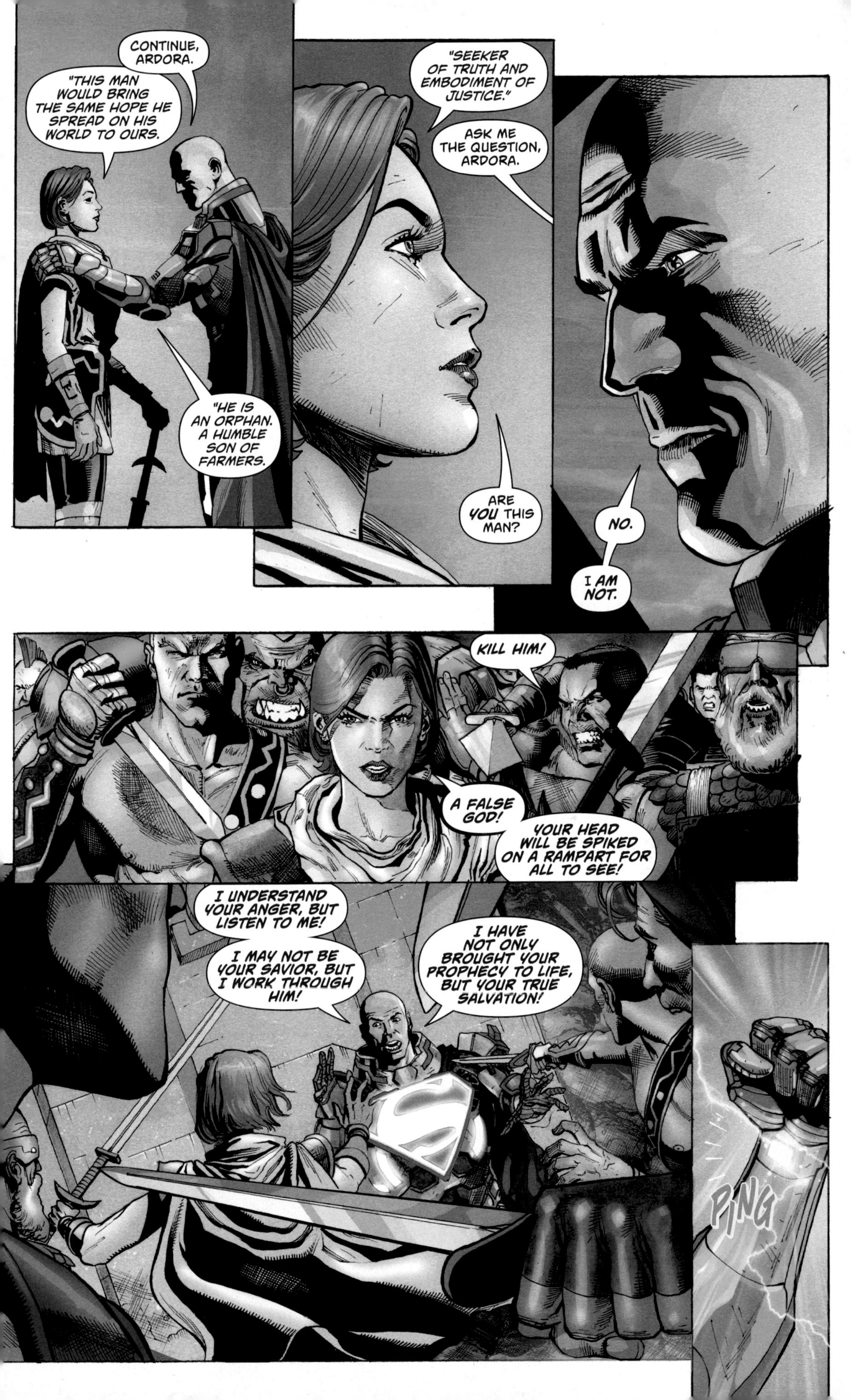
CONTINUE, ARDORA.
"THIS MAN WOULD BRING THE SAME HOPE HE SPREAD ON HIS WORLD TO OURS.
"HE IS AN ORPHAN. A HUMBLE SON OF FARMERS.
"SEEKER OF TRUTH AND EMBODIMENT OF JUSTICE."
ASK ME THE QUESTION, ARDORA.
ARE YOU THIS MAN?
NO.
I AM NOT.
KILL HIM!
A FALSE GOD!
YOUR HEAD WILL BE SPIKED ON A RAMPART FOR ALL TO SEE!
I UNDERSTAND YOUR ANGER, BUT LISTEN TO ME!
I MAY NOT BE YOUR SAVIOR, BUT I WORK THROUGH HIM!
I HAVE NOT ONLY BROUGHT YOUR PROPHECY TO LIFE, BUT YOUR TRUE SALVATION!
PING

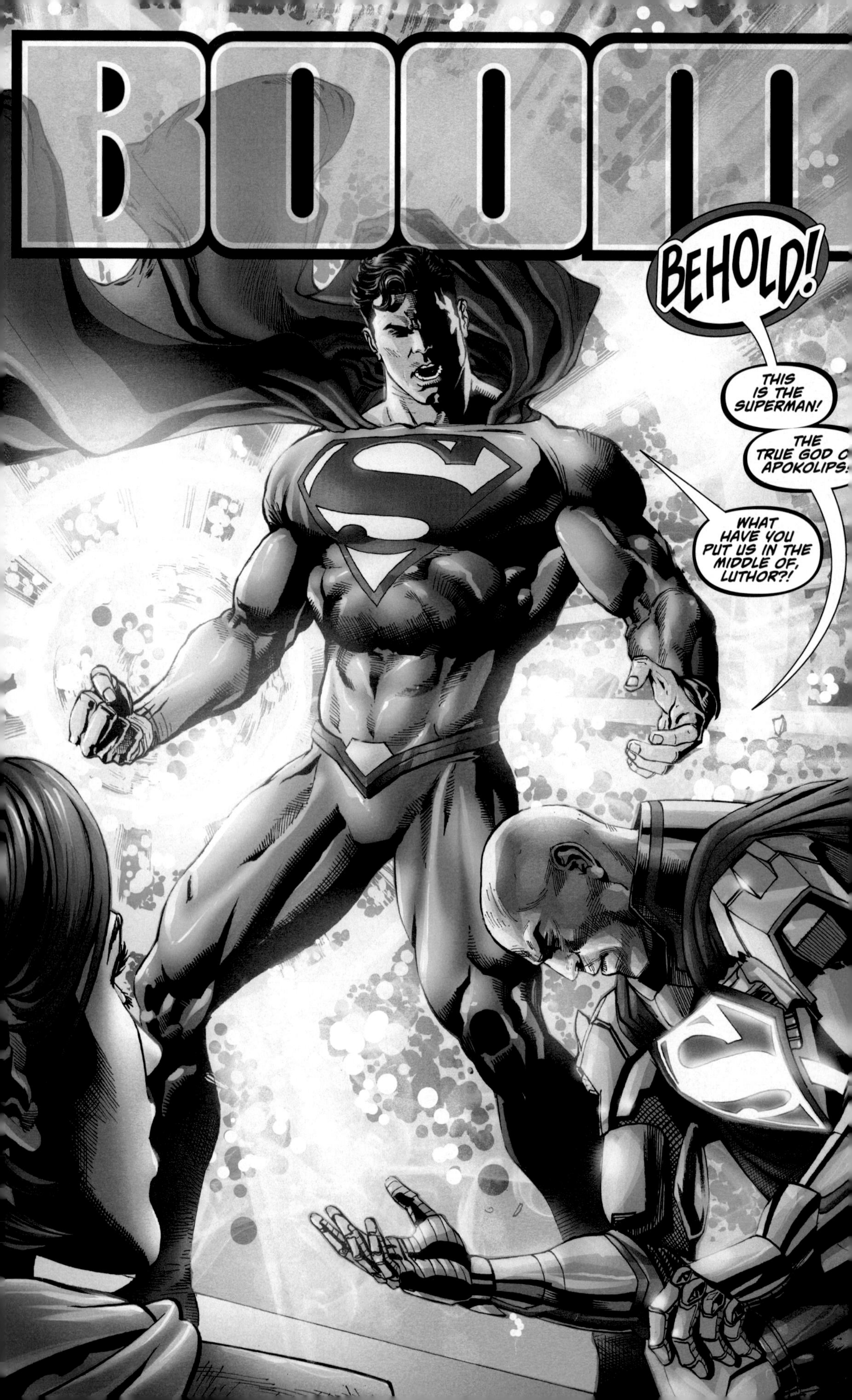
BOO
BEHOLD!
THIS IS THE SUPERMAN!
THE TRUE GOD O APOKOLIPS!
WHAT HAVE YOU PUT US IN THE MIDDLE OF, LUTHOR?!

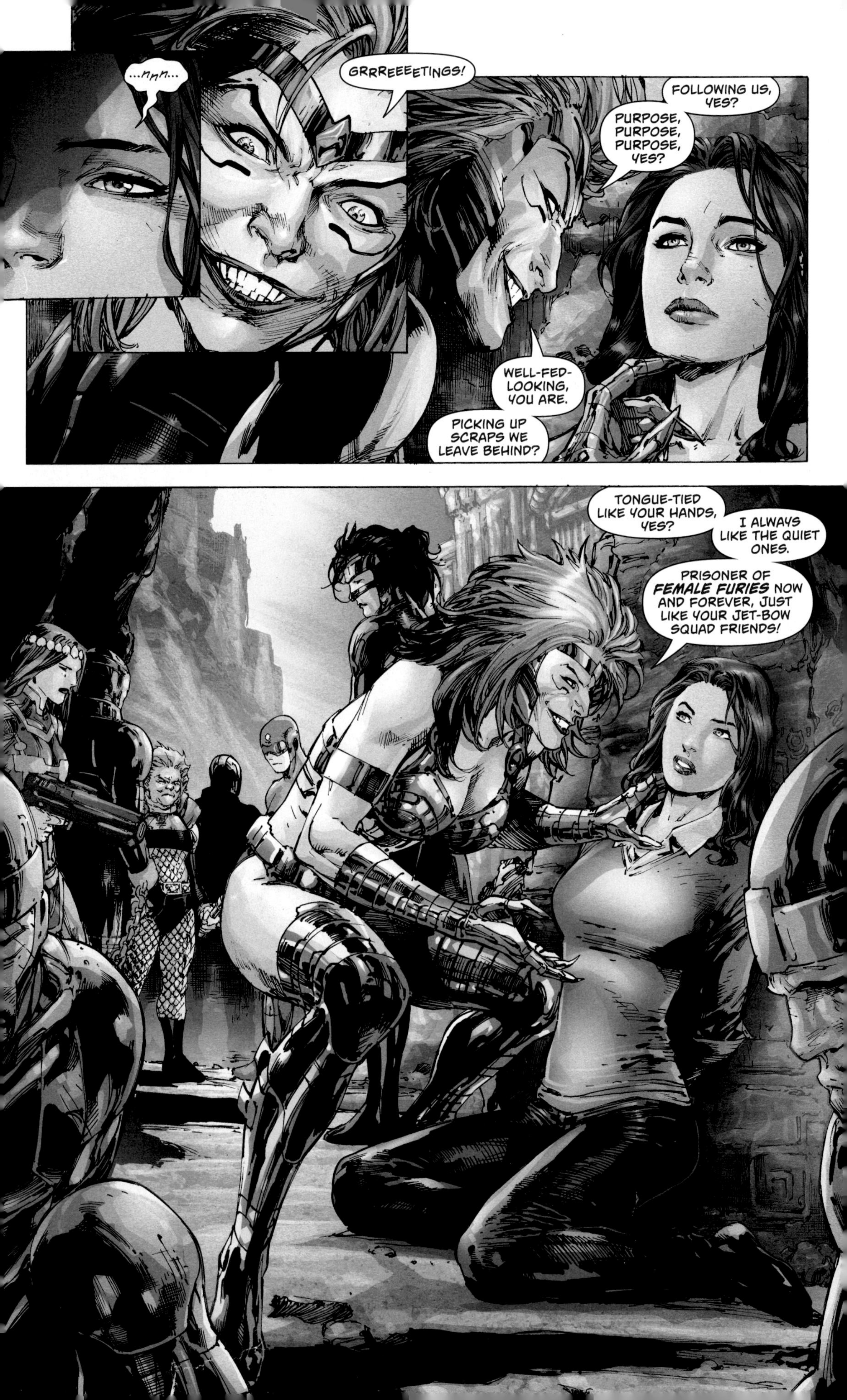
...nnn...
GRRREEEEETINGS!
FOLLOWING US, YES?
PURPOSE, PURPOSE, PURPOSE, YES?
WELL-FED-LOOKING, YOU ARE.
PICKING UP SCRAPS WE LEAVE BEHIND?
TONGUE-TIED LIKE YOUR HANDS, YES?
I ALWAYS LIKE THE QUIET ONES.
PRISONER OF FEMALE FURIES NOW AND FOREVER, JUST LIKE YOUR JET-BOW SQUAD FRIENDS!

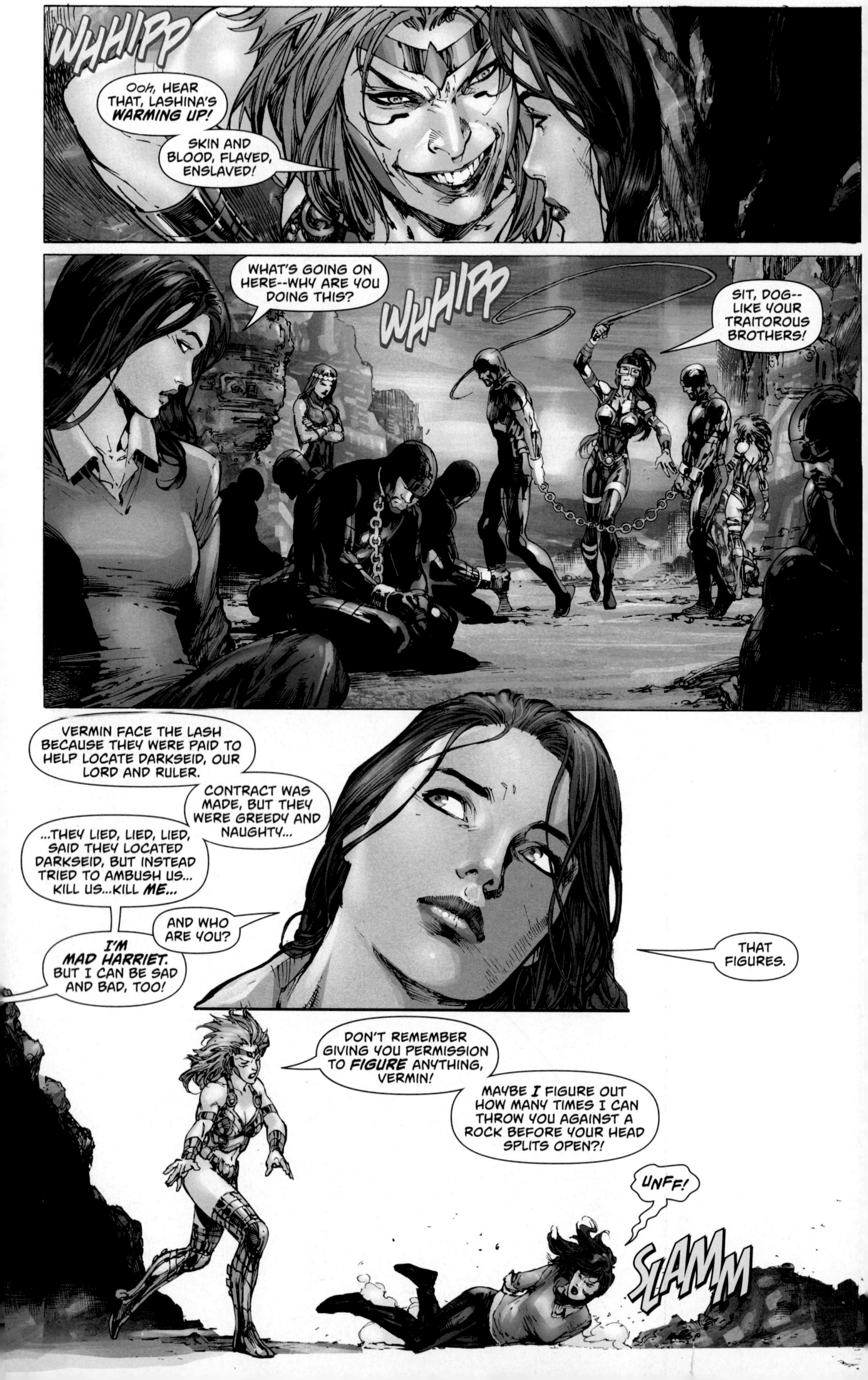
WHHIPP
Ooh, HEAR THAT, LASHINA'S WARMING UP!
SKIN AND BLOOD, FLAYED, ENSLAVED!
WHAT'S GOING ON HERE--WHY ARE YOU DOING THIS?
WHHIPP
SIT, DOG-- LIKE YOUR TRAITOROUS BROTHERS!
VERMIN FACE THE LASH BECAUSE THEY WERE PAID TO HELP LOCATE DARKSEID, OUR LORD AND RULER.
CONTRACT WAS MADE, BUT THEY WERE GREEDY AND NAUGHTY...
...THEY LIED, LIED, LIED, SAID THEY LOCATED DARKSEID, BUT INSTEAD TRIED TO AMBUSH US... KILL US...KILL ME...
AND WHO ARE YOU?
I'M MAD HARRIET. BUT I CAN BE SAD AND BAD, TOO!
THAT FIGURES.
DON'T REMEMBER GIVING YOU PERMISSION TO FIGURE ANYTHING, VERMIN!
MAYBE I FIGURE OUT HOW MANY TIMES I CAN THROW YOU AGAINST A ROCK BEFORE YOUR HEAD SPLITS OPEN?!
UNFF!
SLAMM

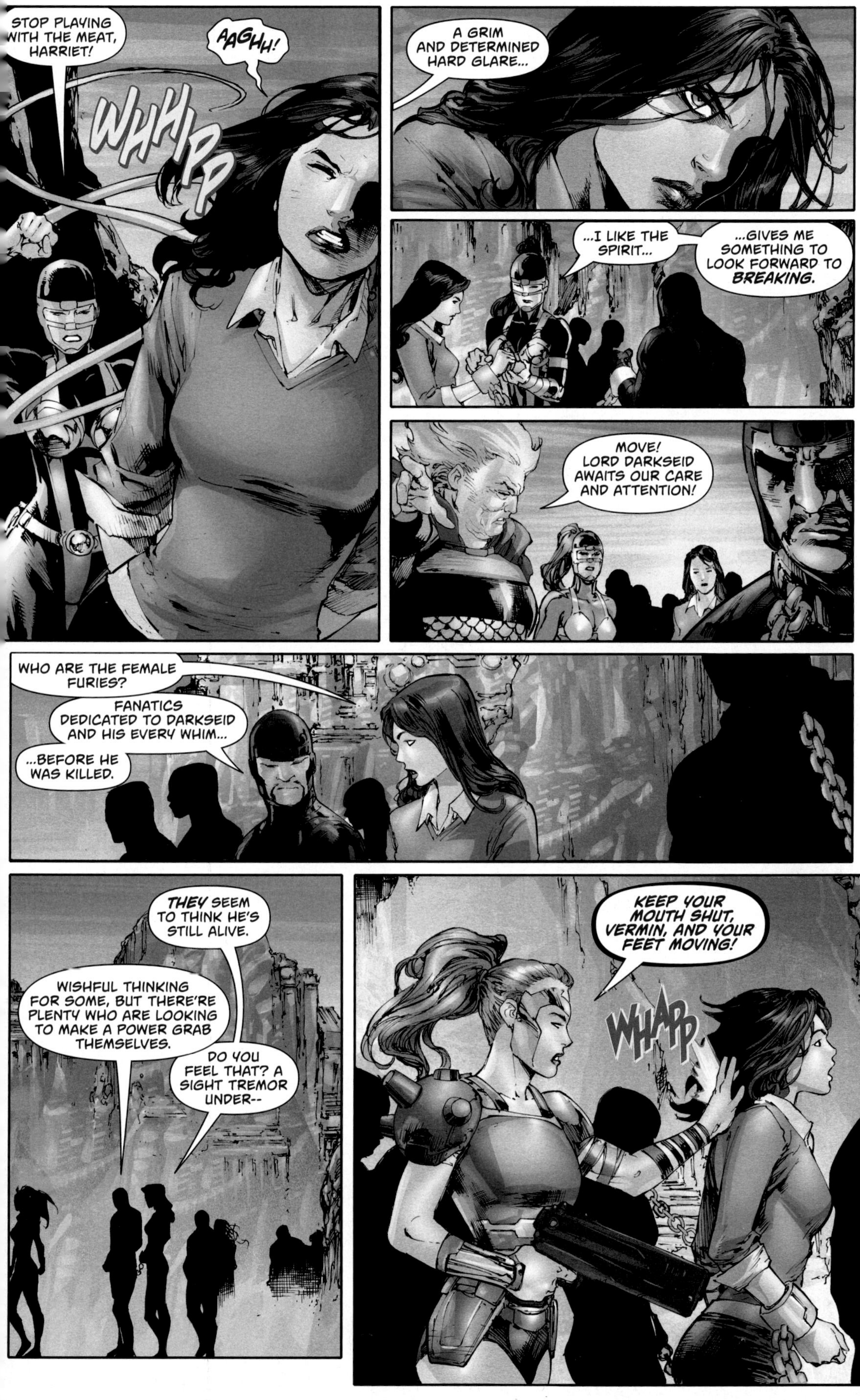
STOP PLAYING WITH THE MEAT, HARRIET!
AAGHH!
WHHIPP
A GRIM AND DETERMINED HARD GLARE...
...I LIKE THE SPIRIT...
...GIVES ME SOMETHING TO LOOK FORWARD TO BREAKING.
MOVE! LORD DARKSEID AWAITS OUR CARE AND ATTENTION!
WHO ARE THE FEMALE FURIES?
FANATICS DEDICATED TO DARKSEID AND HIS EVERY WHIM...
...BEFORE HE WAS KILLED.
THEY SEEM TO THINK HE'S STILL ALIVE.
WISHFUL THINKING FOR SOME, BUT THERE'RE PLENTY WHO ARE LOOKING TO MAKE A POWER GRAB THEMSELVES.
DO YOU FEEL THAT? A SIGHT TREMOR UNDER--
KEEP YOUR MOUTH SHUT, VERMIN, AND YOUR FEET MOVING!
WHAPP

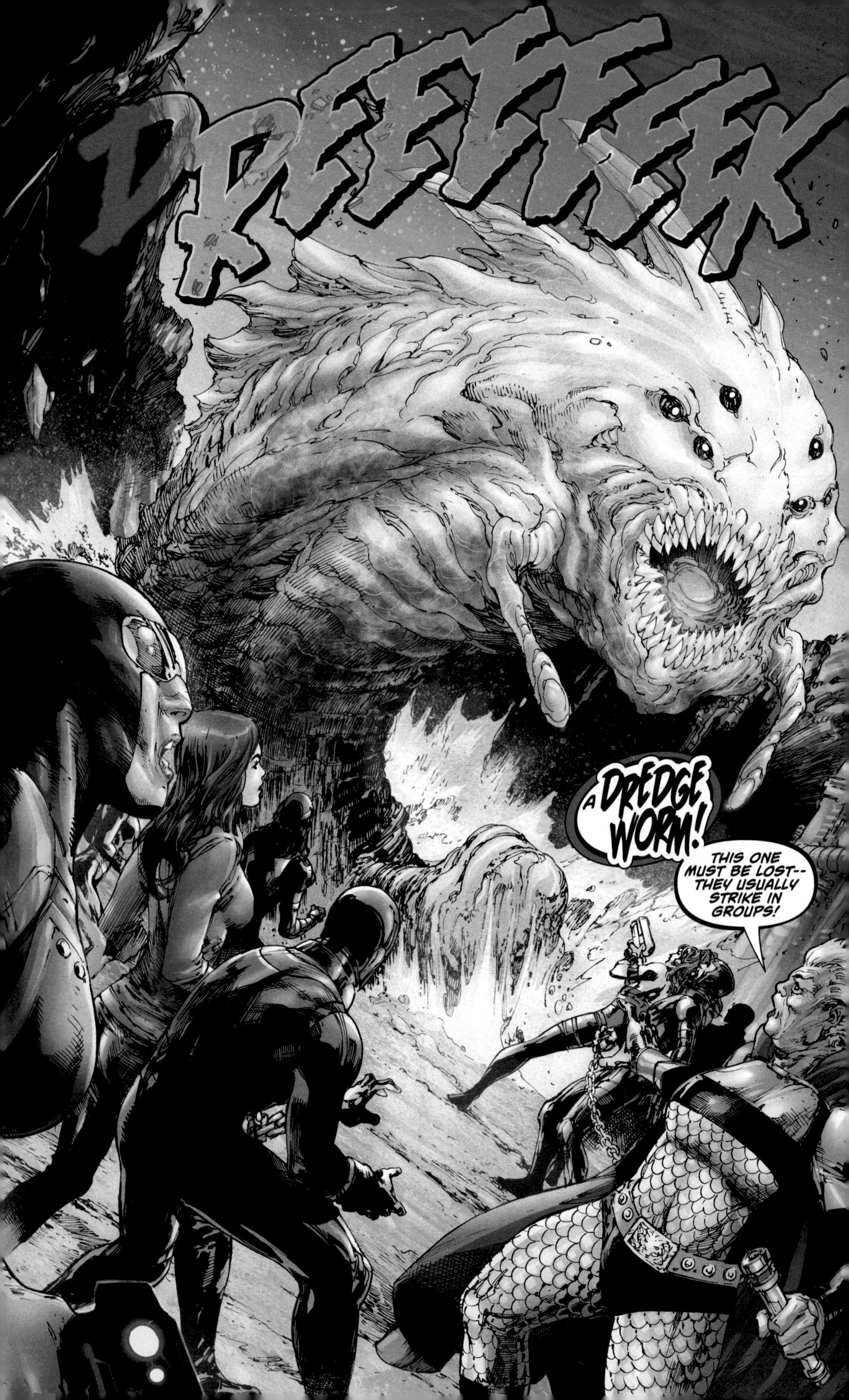
DREEEEEK
A DREDGE WORM!
THIS ONE MUST BE LOST-- THEY USUALLY STRIKE IN GROUPS!

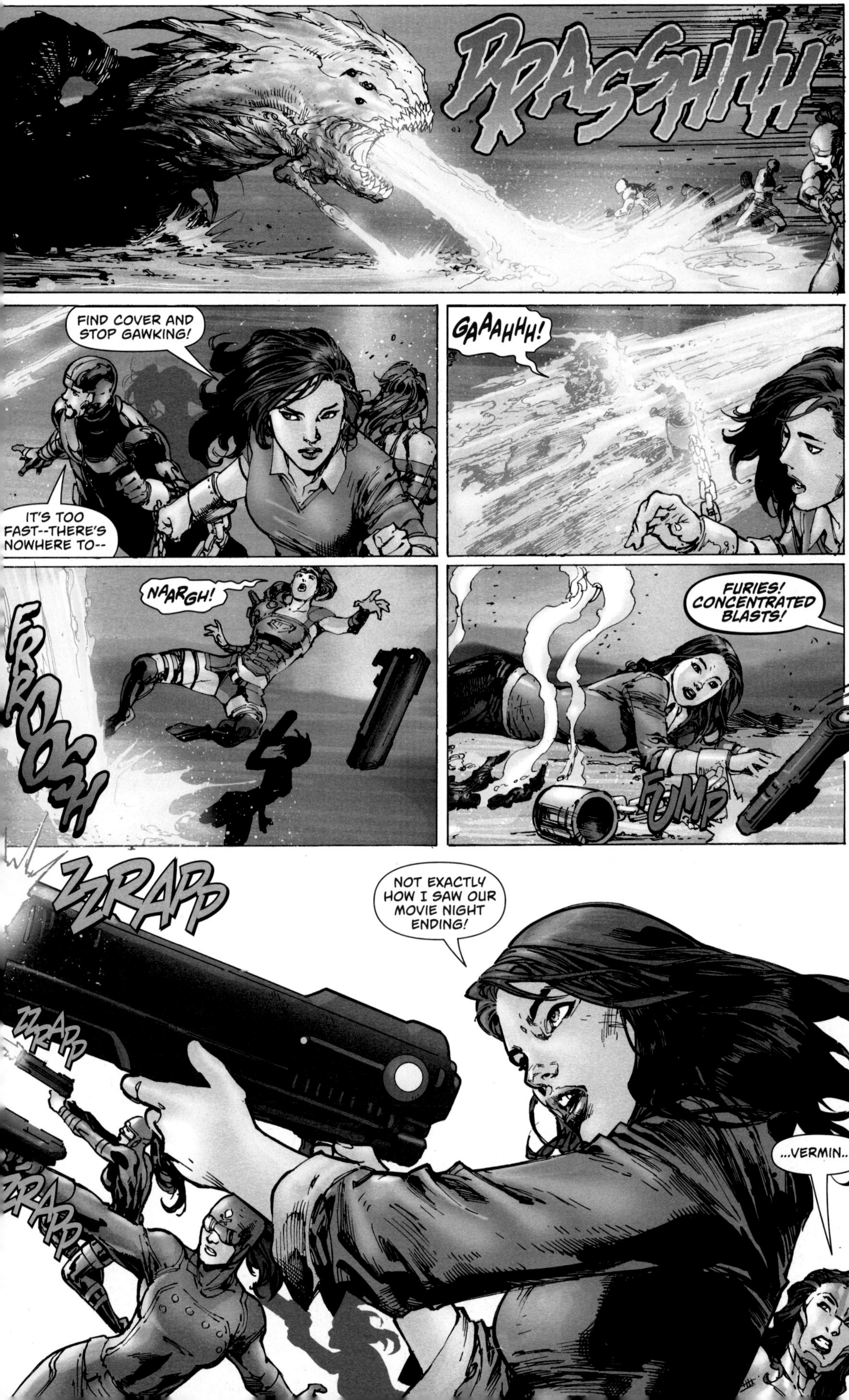
DRASSHHH
FIND COVER AND STOP GAWKING!
IT'S TOO FAST--THERE'S NOWHERE TO--
GAAAHHH!
NAARGH!
FRROOSH
FURIES! CONCENTRATED BLASTS!
FUMP
ZZRAPP
NOT EXACTLY HOW I SAW OUR MOVIE NIGHT ENDING!
ZZRAPP
ZZRAPP
...VERMIN...

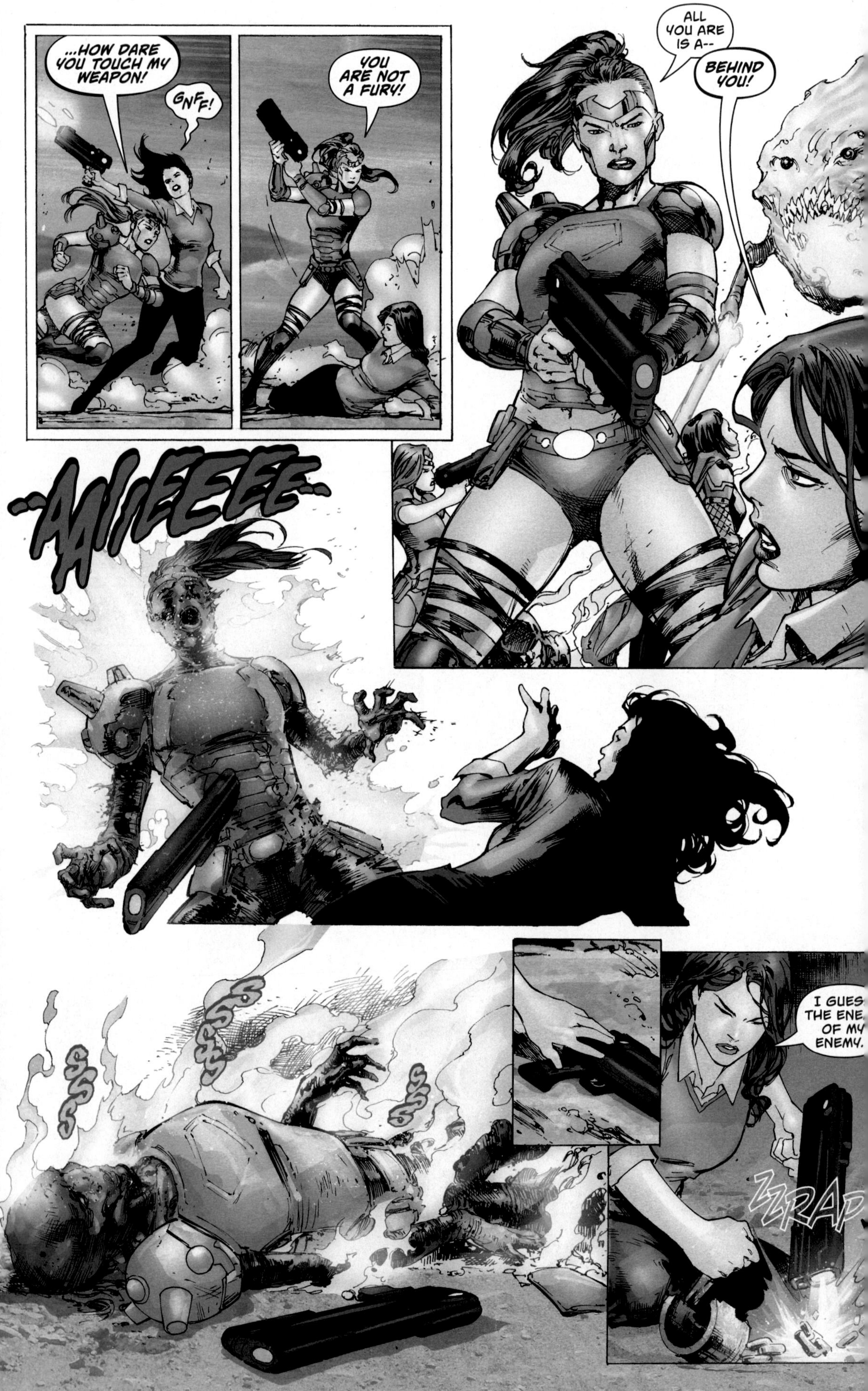
...HOW DARE YOU TOUCH MY WEAPON!
GNFF!
YOU ARE NOT A FURY!
ALL YOU ARE IS A--
BEHIND YOU!
AAIIEEEE
SSSS
SSS
SSS
I GUES THE ENE OF MY ENEMY.
ZZRAP

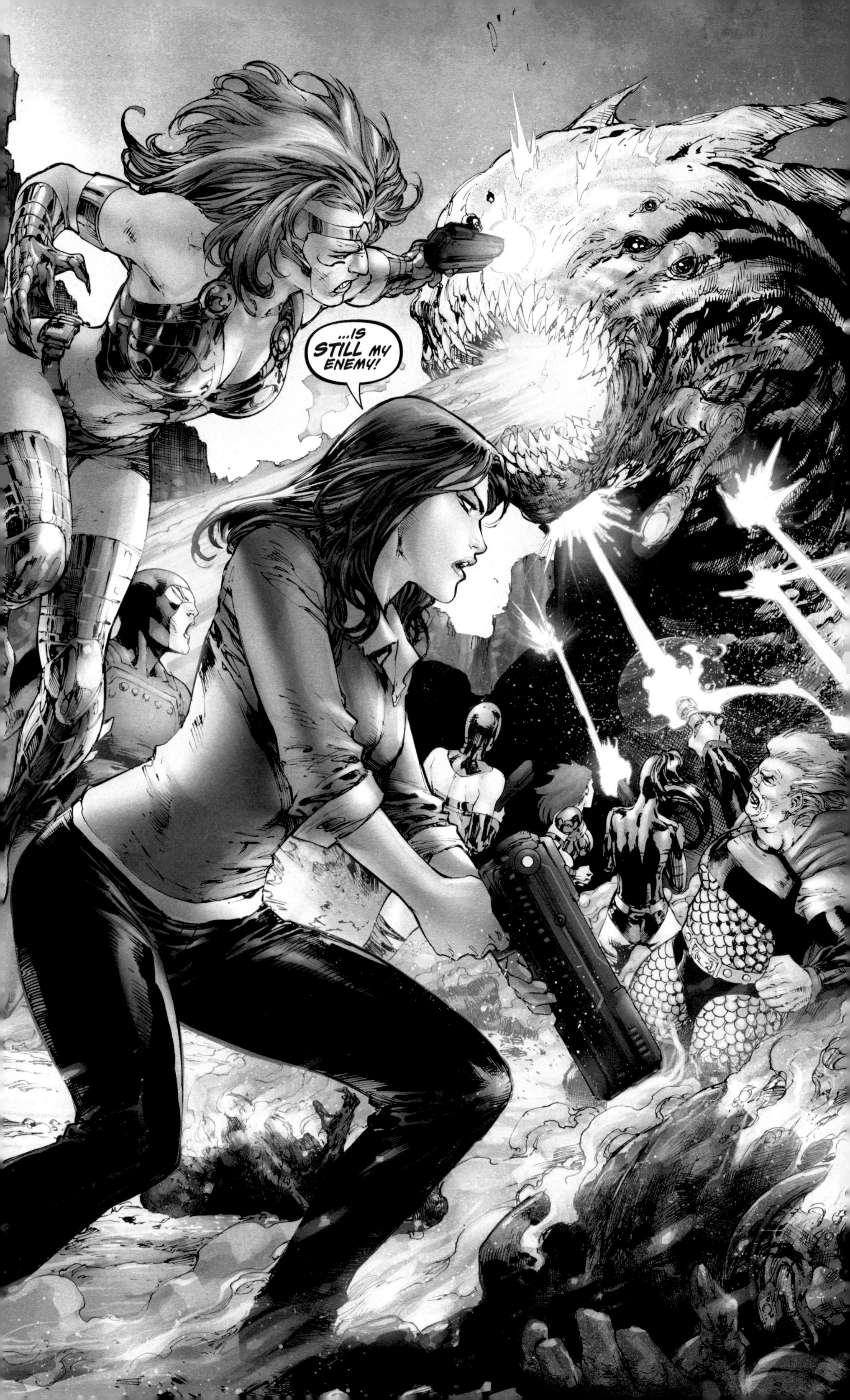
...IS STILL MY ENEMY!

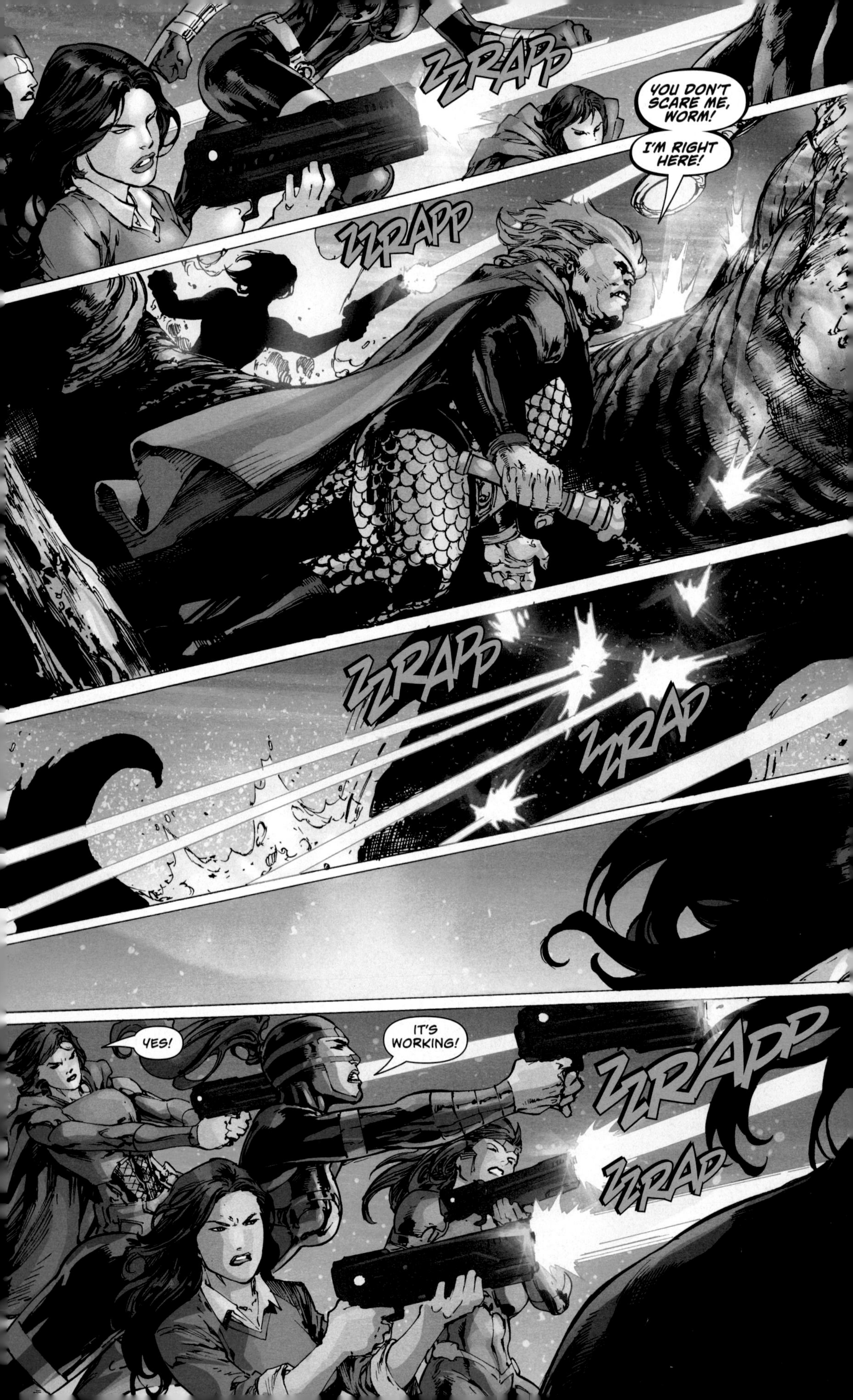
ZZRAPP
YOU DON'T SCARE ME, WORM!
I'M RIGHT HERE!
ZZRAPP
ZZRAPP
ZZRAP
YES!
IT'S WORKING!
ZZRAPP
ZZRAP

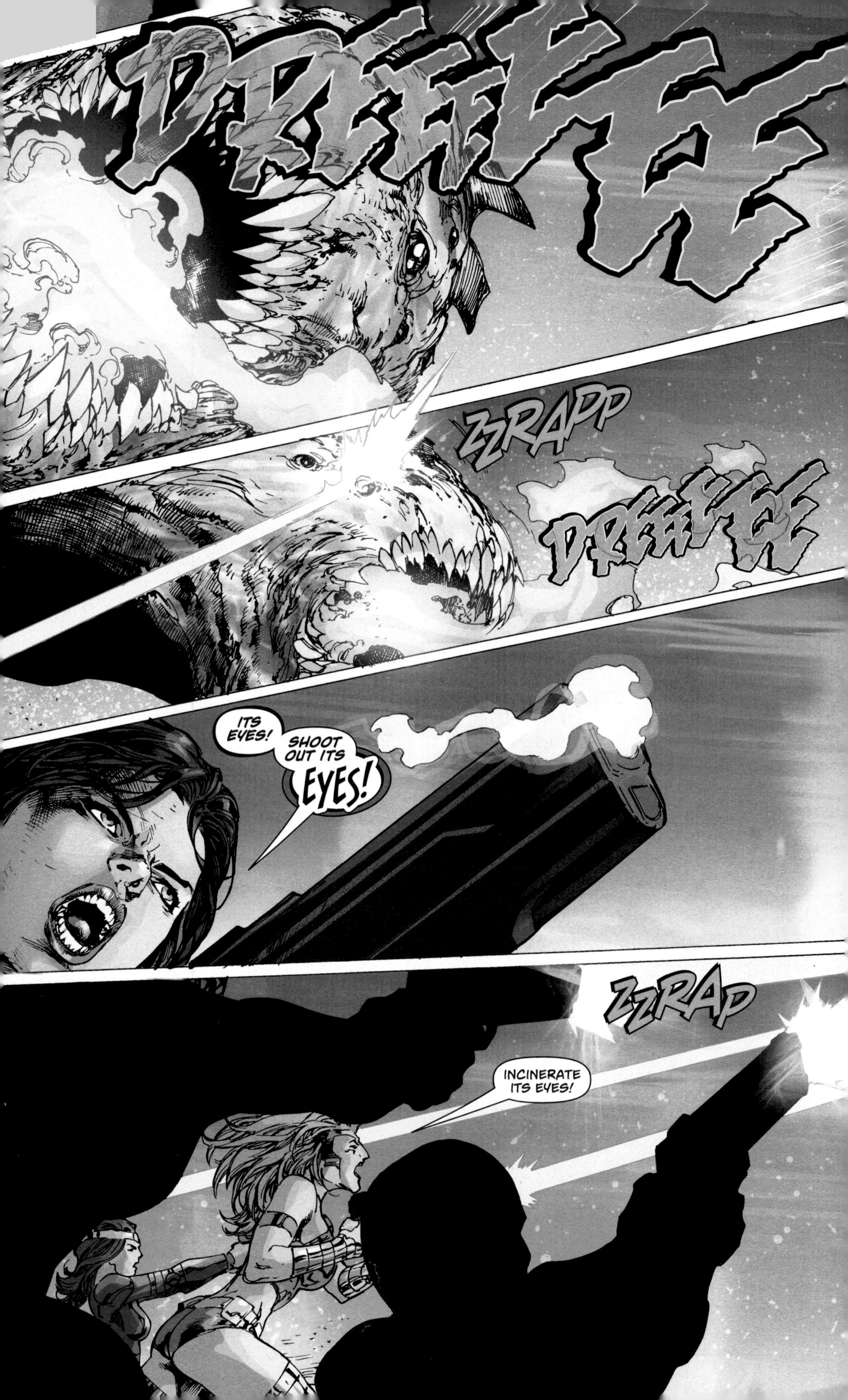

DREEEEEE
ZZRAPP
DREEEEEE
ITS EYES!
SHOOT OUT ITS EYES!
ZZRAP
INCINERATE ITS EYES!

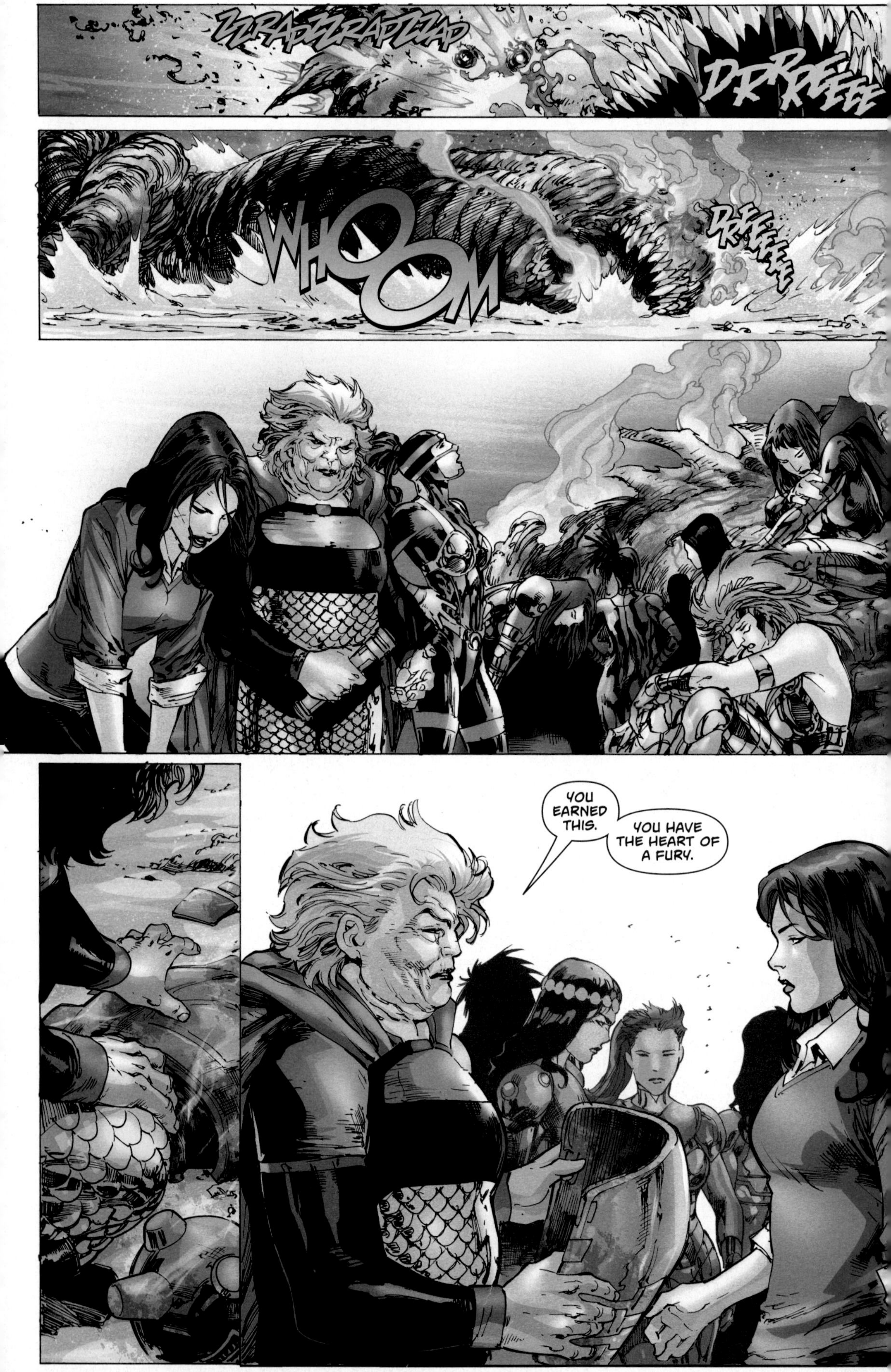
ZZRAPZZRAPZZAP
DRRREEEE
WHOOOM
DREEEEE
YOU EARNED THIS.
YOU HAVE THE HEART OF A FURY.

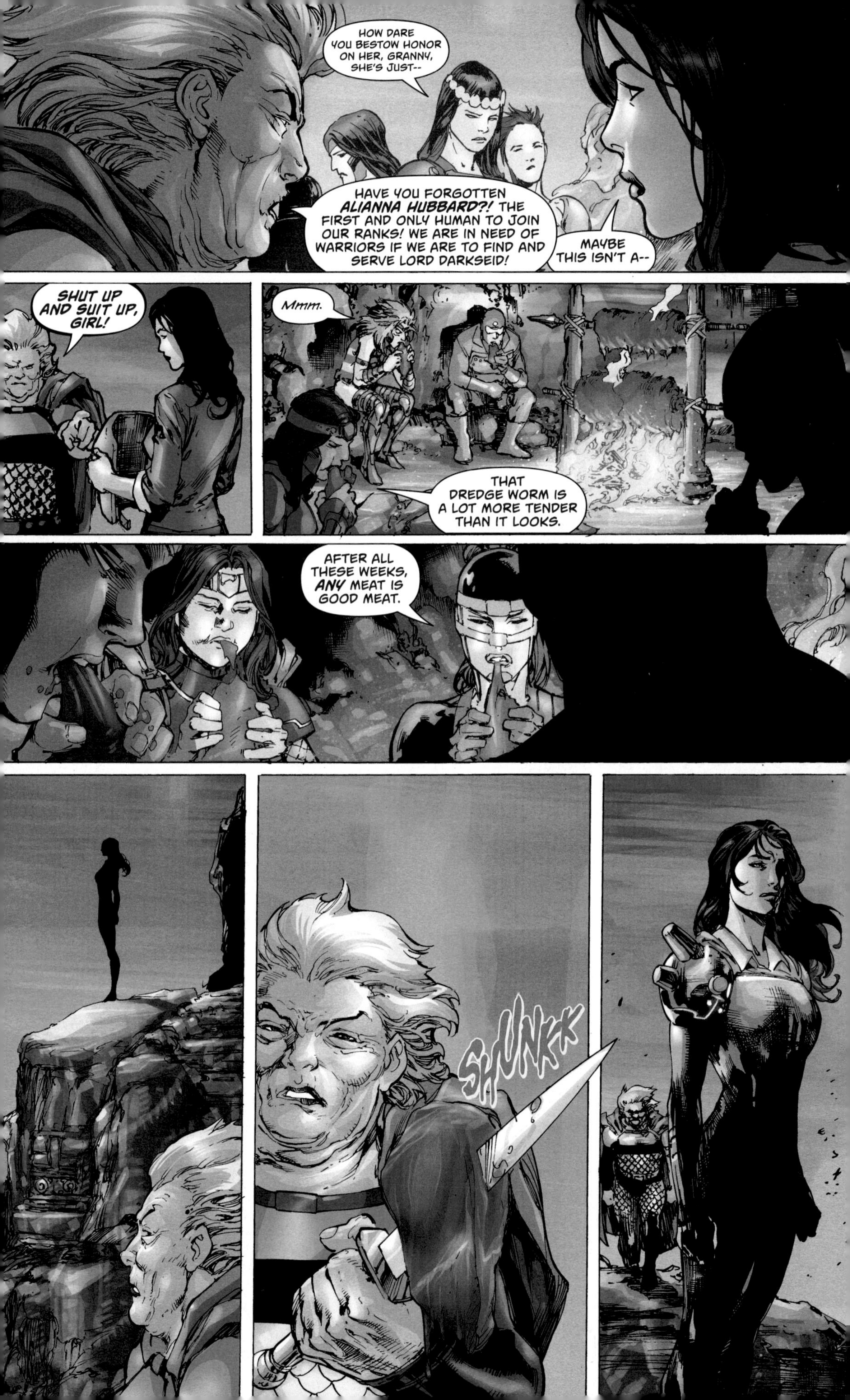
HOW DARE YOU BESTOW HONOR ON HER, GRANNY, SHE'S JUST--
HAVE YOU FORGOTTEN ALIANNA HUBBARD?! THE FIRST AND ONLY HUMAN TO JOIN OUR RANKS! WE ARE IN NEED OF WARRIORS IF WE ARE TO FIND AND SERVE LORD DARKSEID!
MAYBE THIS ISN'T A--
SHUT UP AND SUIT UP, GIRL!
Mmm.
THAT DREDGE WORM IS A LOT MORE TENDER THAN IT LOOKS.
AFTER ALL THESE WEEKS, ANY MEAT IS GOOD MEAT.
SHUNKK

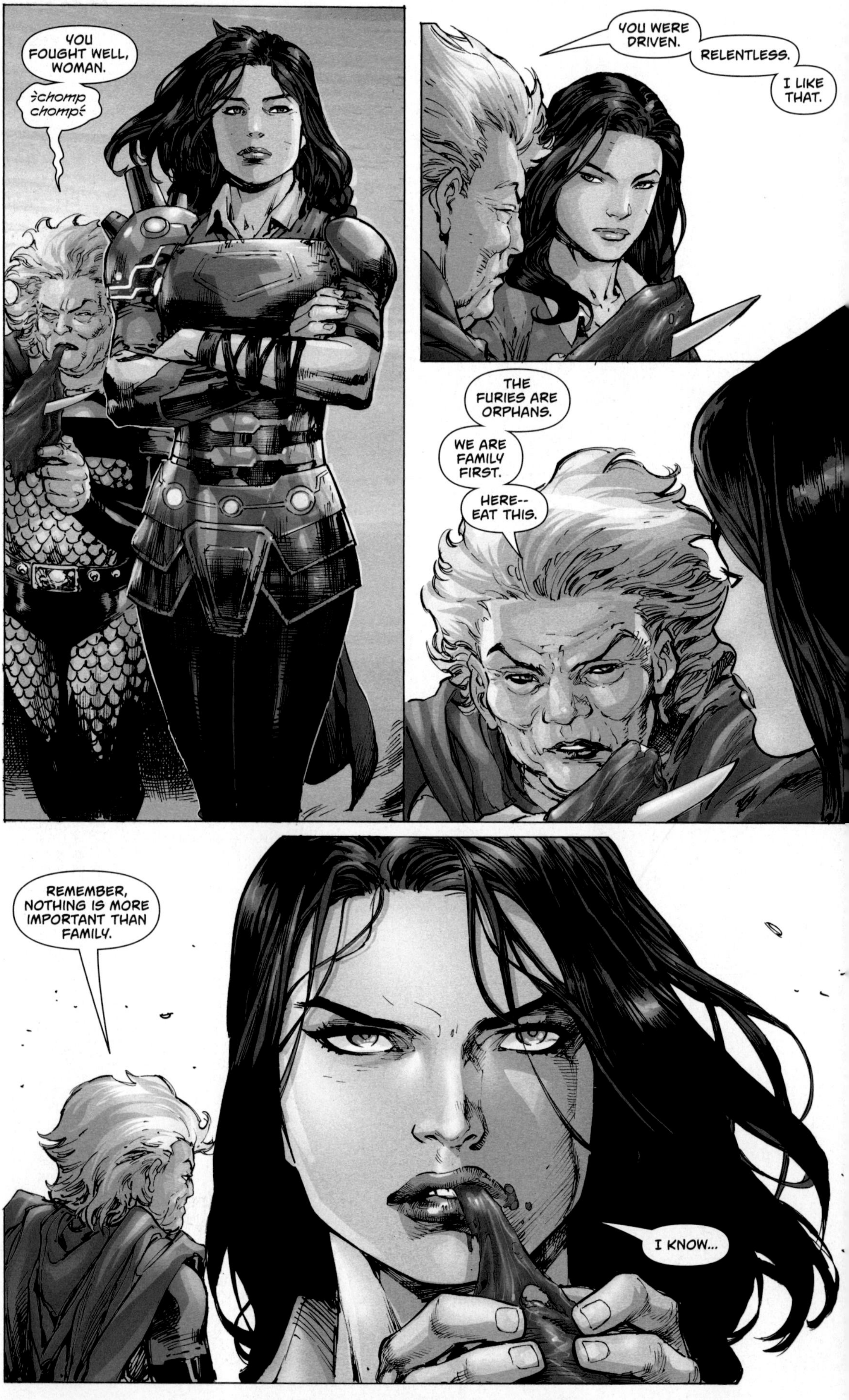

YOU FOUGHT WELL, WOMAN.
chomp chomp
YOU WERE DRIVEN.
RELENTLESS.
I LIKE THAT.
THE FURIES ARE ORPHANS.
WE ARE FAMILY FIRST.
HERE-- EAT THIS.
REMEMBER, NOTHING IS MORE IMPORTANT THAN FAMILY.
I KNOW...

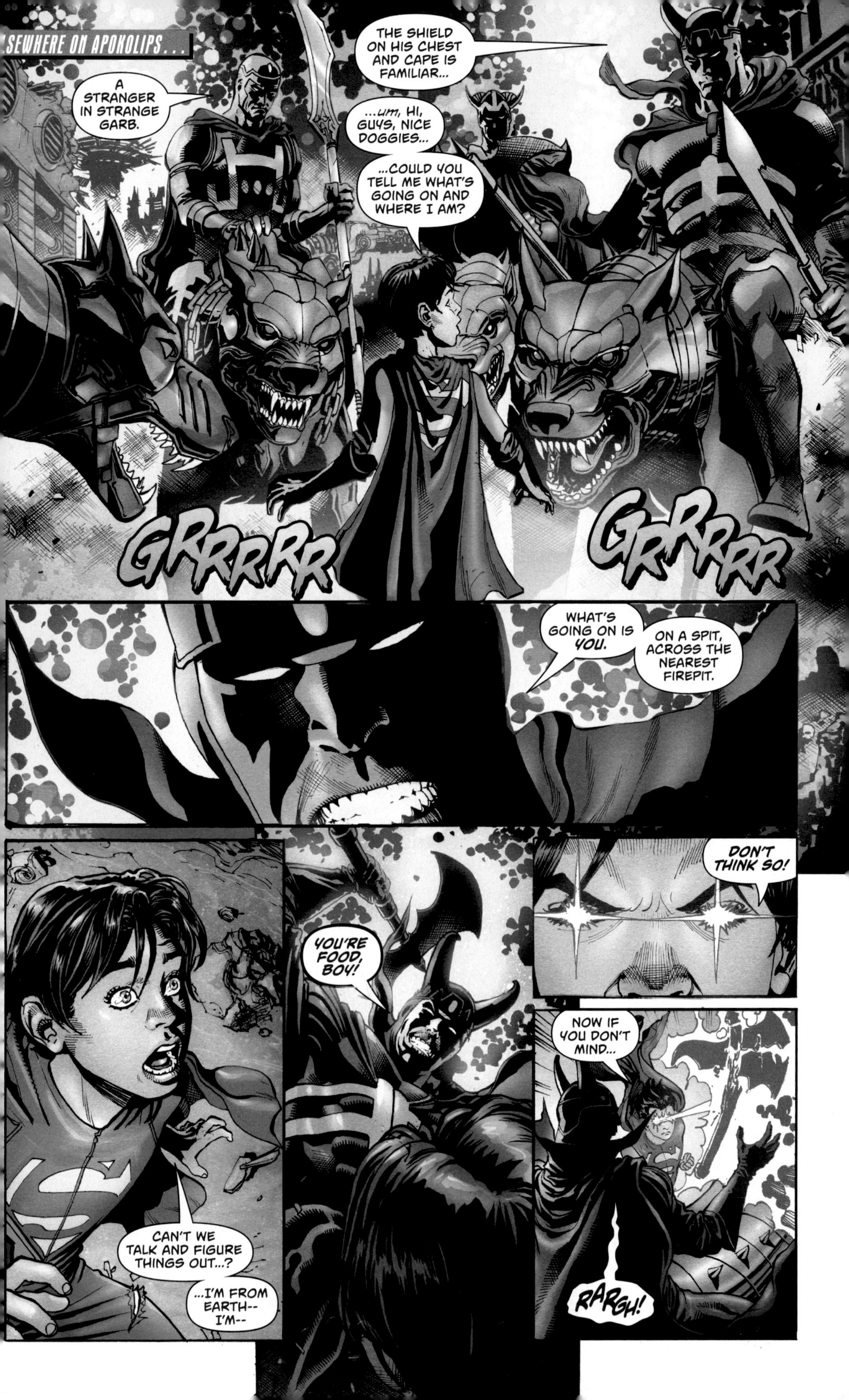
SEWHERE ON APOKOLIPS. . .
A STRANGER IN STRANGE GARB.
THE SHIELD ON HIS CHEST AND CAPE IS FAMILIAR...
...UM, HI, GUYS, NICE DOGGIES...
...COULD YOU TELL ME WHAT'S GOING ON AND WHERE I AM?
GRRRRR
GRRRRR
WHAT'S GOING ON IS YOU.
ON A SPIT, ACROSS THE NEAREST FIREPIT.
CAN'T WE TALK AND FIGURE THINGS OUT...?
...I'M FROM EARTH-- I'M--
YOU'RE FOOD, BOY!
DON'T THINK SO!
NOW IF YOU DON'T MIND...
RARGH!

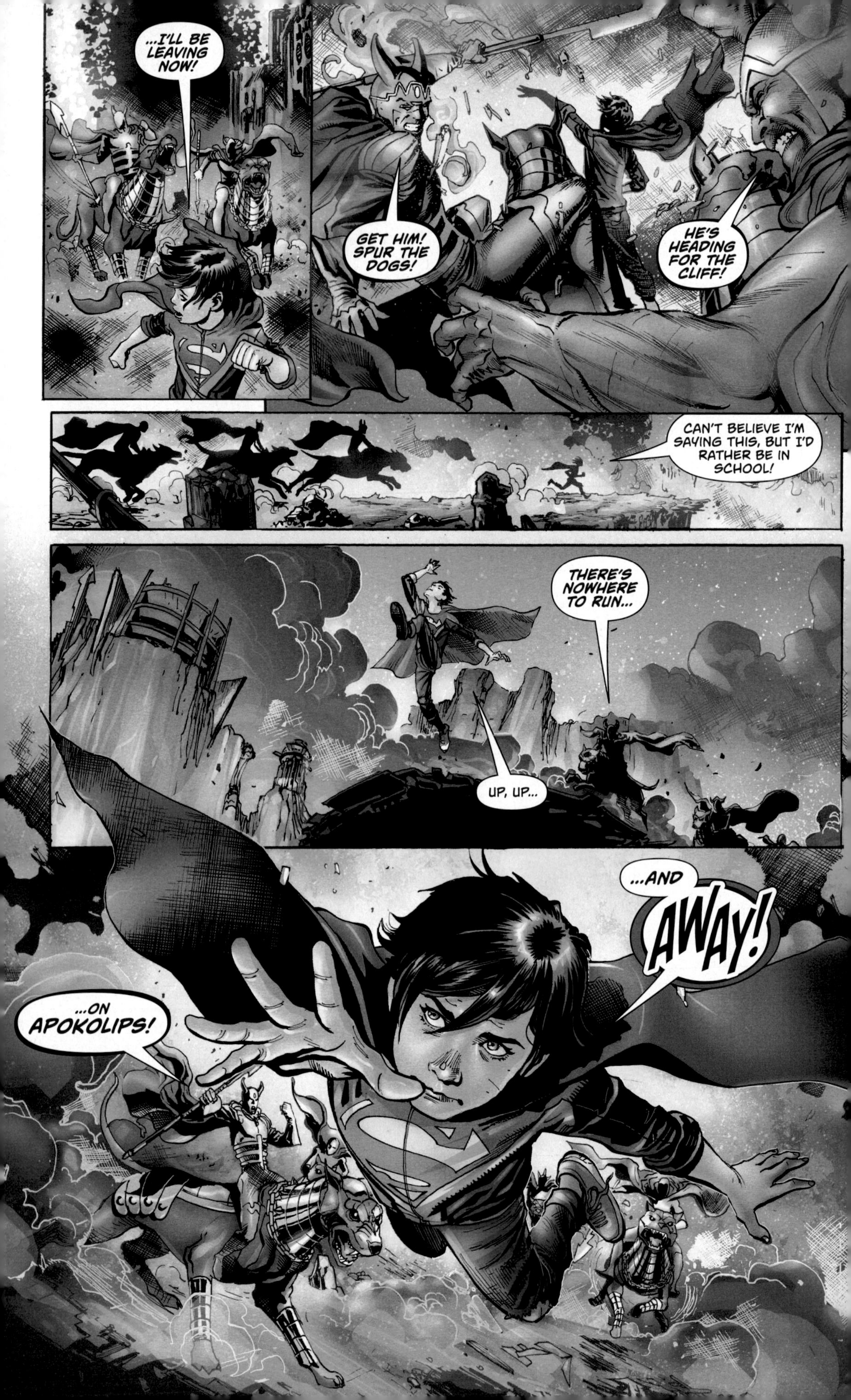
...I'LL BE LEAVING NOW!
GET HIM! SPUR THE DOGS!
HE'S HEADING FOR THE CLIFF!
CAN'T BELIEVE I'M SAYING THIS, BUT I'D RATHER BE IN SCHOOL!
THERE'S NOWHERE TO RUN...
UP, UP...
...AND
AWAY!
...ON APOKOLIPS!

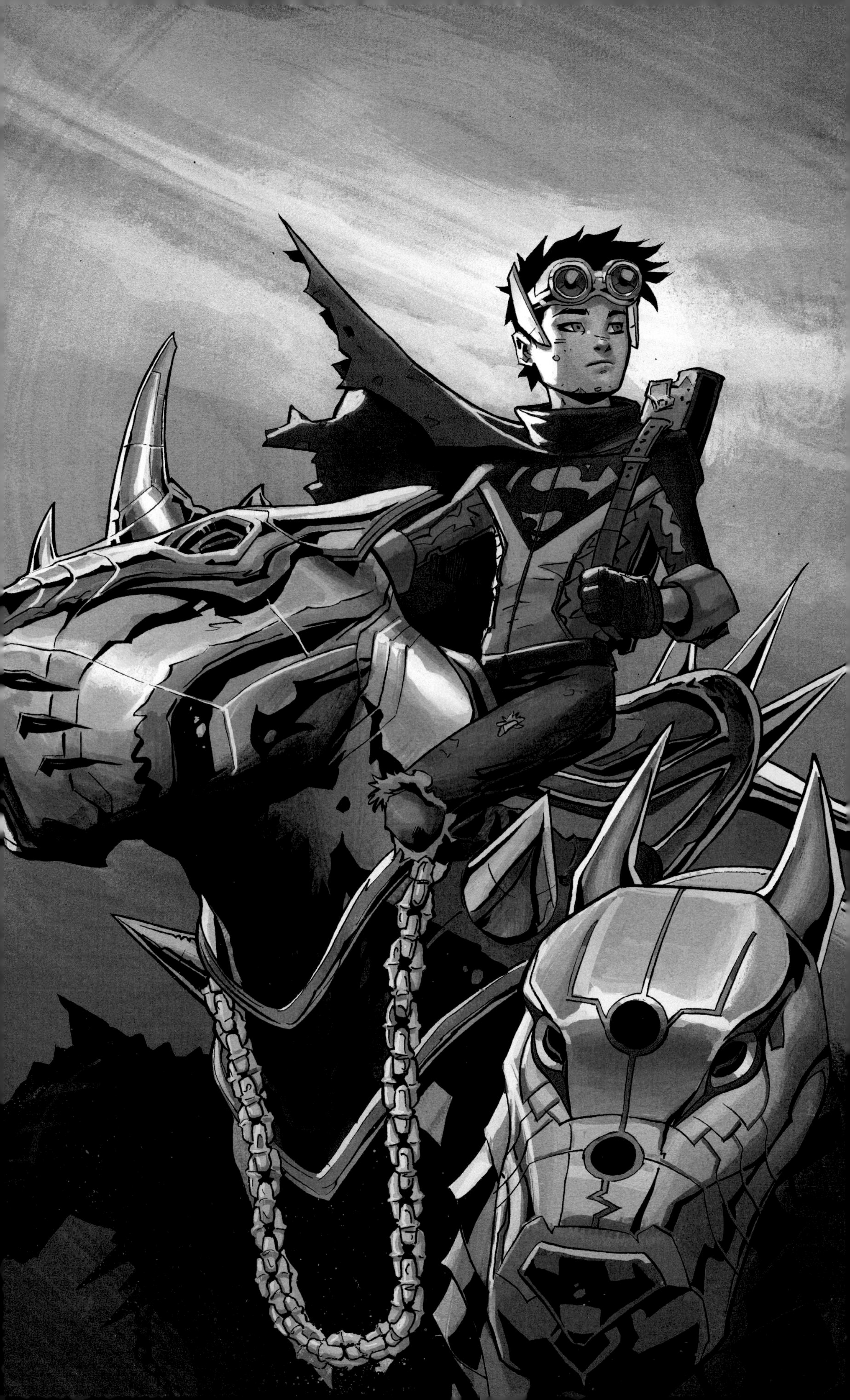

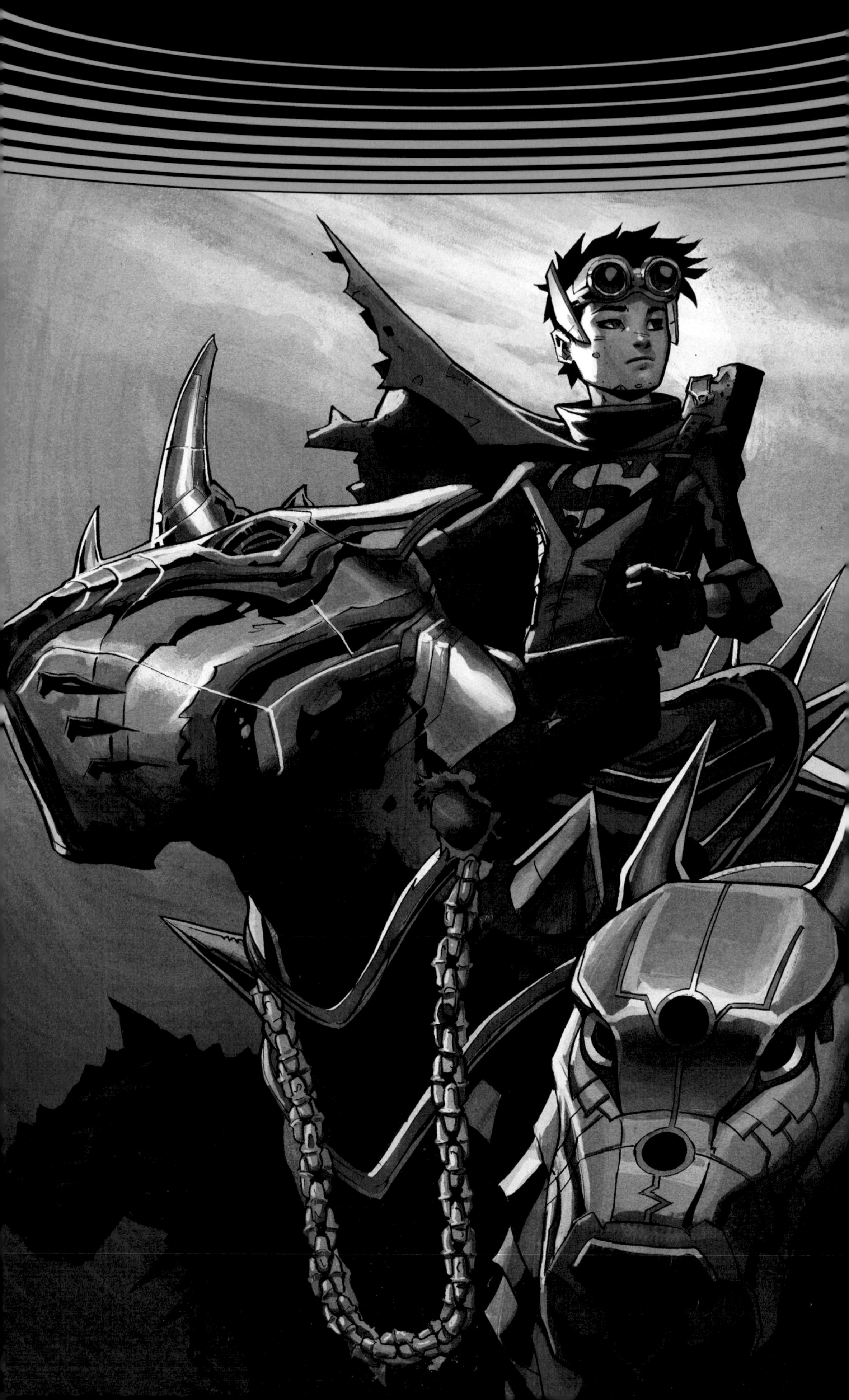

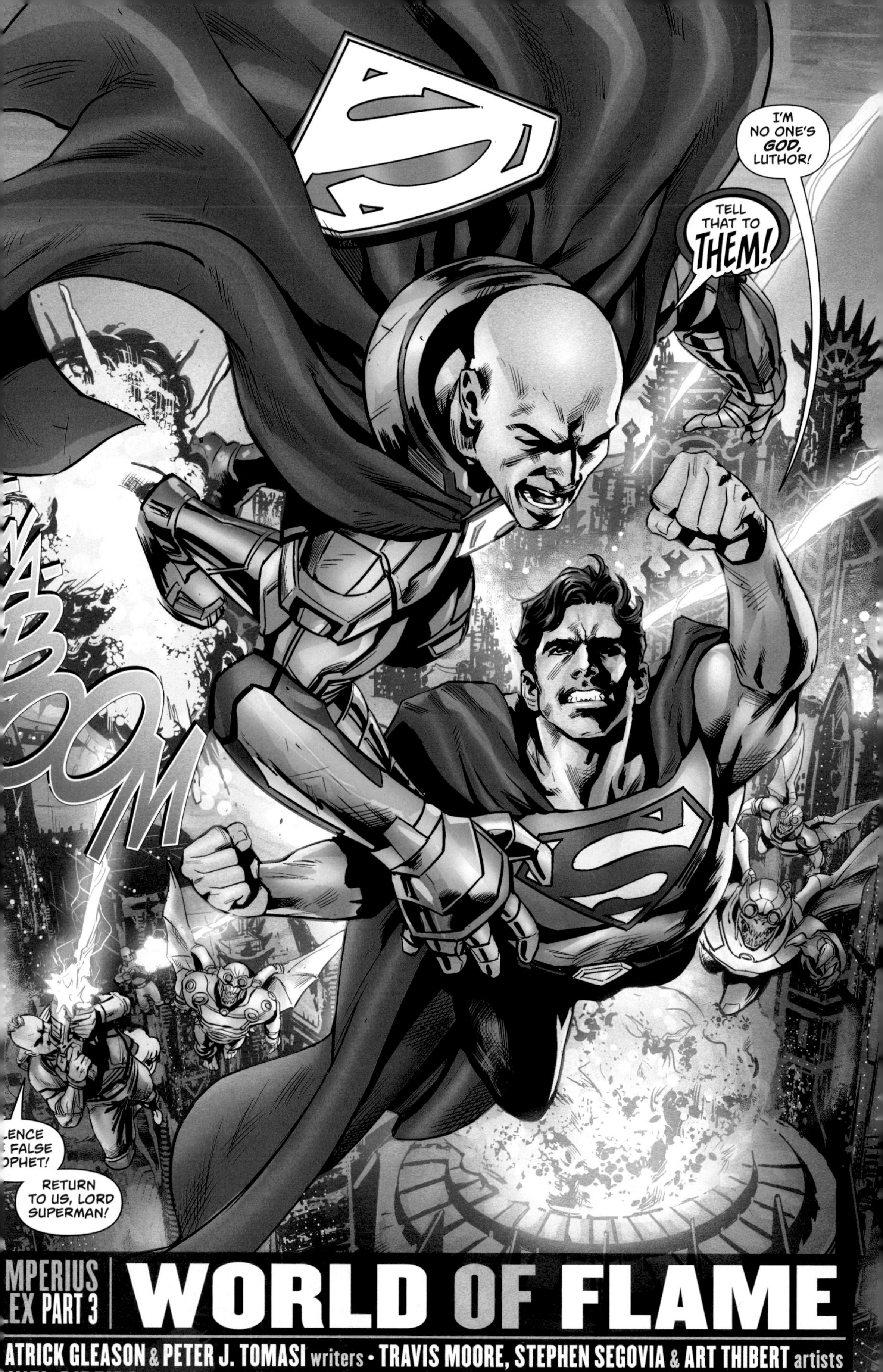

I'M NO ONE'S GOD, LUTHOR!
TELL THAT TO THEM!
LENCE FALSE OPHET!
RETURN TO US, LORD SUPERMAN!

MPERIUS LEX PART 3

WORLD OF FLAME

ATRICK GLEASON & PETER J. TOMASI writers • TRAVIS MOORE, STEPHEN SEGOVIA & ART THIBERT artists
INEI RIBEIRO colorist • ROB LEIGH letterer • PATRICK GLEASON & DEAN WHITE cover
ESSICA CHEN associate editor • PAUL KAMINSKI editor • EDDIE BERGANZA group editor

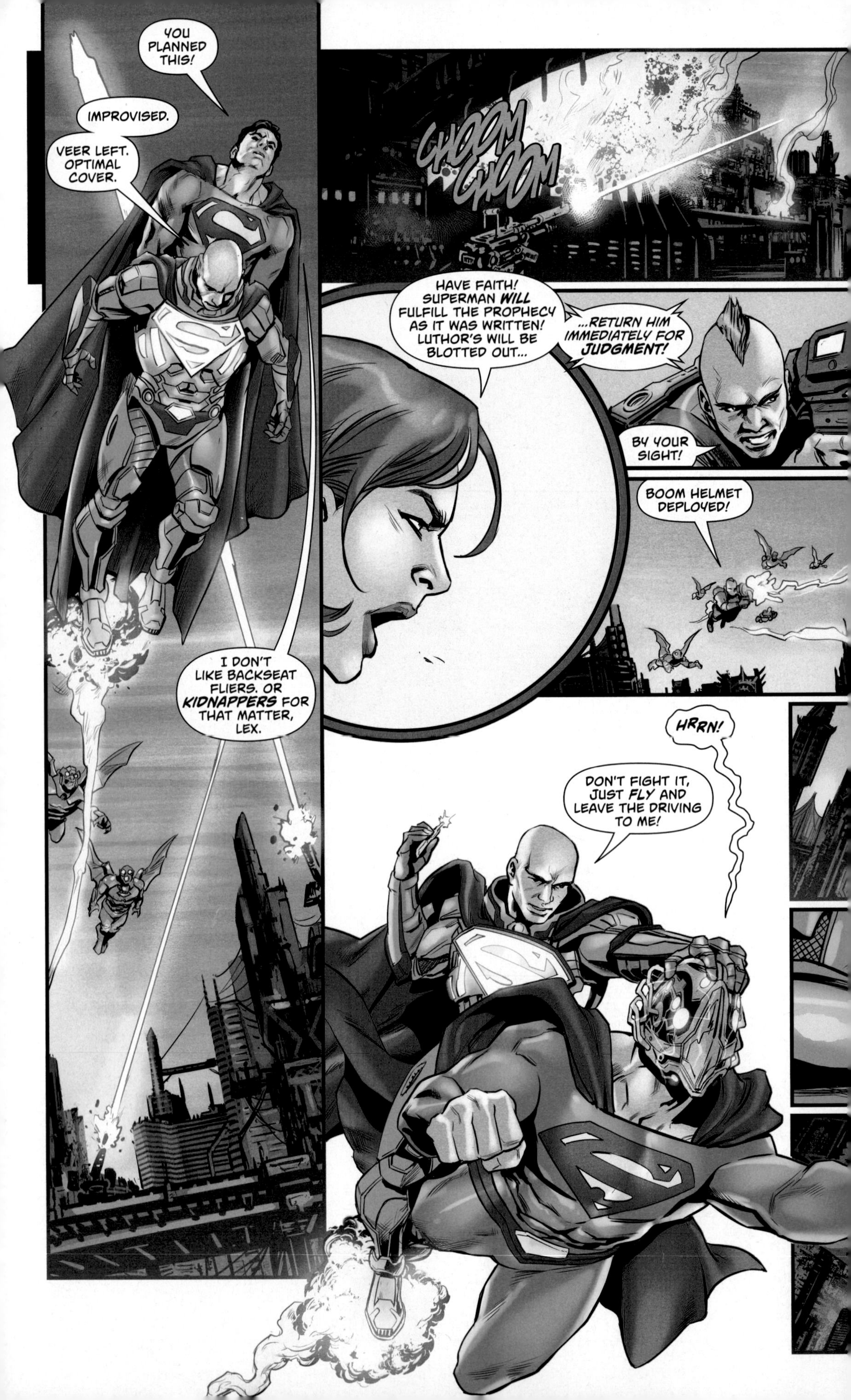
YOU PLANNED THIS!
IMPROVISED.
VEER LEFT. OPTIMAL COVER.
I DON'T LIKE BACKSEAT FLIERS. OR KIDNAPPERS FOR THAT MATTER, LEX.
CHOOM CHOOM
HAVE FAITH! SUPERMAN WILL FULFILL THE PROPHECY AS IT WAS WRITTEN! LUTHOR'S WILL BE BLOTTED OUT...
...RETURN HIM IMMEDIATELY FOR JUDGMENT!
BY YOUR SIGHT!
BOOM HELMET DEPLOYED!
HRRN!
DON'T FIGHT IT, JUST FLY AND LEAVE THE DRIVING TO ME!

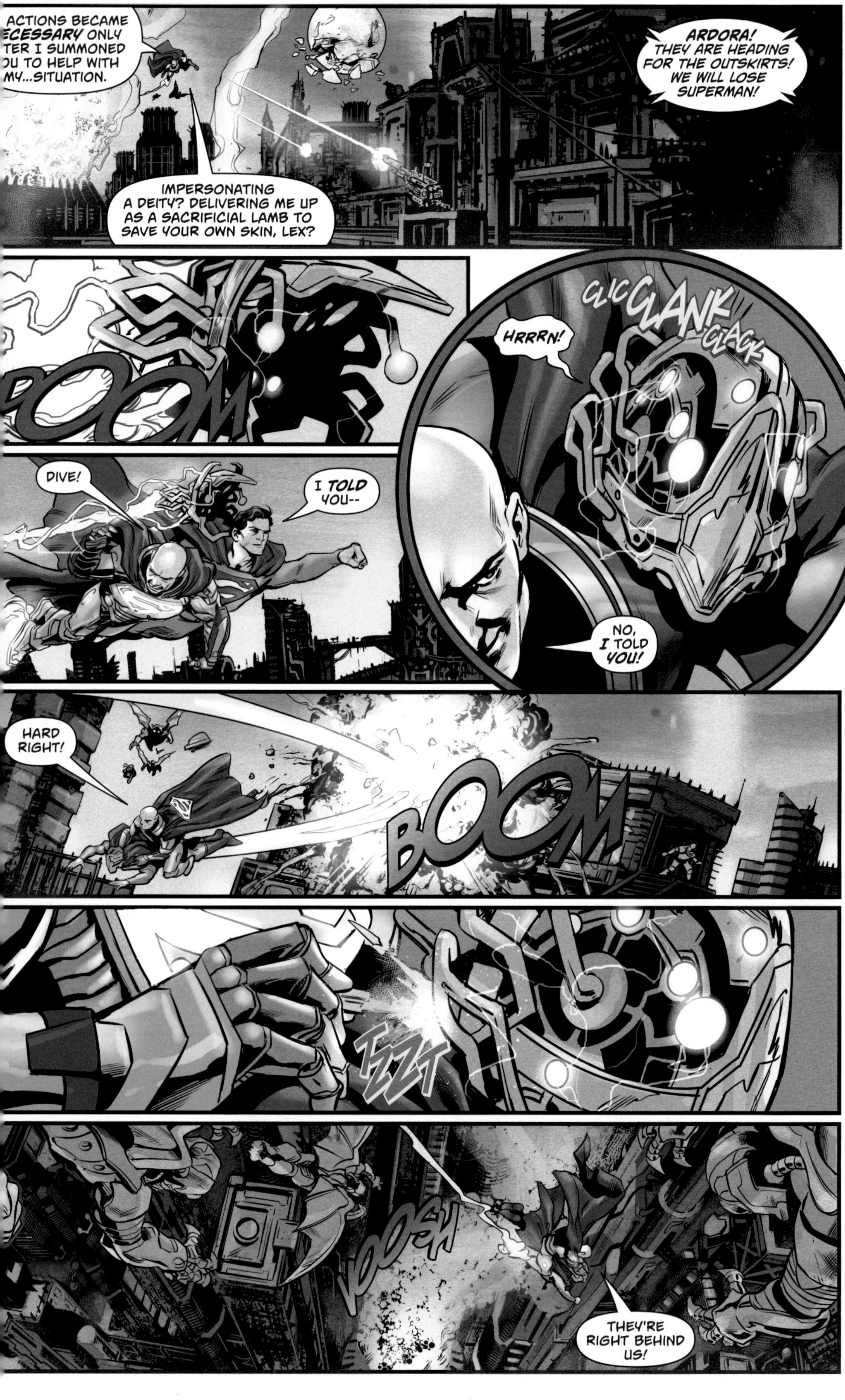
ACTIONS BECAME
ECESSARY ONLY
TER I SUMMONED
OU TO HELP WITH
MY...SITUATION.
ARDORA! THEY ARE HEADING FOR THE OUTSKIRTS! WE WILL LOSE SUPERMAN!
IMPERSONATING A DEITY? DELIVERING ME UP AS A SACRIFICIAL LAMB TO SAVE YOUR OWN SKIN, LEX?
POOM
CLIC CLANK CLACK
HRRRN!
DIVE!
I TOLD YOU--
NO, I TOLD YOU!
HARD RIGHT!
BOOM
TZZT
VOOSH
THEY'RE RIGHT BEHIND US!

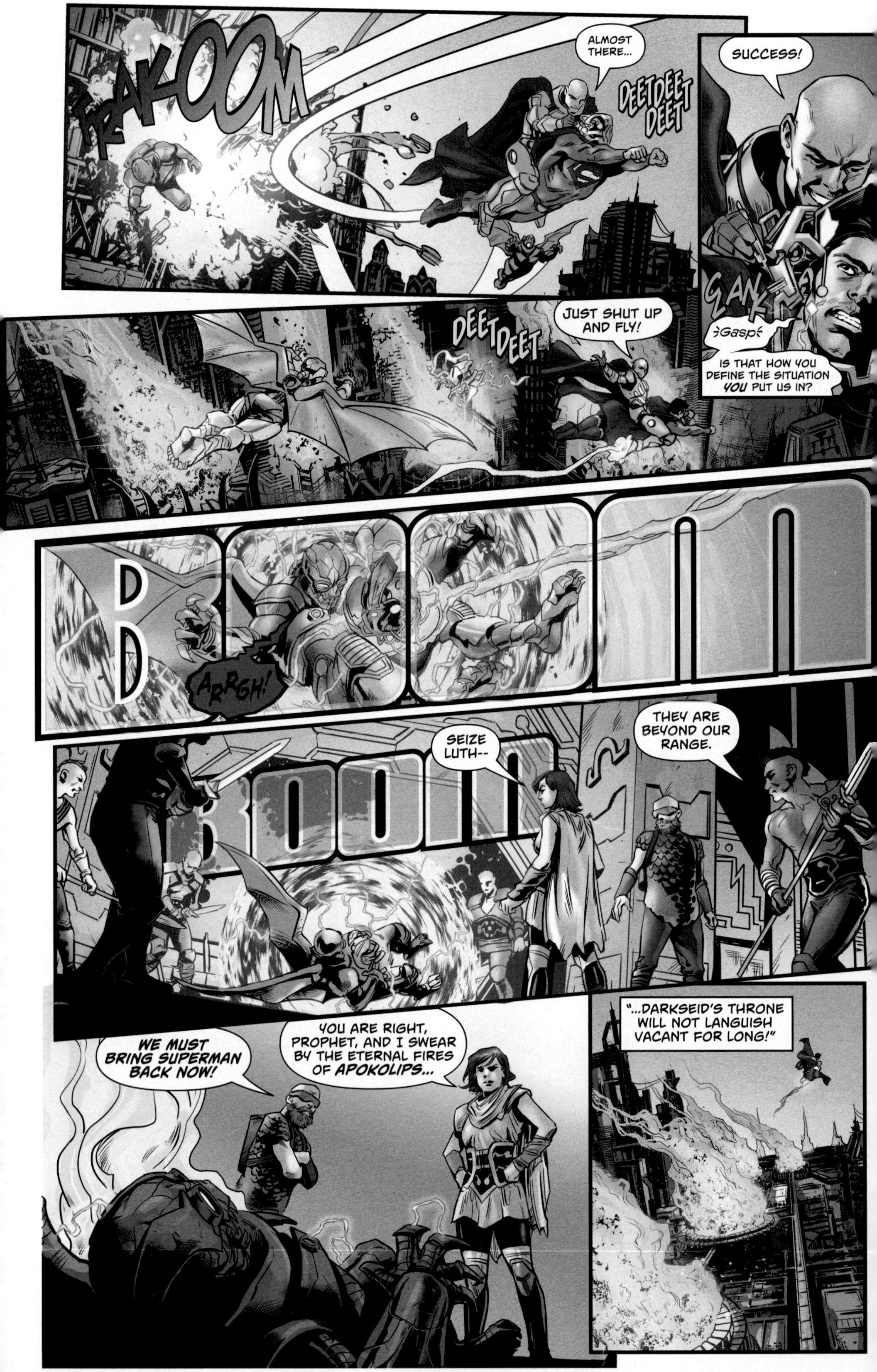
FRAKOOM
ALMOST THERE...
DEETDEET DEET
SUCCESS!
CLANK
Gasp
IS THAT HOW YOU DEFINE THE SITUATION YOU PUT US IN?
DEETDEET
JUST SHUT UP AND FLY!
BOOM
ARRGH!
SEIZE LUTH--
THEY ARE BEYOND OUR RANGE.
WE MUST BRING SUPERMAN BACK NOW!
YOU ARE RIGHT, PROPHET, AND I SWEAR BY THE ETERNAL FIRES OF APOKOLIPS...
"...DARKSEID'S THRONE WILL NOT LANGUISH VACANT FOR LONG!"

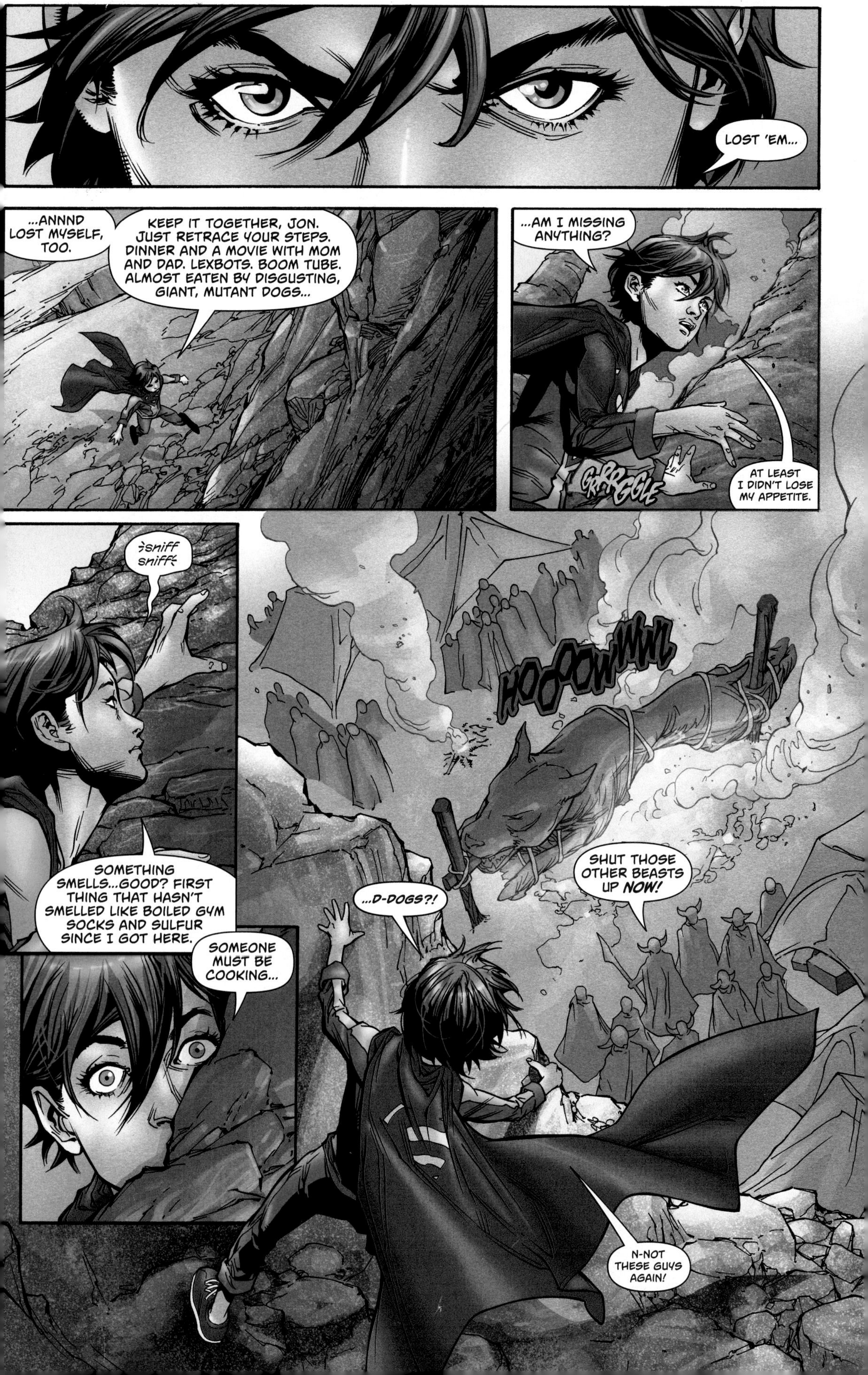
LOST 'EM...
...ANNND LOST MYSELF, TOO.
KEEP IT TOGETHER, JON. JUST RETRACE YOUR STEPS. DINNER AND A MOVIE WITH MOM AND DAD. LEXBOTS. BOOM TUBE. ALMOST EATEN BY DISGUSTING, GIANT, MUTANT DOGS...
...AM I MISSING ANYTHING?
GRRRGGLE
AT LEAST I DIDN'T LOSE MY APPETITE.
sniff sniff
SOMETHING SMELLS...GOOD? FIRST THING THAT HASN'T SMELLED LIKE BOILED GYM SOCKS AND SULFUR SINCE I GOT HERE.
SOMEONE MUST BE COOKING...
HOOOOWWWL
SHUT THOSE OTHER BEASTS UP NOW!
...D-DOGS?!
N-NOT THESE GUYS AGAIN!

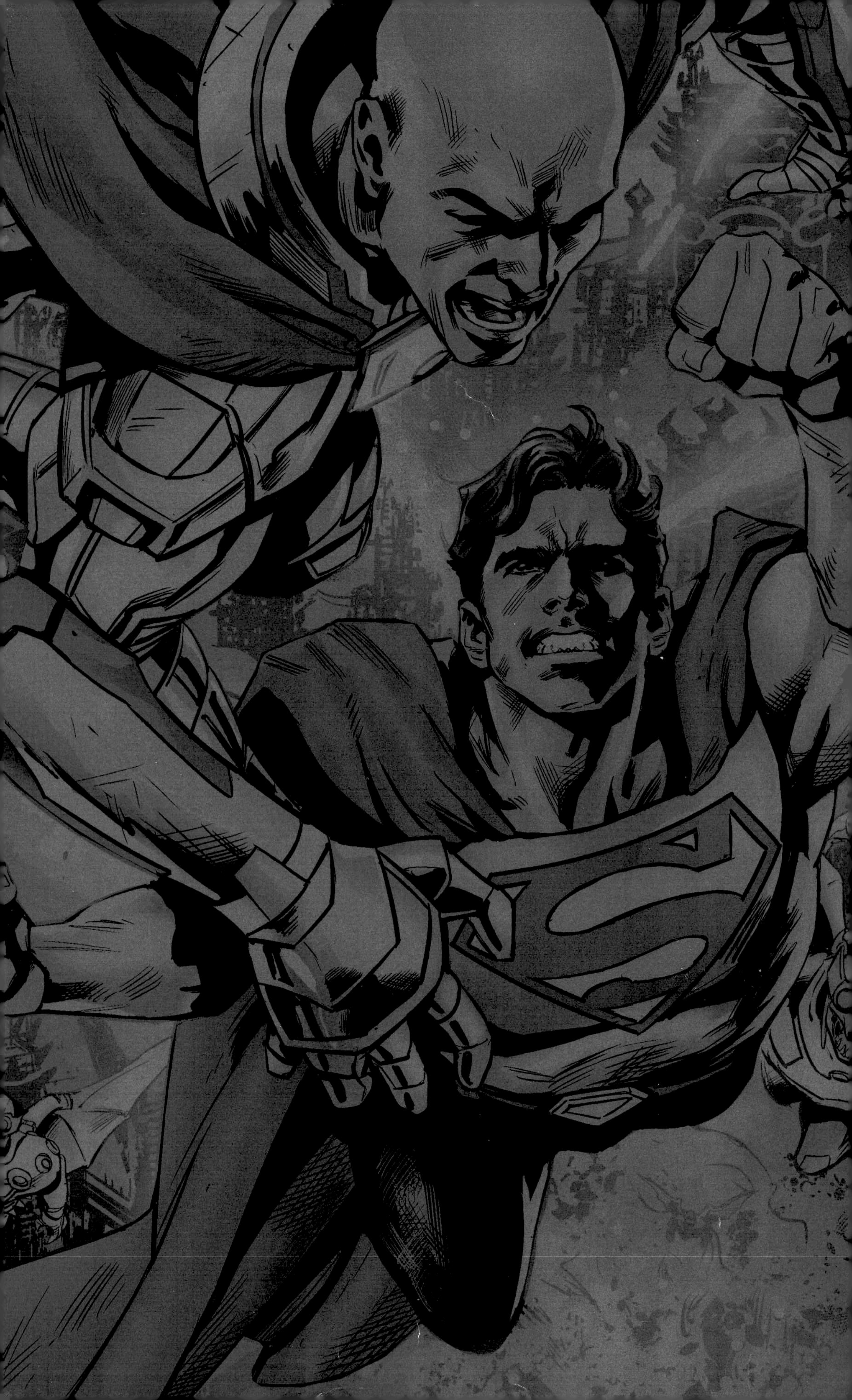

BLOOD DRAINS FASTER WHEN THE HEART IS PUMPING. WE HAVE NO TIME TO WASTE IF WE ARE TO STRIKE AGAINST KALIBAK!

WHY SHOULD WE BE MADE TO STARVE AND EAT OUR OWN DOGS, JUST SO THAT BUFFOON CAN DIVERT ALL OF APOKOLIPS' RESOURCES TO HIS MAD SCHEME OF FINDING DARKSEID?

KALIBAK WILL NEVER GIVE UP HIS BIRTHRIGHT, NO MATTER WHAT THOSE TRAITORS' PROPHETS SAY!

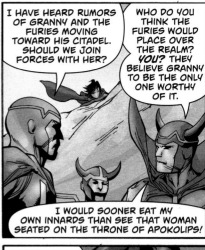

I HAVE HEARD RUMORS OF GRANNY AND THE FURIES MOVING TOWARD HIS CITADEL. SHOULD WE JOIN FORCES WITH HER?

WHO DO YOU THINK THE FURIES WOULD PLACE OVER THE REALM? *YOU*? THEY BELIEVE GRANNY TO BE THE ONLY ONE WORTHY OF IT.

I WOULD SOONER EAT MY OWN INNARDS THAN SEE THAT WOMAN SEATED ON THE THRONE OF APOKOLIPS!

I GOTTA GET OUT OF HERE BEFORE THEY FIND--

GAHH!

EW, EW, *EW!*

NOW BLEED THOSE PUPS FOR THE BUTCHER'S BLOCK!

WE WILL EAT OUR STRENGTH THIS DAY, DOG!

DAD, WHERE ARE YOU WHEN YA NEED YA?

HOLD STILL, MONGREL!

HOWWWWL!

CAN'T BELIEVE I'M REALLY GOING TO DO THIS...

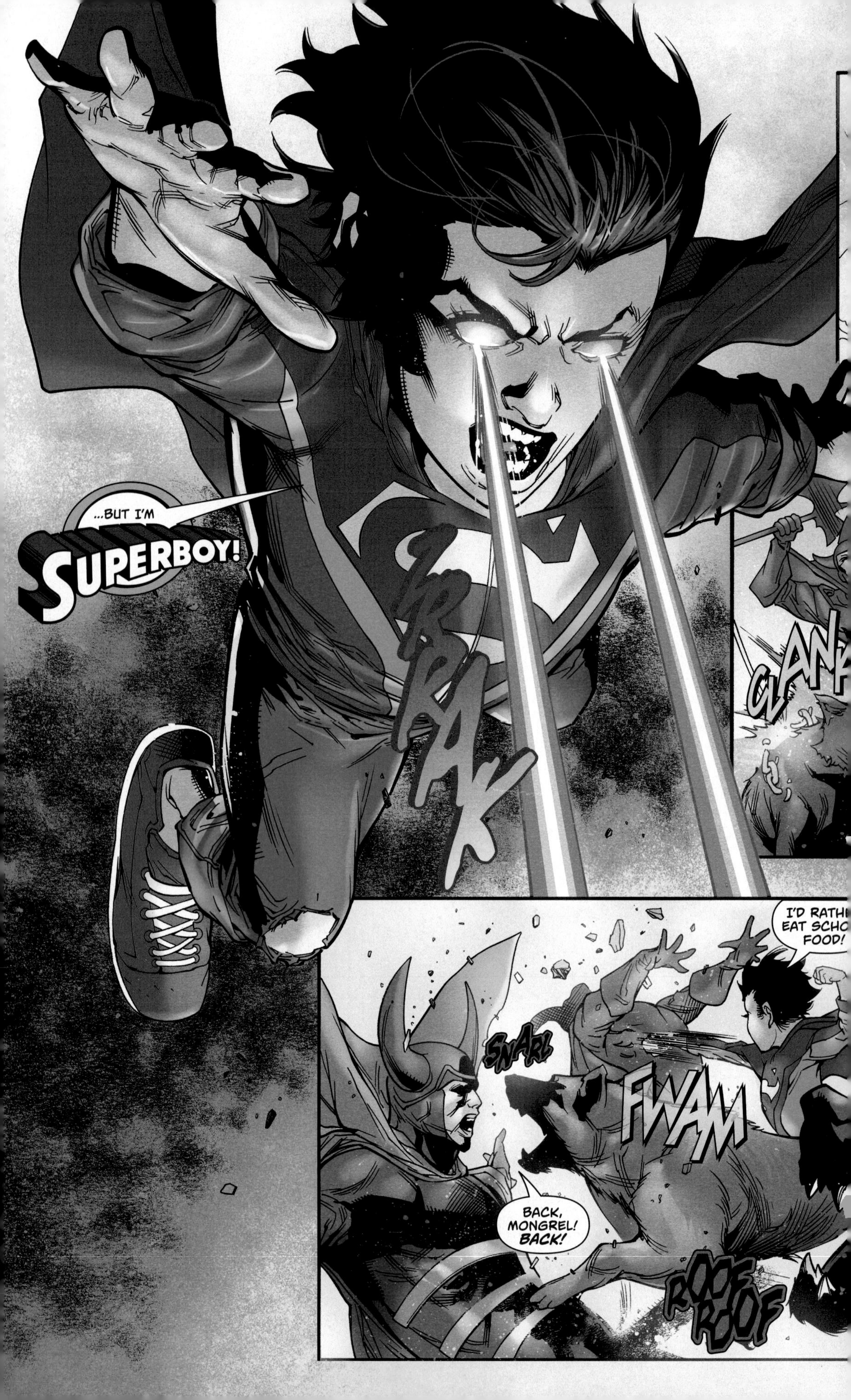
...BUT I'M
SUPERBOY!
I'D RATH
EAT SCHO
FOOD!
SNARL
FWAM
BACK, MONGREL! BACK!
ROOF ROOF

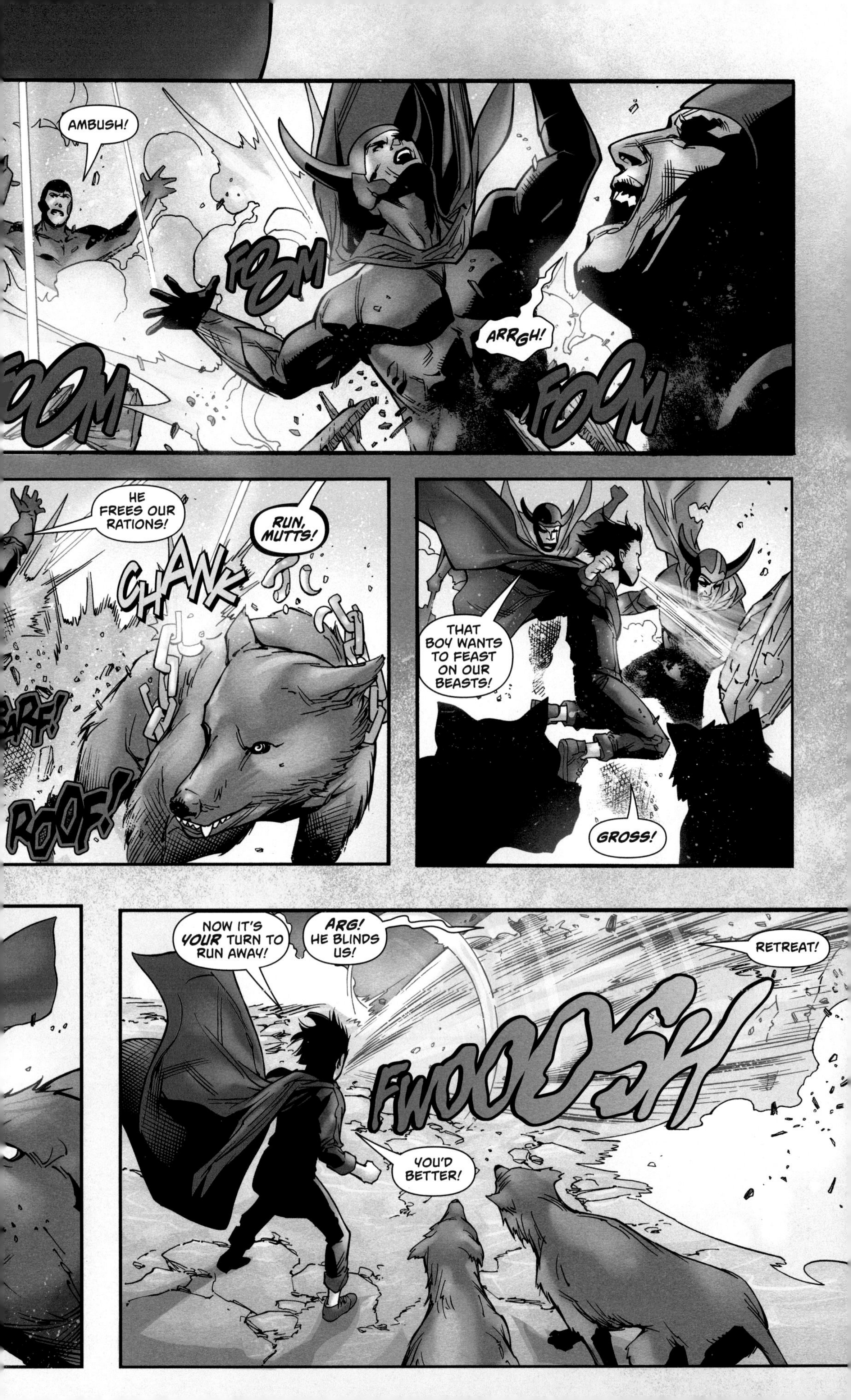
AMBUSH!
FOOM
ARRGH!
FOOM
FOOM
HE FREES OUR RATIONS!
RUN, MUTTS!
CHANK
BARF!
ROOF!
THAT BOY WANTS TO FEAST ON OUR BEASTS!
GROSS!
NOW IT'S YOUR TURN TO RUN AWAY!
ARG! HE BLINDS US!
RETREAT!
FWOOOSH
YOU'D BETTER!

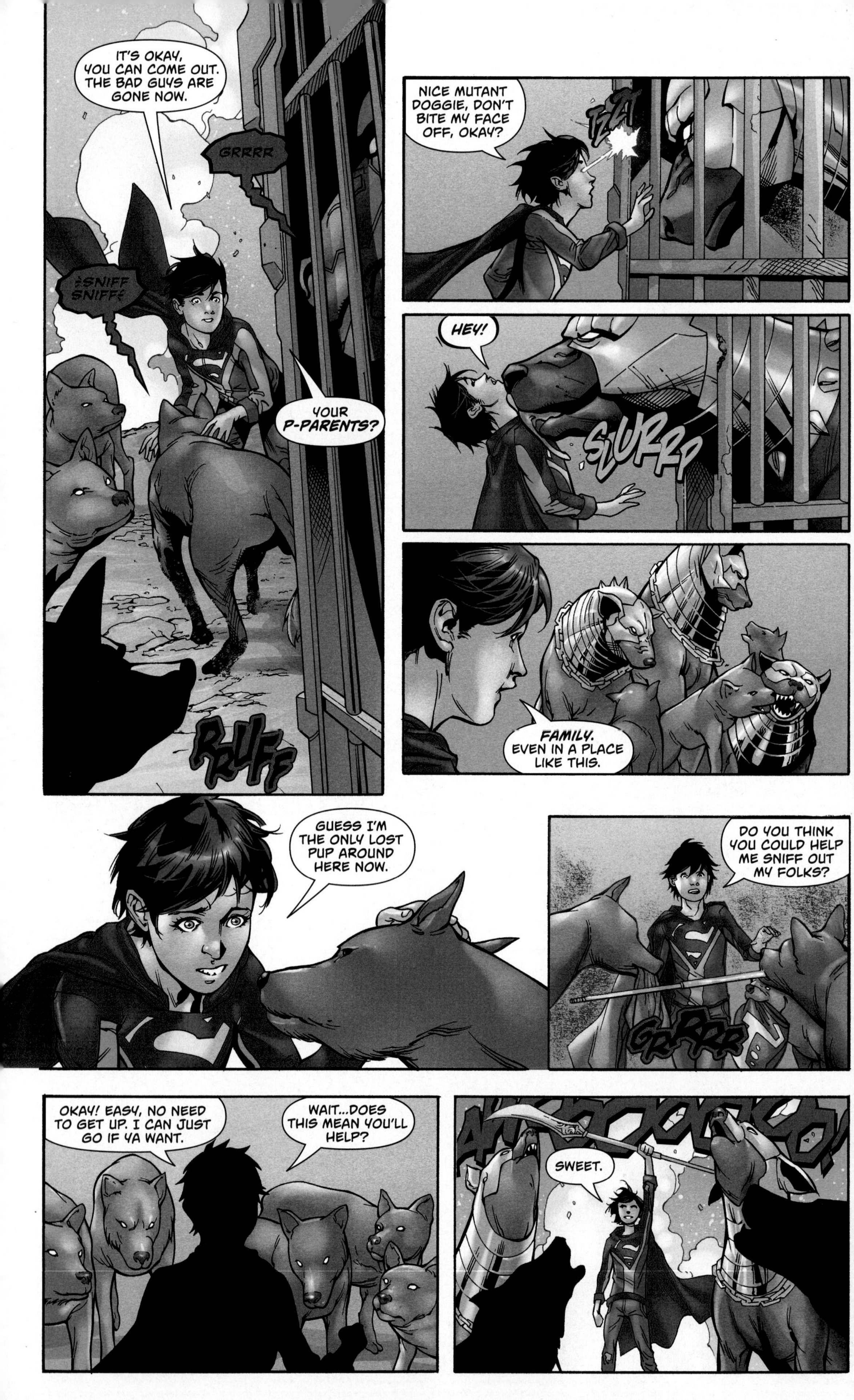
IT'S OKAY, YOU CAN COME OUT. THE BAD GUYS ARE GONE NOW.
GRRRR
SNIFF SNIFF
YOUR P-PARENTS?
RRUFF
NICE MUTANT DOGGIE, DON'T BITE MY FACE OFF, OKAY?
TZZT
HEY!
SLURRP
FAMILY. EVEN IN A PLACE LIKE THIS.
GUESS I'M THE ONLY LOST PUP AROUND HERE NOW.
DO YOU THINK YOU COULD HELP ME SNIFF OUT MY FOLKS?
GRRRR
OKAY! EASY, NO NEED TO GET UP. I CAN JUST GO IF YA WANT.
WAIT...DOES THIS MEAN YOU'LL HELP?
SWEET.

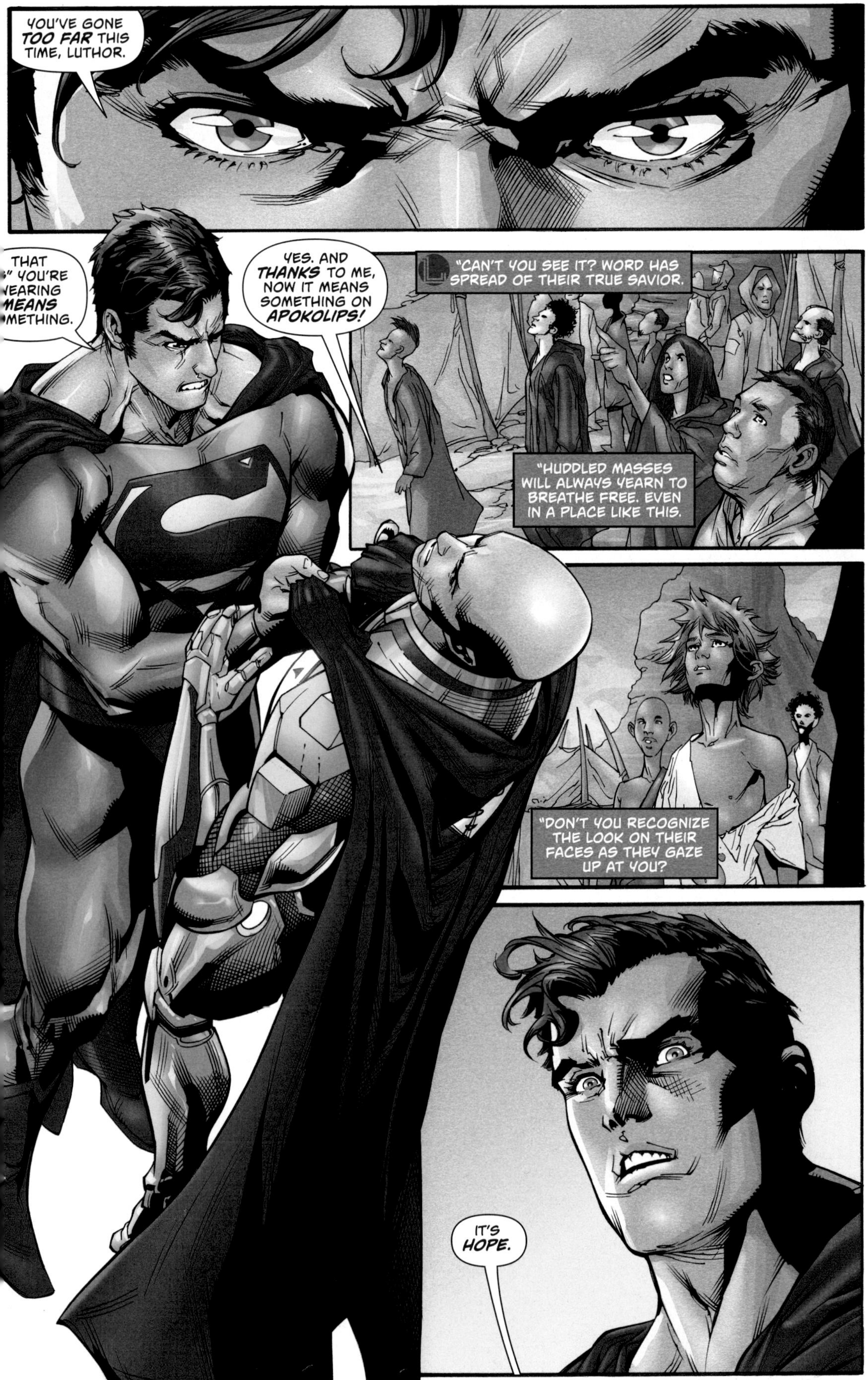

YOU'VE GONE TOO FAR THIS TIME, LUTHOR.
THAT ” YOU'RE EARING MEANS METHING.
YES. AND THANKS TO ME, NOW IT MEANS SOMETHING ON APOKOLIPS!
“CAN'T YOU SEE IT? WORD HAS SPREAD OF THEIR TRUE SAVIOR.
“HUDDLED MASSES WILL ALWAYS YEARN TO BREATHE FREE. EVEN IN A PLACE LIKE THIS.
“DON'T YOU RECOGNIZE THE LOOK ON THEIR FACES AS THEY GAZE UP AT YOU?
IT'S HOPE.

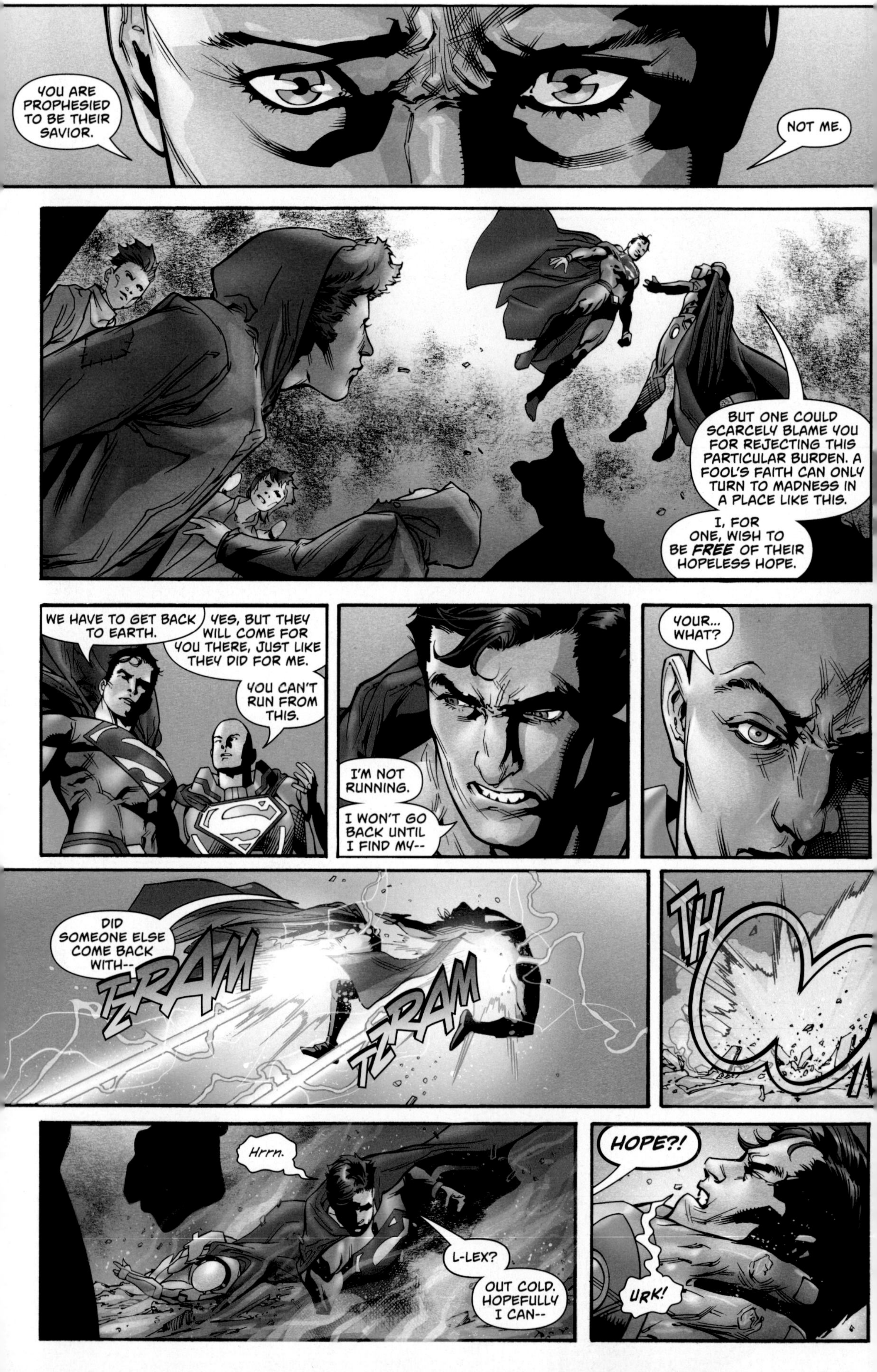
YOU ARE PROPHESIED TO BE THEIR SAVIOR.
NOT ME.
BUT ONE COULD SCARCELY BLAME YOU FOR REJECTING THIS PARTICULAR BURDEN. A FOOL'S FAITH CAN ONLY TURN TO MADNESS IN A PLACE LIKE THIS.
I, FOR ONE, WISH TO BE FREE OF THEIR HOPELESS HOPE.
WE HAVE TO GET BACK TO EARTH.
YES, BUT THEY WILL COME FOR YOU THERE, JUST LIKE THEY DID FOR ME.
YOU CAN'T RUN FROM THIS.
I'M NOT RUNNING.
I WON'T GO BACK UNTIL I FIND MY--
YOUR... WHAT?
DID SOMEONE ELSE COME BACK WITH--
TZRAM
TZRAM
TH
Hrrn.
L-LEX?
OUT COLD. HOPEFULLY I CAN--
HOPE?!
URK!

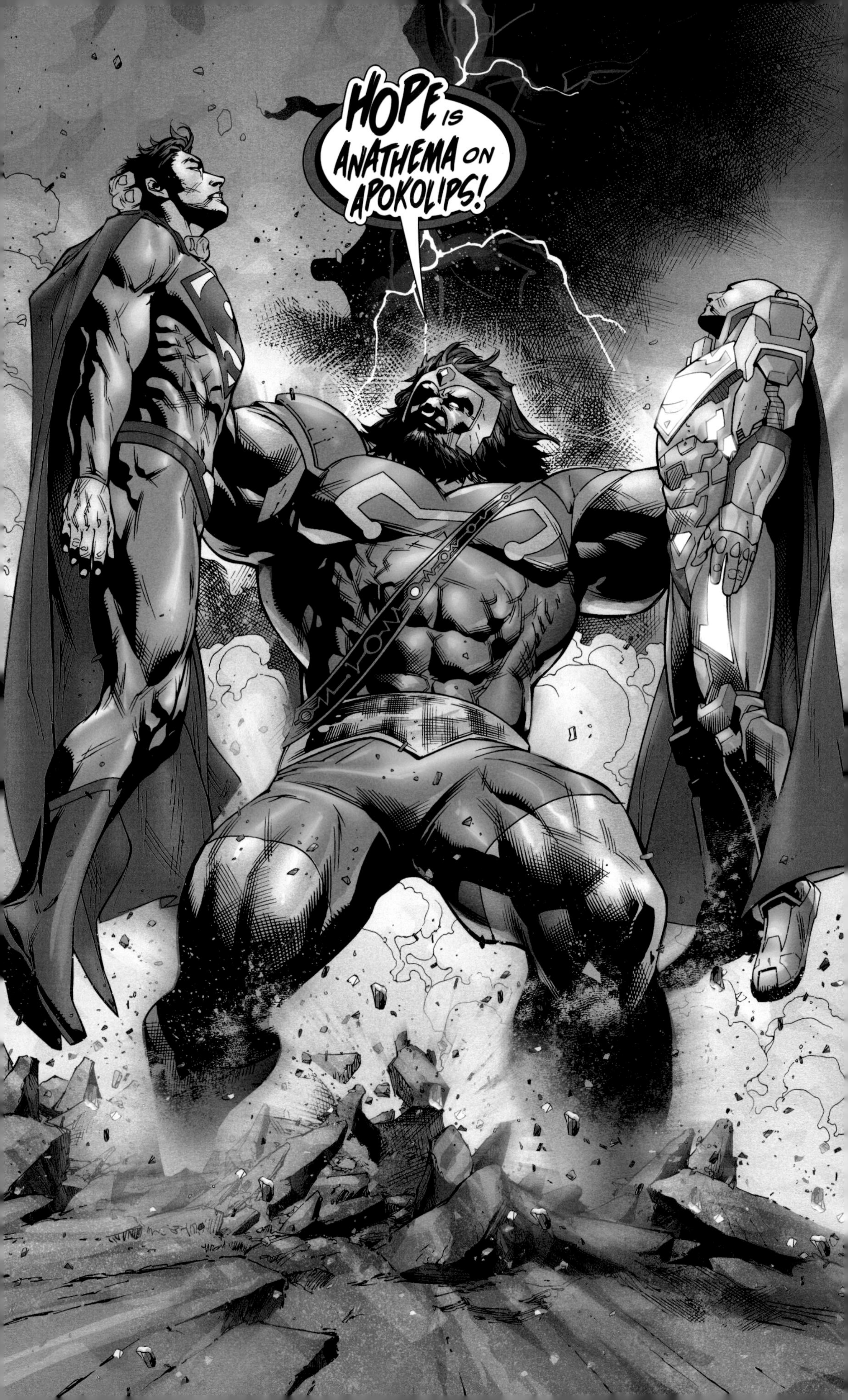
HOPE IS ANATHEMA ON APOKOLIPS!

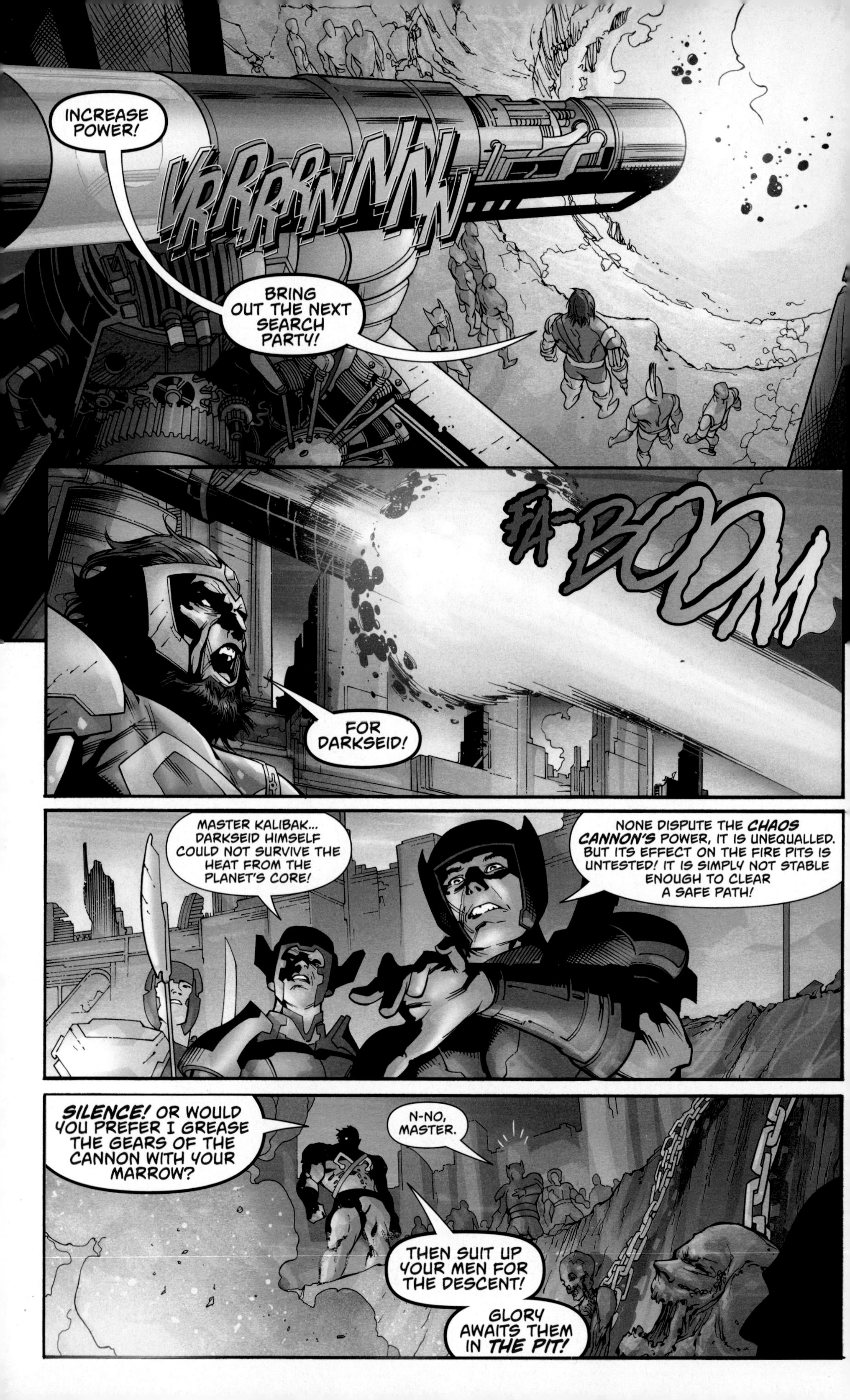
INCREASE POWER!
VRRRRNNNN...
BRING OUT THE NEXT SEARCH PARTY!
FA-BOOM
FOR DARKSEID!
MASTER KALIBAK... DARKSEID HIMSELF COULD NOT SURVIVE THE HEAT FROM THE PLANET'S CORE!
NONE DISPUTE THE CHAOS CANNON'S POWER, IT IS UNEQUALLED. BUT ITS EFFECT ON THE FIRE PITS IS UNTESTED! IT IS SIMPLY NOT STABLE ENOUGH TO CLEAR A SAFE PATH!
SILENCE! OR WOULD YOU PREFER I GREASE THE GEARS OF THE CANNON WITH YOUR MARROW?
N-NO, MASTER.
THEN SUIT UP YOUR MEN FOR THE DESCENT!
GLORY AWAITS THEM IN THE PIT!

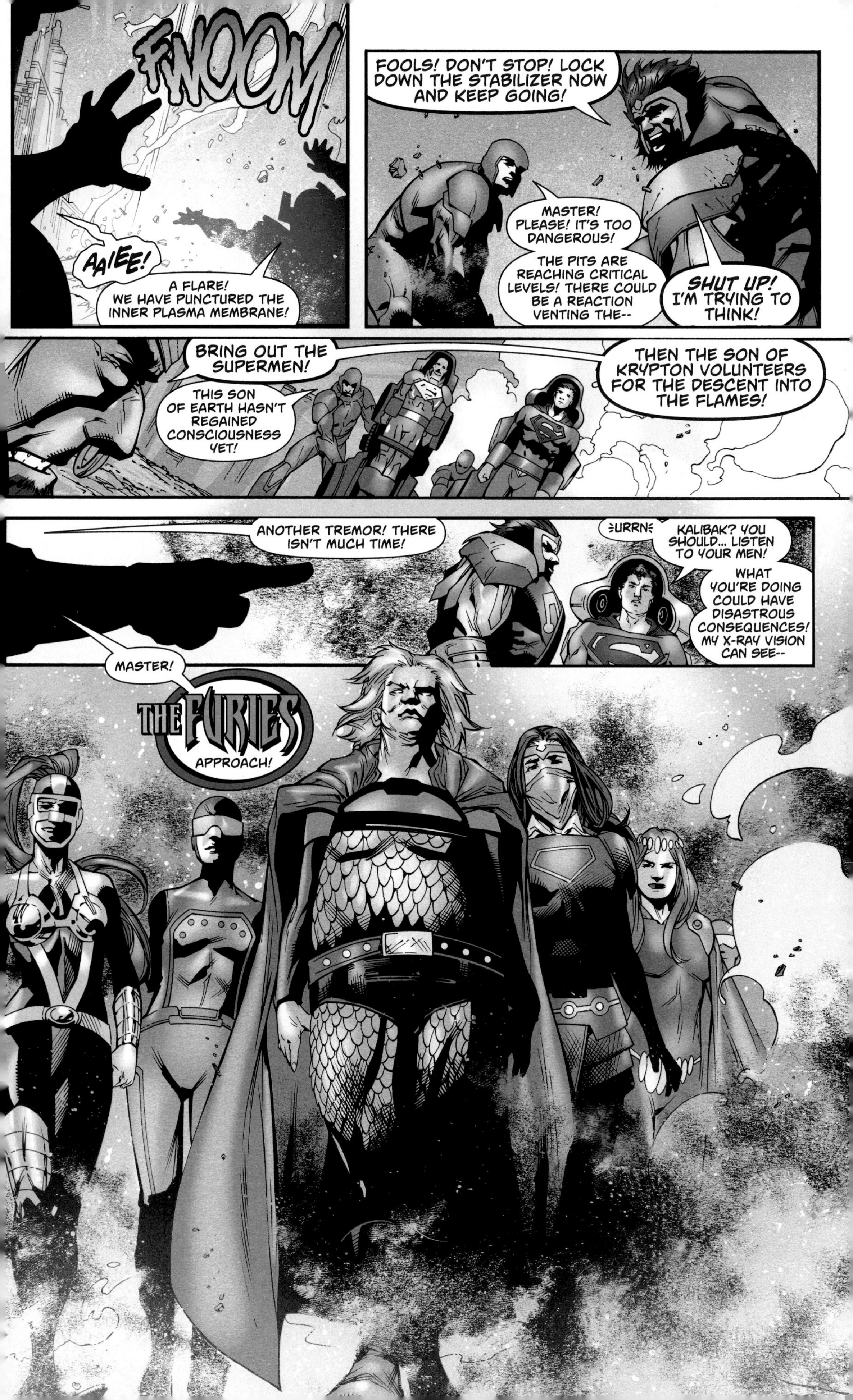
FWOOM
AAIEE!
A FLARE! WE HAVE PUNCTURED THE INNER PLASMA MEMBRANE!
FOOLS! DON'T STOP! LOCK DOWN THE STABILIZER NOW AND KEEP GOING!
MASTER! PLEASE! IT'S TOO DANGEROUS!
THE PITS ARE REACHING CRITICAL LEVELS! THERE COULD BE A REACTION VENTING THE--
SHUT UP! I'M TRYING TO THINK!
BRING OUT THE SUPERMEN!
THIS SON OF EARTH HASN'T REGAINED CONSCIOUSNESS YET!
THEN THE SON OF KRYPTON VOLUNTEERS FOR THE DESCENT INTO THE FLAMES!
ANOTHER TREMOR! THERE ISN'T MUCH TIME!
URRN
KALIBAK? YOU SHOULD... LISTEN TO YOUR MEN!
WHAT YOU'RE DOING COULD HAVE DISASTROUS CONSEQUENCES! MY X-RAY VISION CAN SEE--
MASTER!
THE FURIES APPROACH!

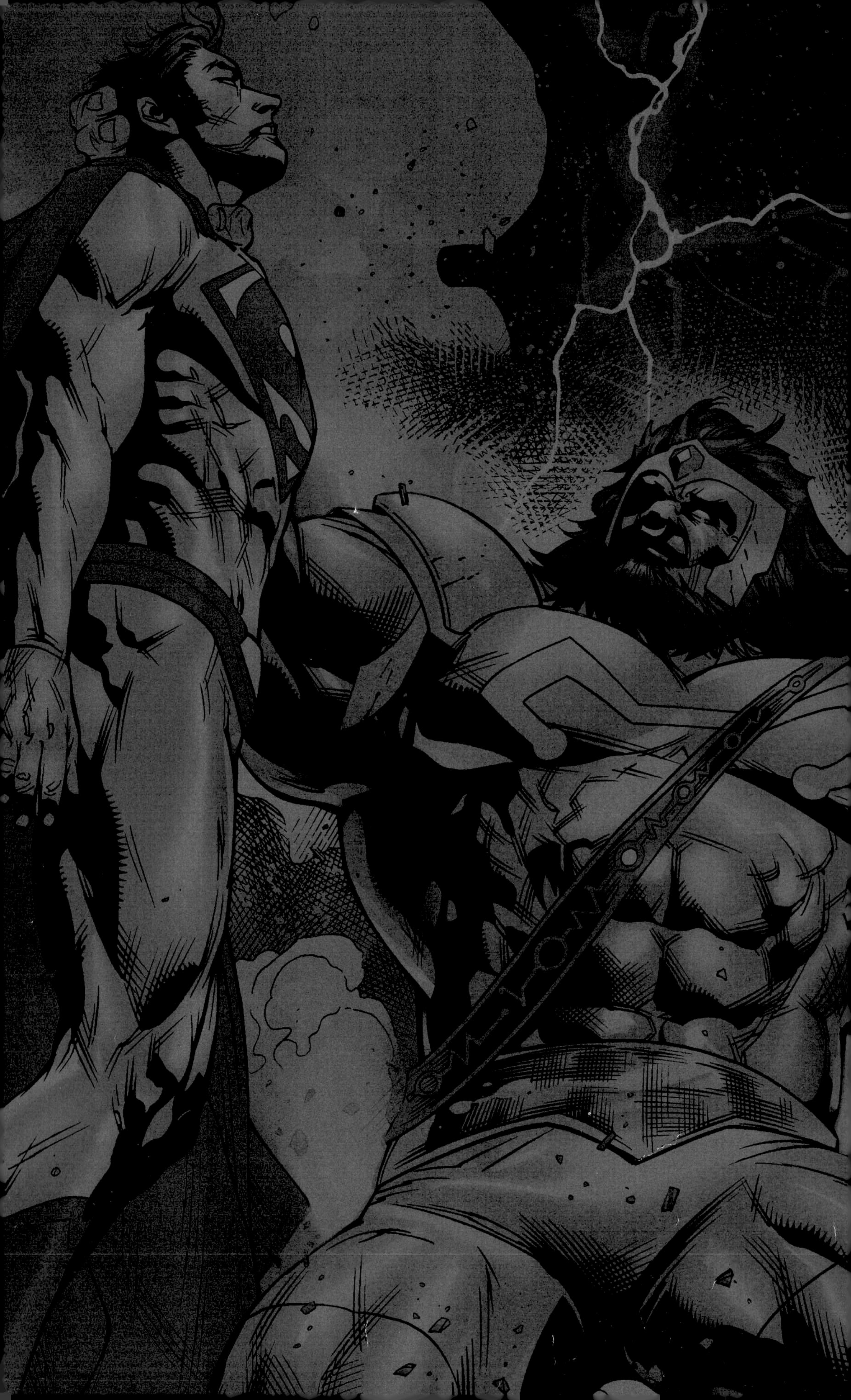

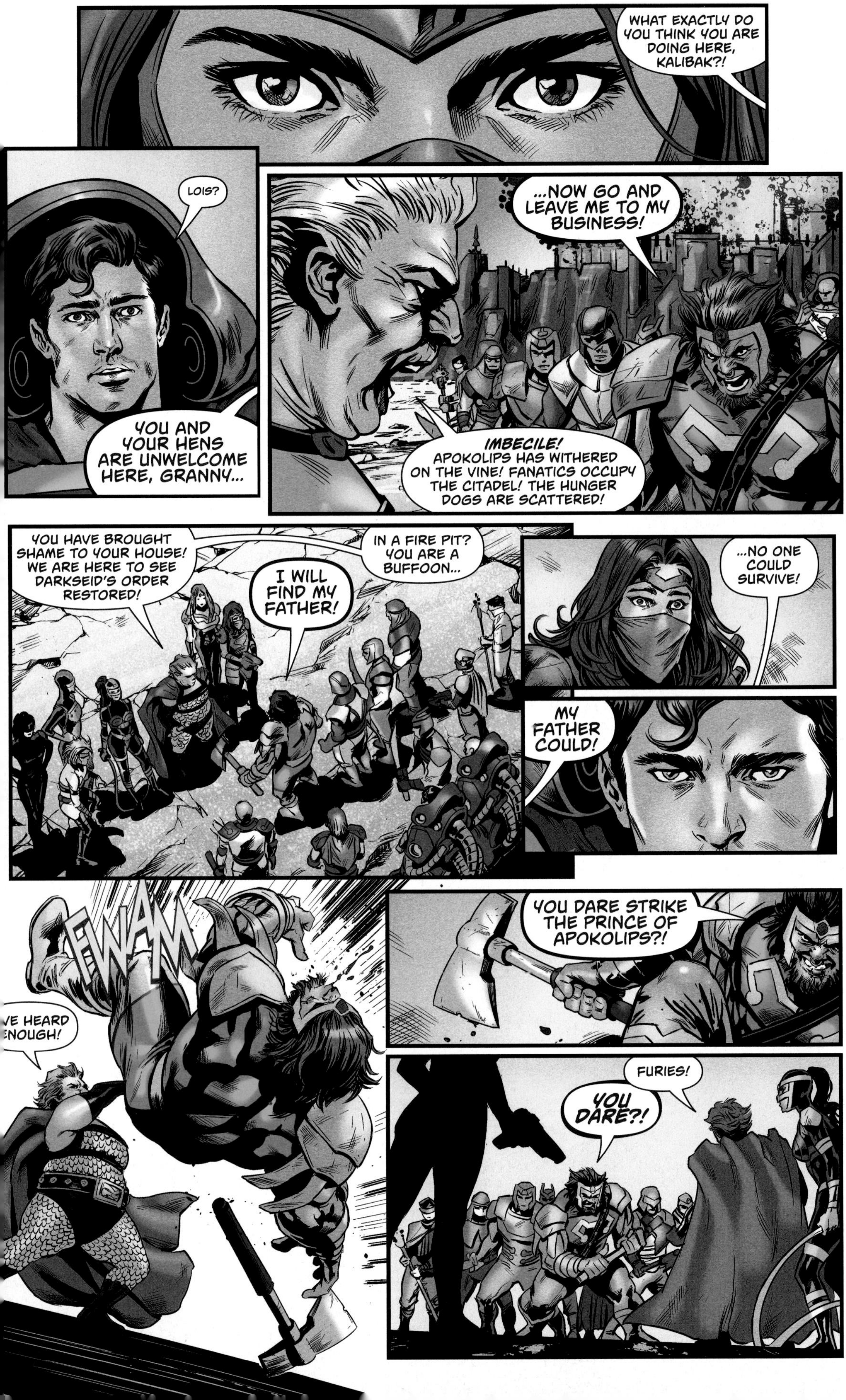
WHAT EXACTLY DO YOU THINK YOU ARE DOING HERE, KALIBAK?!
LOIS?
YOU AND YOUR HENS ARE UNWELCOME HERE, GRANNY...
...NOW GO AND LEAVE ME TO MY BUSINESS!
IMBECILE! APOKOLIPS HAS WITHERED ON THE VINE! FANATICS OCCUPY THE CITADEL! THE HUNGER DOGS ARE SCATTERED!
YOU HAVE BROUGHT SHAME TO YOUR HOUSE! WE ARE HERE TO SEE DARKSEID'S ORDER RESTORED!
I WILL FIND MY FATHER!
IN A FIRE PIT? YOU ARE A BUFFOON...
...NO ONE COULD SURVIVE!
MY FATHER COULD!
FWAM
VE HEARD ENOUGH!
YOU DARE STRIKE THE PRINCE OF APOKOLIPS?!
FURIES!
YOU DARE?!

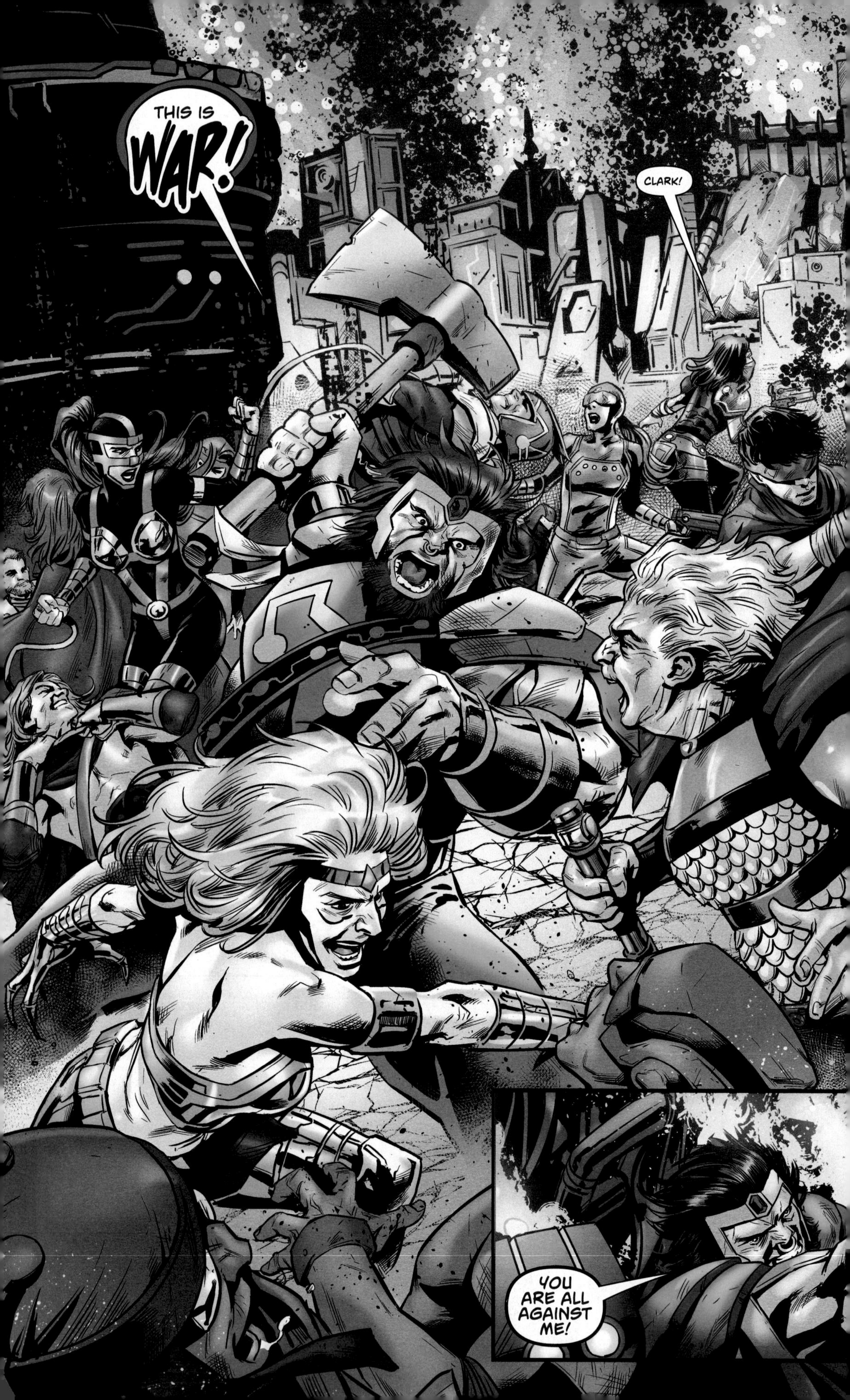
THIS IS WAR!
CLARK!
YOU ARE ALL AGAINST ME!

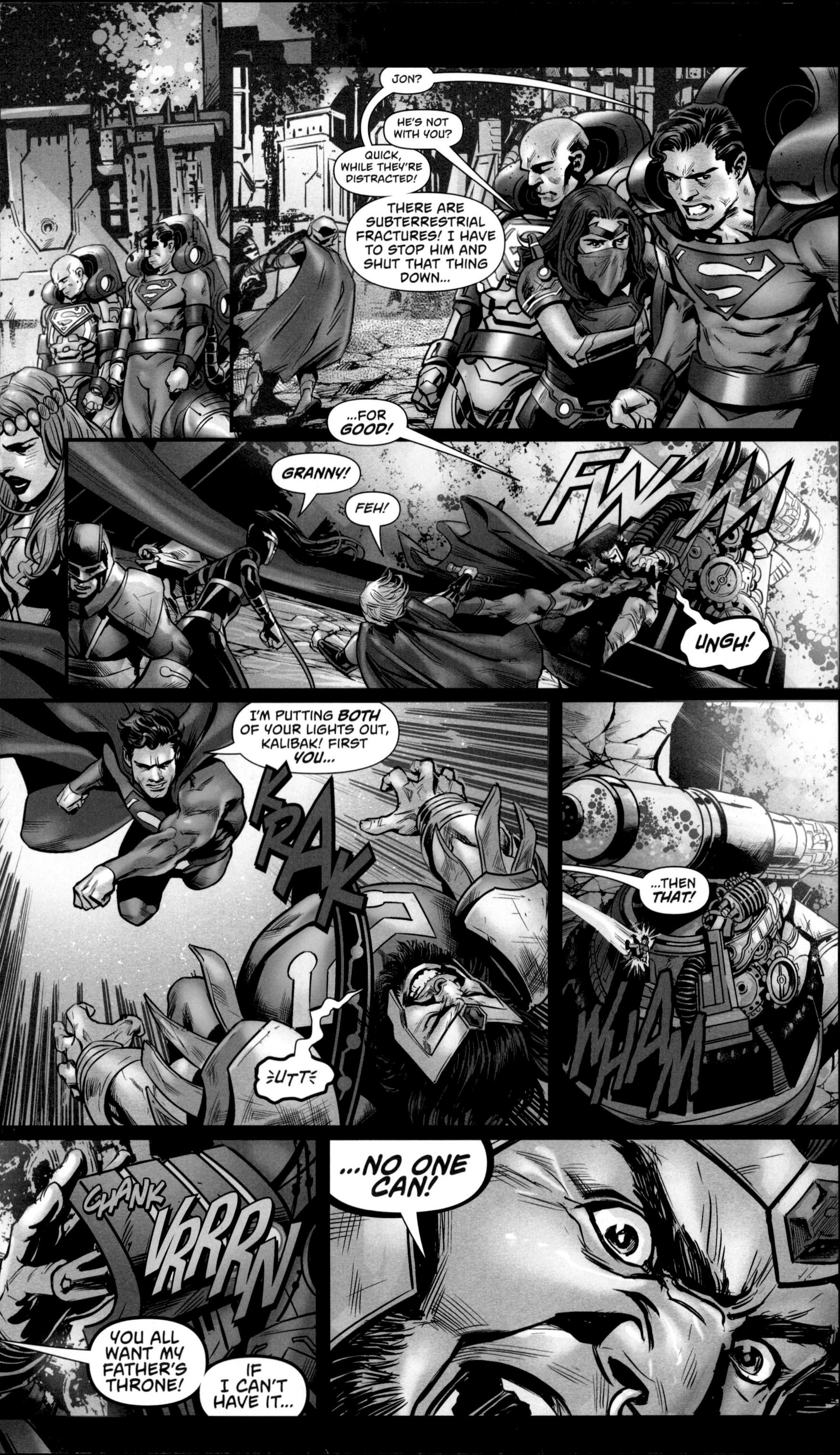
JON?
HE'S NOT WITH YOU?
QUICK, WHILE THEY'RE DISTRACTED!
THERE ARE SUBTERRESTRIAL FRACTURES! I HAVE TO STOP HIM AND SHUT THAT THING DOWN...
...FOR GOOD!
GRANNY!
FEH!
FWAM
UNGH!
I'M PUTTING BOTH OF YOUR LIGHTS OUT, KALIBAK! FIRST YOU...
KRAK
UTT
...THEN THAT!
WHAM
CHANK
VRRRN
YOU ALL WANT MY FATHER'S THRONE!
IF I CAN'T HAVE IT...
...NO ONE CAN!

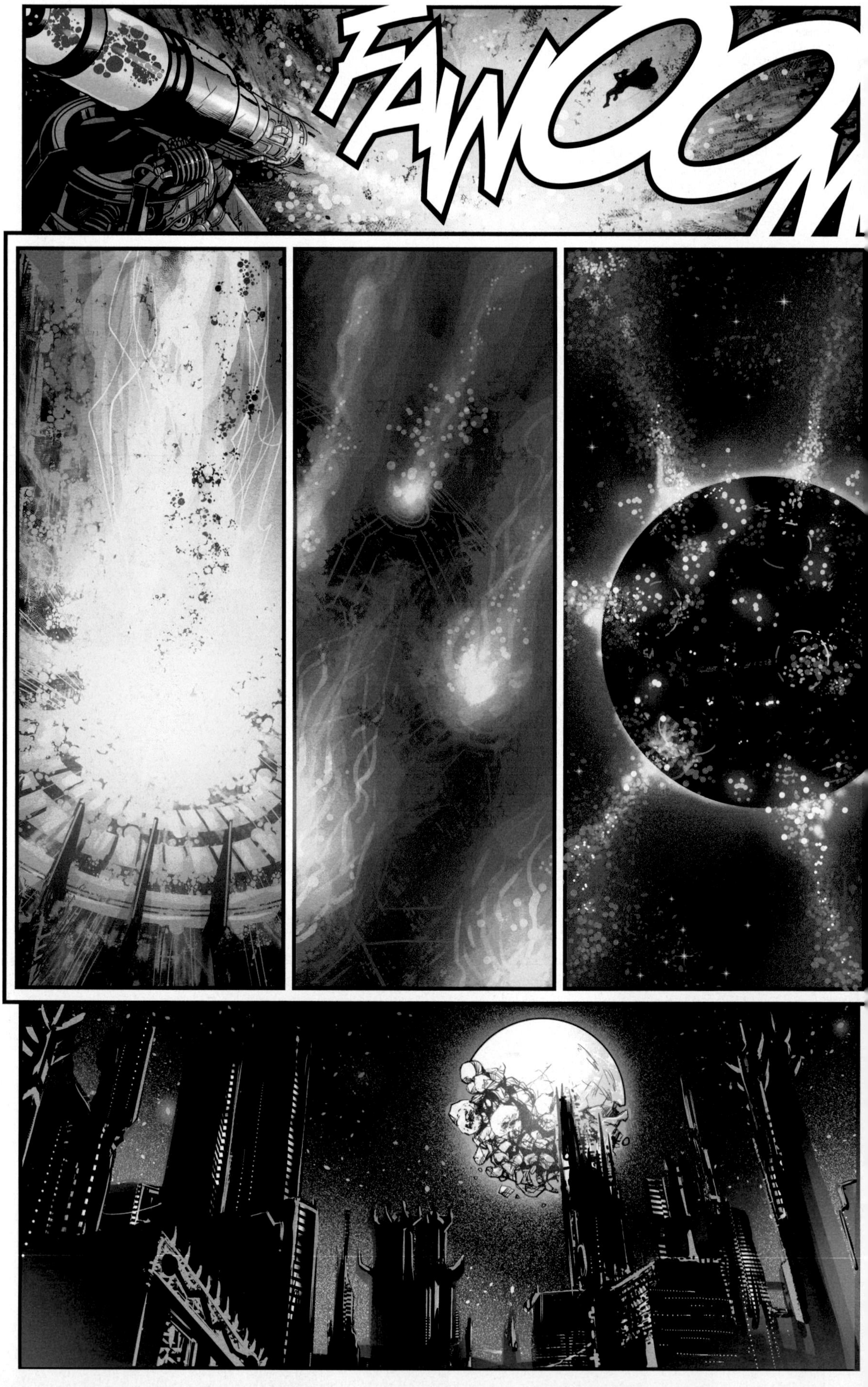
FWOOM

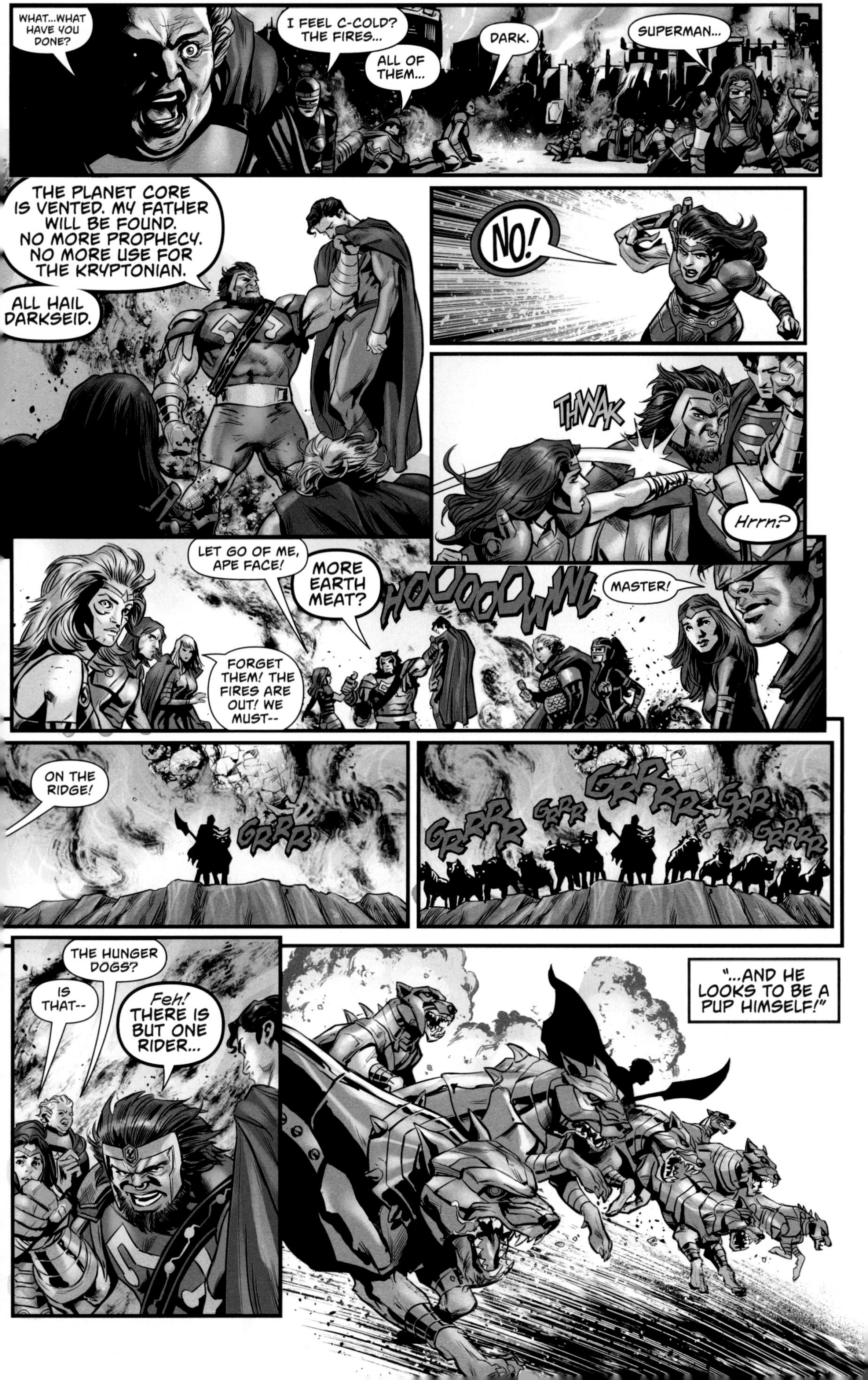
WHAT...WHAT HAVE YOU DONE?
I FEEL C-COLD? THE FIRES...
ALL OF THEM...
DARK.
SUPERMAN...
THE PLANET CORE IS VENTED. MY FATHER WILL BE FOUND. NO MORE PROPHECY. NO MORE USE FOR THE KRYPTONIAN.
ALL HAIL DARKSEID.
NO!
THWAK
Hrrn?
LET GO OF ME, APE FACE!
MORE EARTH MEAT?
HOOOOOOWL
MASTER!
FORGET THEM! THE FIRES ARE OUT! WE MUST--
ON THE RIDGE!
GRRR
GRRRR
GRRR
GRRRRR
GRRR
GRRRR
THE HUNGER DOGS?
IS THAT--
Feh! THERE IS BUT ONE RIDER...
"...AND HE LOOKS TO BE A PUP HIMSELF!"

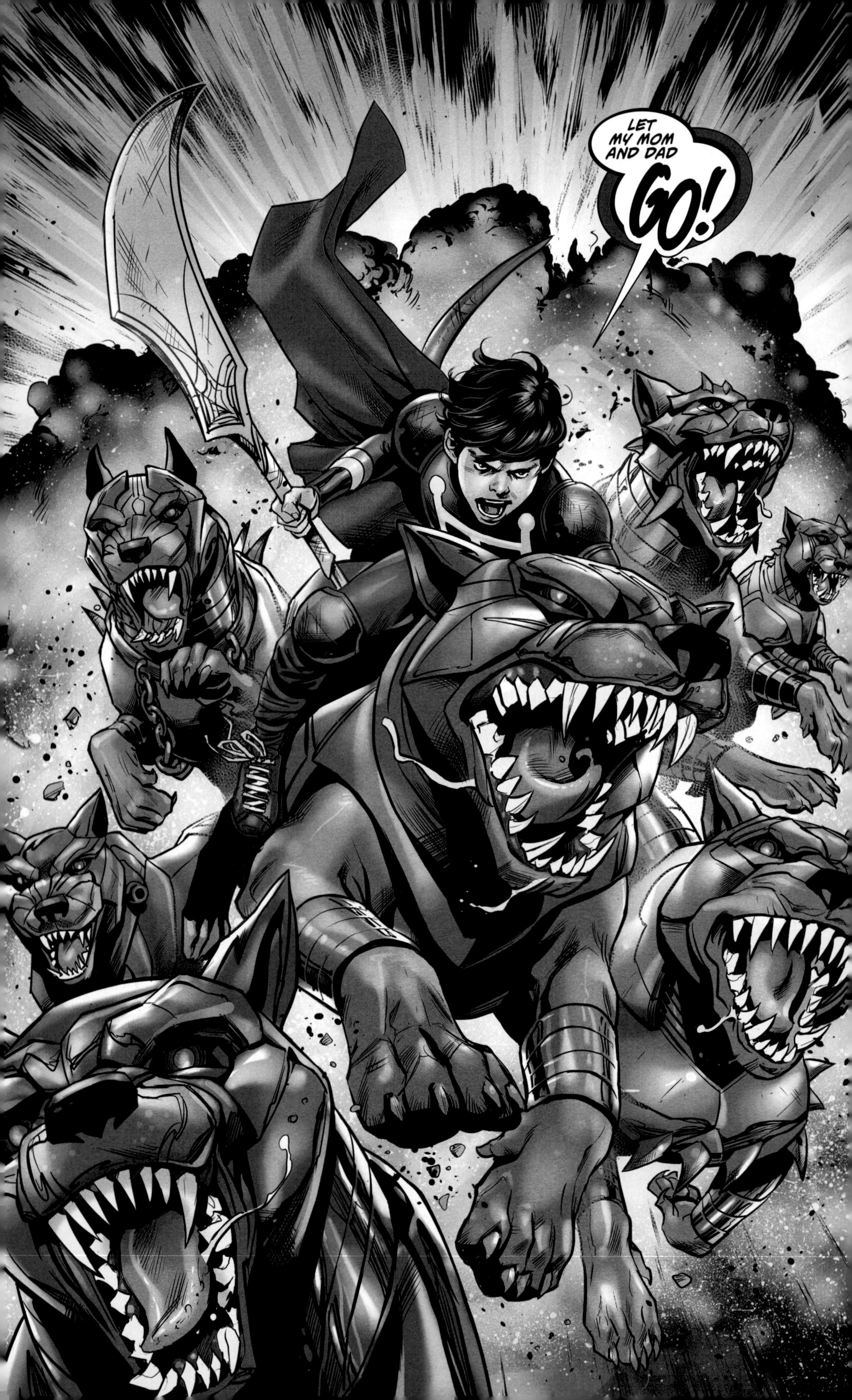
LET MY MOM AND DAD GO!

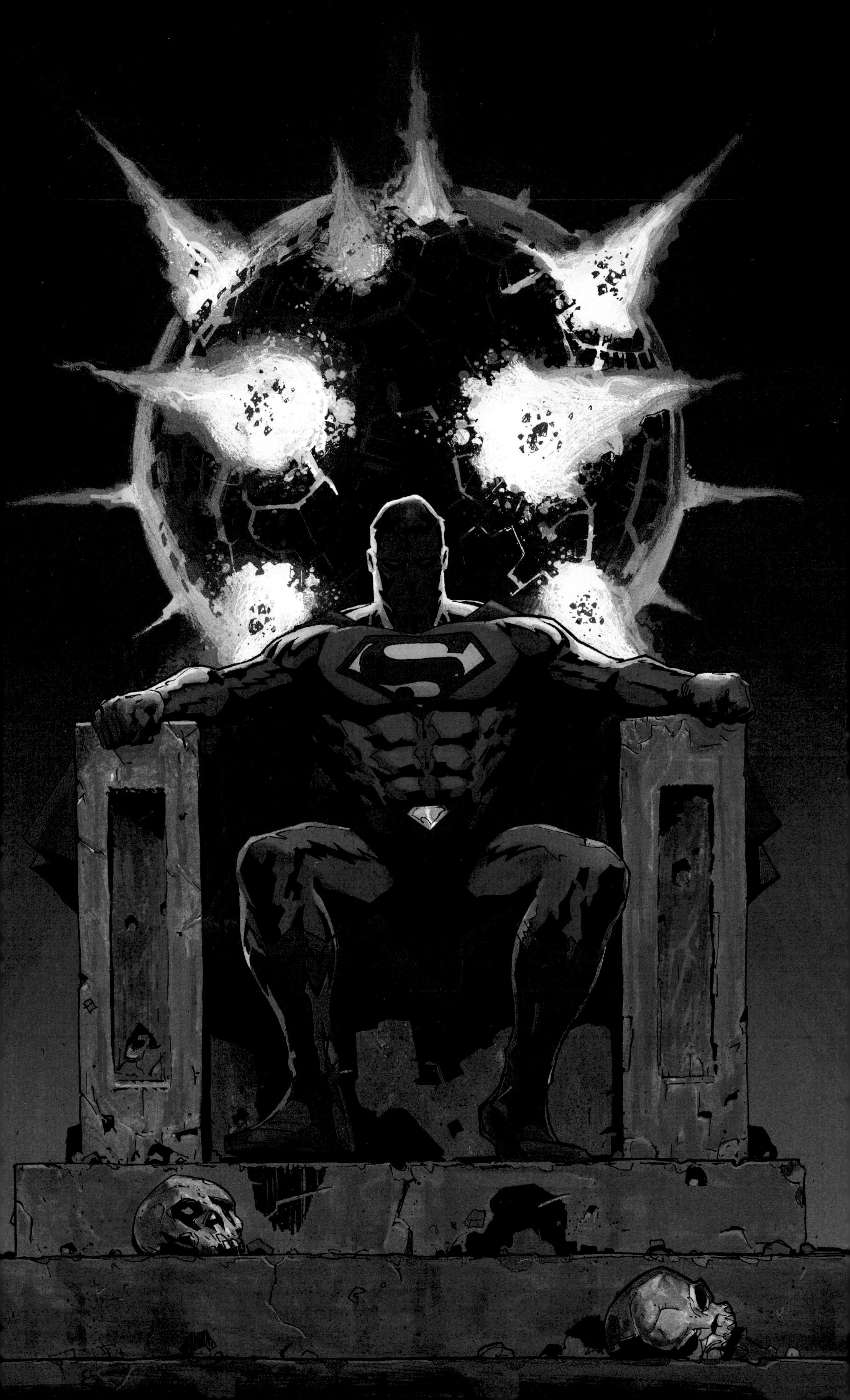

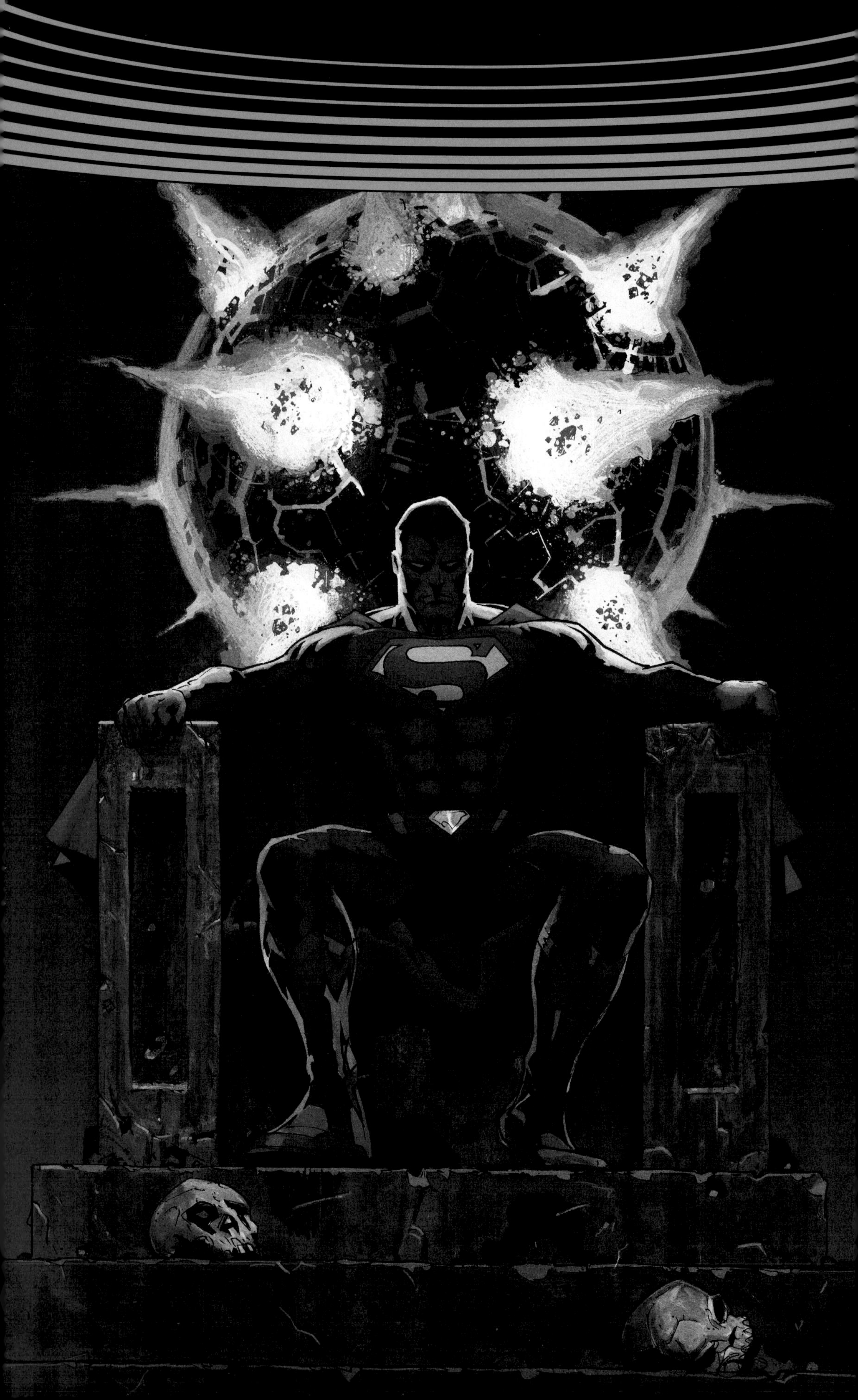

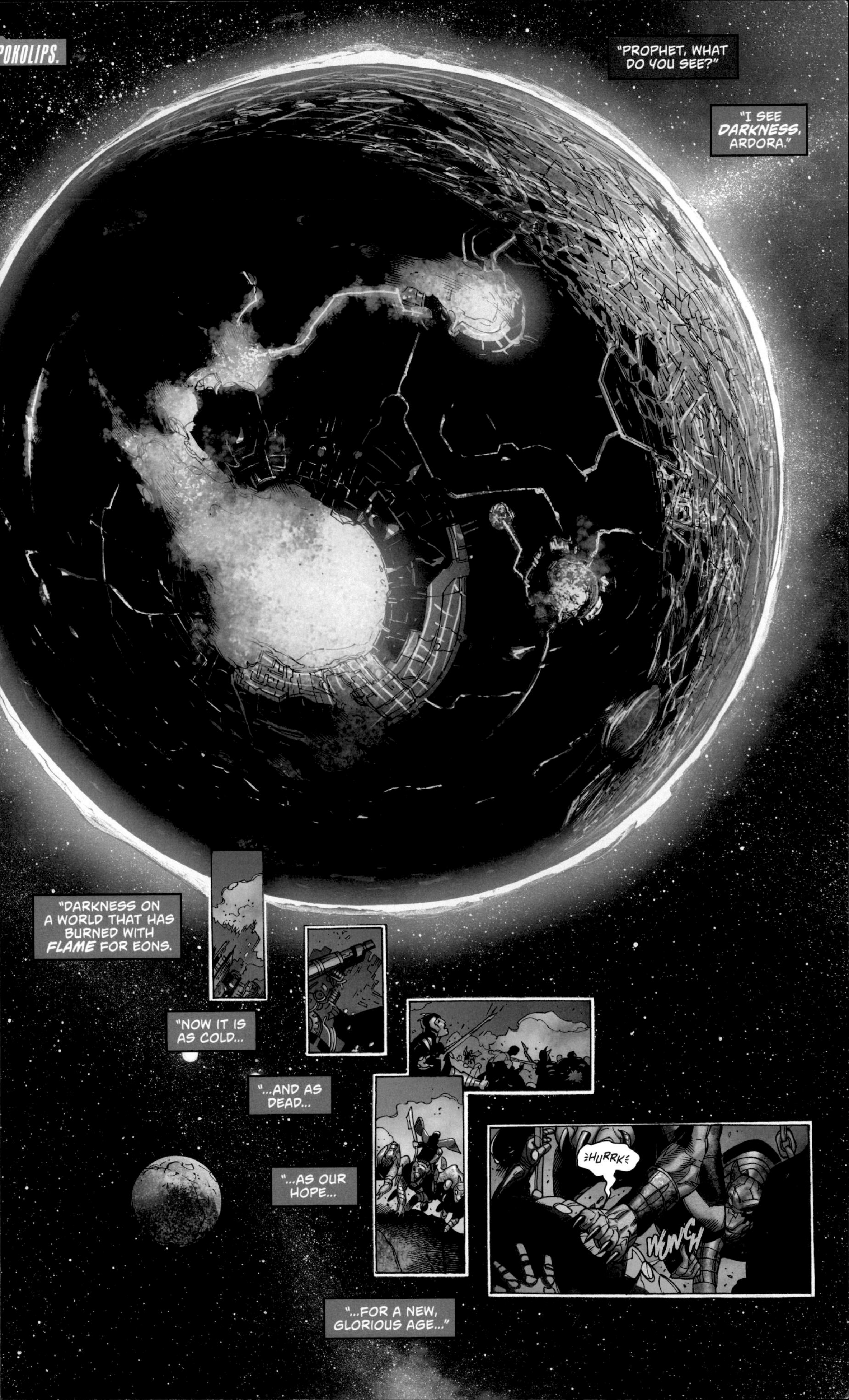

POKOLIPS.
"PROPHET, WHAT DO YOU SEE?"
"I SEE DARKNESS, ARDORA."
"DARKNESS ON A WORLD THAT HAS BURNED WITH FLAME FOR EONS.
"NOW IT IS AS COLD...
"...AND AS DEAD...
"...AS OUR HOPE...
HURRK
WENCH
"...FOR A NEW, GLORIOUS AGE..."

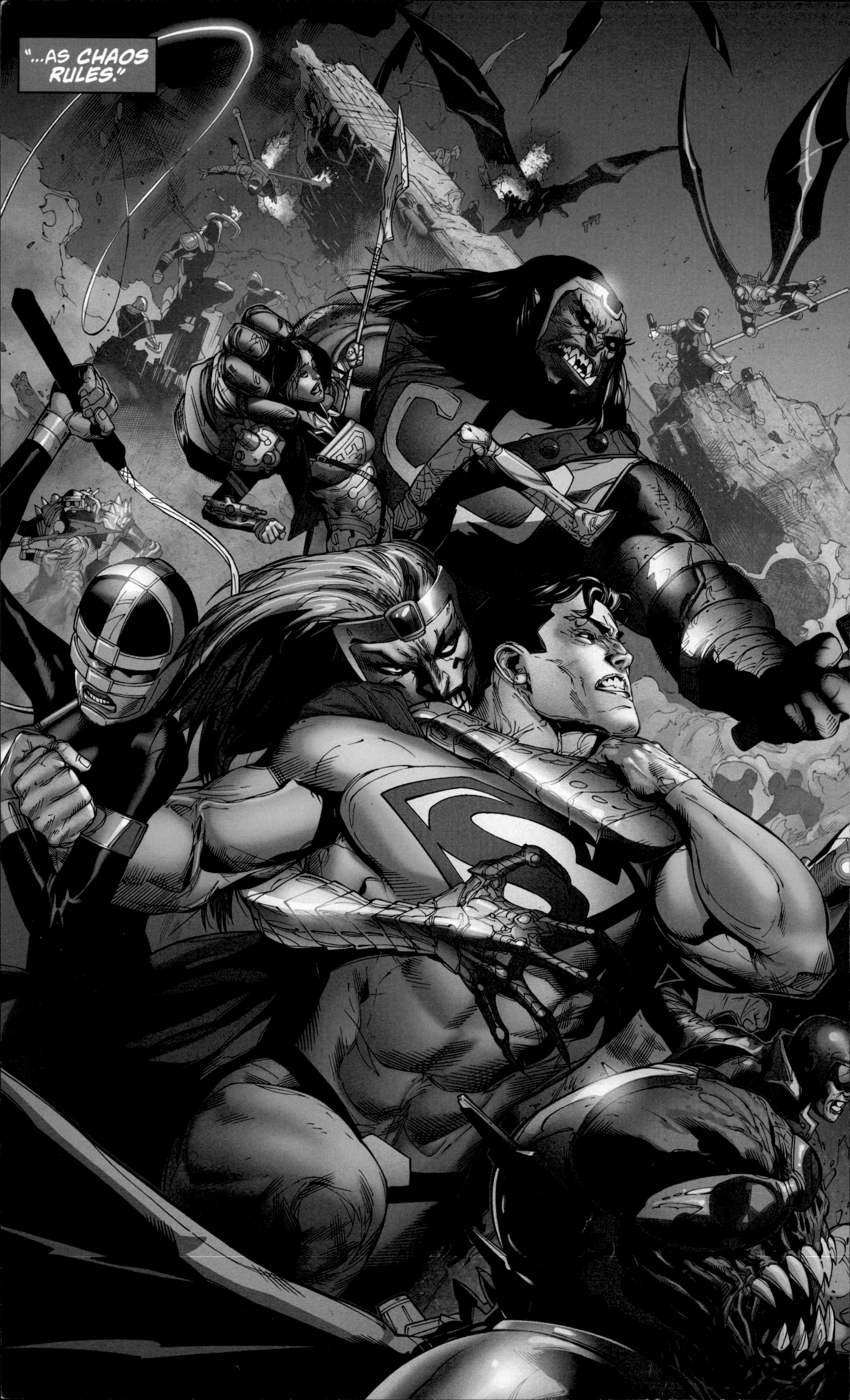
"...AS CHAOS RULES."

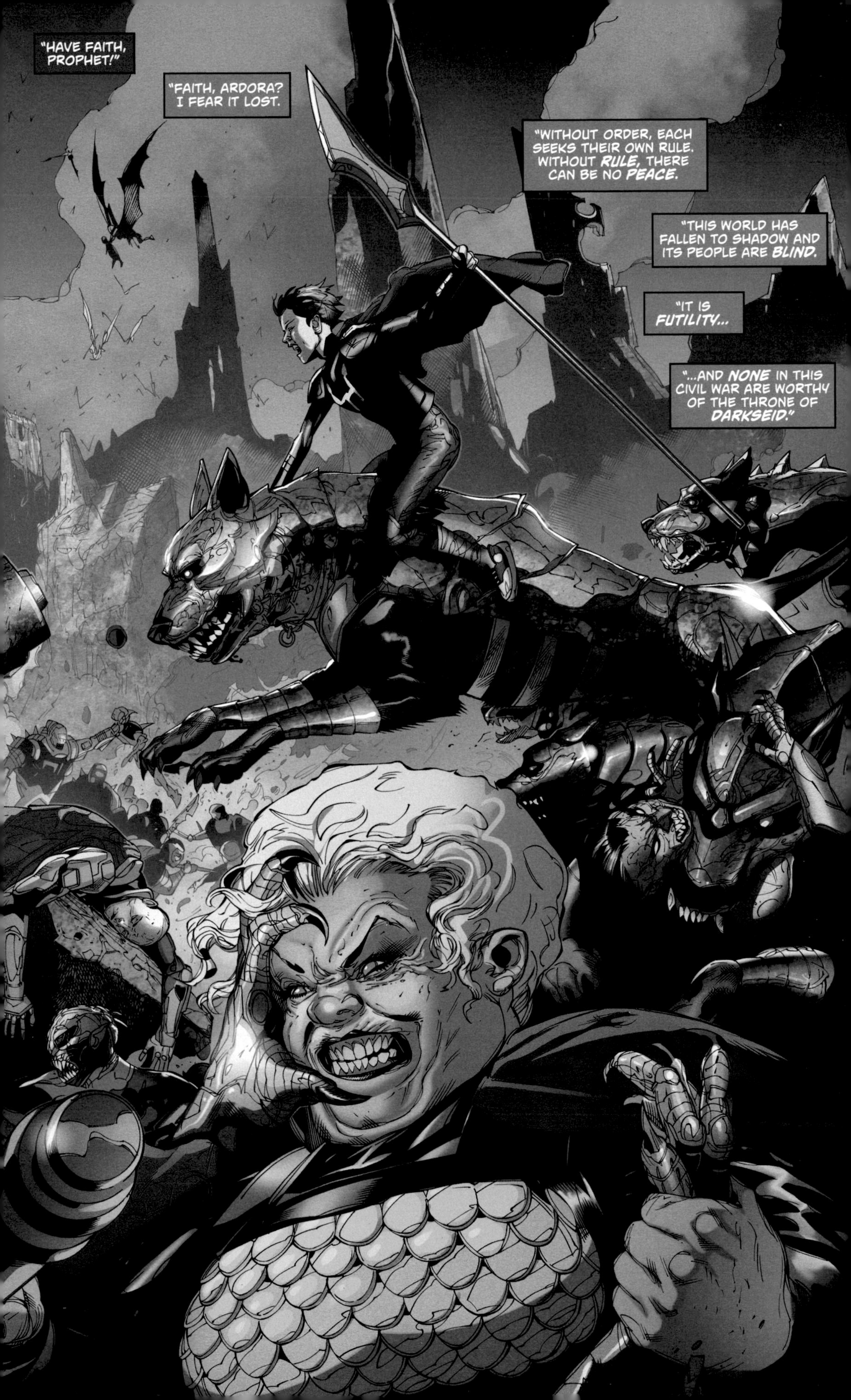
"HAVE FAITH, PROPHET!"
"FAITH, ARDORA? I FEAR IT LOST.
"WITHOUT ORDER, EACH SEEKS THEIR OWN RULE. WITHOUT *RULE,* THERE CAN BE NO *PEACE.*
"THIS WORLD HAS FALLEN TO SHADOW AND ITS PEOPLE ARE *BLIND.*
"IT IS *FUTILITY*...
"...AND *NONE* IN THIS CIVIL WAR ARE WORTHY OF THE THRONE OF *DARKSEID.*"

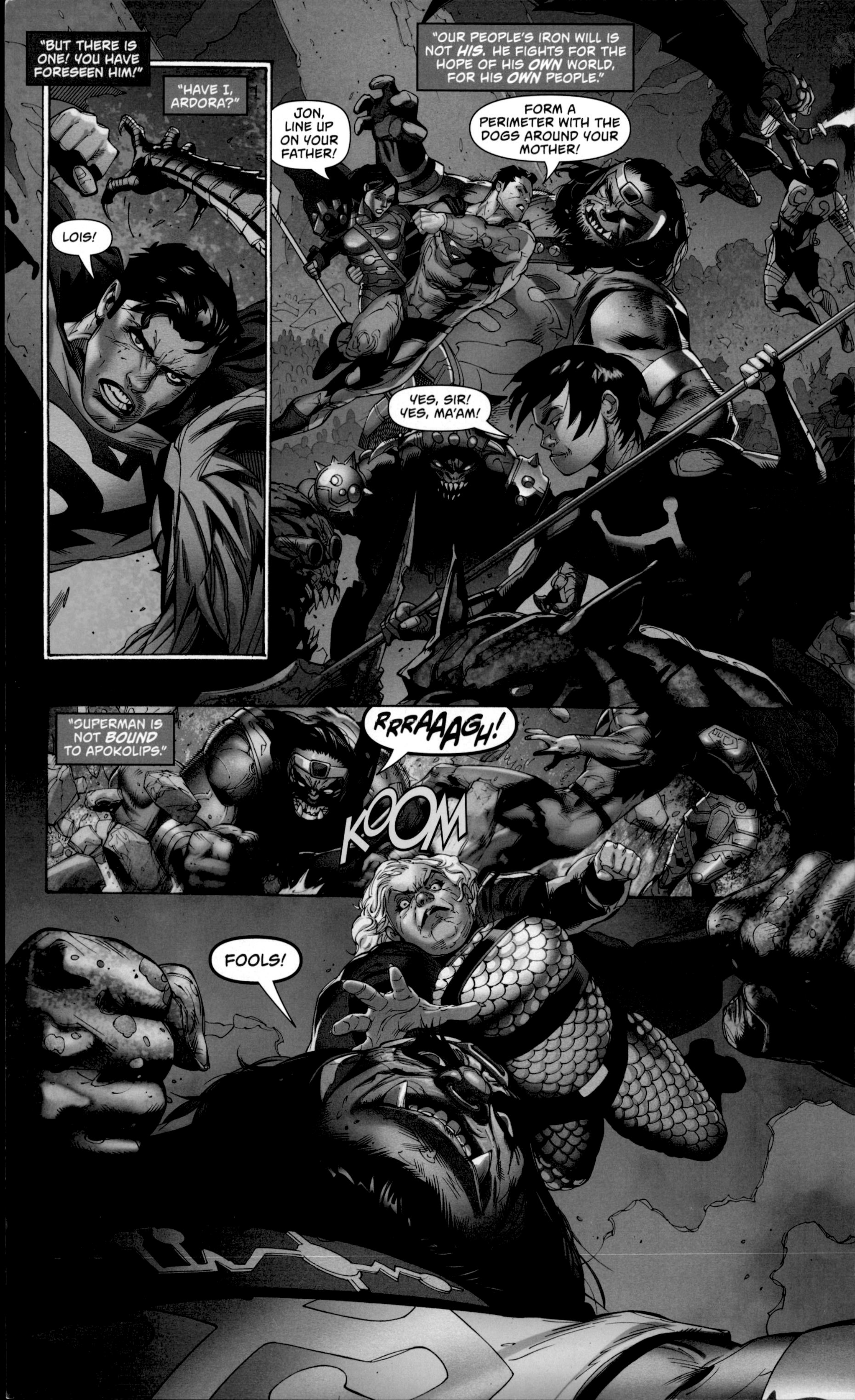
"BUT THERE IS ONE! YOU HAVE FORESEEN HIM!"
"HAVE I, ARDORA?"
LOIS!
"OUR PEOPLE'S IRON WILL IS NOT HIS. HE FIGHTS FOR THE HOPE OF HIS OWN WORLD, FOR HIS OWN PEOPLE."
JON, LINE UP ON YOUR FATHER!
FORM A PERIMETER WITH THE DOGS AROUND YOUR MOTHER!
YES, SIR! YES, MA'AM!
"SUPERMAN IS NOT BOUND TO APOKOLIPS."
RRRAAAAGH!
KOOM
FOOLS!

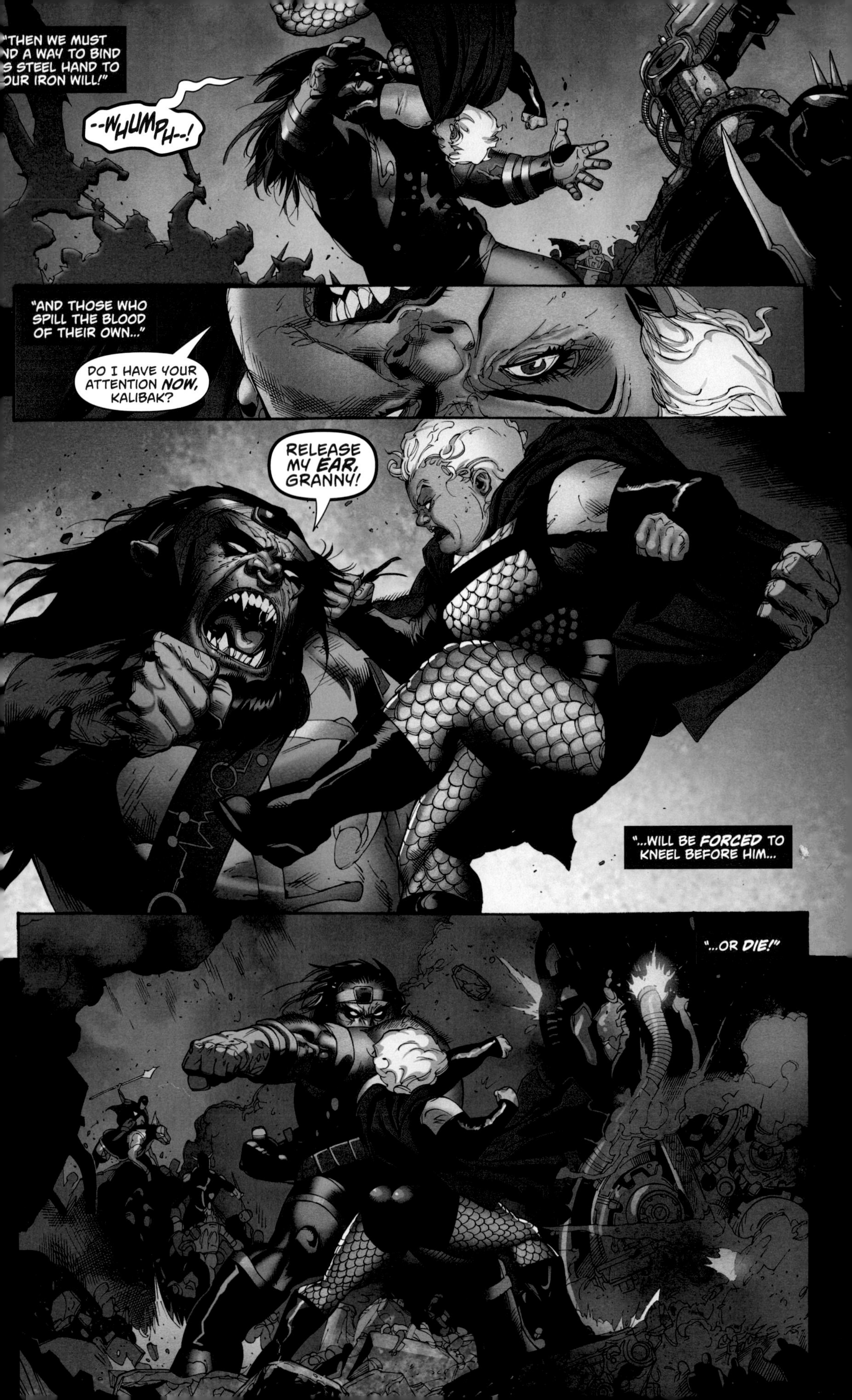
"THEN WE MUST
ND A WAY TO BIND
S STEEL HAND TO
OUR IRON WILL!"
--WHUMPH--!
"AND THOSE WHO SPILL THE BLOOD OF THEIR OWN..."
DO I HAVE YOUR ATTENTION NOW, KALIBAK?
RELEASE MY EAR, GRANNY!
"...WILL BE FORCED TO KNEEL BEFORE HIM...
"...OR DIE!"

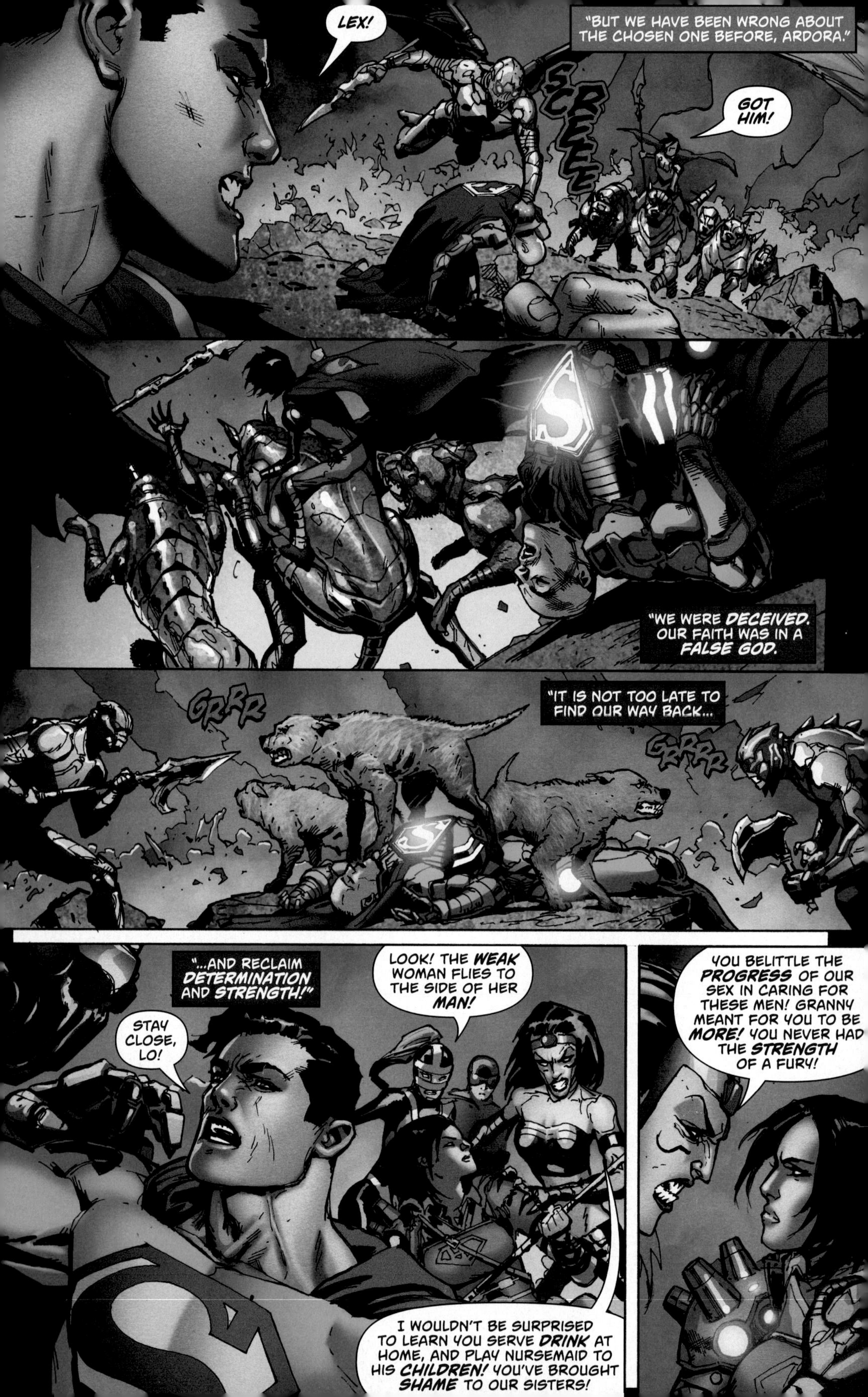
LEX!
"BUT WE HAVE BEEN WRONG ABOUT THE CHOSEN ONE BEFORE, ARDORA."
SCREEEE
GOT HIM!
"WE WERE DECEIVED. OUR FAITH WAS IN A FALSE GOD.
GRRR
"IT IS NOT TOO LATE TO FIND OUR WAY BACK...
GRRRR
"...AND RECLAIM DETERMINATION AND STRENGTH!"
STAY CLOSE, LO!
LOOK! THE WEAK WOMAN FLIES TO THE SIDE OF HER MAN!
I WOULDN'T BE SURPRISED TO LEARN YOU SERVE DRINK AT HOME, AND PLAY NURSEMAID TO HIS CHILDREN! YOU'VE BROUGHT SHAME TO OUR SISTERS!
YOU BELITTLE THE PROGRESS OF OUR SEX IN CARING FOR THESE MEN! GRANNY MEANT FOR YOU TO BE MORE! YOU NEVER HAD THE STRENGTH OF A FURY!

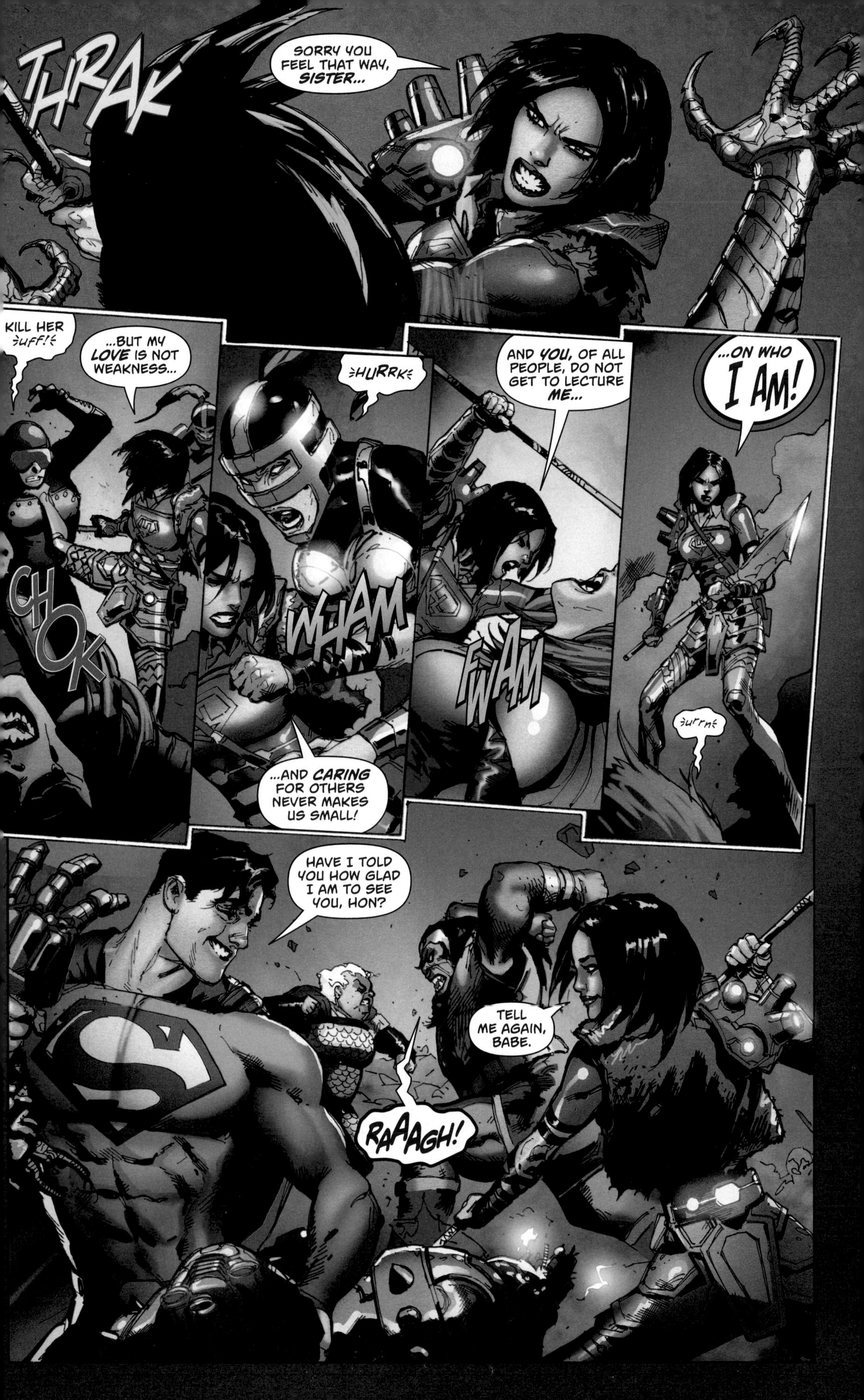
THRAK
SORRY YOU FEEL THAT WAY, SISTER...
KILL HER uff!
...BUT MY LOVE IS NOT WEAKNESS...
CHOK
HURRK
WHAM
...AND CARING FOR OTHERS NEVER MAKES US SMALL!
AND YOU, OF ALL PEOPLE, DO NOT GET TO LECTURE ME...
FWAM
...ON WHO I AM!
urrn
HAVE I TOLD YOU HOW GLAD I AM TO SEE YOU, HON?
TELL ME AGAIN, BABE.
RAAAGH!

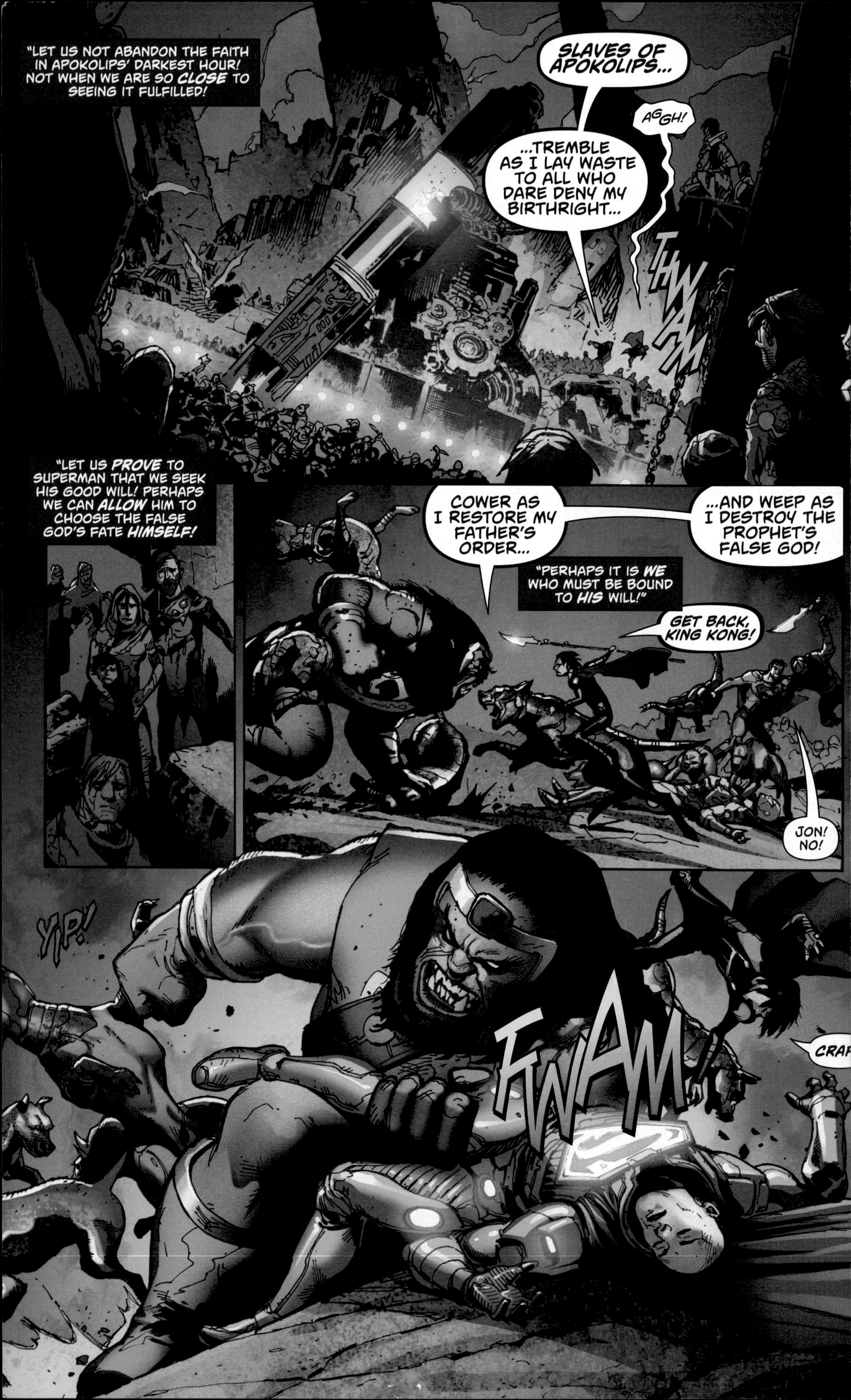
"LET US NOT ABANDON THE FAITH IN APOKOLIPS' DARKEST HOUR! NOT WHEN WE ARE SO CLOSE TO SEEING IT FULFILLED!
SLAVES OF APOKOLIPS...
...TREMBLE AS I LAY WASTE TO ALL WHO DARE DENY MY BIRTHRIGHT...
AGGH!
THWAM
"LET US PROVE TO SUPERMAN THAT WE SEEK HIS GOOD WILL! PERHAPS WE CAN ALLOW HIM TO CHOOSE THE FALSE GOD'S FATE HIMSELF!
COWER AS I RESTORE MY FATHER'S ORDER...
...AND WEEP AS I DESTROY THE PROPHET'S FALSE GOD!
"PERHAPS IT IS WE WHO MUST BE BOUND TO HIS WILL!"
GET BACK, KING KONG!
JON! NO!
YIP!
FWAM
CRAP

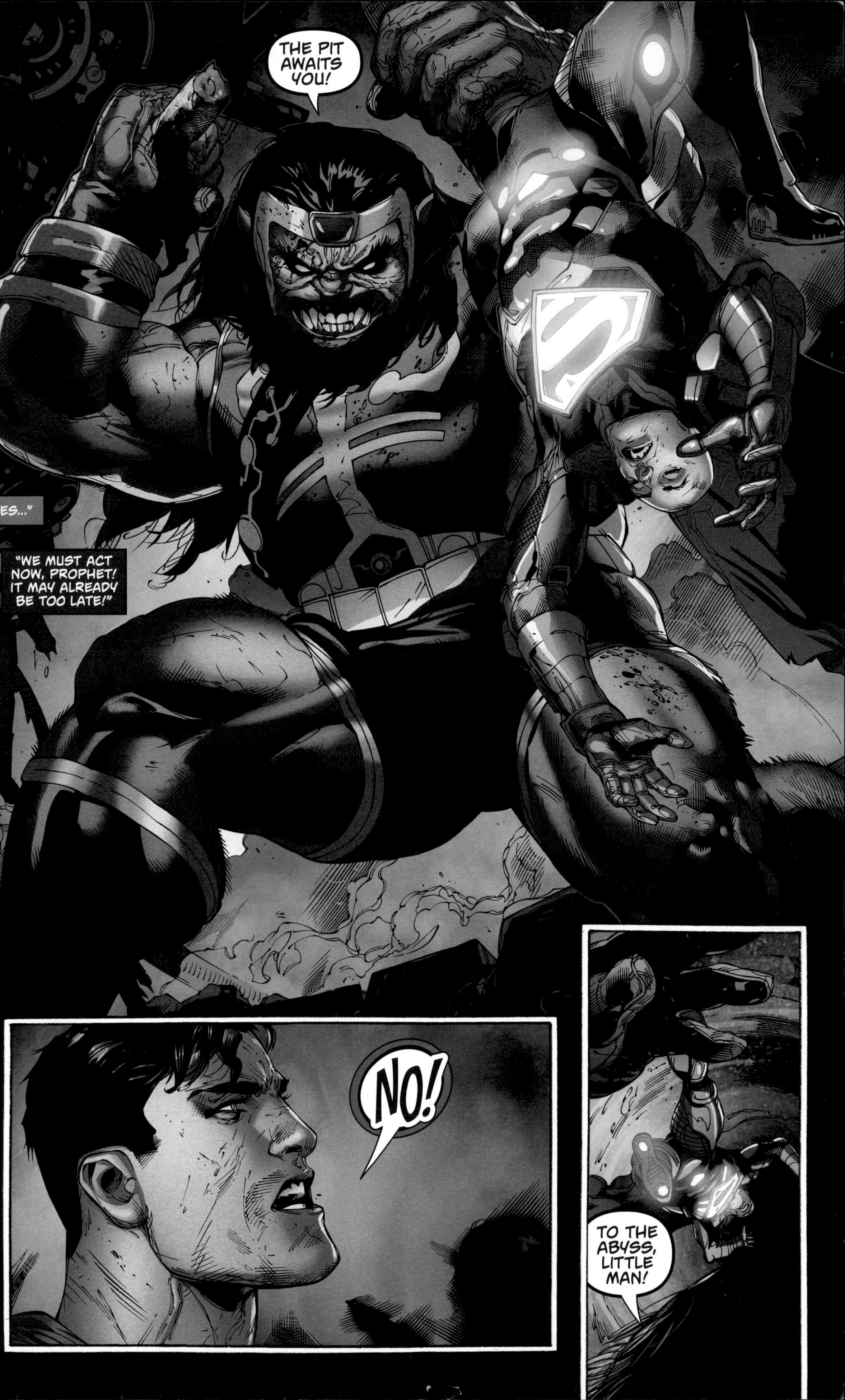
THE PIT AWAITS YOU!
ES..."
"WE MUST ACT NOW, PROPHET! IT MAY ALREADY BE TOO LATE!"
NO!
TO THE ABYSS, LITTLE MAN!

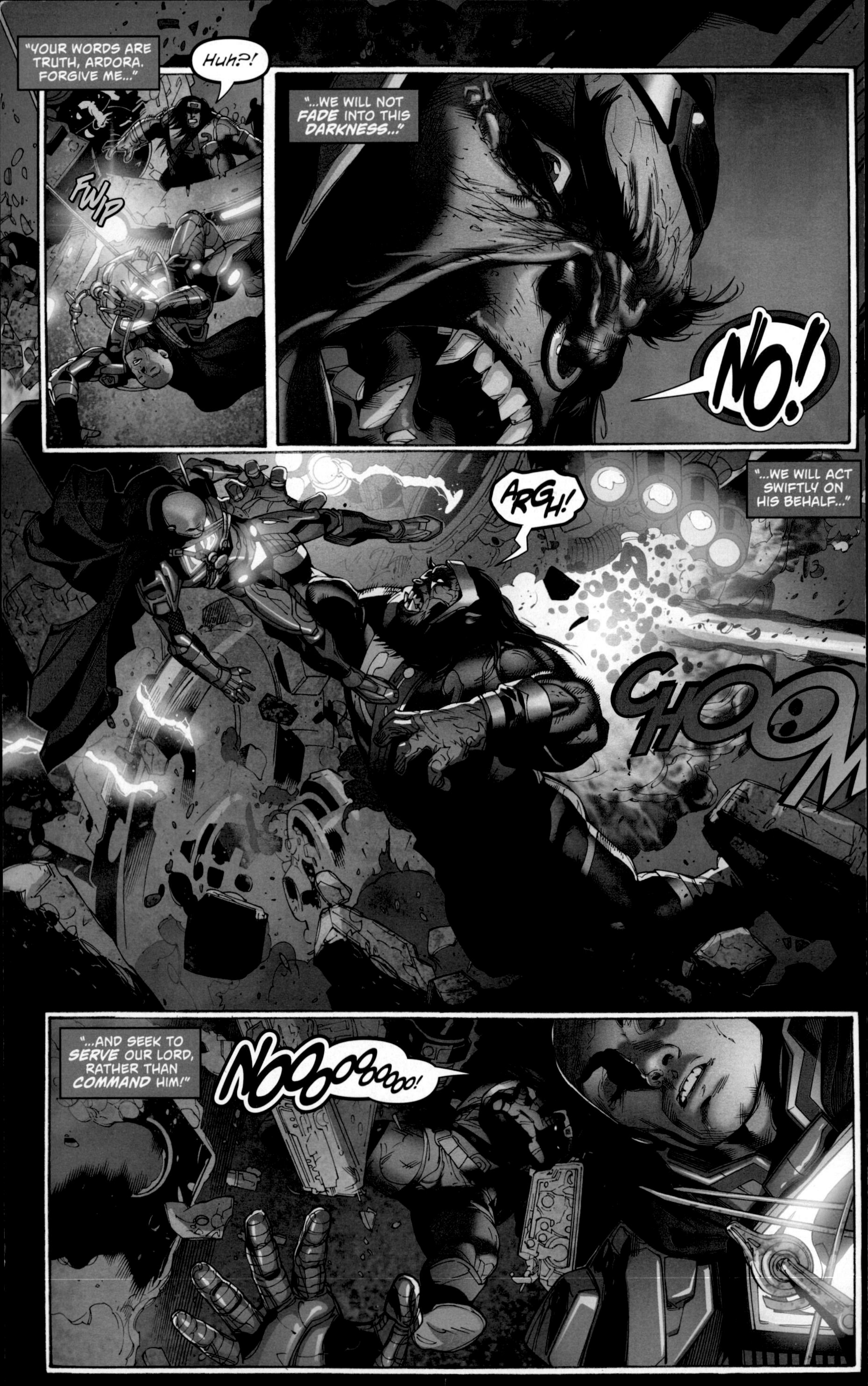
"YOUR WORDS ARE TRUTH, ARDORA. FORGIVE ME..."
Huh?!
FWIP
"...WE WILL NOT FADE INTO THIS DARKNESS..."
NO!
ARGH!
"...WE WILL ACT SWIFTLY ON HIS BEHALF..."
CHOOM
"...AND SEEK TO SERVE OUR LORD, RATHER THAN COMMAND HIM!"
NOOOOOOOOOO!

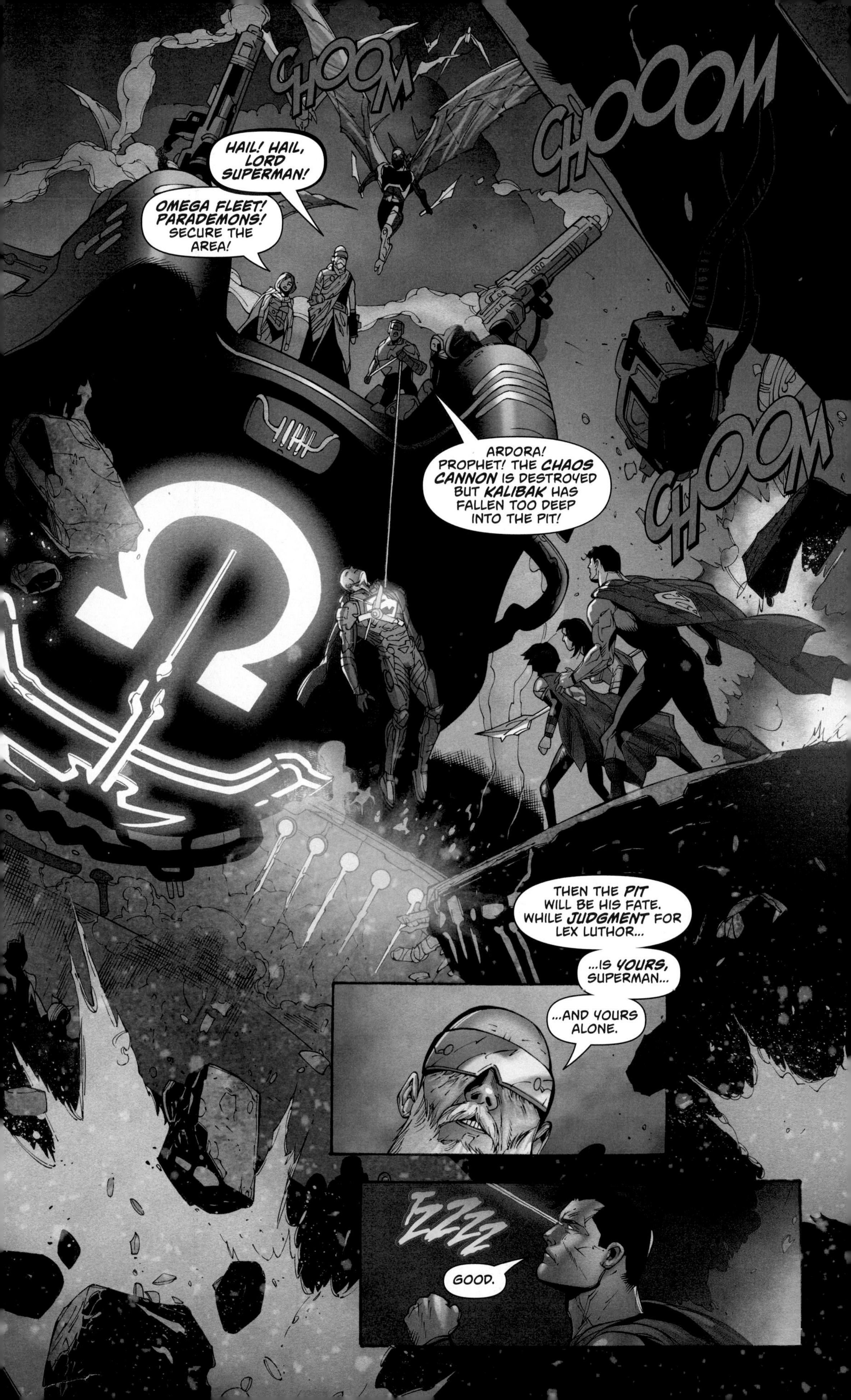

CHOOM
CHOOOOM
HAIL! HAIL, LORD SUPERMAN!
OMEGA FLEET! PARADEMONS! SECURE THE AREA!
ARDORA! PROPHET! THE CHAOS CANNON IS DESTROYED BUT KALIBAK HAS FALLEN TOO DEEP INTO THE PIT!
CHOOM
THEN THE PIT WILL BE HIS FATE. WHILE JUDGMENT FOR LEX LUTHOR...
...IS YOURS, SUPERMAN...
...AND YOURS ALONE.
FZZZZ
GOOD.

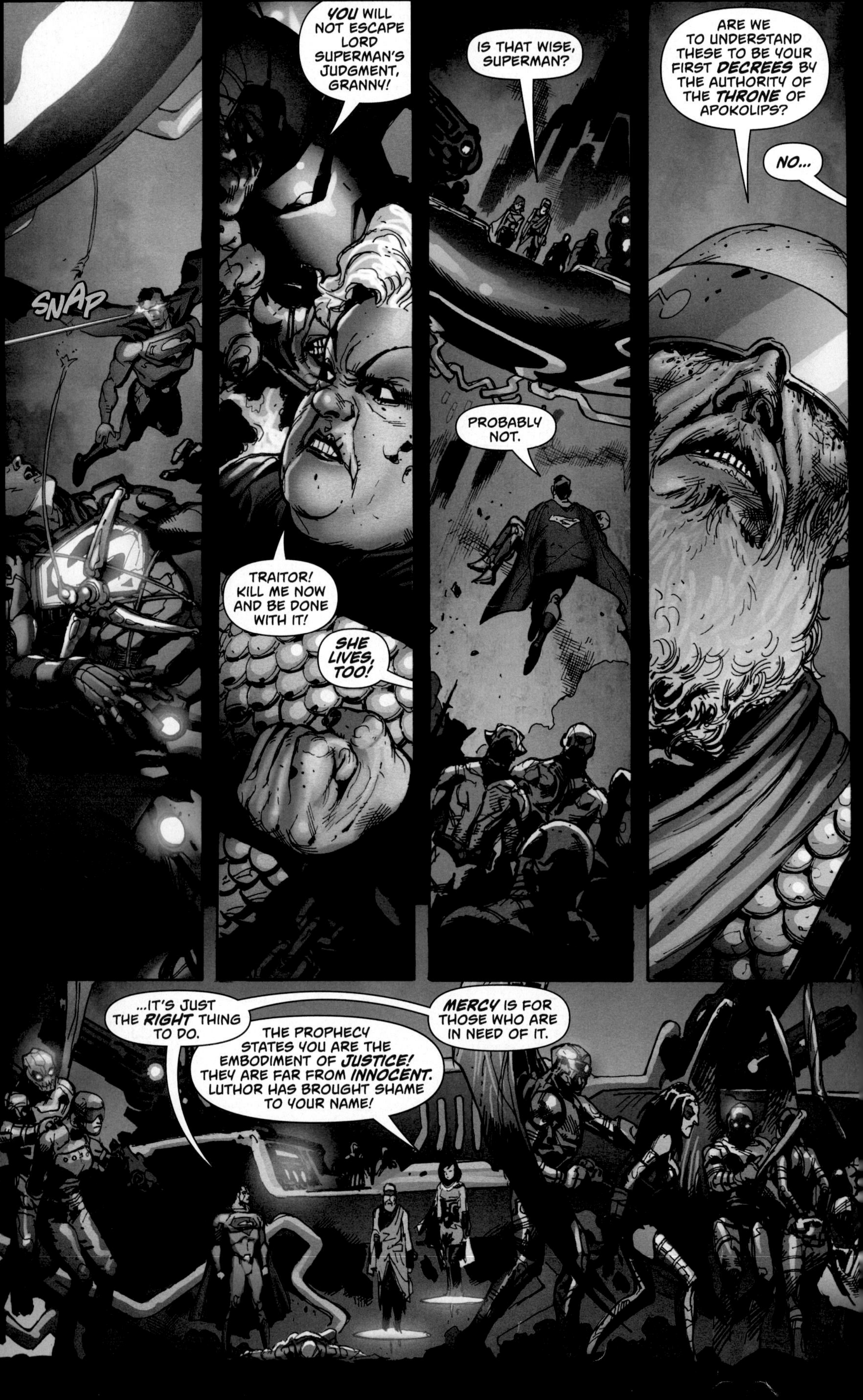

SNAP
YOU WILL NOT ESCAPE LORD SUPERMAN'S JUDGMENT, GRANNY!
TRAITOR! KILL ME NOW AND BE DONE WITH IT!
SHE LIVES, TOO!
IS THAT WISE, SUPERMAN?
PROBABLY NOT.
ARE WE TO UNDERSTAND THESE TO BE YOUR FIRST DECREES BY THE AUTHORITY OF THE THRONE OF APOKOLIPS?
NO...
...IT'S JUST THE RIGHT THING TO DO.
MERCY IS FOR THOSE WHO ARE IN NEED OF IT.
THE PROPHECY STATES YOU ARE THE EMBODIMENT OF JUSTICE! THEY ARE FAR FROM INNOCENT. LUTHOR HAS BROUGHT SHAME TO YOUR NAME!

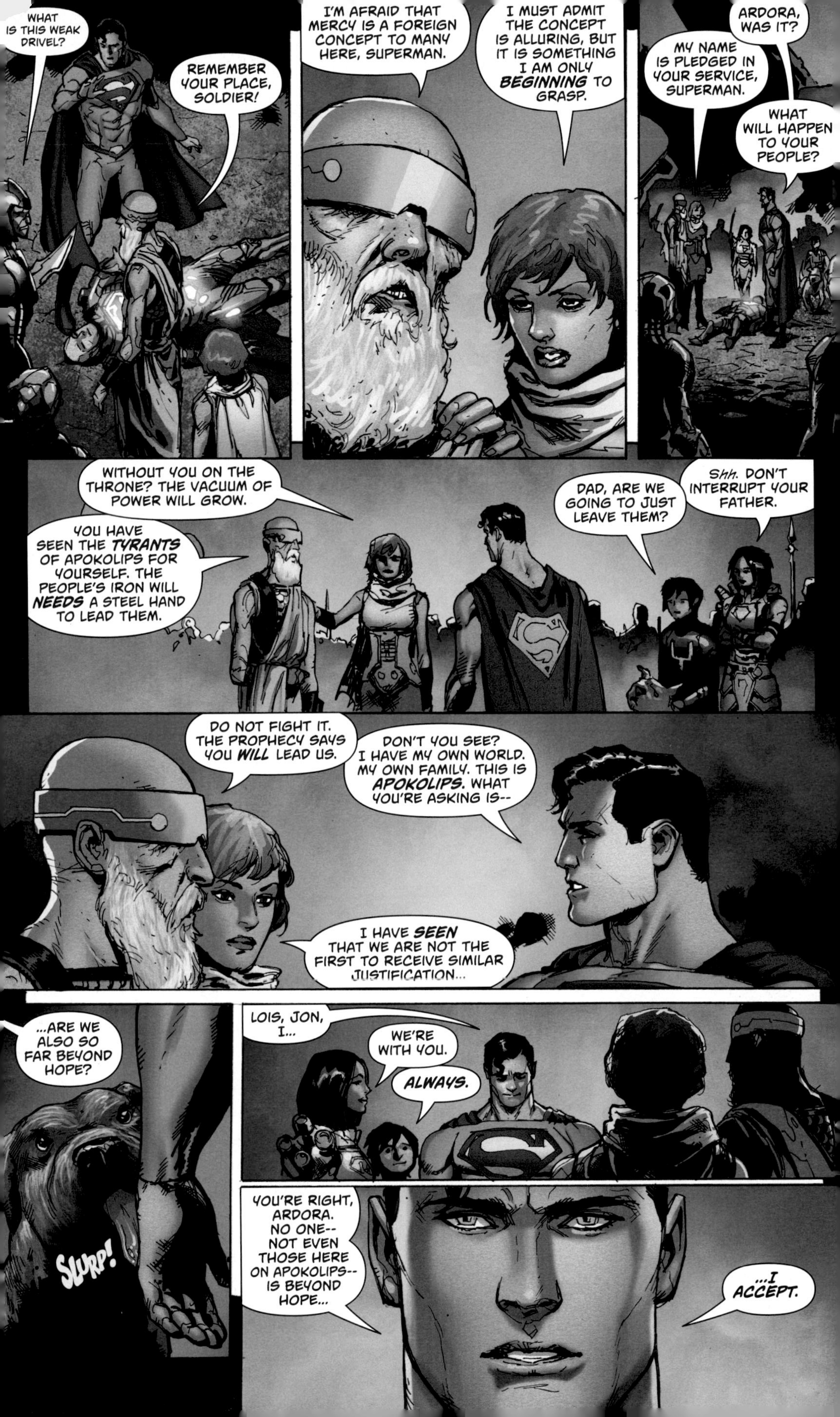

WHAT IS THIS WEAK DRIVEL?
REMEMBER YOUR PLACE, SOLDIER!
I'M AFRAID THAT MERCY IS A FOREIGN CONCEPT TO MANY HERE, SUPERMAN.
I MUST ADMIT THE CONCEPT IS ALLURING, BUT IT IS SOMETHING I AM ONLY BEGINNING TO GRASP.
ARDORA, WAS IT?
MY NAME IS PLEDGED IN YOUR SERVICE, SUPERMAN.
WHAT WILL HAPPEN TO YOUR PEOPLE?
WITHOUT YOU ON THE THRONE? THE VACUUM OF POWER WILL GROW.
YOU HAVE SEEN THE TYRANTS OF APOKOLIPS FOR YOURSELF. THE PEOPLE'S IRON WILL NEEDS A STEEL HAND TO LEAD THEM.
DAD, ARE WE GOING TO JUST LEAVE THEM?
Shh. DON'T INTERRUPT YOUR FATHER.
DO NOT FIGHT IT. THE PROPHECY SAYS YOU WILL LEAD US.
DON'T YOU SEE? I HAVE MY OWN WORLD. MY OWN FAMILY. THIS IS APOKOLIPS. WHAT YOU'RE ASKING IS--
I HAVE SEEN THAT WE ARE NOT THE FIRST TO RECEIVE SIMILAR JUSTIFICATION...
...ARE WE ALSO SO FAR BEYOND HOPE?
SLURP!
LOIS, JON, I...
WE'RE WITH YOU.
ALWAYS.
YOU'RE RIGHT, ARDORA. NO ONE-- NOT EVEN THOSE HERE ON APOKOLIPS-- IS BEYOND HOPE...
...I ACCEPT.

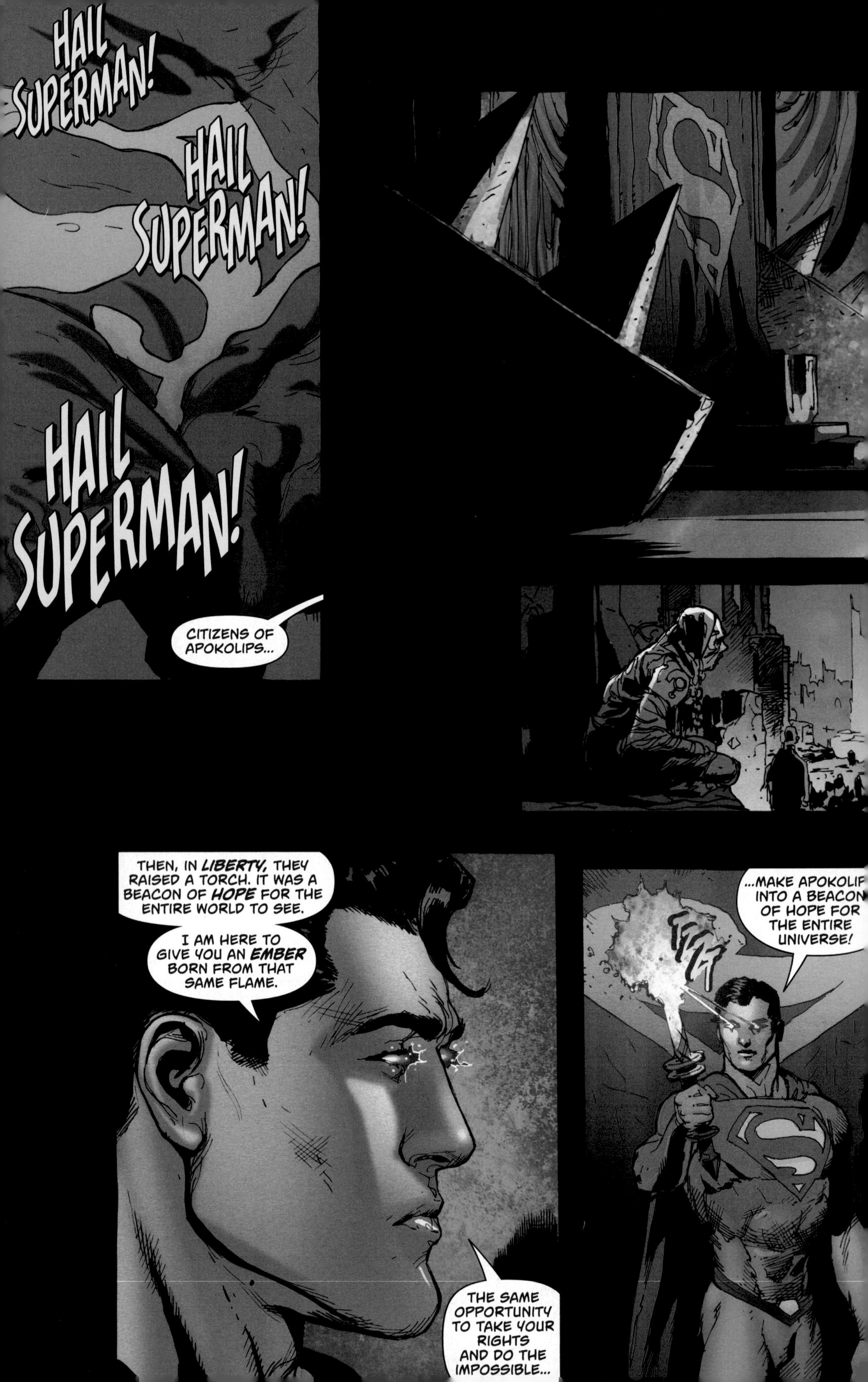
HAIL SUPERMAN!
HAIL SUPERMAN!
HAIL SUPERMAN!
CITIZENS OF APOKOLIPS...
THEN, IN LIBERTY, THEY RAISED A TORCH. IT WAS A BEACON OF HOPE FOR THE ENTIRE WORLD TO SEE.
I AM HERE TO GIVE YOU AN EMBER BORN FROM THAT SAME FLAME.
THE SAME OPPORTUNITY TO TAKE YOUR RIGHTS AND DO THE IMPOSSIBLE...
...MAKE APOKOLIP INTO A BEACON OF HOPE FOR THE ENTIRE UNIVERSE!

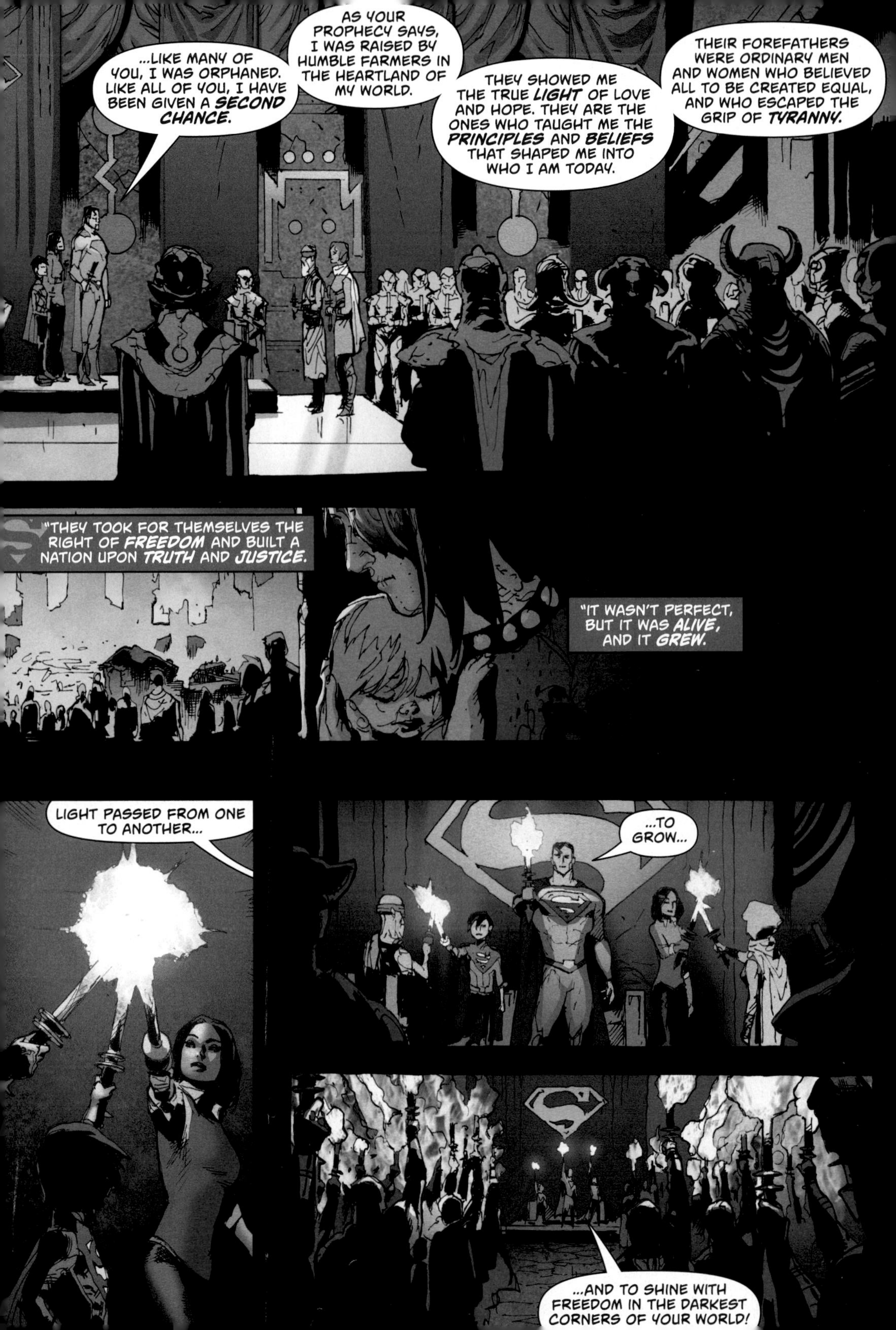
...LIKE MANY OF YOU, I WAS ORPHANED. LIKE ALL OF YOU, I HAVE BEEN GIVEN A SECOND CHANCE.
AS YOUR PROPHECY SAYS, I WAS RAISED BY HUMBLE FARMERS IN THE HEARTLAND OF MY WORLD.
THEY SHOWED ME THE TRUE LIGHT OF LOVE AND HOPE. THEY ARE THE ONES WHO TAUGHT ME THE PRINCIPLES AND BELIEFS THAT SHAPED ME INTO WHO I AM TODAY.
THEIR FOREFATHERS WERE ORDINARY MEN AND WOMEN WHO BELIEVED ALL TO BE CREATED EQUAL, AND WHO ESCAPED THE GRIP OF TYRANNY.
"THEY TOOK FOR THEMSELVES THE RIGHT OF FREEDOM AND BUILT A NATION UPON TRUTH AND JUSTICE.
"IT WASN'T PERFECT, BUT IT WAS ALIVE, AND IT GREW.
LIGHT PASSED FROM ONE TO ANOTHER...
...TO GROW...
...AND TO SHINE WITH FREEDOM IN THE DARKEST CORNERS OF YOUR WORLD!

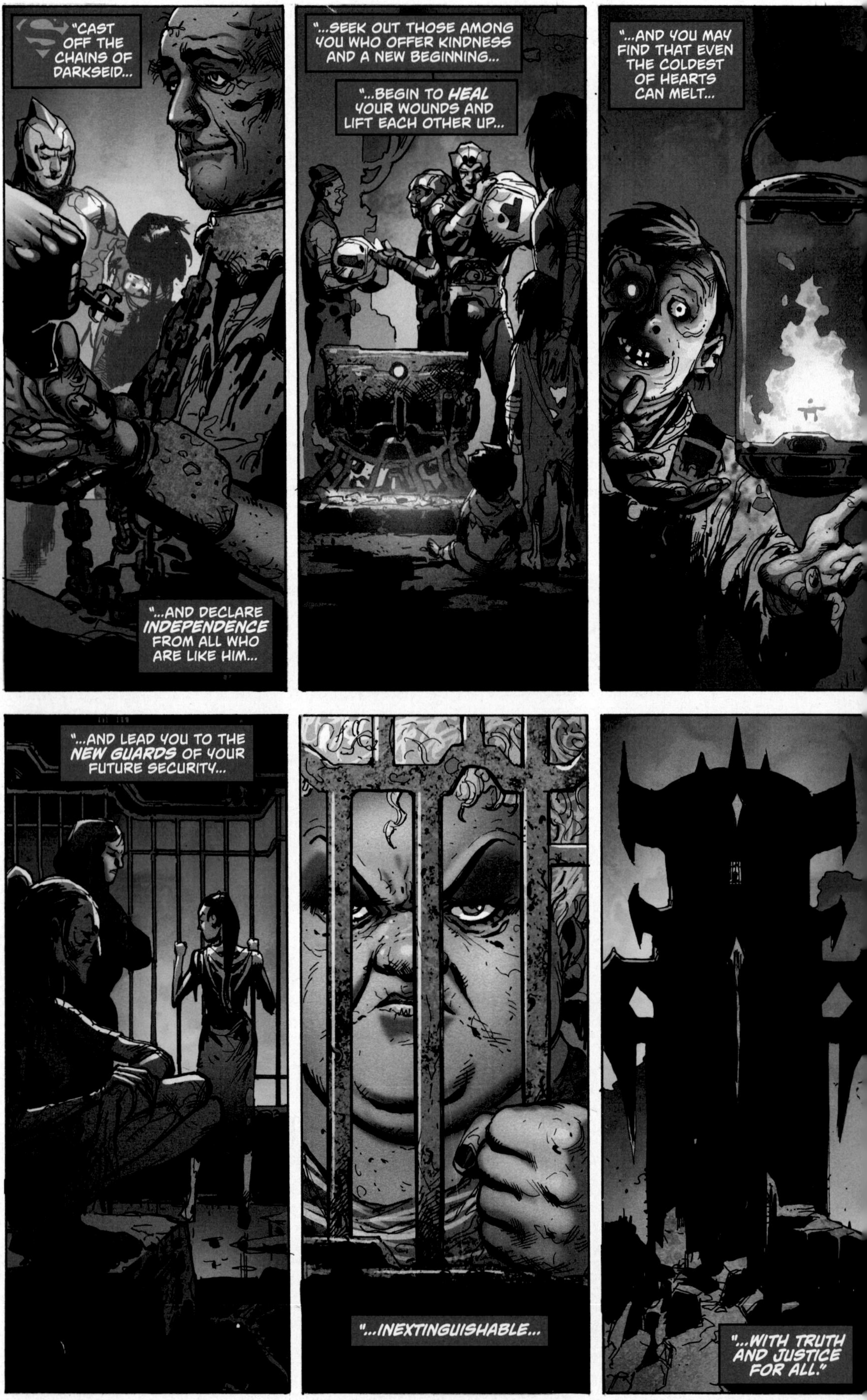
"CAST OFF THE CHAINS OF DARKSEID...
"...AND DECLARE INDEPENDENCE FROM ALL WHO ARE LIKE HIM...
"...SEEK OUT THOSE AMONG YOU WHO OFFER KINDNESS AND A NEW BEGINNING...
"...BEGIN TO HEAL YOUR WOUNDS AND LIFT EACH OTHER UP...
"...AND YOU MAY FIND THAT EVEN THE COLDEST OF HEARTS CAN MELT...
"...AND LEAD YOU TO THE NEW GUARDS OF YOUR FUTURE SECURITY...
"...INEXTINGUISHABLE...
"...WITH TRUTH AND JUSTICE FOR ALL."

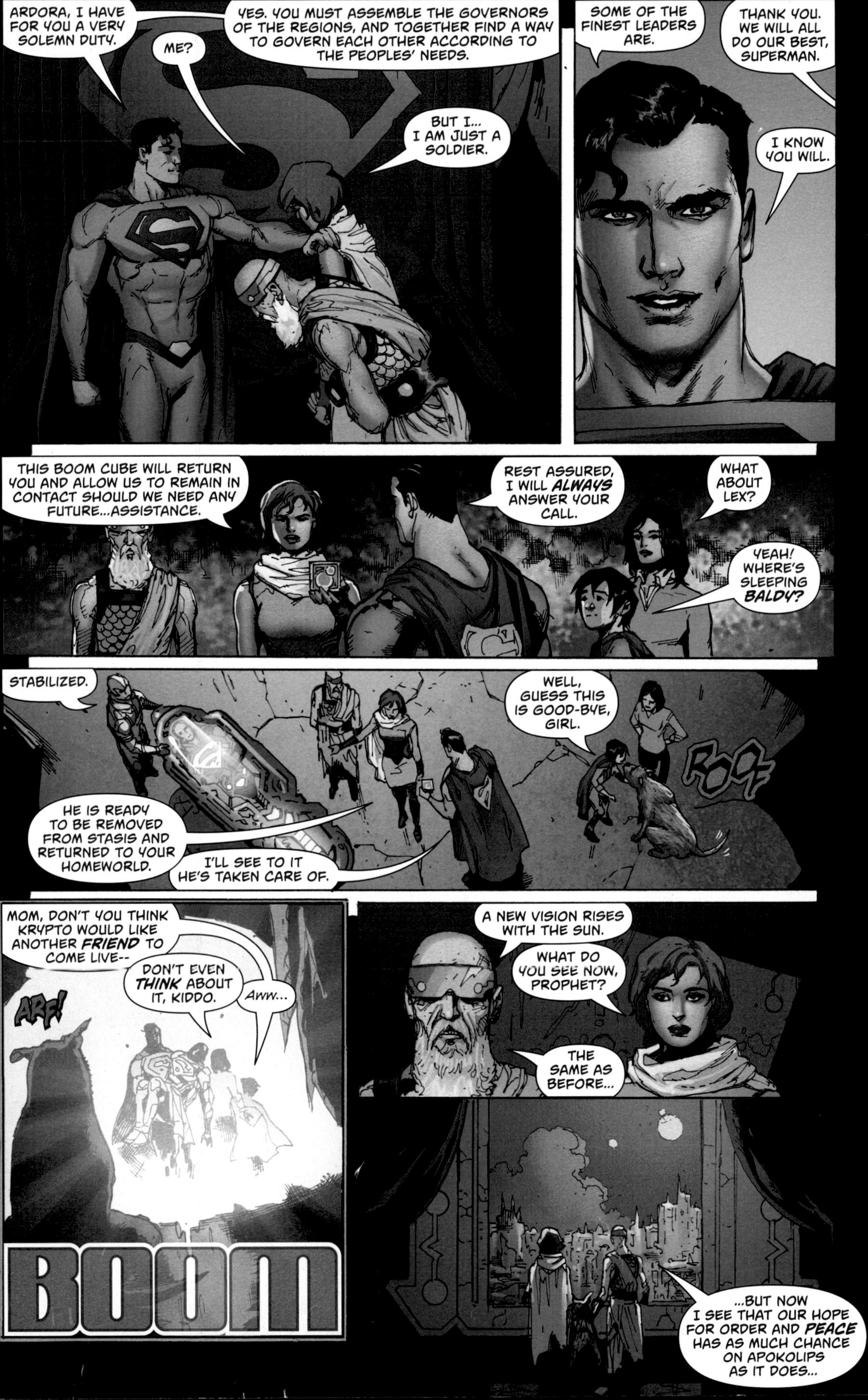
ARDORA, I HAVE FOR YOU A VERY SOLEMN DUTY.
ME?
YES. YOU MUST ASSEMBLE THE GOVERNORS OF THE REGIONS, AND TOGETHER FIND A WAY TO GOVERN EACH OTHER ACCORDING TO THE PEOPLES' NEEDS.
BUT I... I AM JUST A SOLDIER.
SOME OF THE FINEST LEADERS ARE.
THANK YOU. WE WILL ALL DO OUR BEST, SUPERMAN.
I KNOW YOU WILL.
THIS BOOM CUBE WILL RETURN YOU AND ALLOW US TO REMAIN IN CONTACT SHOULD WE NEED ANY FUTURE...ASSISTANCE.
REST ASSURED, I WILL ALWAYS ANSWER YOUR CALL.
WHAT ABOUT LEX?
YEAH! WHERE'S SLEEPING BALDY?
STABILIZED.
HE IS READY TO BE REMOVED FROM STASIS AND RETURNED TO YOUR HOMEWORLD.
I'LL SEE TO IT HE'S TAKEN CARE OF.
WELL, GUESS THIS IS GOOD-BYE, GIRL.
ROOF
MOM, DON'T YOU THINK KRYPTO WOULD LIKE ANOTHER FRIEND TO COME LIVE--
DON'T EVEN THINK ABOUT IT, KIDDO.
AWW...
ARF!
BOOM
A NEW VISION RISES WITH THE SUN.
WHAT DO YOU SEE NOW, PROPHET?
THE SAME AS BEFORE...
...BUT NOW I SEE THAT OUR HOPE FOR ORDER AND PEACE HAS AS MUCH CHANCE ON APOKOLIPS AS IT DOES...

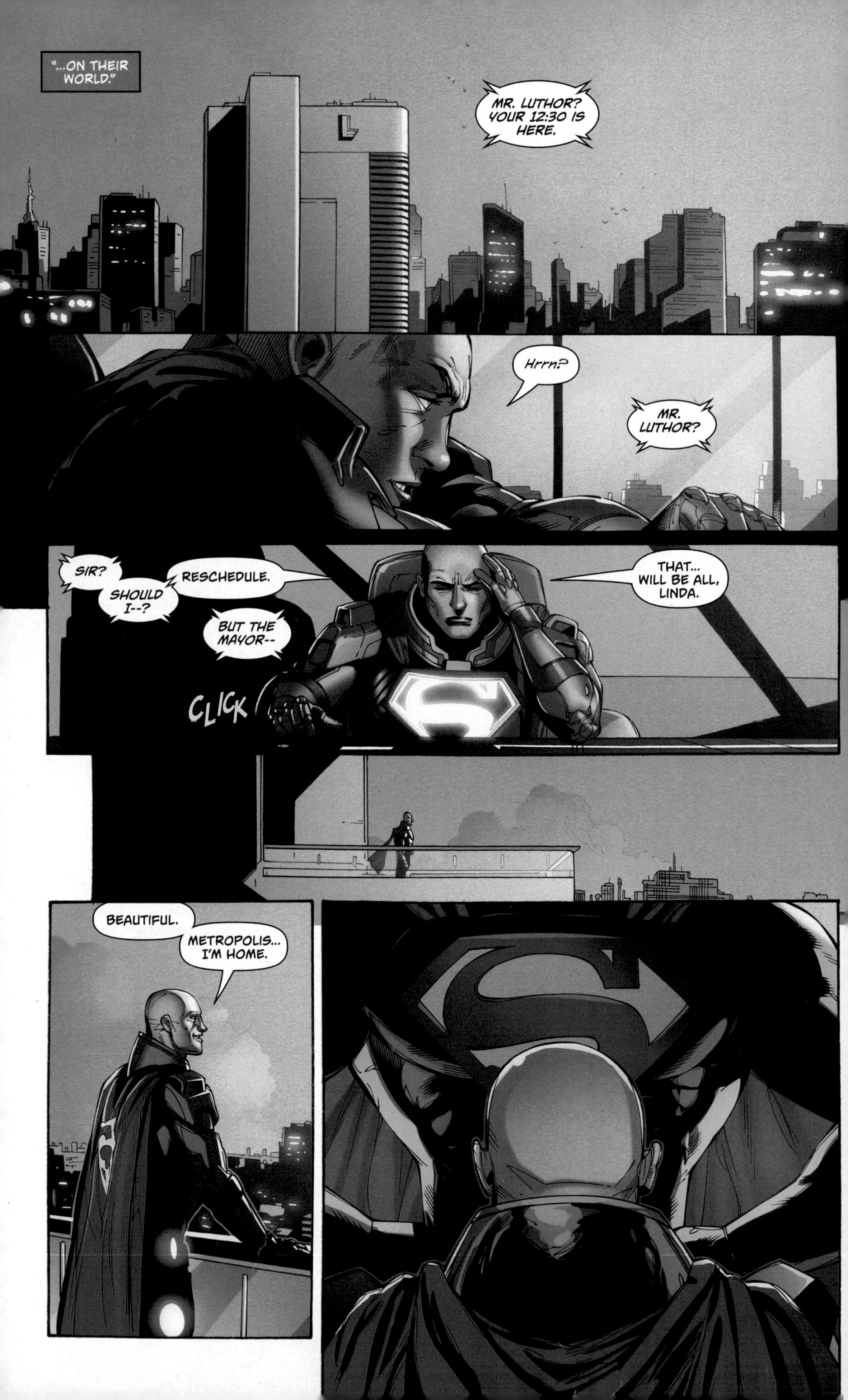
"...ON THEIR WORLD."
MR. LUTHOR? YOUR 12:30 IS HERE.
Hrrn?
MR. LUTHOR?
SIR?
SHOULD I--?
RESCHEDULE.
BUT THE MAYOR--
THAT... WILL BE ALL, LINDA.
CLICK
BEAUTIFUL.
METROPOLIS... I'M HOME.

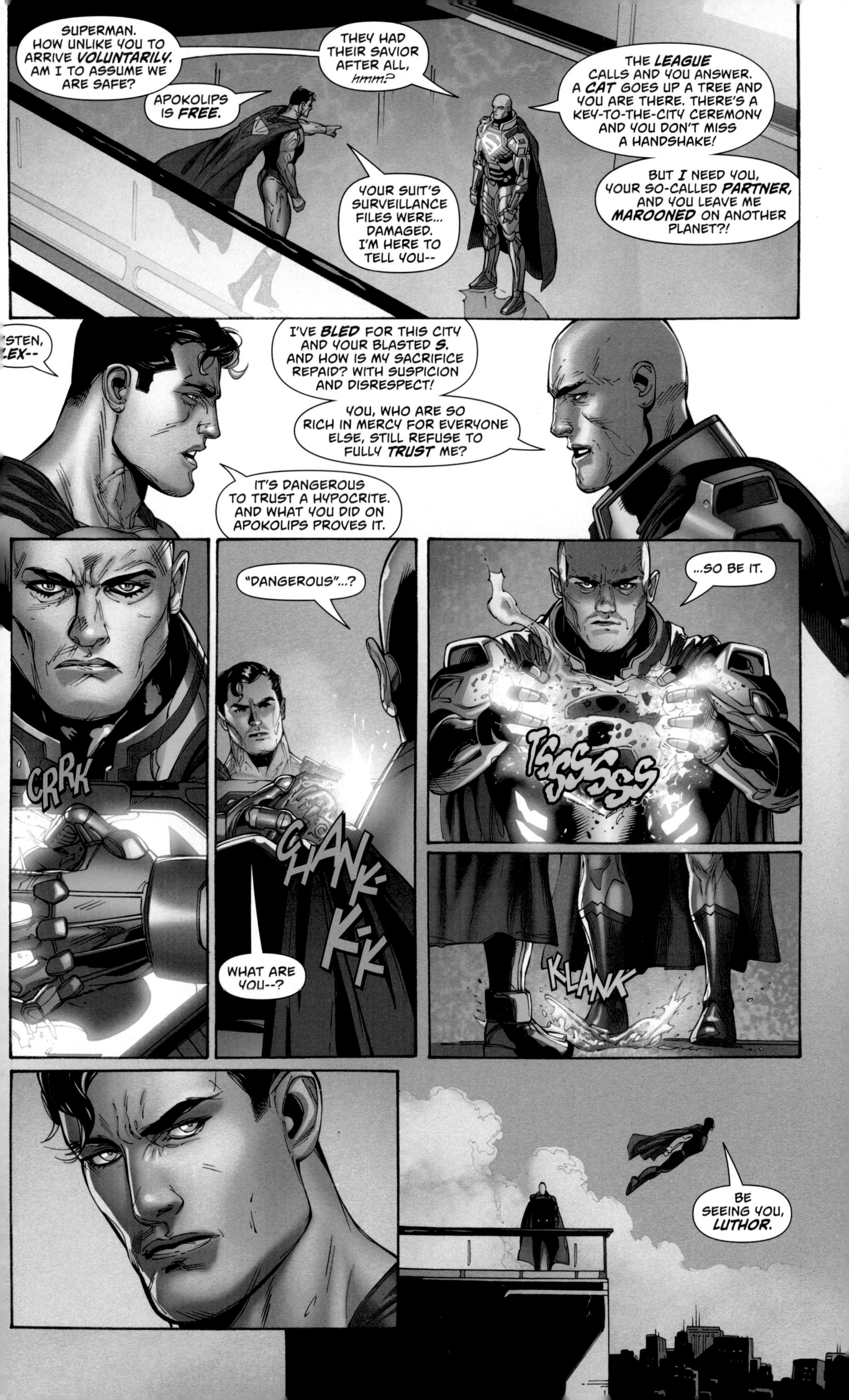

SUPERMAN. HOW UNLIKE YOU TO ARRIVE VOLUNTARILY. AM I TO ASSUME WE ARE SAFE?
APOKOLIPS IS FREE.
THEY HAD THEIR SAVIOR AFTER ALL, hmm?
YOUR SUIT'S SURVEILLANCE FILES WERE... DAMAGED. I'M HERE TO TELL YOU--
THE LEAGUE CALLS AND YOU ANSWER. A CAT GOES UP A TREE AND YOU ARE THERE. THERE'S A KEY-TO-THE-CITY CEREMONY AND YOU DON'T MISS A HANDSHAKE!
BUT I NEED YOU, YOUR SO-CALLED PARTNER, AND YOU LEAVE ME MAROONED ON ANOTHER PLANET?!
I'VE BLED FOR THIS CITY AND YOUR BLASTED S. AND HOW IS MY SACRIFICE REPAID? WITH SUSPICION AND DISRESPECT!
YOU, WHO ARE SO RICH IN MERCY FOR EVERYONE ELSE, STILL REFUSE TO FULLY TRUST ME?
IT'S DANGEROUS TO TRUST A HYPOCRITE. AND WHAT YOU DID ON APOKOLIPS PROVES IT.
CRRK
"DANGEROUS"...?
CHANK-K-K
WHAT ARE YOU--?
...SO BE IT.
TSSSSSS
KLANK
BE SEEING YOU, LUTHOR.

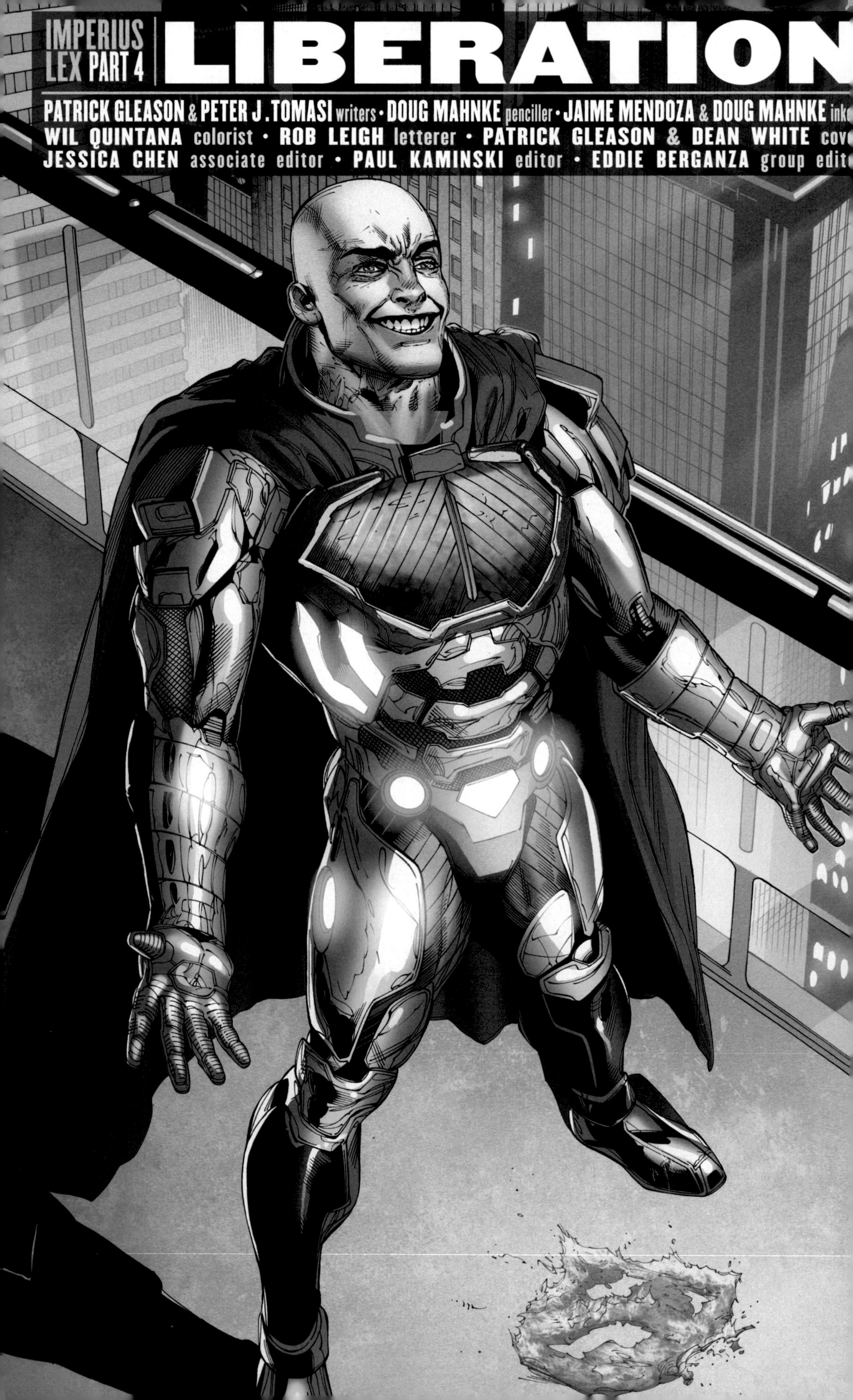
IMPERIUS LEX PART 4
LIBERATION
PATRICK GLEASON & PETER J. TOMASI writers • DOUG MAHNKE penciller • JAIME MENDOZA & DOUG MAHNKE inke
WIL QUINTANA colorist • ROB LEIGH letterer • PATRICK GLEASON & DEAN WHITE cove
JESSICA CHEN associate editor • PAUL KAMINSKI editor • EDDIE BERGANZA group edit

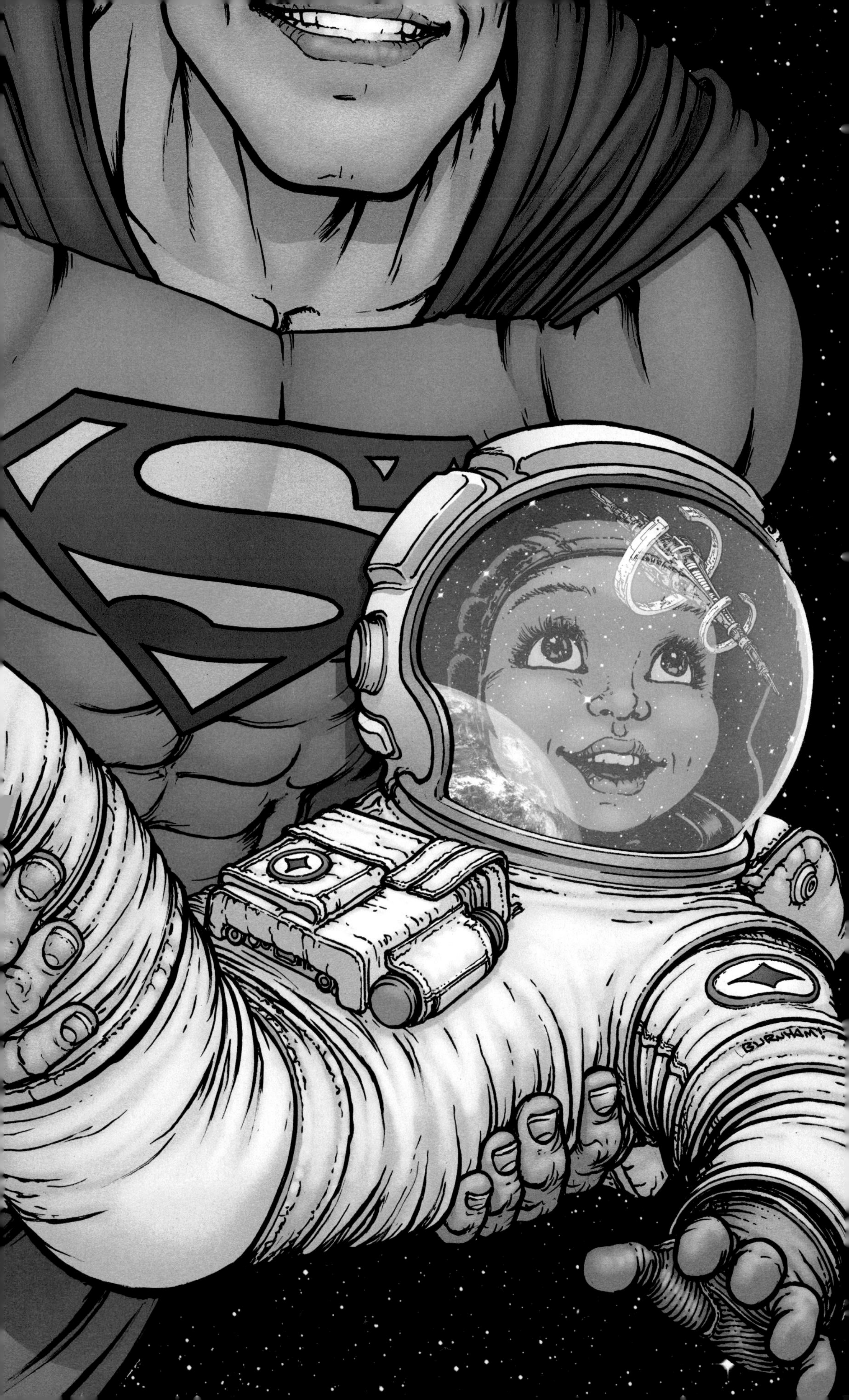
BURNHAM!

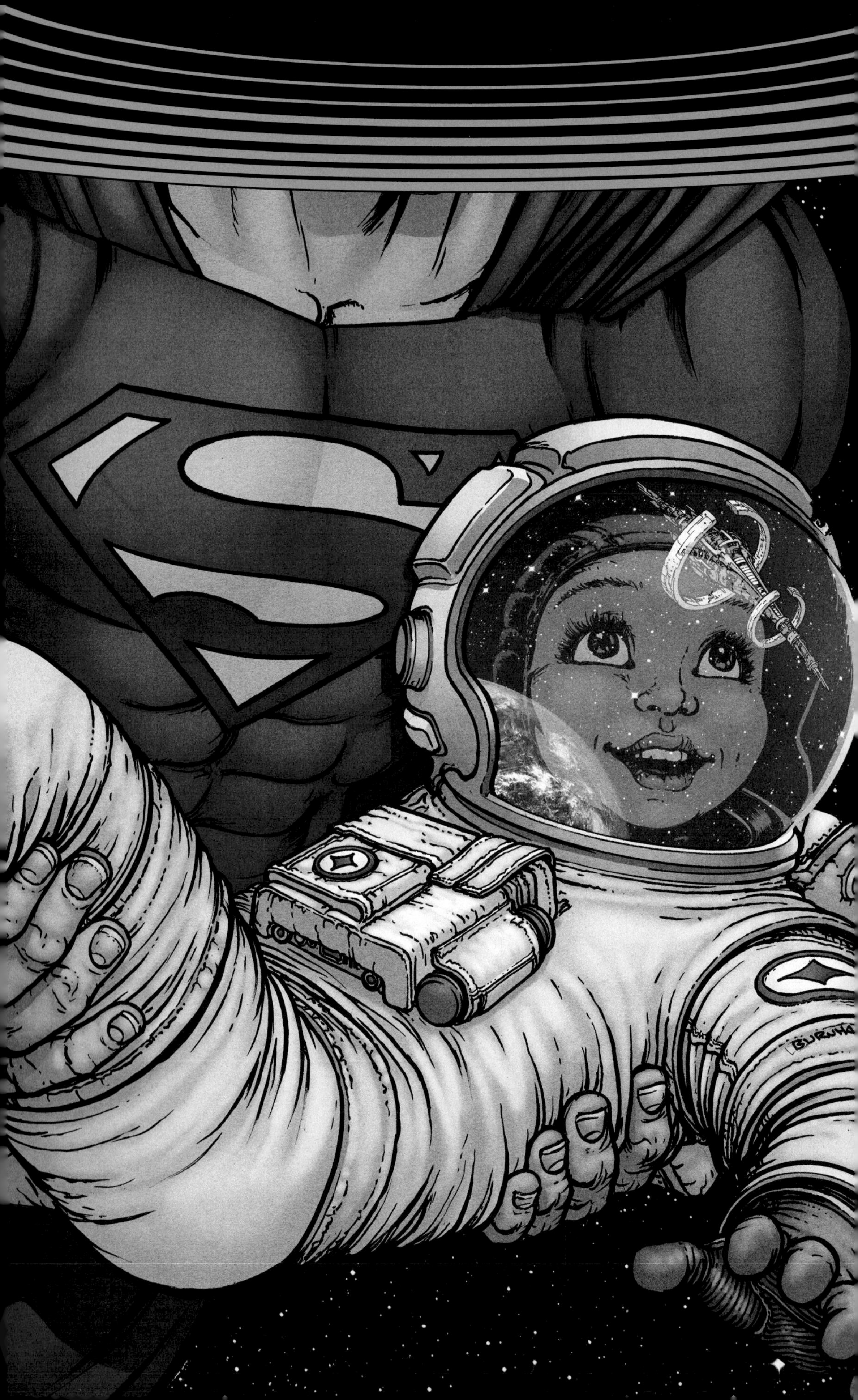

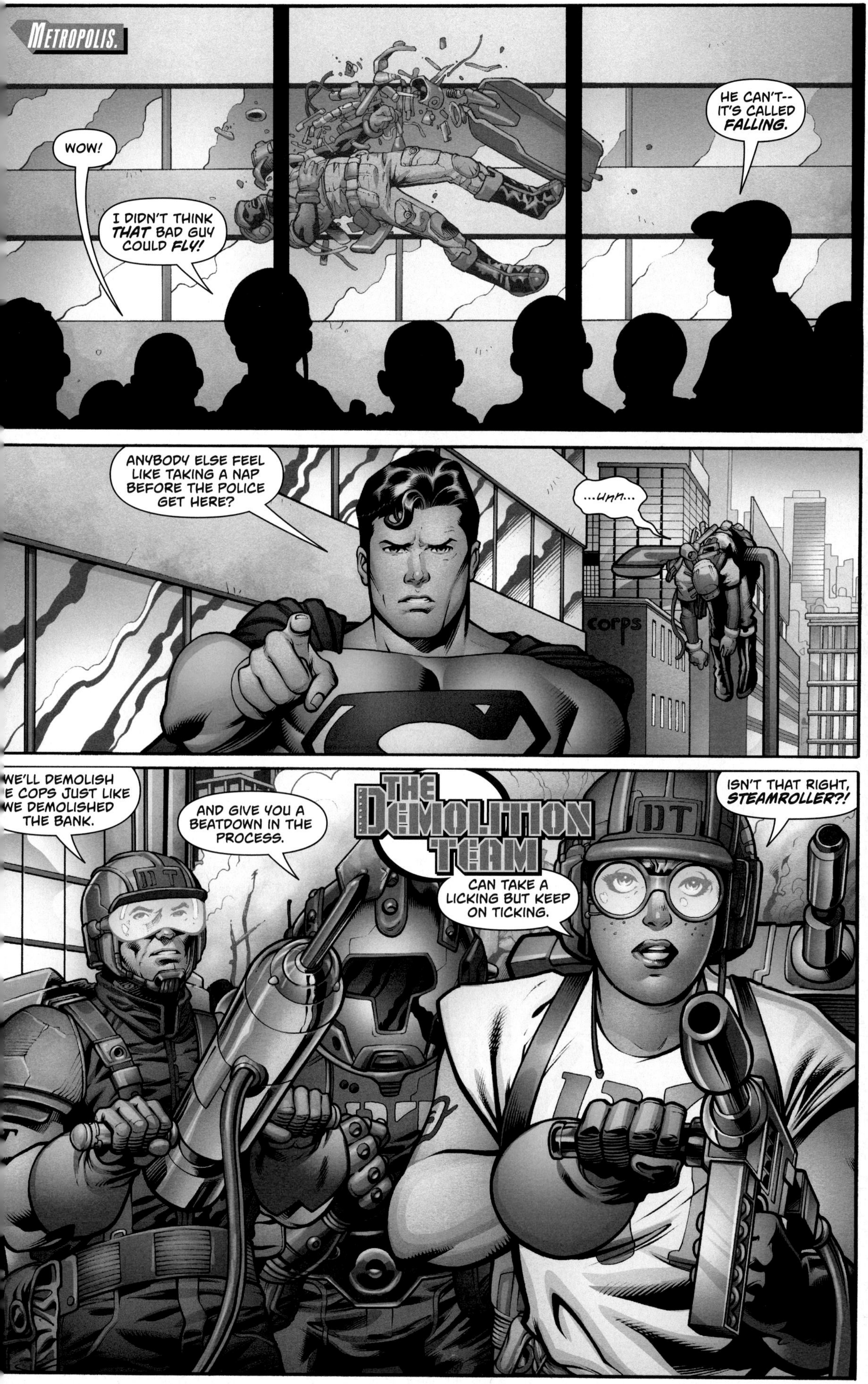
METROPOLIS.
WOW!
I DIDN'T THINK THAT BAD GUY COULD FLY!
HE CAN'T-- IT'S CALLED FALLING.
ANYBODY ELSE FEEL LIKE TAKING A NAP BEFORE THE POLICE GET HERE?
...UNN...
CORPS
WE'LL DEMOLISH E COPS JUST LIKE WE DEMOLISHED THE BANK.
AND GIVE YOU A BEATDOWN IN THE PROCESS.
THE DEMOLITION TEAM
CAN TAKE A LICKING BUT KEEP ON TICKING.
ISN'T THAT RIGHT, STEAMROLLER?!

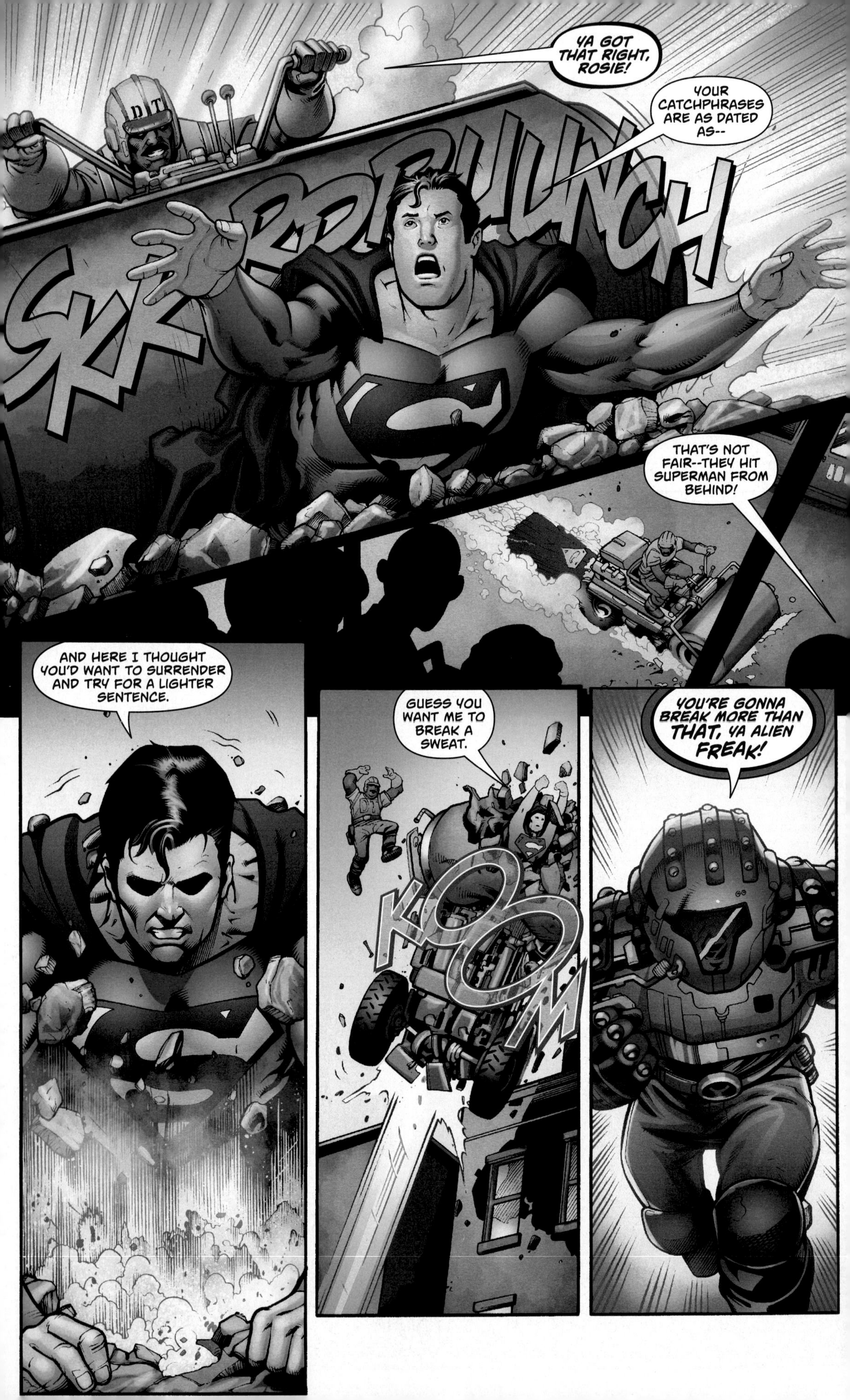
YA GOT THAT RIGHT, ROSIE!
YOUR CATCHPHRASES ARE AS DATED AS--
SKRRRUNCH
THAT'S NOT FAIR--THEY HIT SUPERMAN FROM BEHIND!
AND HERE I THOUGHT YOU'D WANT TO SURRENDER AND TRY FOR A LIGHTER SENTENCE.
GUESS YOU WANT ME TO BREAK A SWEAT.
KOOM
YOU'RE GONNA BREAK MORE THAN THAT, YA ALIEN FREAK!

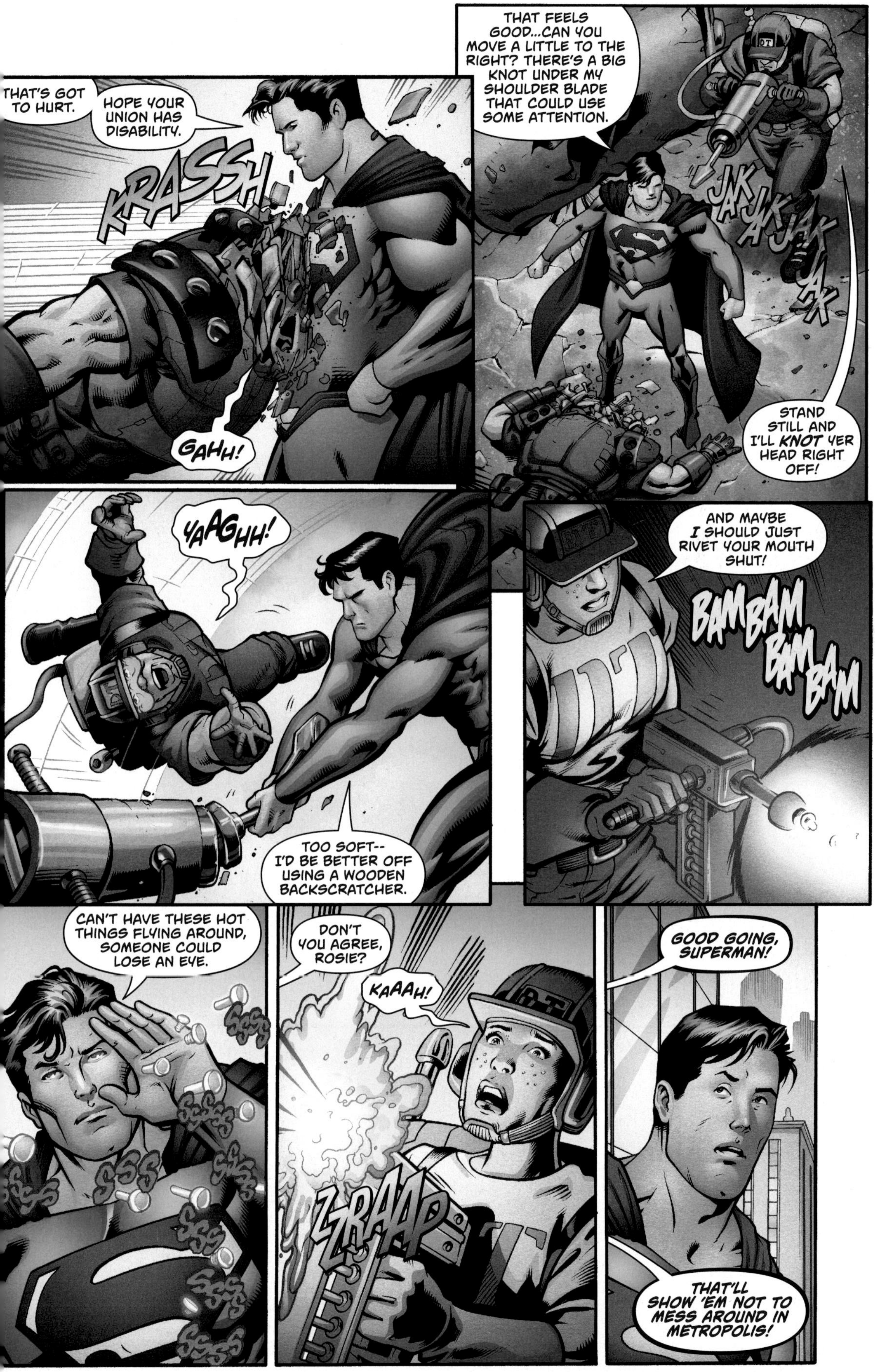
THAT'S GOT TO HURT.
HOPE YOUR UNION HAS DISABILITY.
KRASSH
GAHH!
THAT FEELS GOOD...CAN YOU MOVE A LITTLE TO THE RIGHT? THERE'S A BIG KNOT UNDER MY SHOULDER BLADE THAT COULD USE SOME ATTENTION.
JAKJAKJAKJAKJAK
STAND STILL AND I'LL KNOT YER HEAD RIGHT OFF!
YAAGHH!
TOO SOFT-- I'D BE BETTER OFF USING A WOODEN BACKSCRATCHER.
AND MAYBE I SHOULD JUST RIVET YOUR MOUTH SHUT!
BAMBAM BAMBAM
CAN'T HAVE THESE HOT THINGS FLYING AROUND, SOMEONE COULD LOSE AN EYE.
DON'T YOU AGREE, ROSIE?
KAAAH!
ZZRAAP
GOOD GOING, SUPERMAN!
THAT'LL SHOW 'EM NOT TO MESS AROUND IN METROPOLIS!

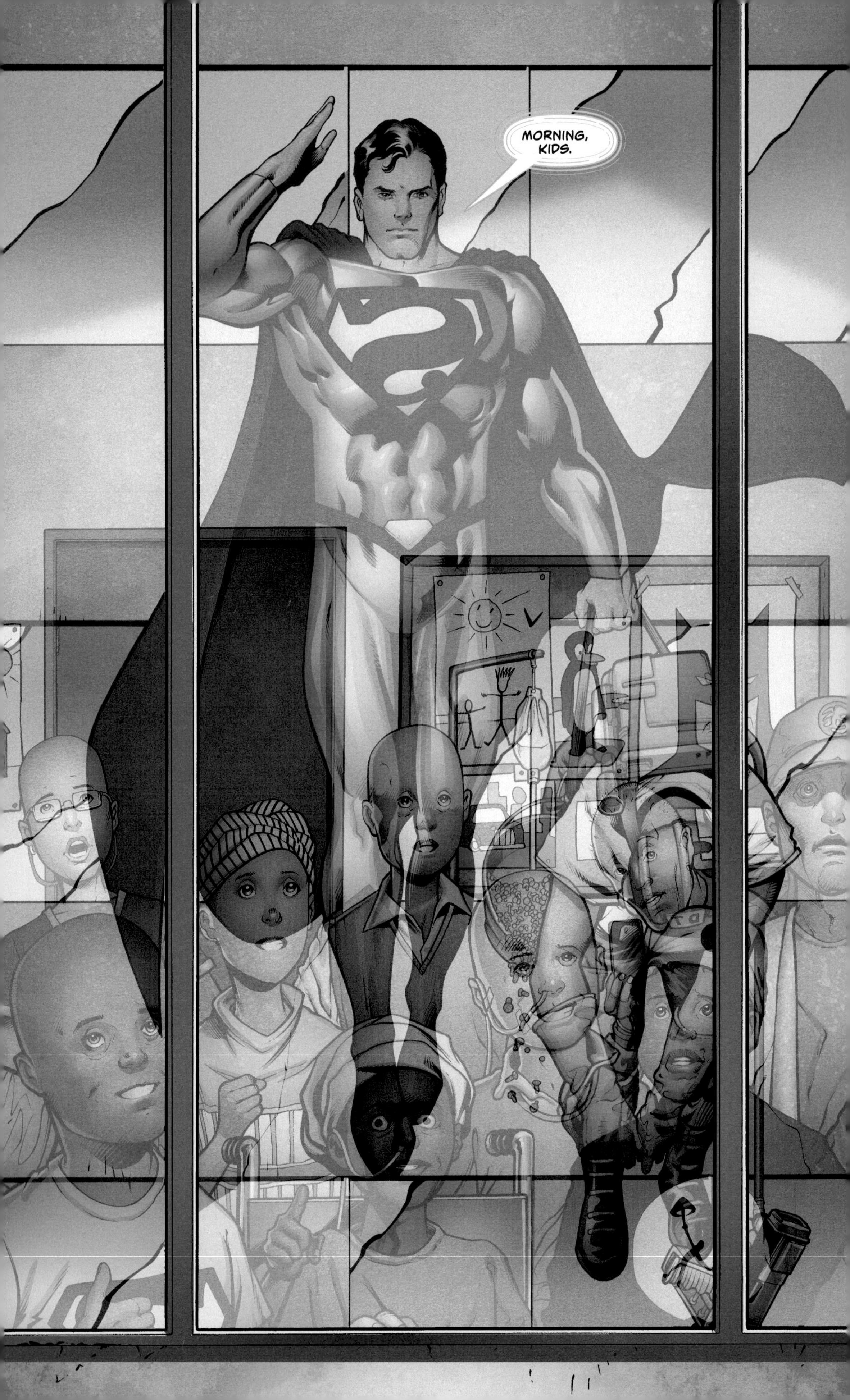
MORNING, KIDS.

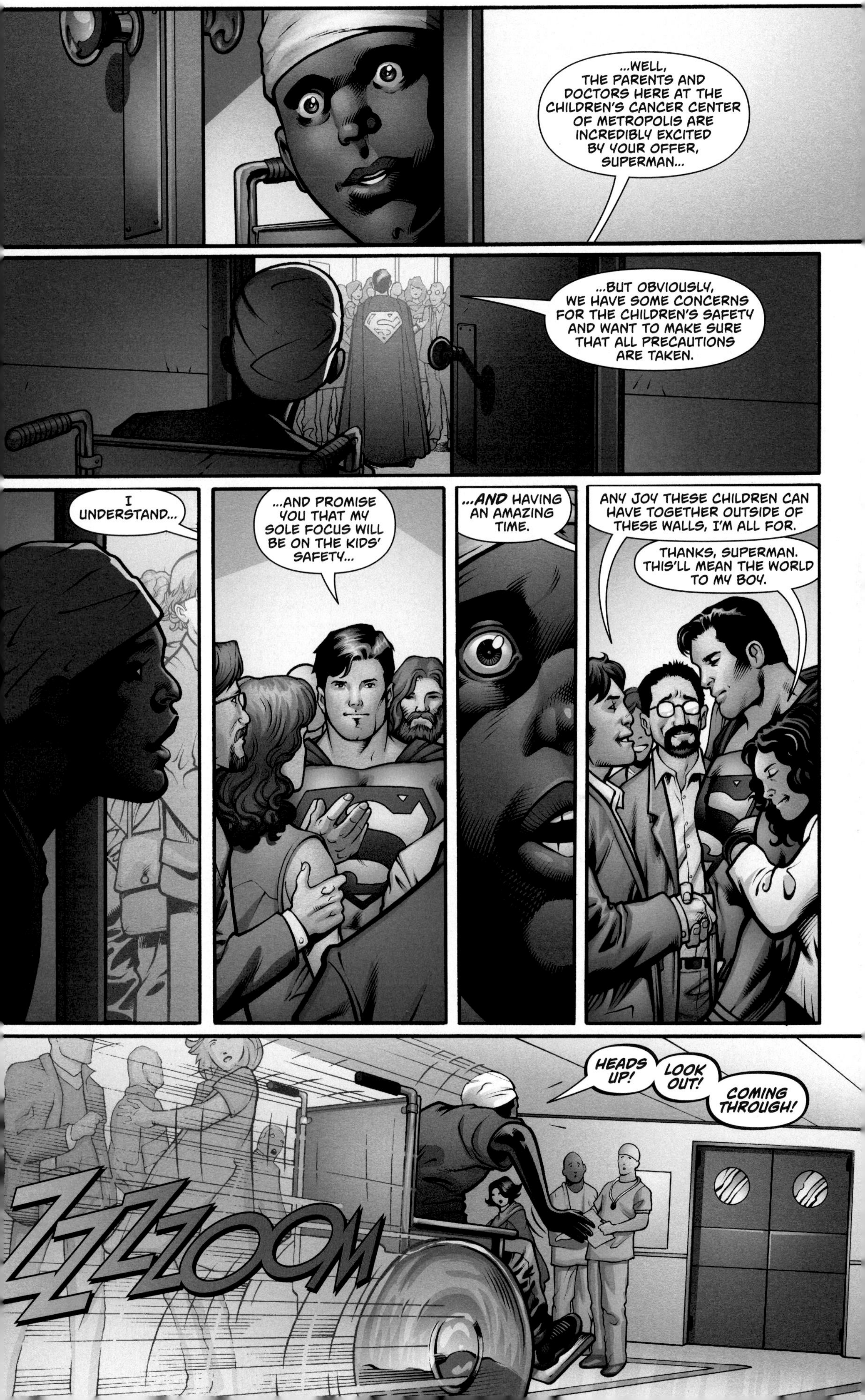
...WELL, THE PARENTS AND DOCTORS HERE AT THE CHILDREN'S CANCER CENTER OF METROPOLIS ARE INCREDIBLY EXCITED BY YOUR OFFER, SUPERMAN...
...BUT OBVIOUSLY, WE HAVE SOME CONCERNS FOR THE CHILDREN'S SAFETY AND WANT TO MAKE SURE THAT ALL PRECAUTIONS ARE TAKEN.
I UNDERSTAND...
...AND PROMISE YOU THAT MY SOLE FOCUS WILL BE ON THE KIDS' SAFETY...
...AND HAVING AN AMAZING TIME.
ANY JOY THESE CHILDREN CAN HAVE TOGETHER OUTSIDE OF THESE WALLS, I'M ALL FOR.
THANKS, SUPERMAN. THIS'LL MEAN THE WORLD TO MY BOY.
HEADS UP!
LOOK OUT!
COMING THROUGH!
ZZZOOM

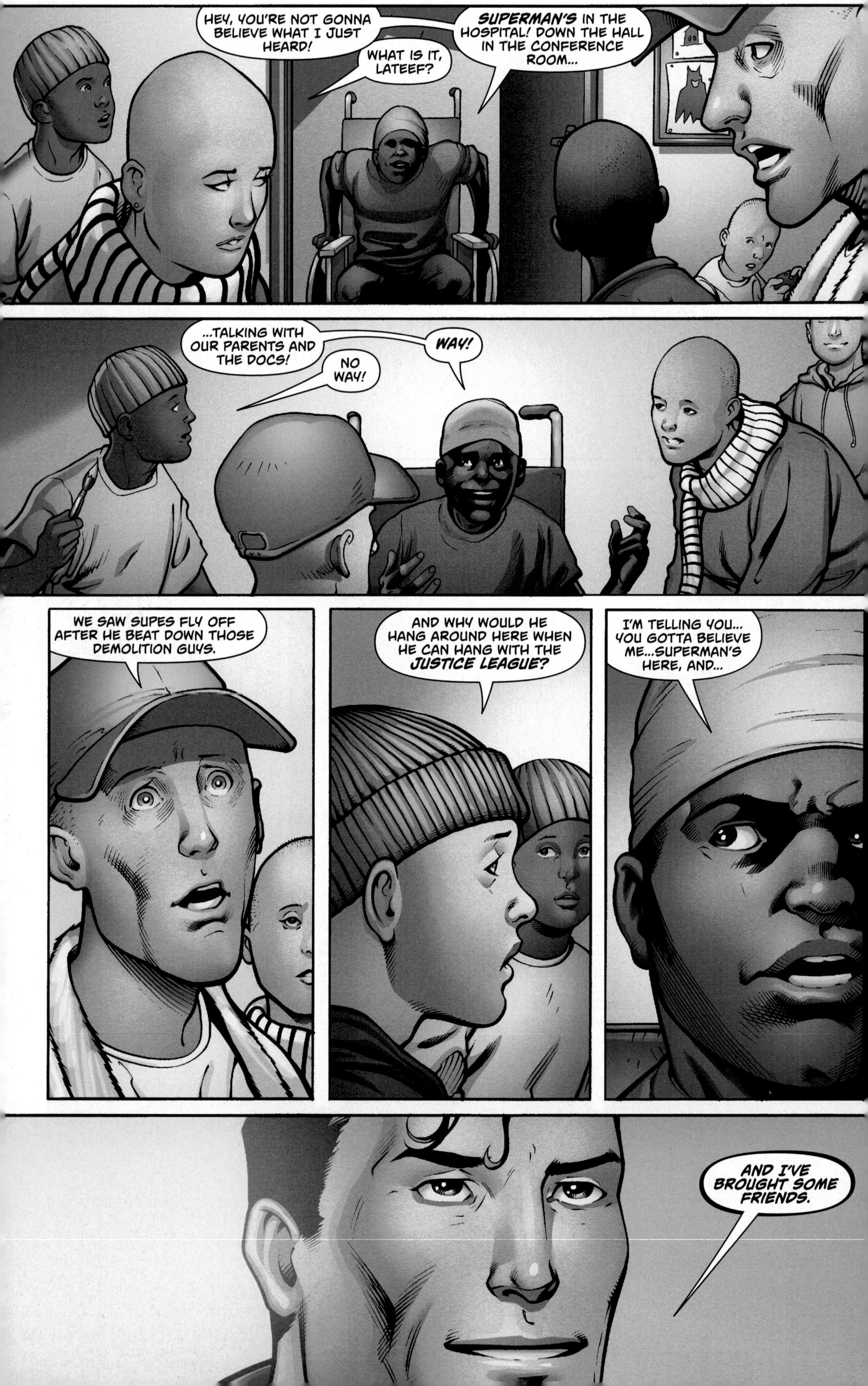
HEY, YOU'RE NOT GONNA BELIEVE WHAT I JUST HEARD!
WHAT IS IT, LATEEF?
SUPERMAN'S IN THE HOSPITAL! DOWN THE HALL IN THE CONFERENCE ROOM...
...TALKING WITH OUR PARENTS AND THE DOCS!
NO WAY!
WAY!
WE SAW SUPES FLY OFF AFTER HE BEAT DOWN THOSE DEMOLITION GUYS.
AND WHY WOULD HE HANG AROUND HERE WHEN HE CAN HANG WITH THE JUSTICE LEAGUE?
I'M TELLING YOU... YOU GOTTA BELIEVE ME...SUPERMAN'S HERE, AND...
AND I'VE BROUGHT SOME FRIENDS.

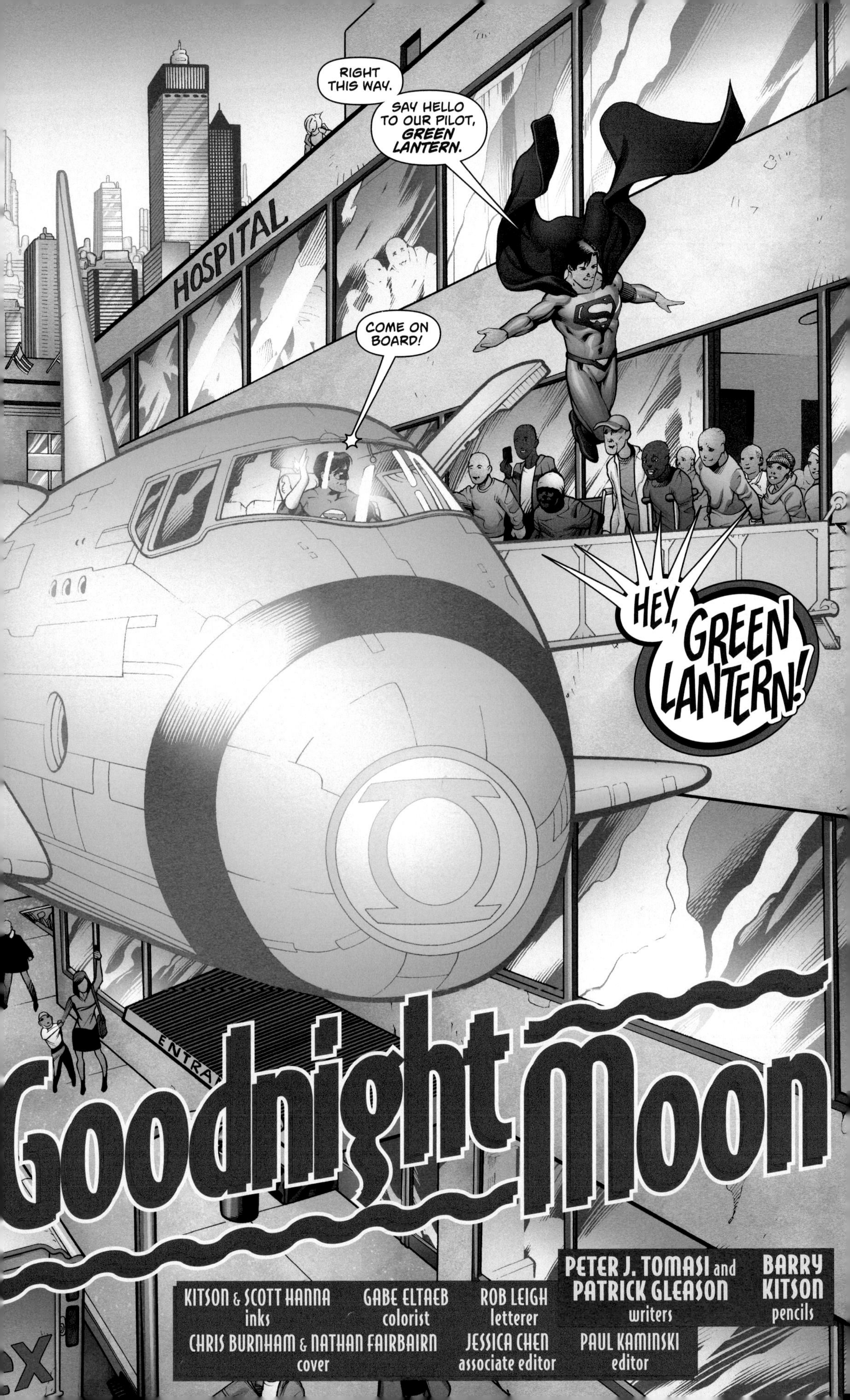
HOSPITAL
RIGHT THIS WAY.
SAY HELLO TO OUR PILOT, GREEN LANTERN.
COME ON BOARD!
HEY, GREEN LANTERN!
Goodnight Moon
PETER J. TOMASI and PATRICK GLEASON writers
BARRY KITSON pencils
KITSON & SCOTT HANNA inks
GABE ELTAEB colorist
ROB LEIGH letterer
CHRIS BURNHAM & NATHAN FAIRBAIRN cover
JESSICA CHEN associate editor
PAUL KAMINSKI editor

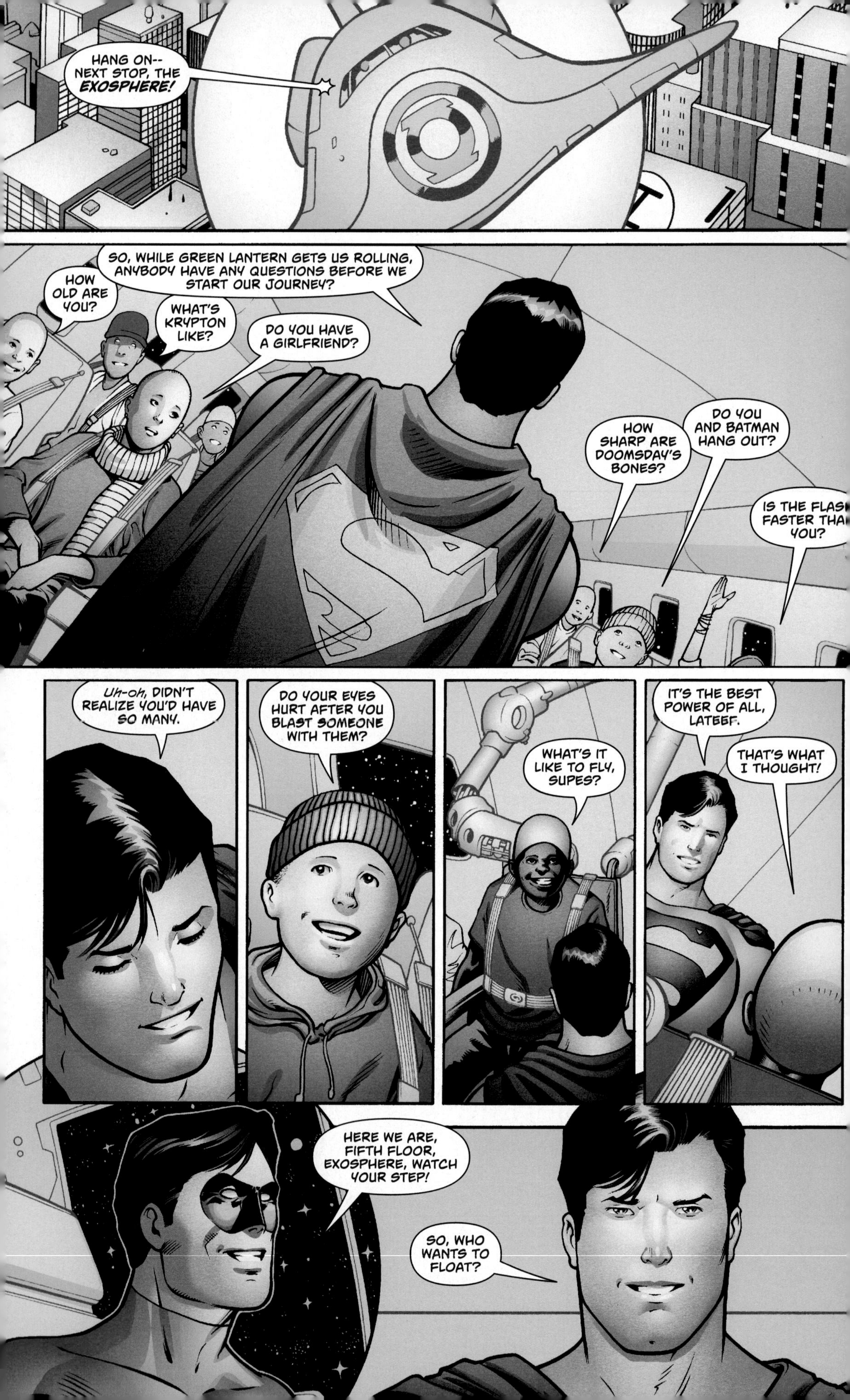
HANG ON-- NEXT STOP, THE *EXOSPHERE!*
SO, WHILE GREEN LANTERN GETS US ROLLING, ANYBODY HAVE ANY QUESTIONS BEFORE WE START OUR JOURNEY?
HOW OLD ARE YOU?
WHAT'S KRYPTON LIKE?
DO YOU HAVE A GIRLFRIEND?
HOW SHARP ARE DOOMSDAY'S BONES?
DO YOU AND BATMAN HANG OUT?
IS THE FLAS FASTER THA YOU?
Uh-oh, DIDN'T REALIZE YOU'D HAVE SO MANY.
DO YOUR EYES HURT AFTER YOU BLAST SOMEONE WITH THEM?
WHAT'S IT LIKE TO FLY, SUPES?
IT'S THE BEST POWER OF ALL, LATEEF.
THAT'S WHAT I THOUGHT!
HERE WE ARE, FIFTH FLOOR, EXOSPHERE, WATCH YOUR STEP!
SO, WHO WANTS TO FLOAT?

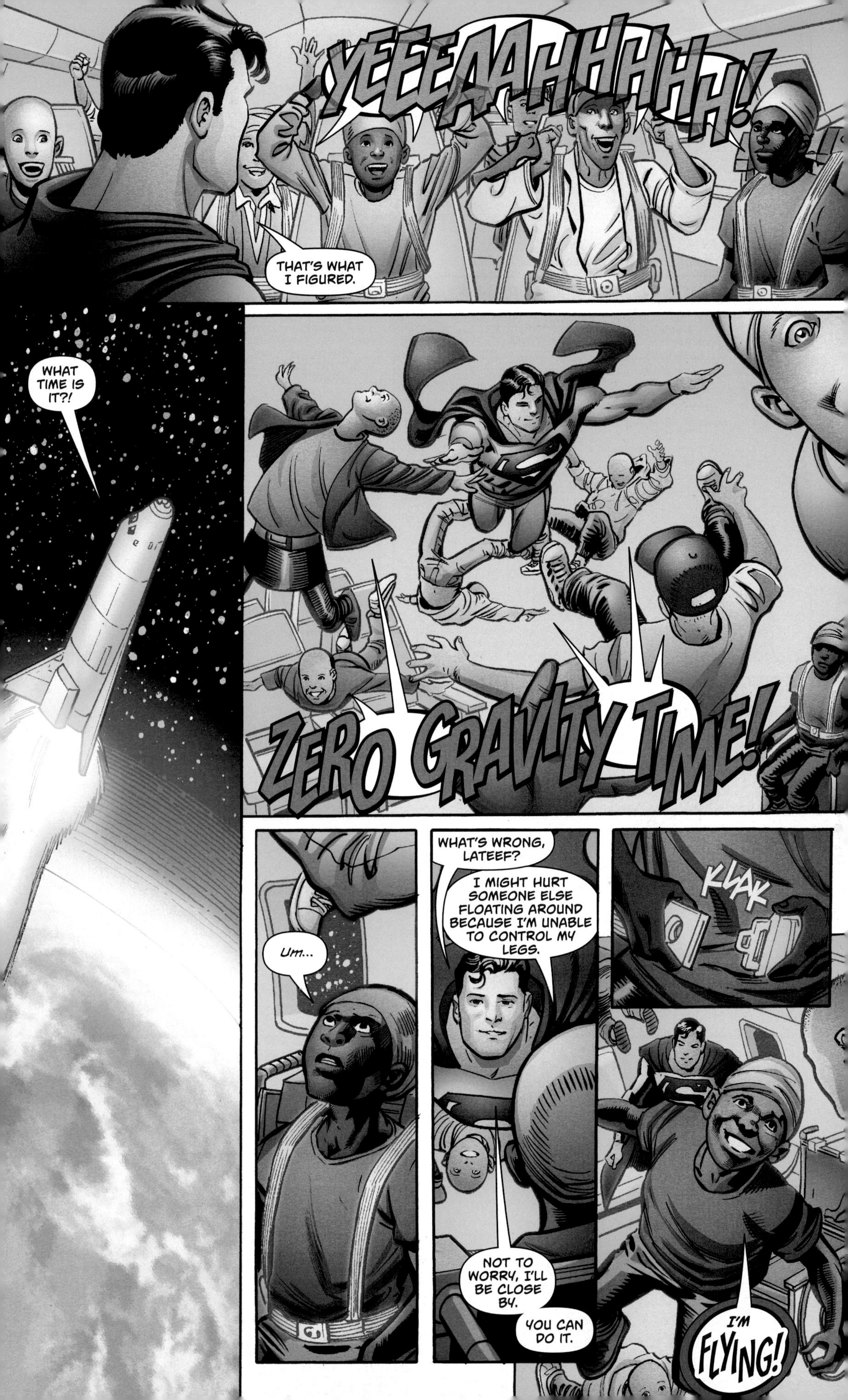
YEEEAAHHHHHH!
THAT'S WHAT I FIGURED.
WHAT TIME IS IT?!
ZERO GRAVITY TIME!
Um...
WHAT'S WRONG, LATEEF?
I MIGHT HURT SOMEONE ELSE FLOATING AROUND BECAUSE I'M UNABLE TO CONTROL MY LEGS.
NOT TO WORRY, I'LL BE CLOSE BY.
YOU CAN DO IT.
KLAK
I'M FLYING!

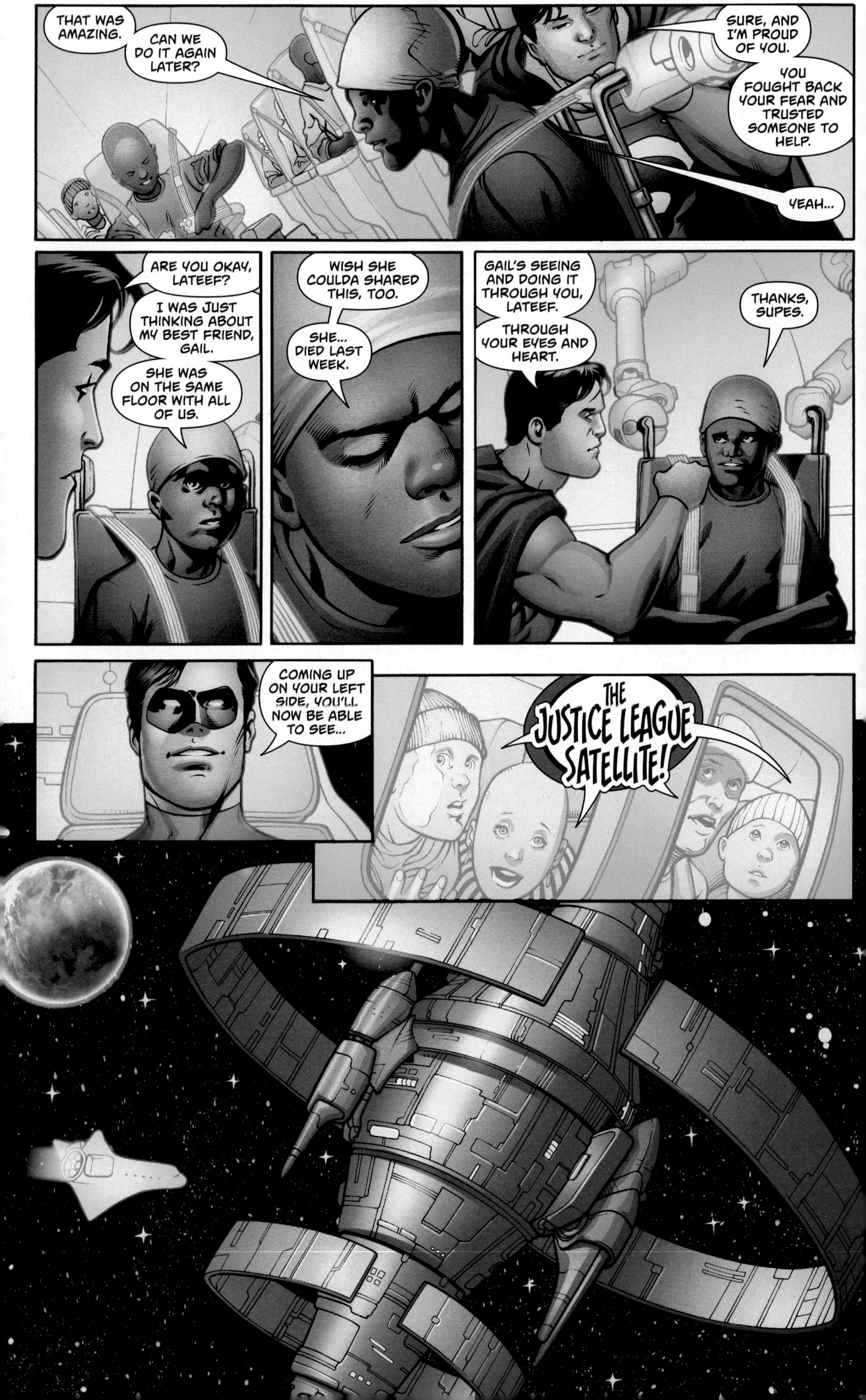
THAT WAS AMAZING.
CAN WE DO IT AGAIN LATER?
SURE, AND I'M PROUD OF YOU.
YOU FOUGHT BACK YOUR FEAR AND TRUSTED SOMEONE TO HELP.
YEAH...
ARE YOU OKAY, LATEEF?
I WAS JUST THINKING ABOUT MY BEST FRIEND, GAIL.
SHE WAS ON THE SAME FLOOR WITH ALL OF US.
WISH SHE COULDA SHARED THIS, TOO.
SHE... DIED LAST WEEK.
GAIL'S SEEING AND DOING IT THROUGH YOU, LATEEF.
THROUGH YOUR EYES AND HEART.
THANKS, SUPES.
COMING UP ON YOUR LEFT SIDE, YOU'LL NOW BE ABLE TO SEE...
THE JUSTICE LEAGUE SATELLITE!

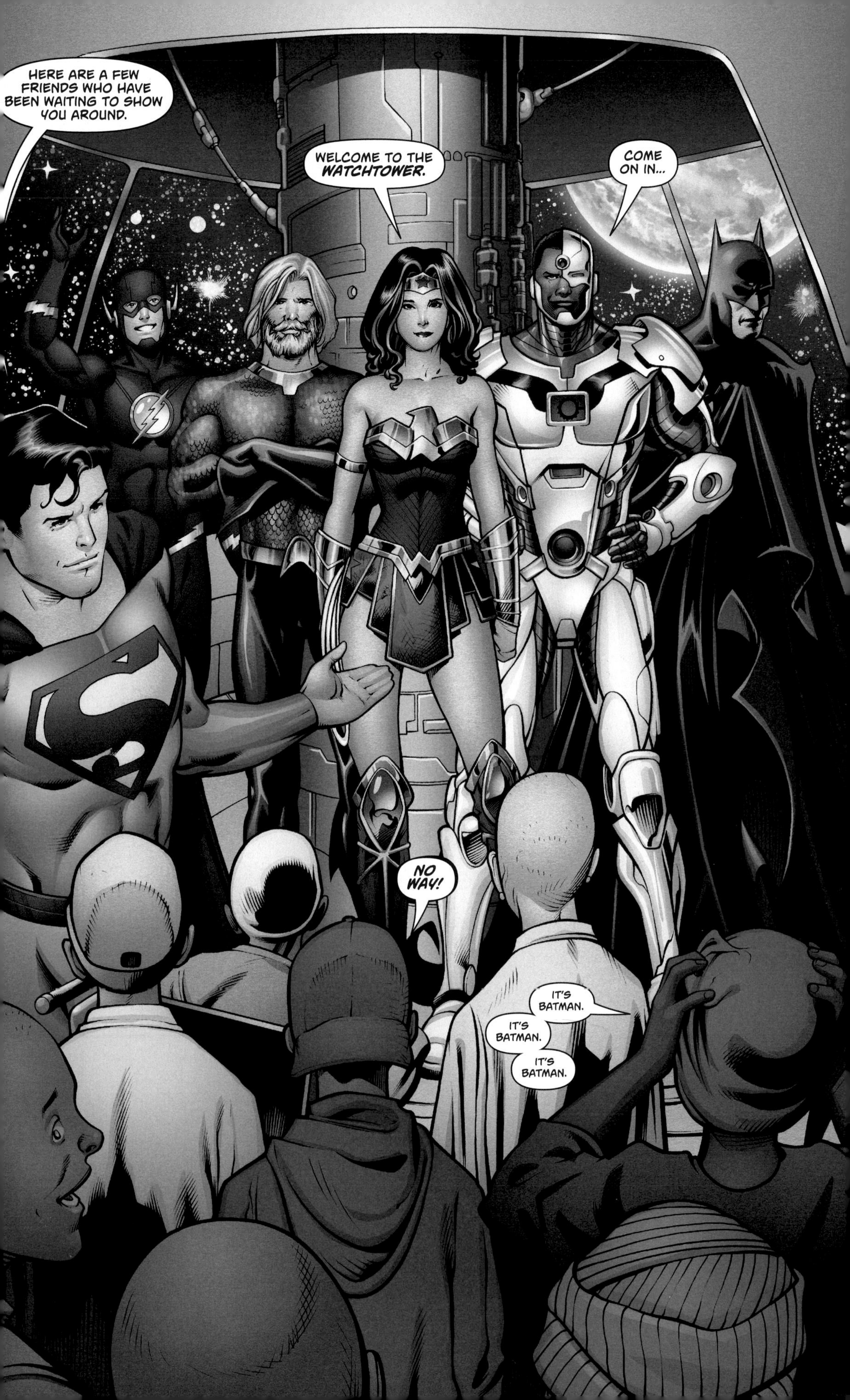
HERE ARE A FEW FRIENDS WHO HAVE BEEN WAITING TO SHOW YOU AROUND.
WELCOME TO THE WATCHTOWER.
COME ON IN...
NO WAY!
IT'S BATMAN.
IT'S BATMAN.
IT'S BATMAN.

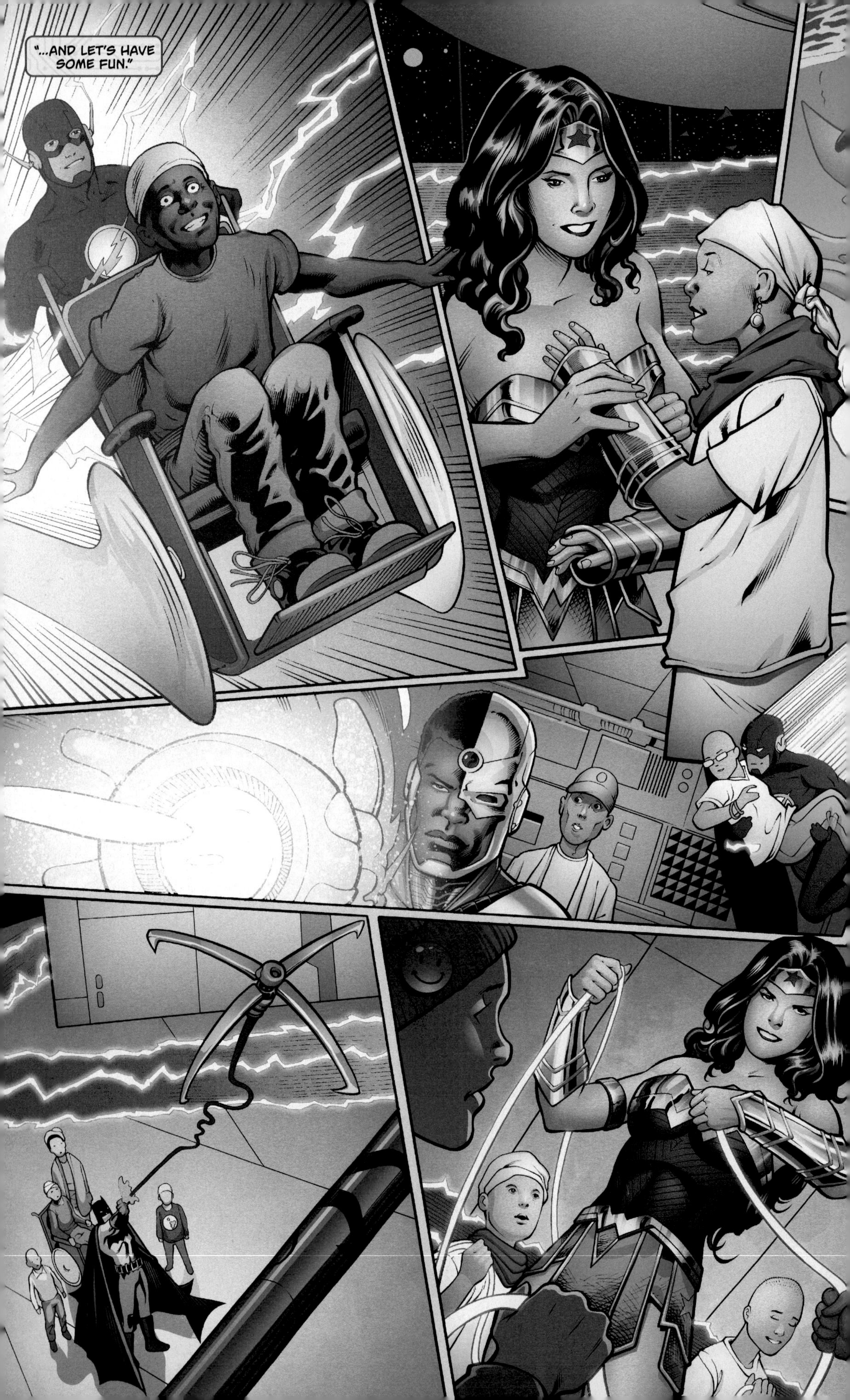
"...AND LET'S HAVE SOME FUN."

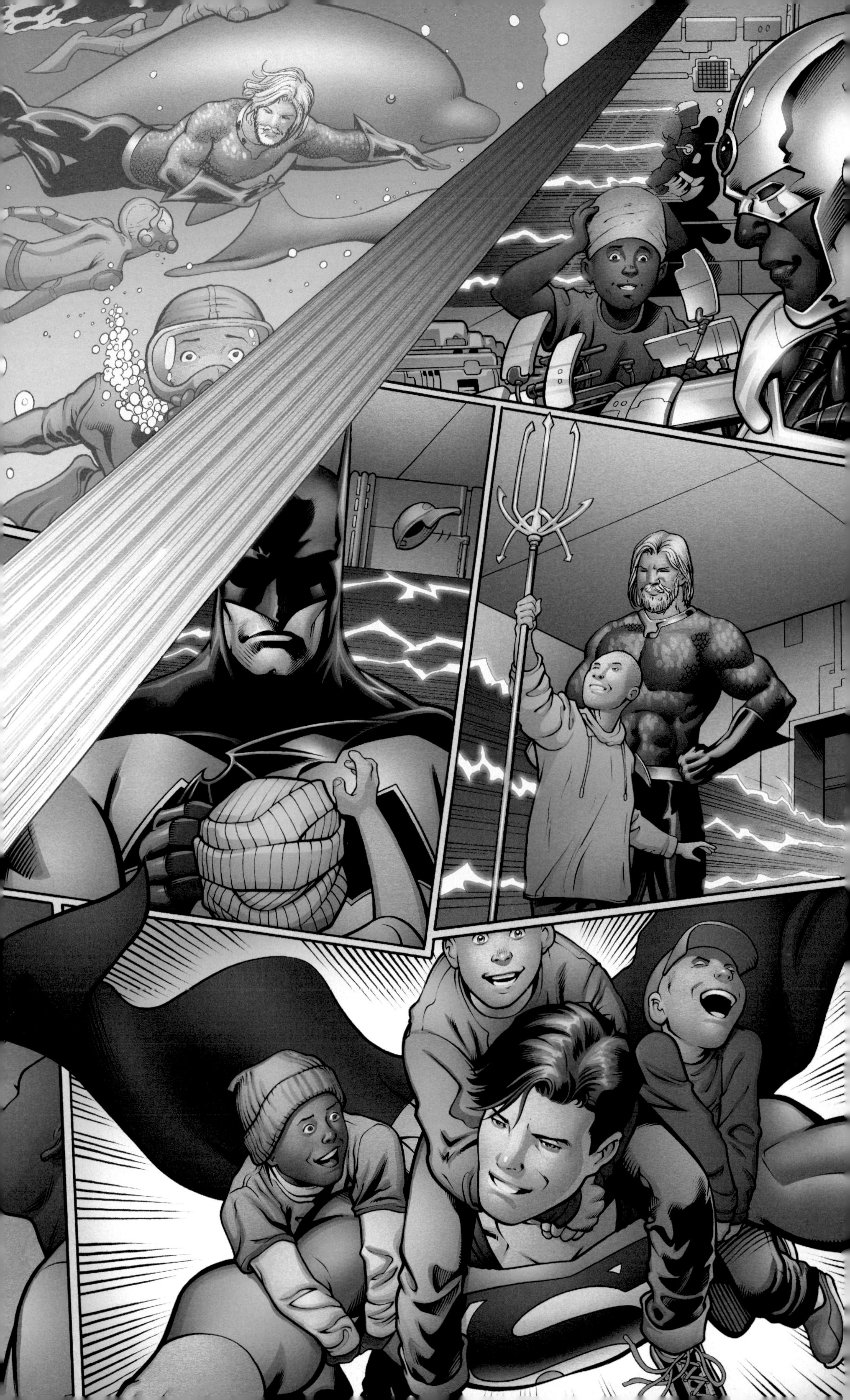

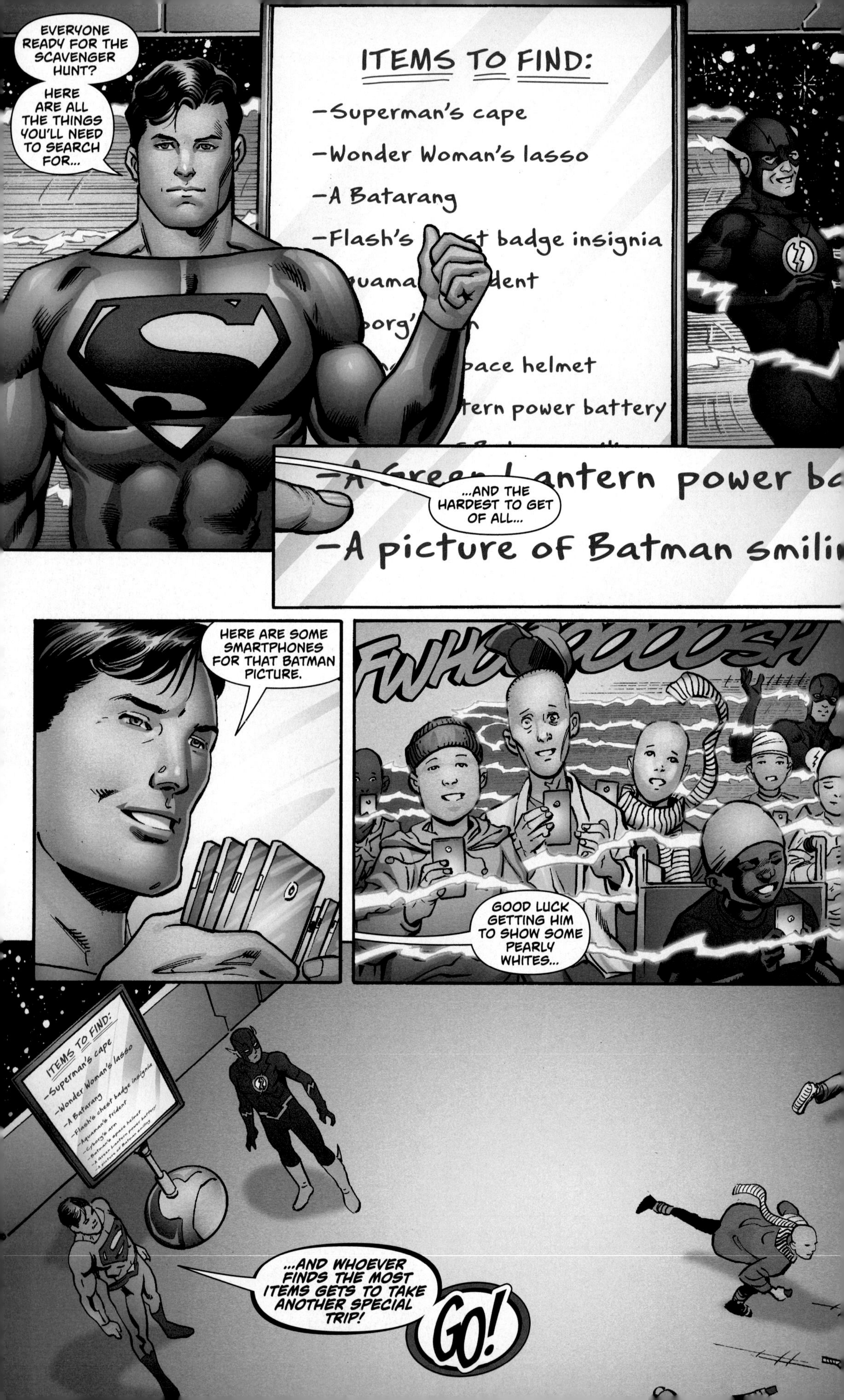
EVERYONE READY FOR THE SCAVENGER HUNT?
HERE ARE ALL THE THINGS YOU'LL NEED TO SEARCH FOR...
ITEMS TO FIND:
–Superman's cape
–Wonder Woman's lasso
–A Batarang
–Flash's chest badge insignia
...AND THE HARDEST TO GET OF ALL...
–A picture of Batman smili
HERE ARE SOME SMARTPHONES FOR THAT BATMAN PICTURE.
GOOD LUCK GETTING HIM TO SHOW SOME PEARLY WHITES...
...AND WHOEVER FINDS THE MOST ITEMS GETS TO TAKE ANOTHER SPECIAL TRIP!
GO!

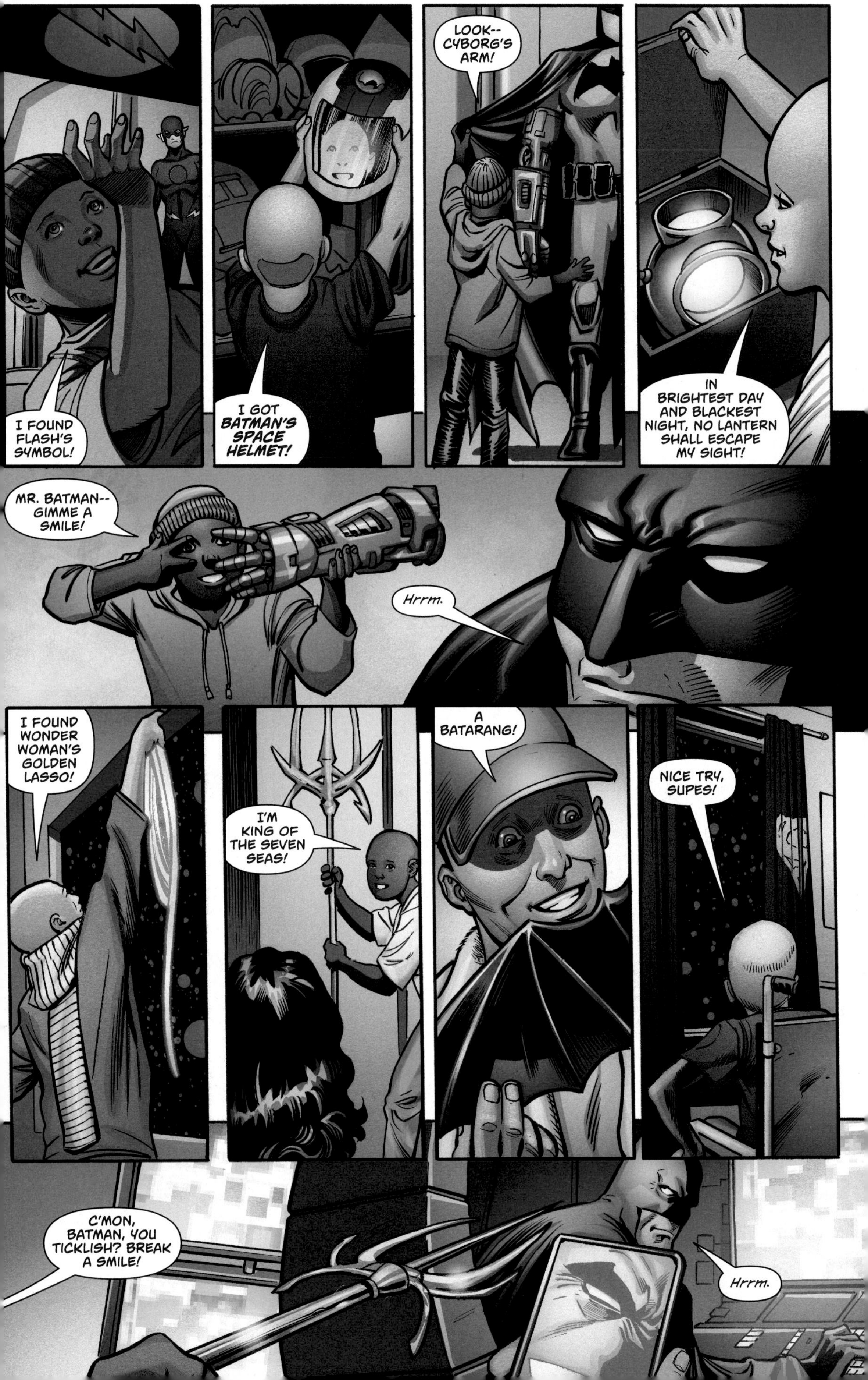
I FOUND FLASH'S SYMBOL!
I GOT BATMAN'S SPACE HELMET!
LOOK-- CYBORG'S ARM!
IN BRIGHTEST DAY AND BLACKEST NIGHT, NO LANTERN SHALL ESCAPE MY SIGHT!
MR. BATMAN-- GIMME A SMILE!
Hrrm.
I FOUND WONDER WOMAN'S GOLDEN LASSO!
I'M KING OF THE SEVEN SEAS!
A BATARANG!
NICE TRY, SUPES!
C'MON, BATMAN, YOU TICKLISH? BREAK A SMILE!
Hrrm.

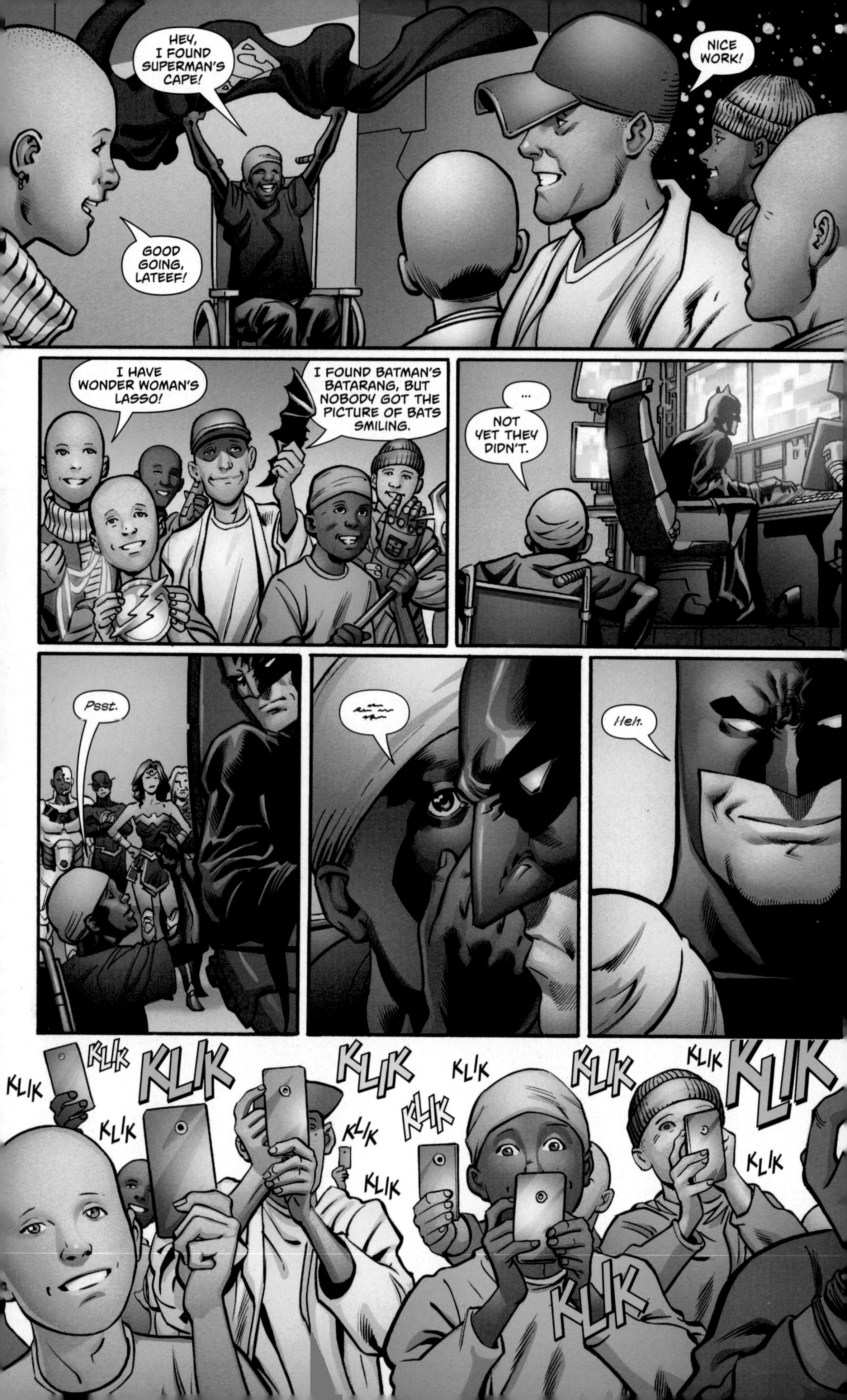
HEY, I FOUND SUPERMAN'S CAPE!
GOOD GOING, LATEEF!
NICE WORK!
I HAVE WONDER WOMAN'S LASSO!
I FOUND BATMAN'S BATARANG, BUT NOBODY GOT THE PICTURE OF BATS SMILING.
...
NOT YET THEY DIDN'T.
Psst.
Heh.
KLIK
KLIK
KLIK
KLIK
KLIK
KLIK
KLIK
KLIK
KLIK
KLIK
KLIK
KLIK
KLIK
KLIK

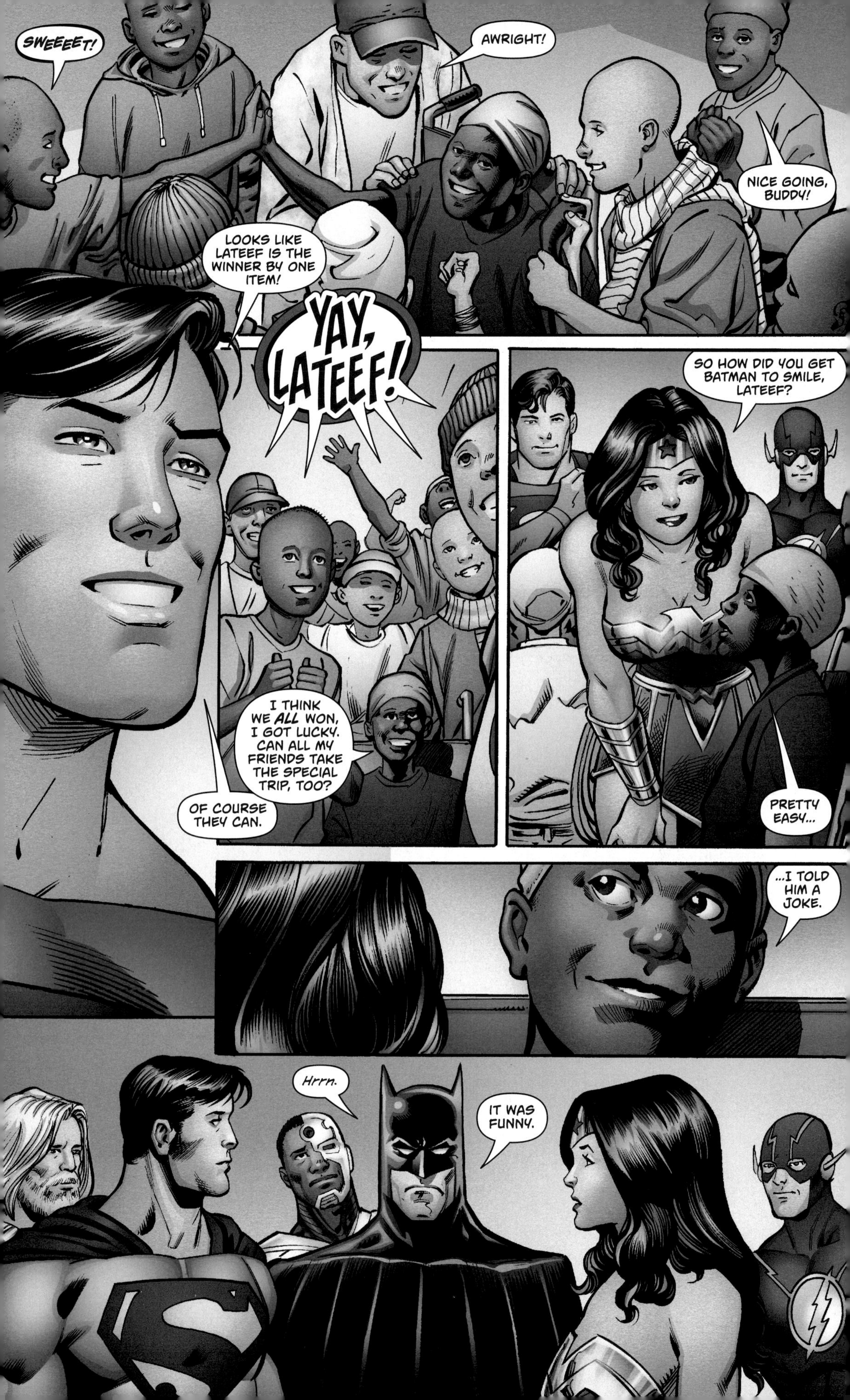
SWEEEEET!
AWRIGHT!
NICE GOING, BUDDY!
LOOKS LIKE LATEEF IS THE WINNER BY ONE ITEM!
YAY, LATEEF!
SO HOW DID YOU GET BATMAN TO SMILE, LATEEF?
I THINK WE ALL WON, I GOT LUCKY. CAN ALL MY FRIENDS TAKE THE SPECIAL TRIP, TOO?
OF COURSE THEY CAN.
PRETTY EASY...
...I TOLD HIM A JOKE.
Hrrn.
IT WAS FUNNY.

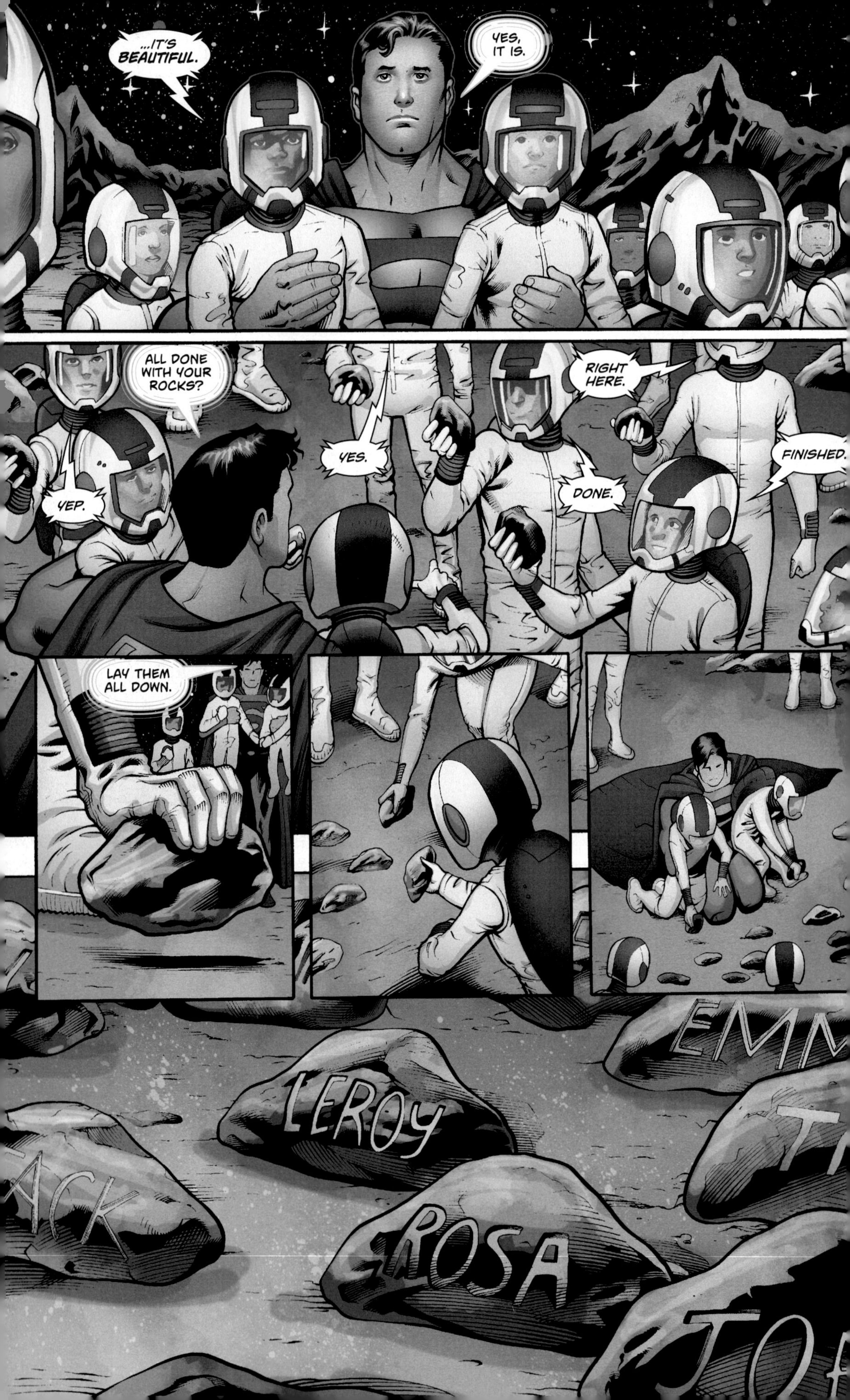
...IT'S BEAUTIFUL.
YES, IT IS.
ALL DONE WITH YOUR ROCKS?
YEP.
YES.
RIGHT HERE.
DONE.
FINISHED.
LAY THEM ALL DOWN.
LEROY
ROSA

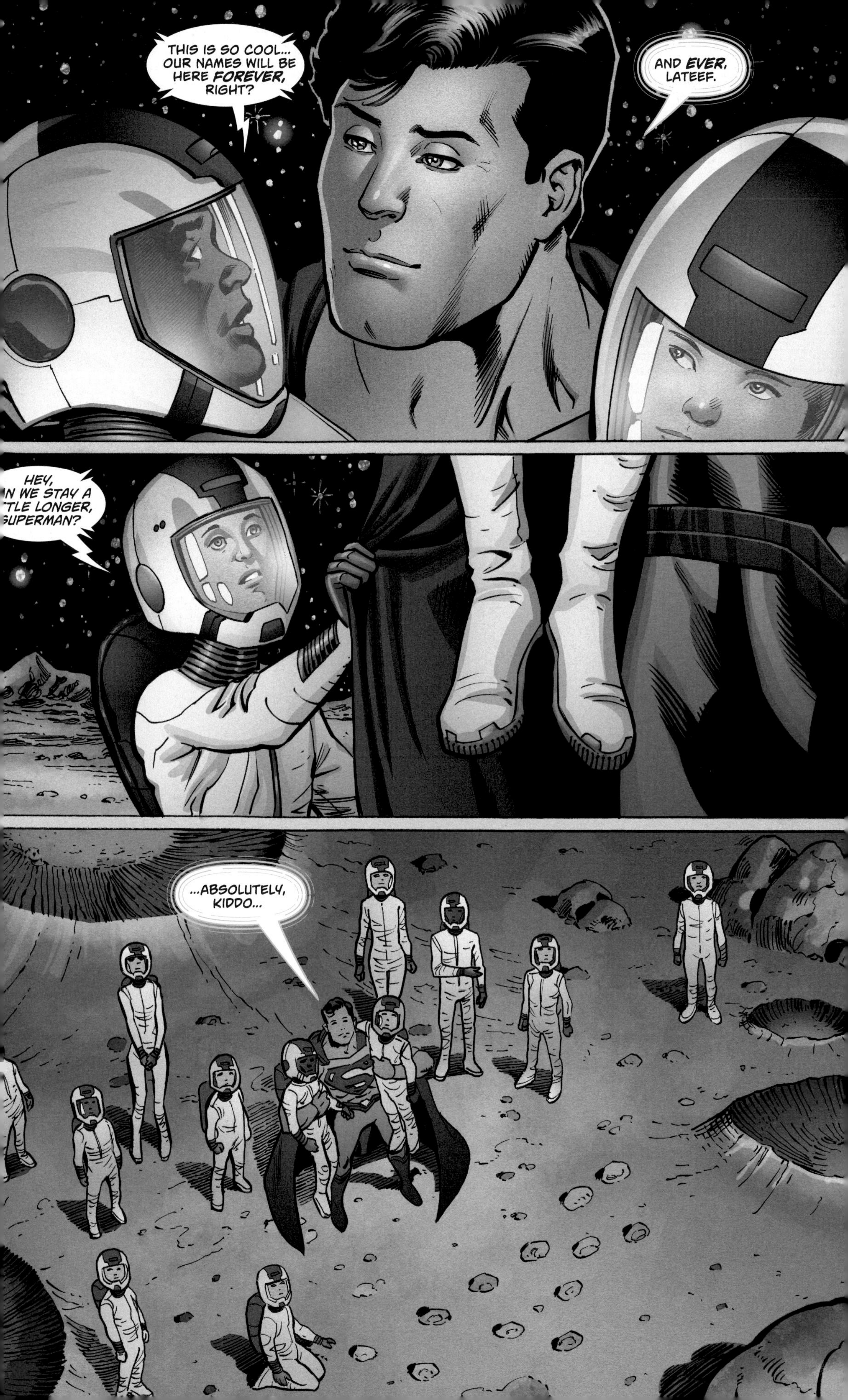

THIS IS SO COOL... OUR NAMES WILL BE HERE FOREVER, RIGHT?
AND EVER, LATEEF.
HEY, N WE STAY A TLE LONGER, SUPERMAN?
...ABSOLUTELY, KIDDO...

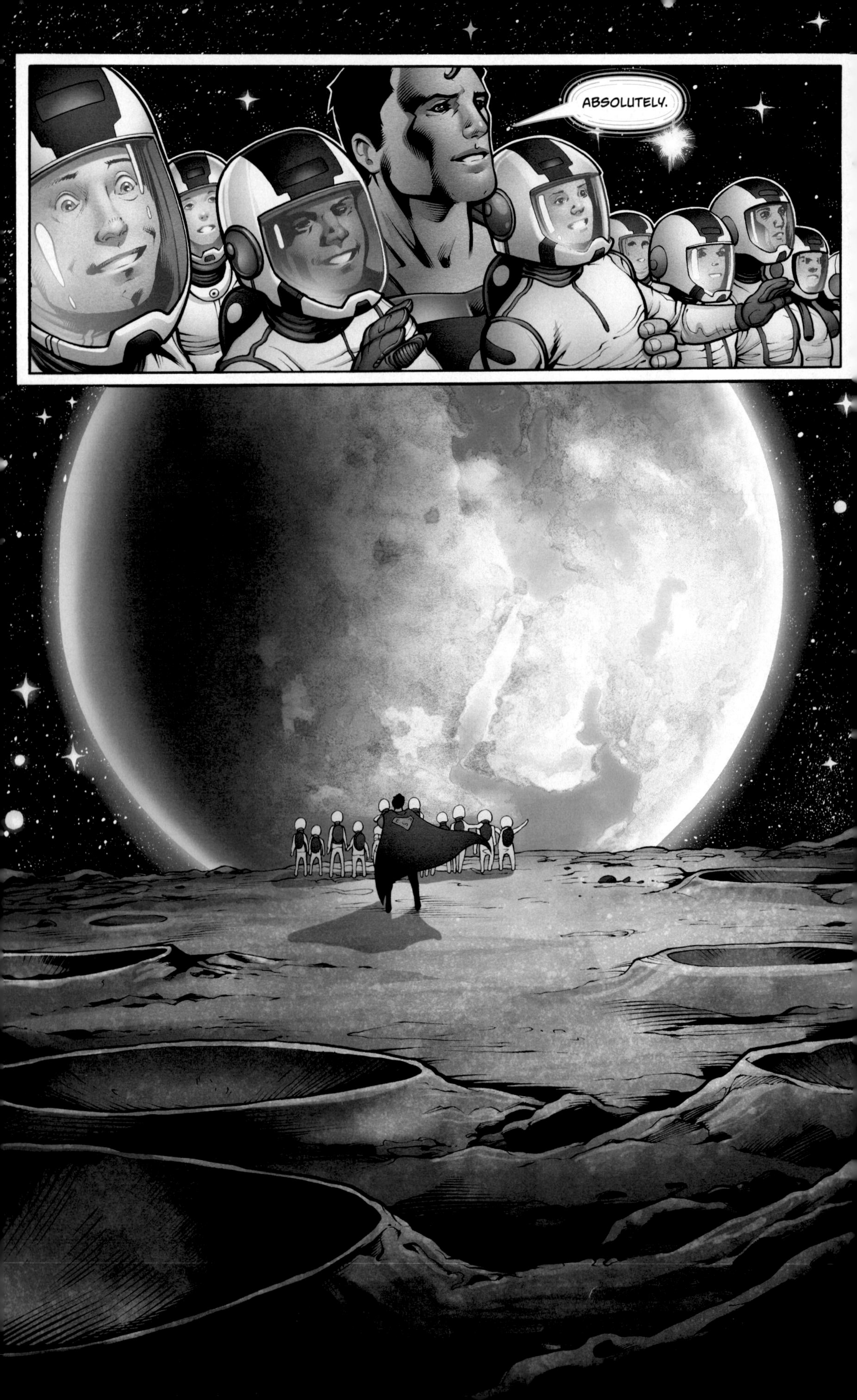
ABSOLUTELY.

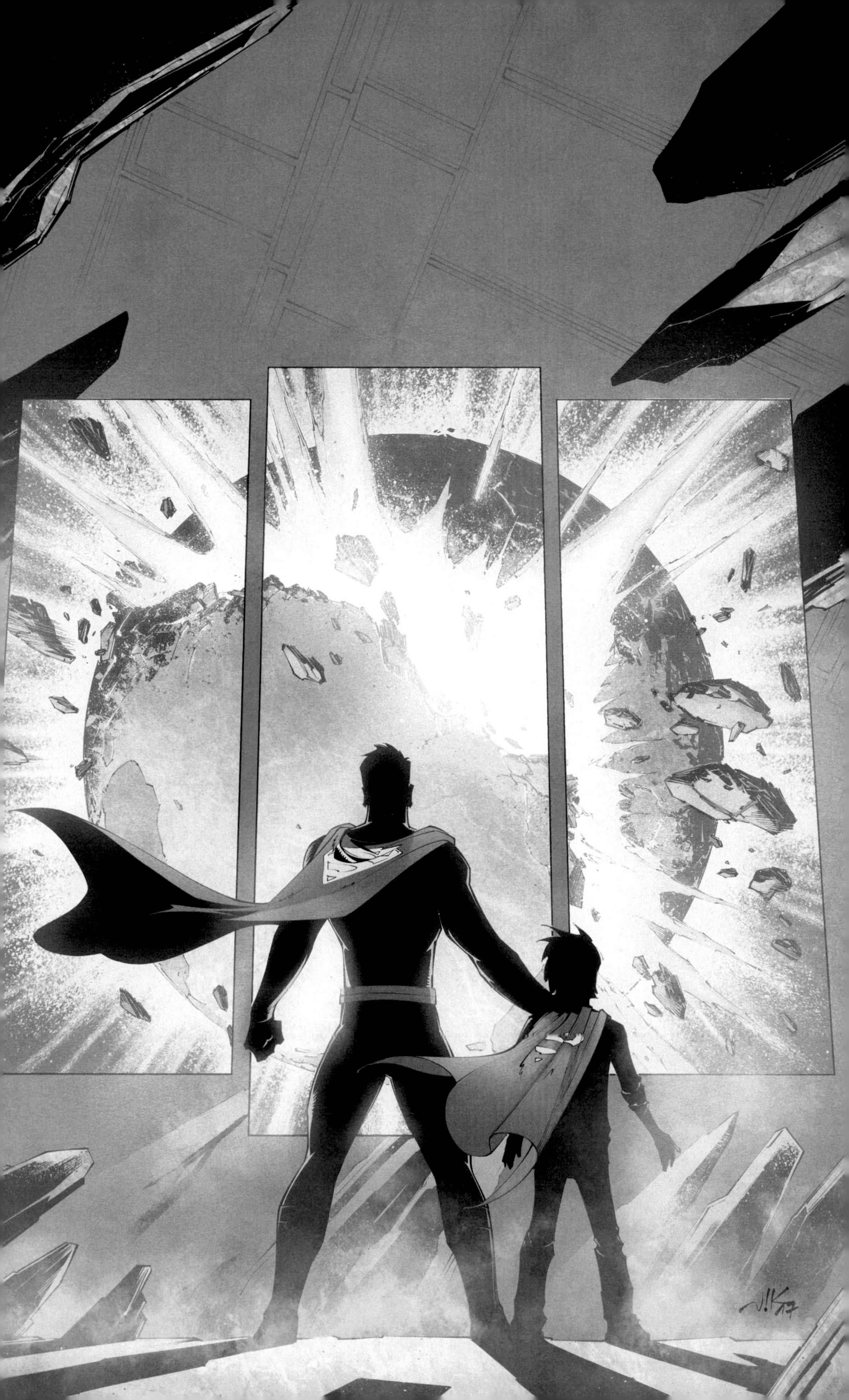

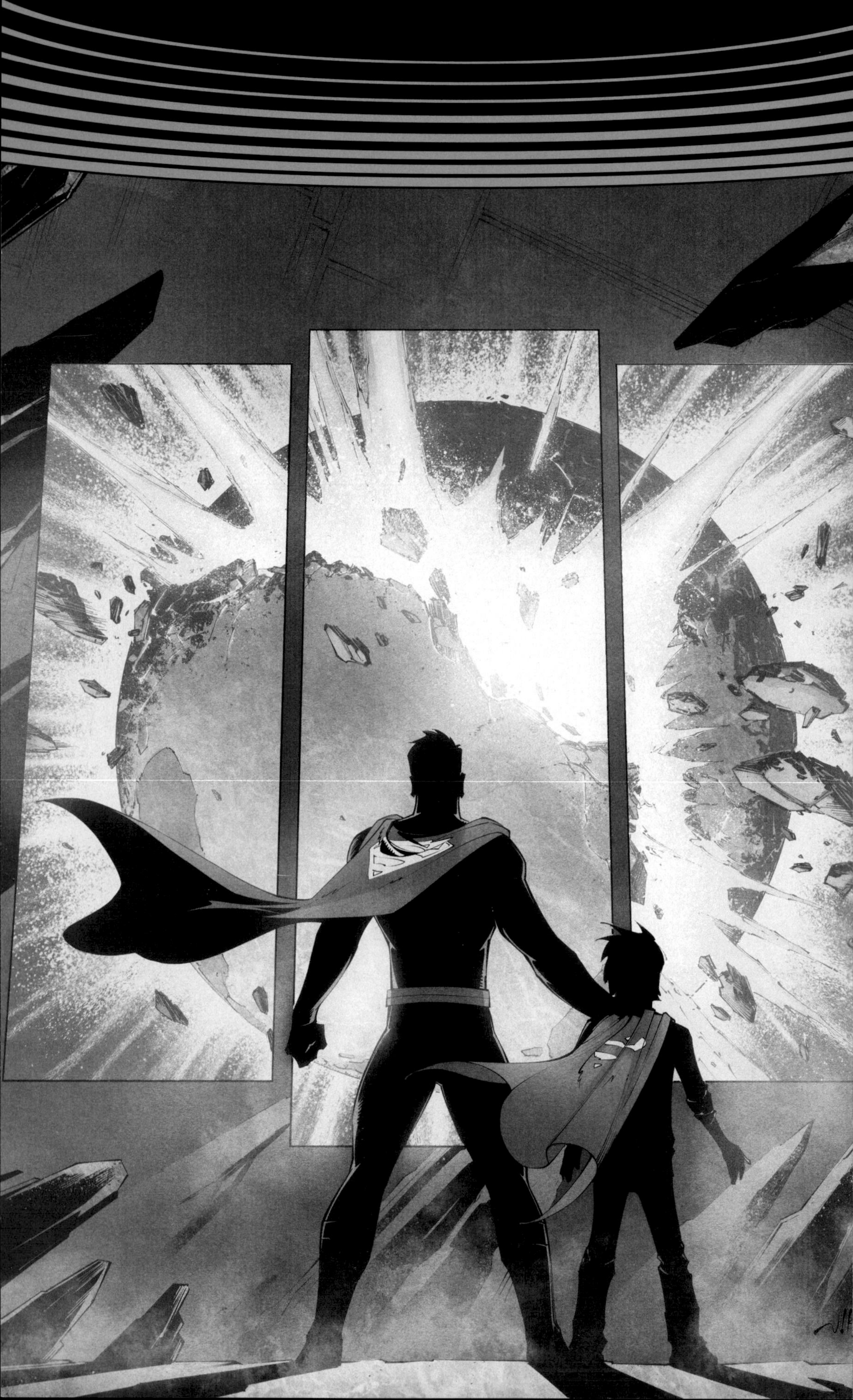

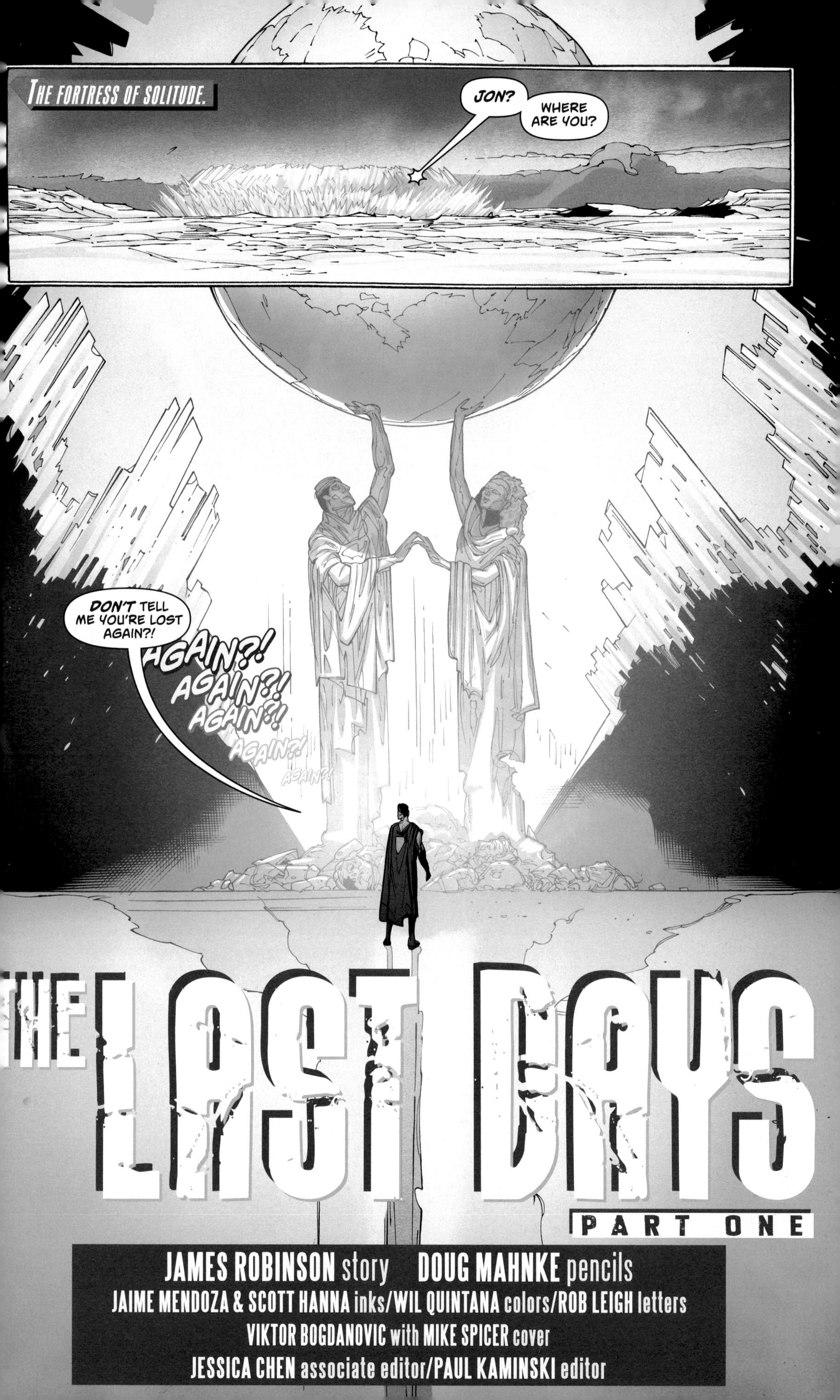
THE FORTRESS OF SOLITUDE.
JON?
WHERE ARE YOU?
DON'T TELL ME YOU'RE LOST AGAIN?!
AGAIN?! AGAIN?! AGAIN?! AGAIN?! AGAIN?!
THE LAST DAYS
PART ONE
JAMES ROBINSON story DOUG MAHNKE pencils
JAIME MENDOZA & SCOTT HANNA inks/WIL QUINTANA colors/ROB LEIGH letters
VIKTOR BOGDANOVIC with MIKE SPICER cover
JESSICA CHEN associate editor/PAUL KAMINSKI editor

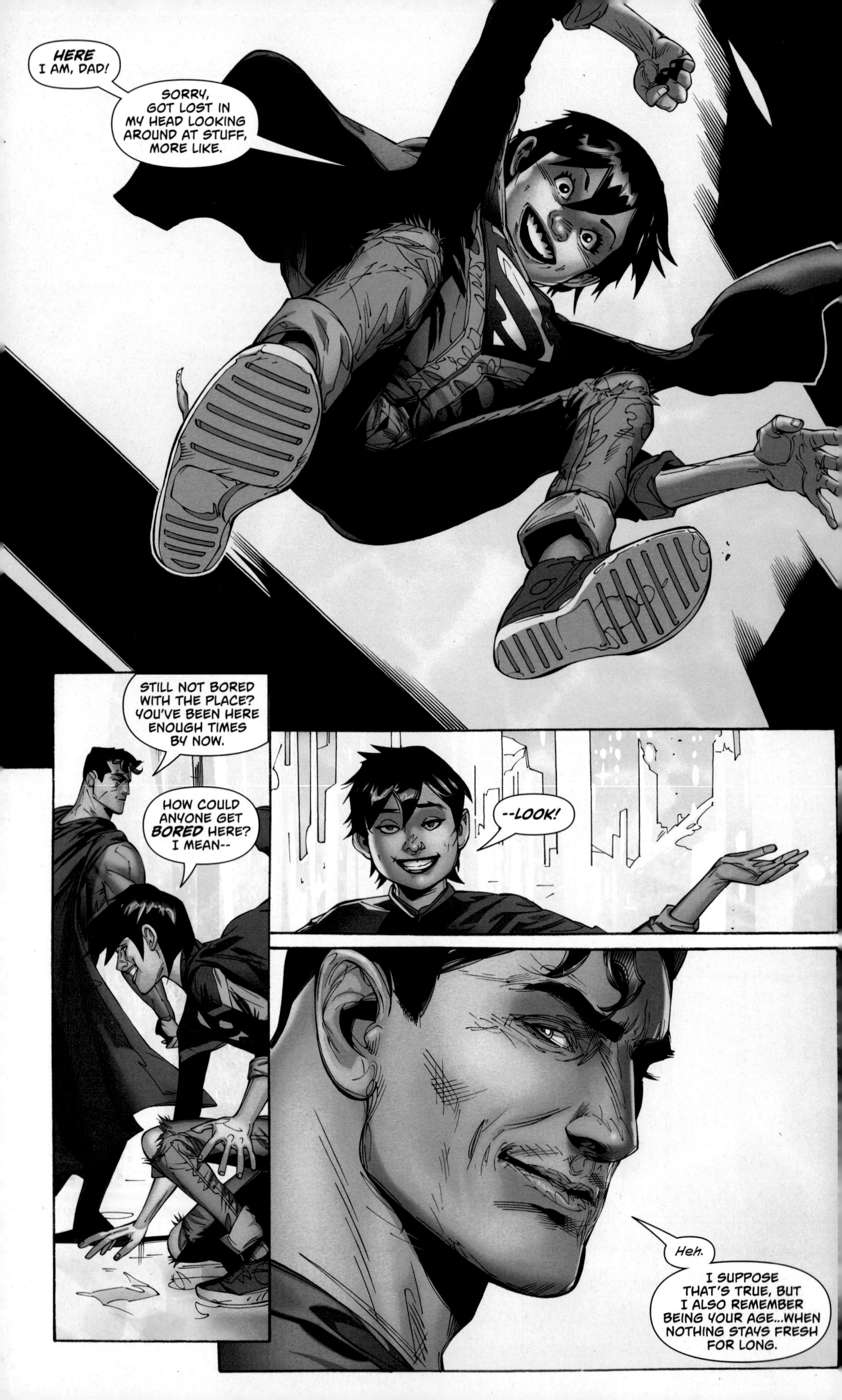
HERE I AM, DAD!
SORRY, GOT LOST IN MY HEAD LOOKING AROUND AT STUFF, MORE LIKE.
STILL NOT BORED WITH THE PLACE? YOU'VE BEEN HERE ENOUGH TIMES BY NOW.
HOW COULD ANYONE GET BORED HERE? I MEAN--
--LOOK!
Heh.
I SUPPOSE THAT'S TRUE, BUT I ALSO REMEMBER BEING YOUR AGE...WHEN NOTHING STAYS FRESH FOR LONG.

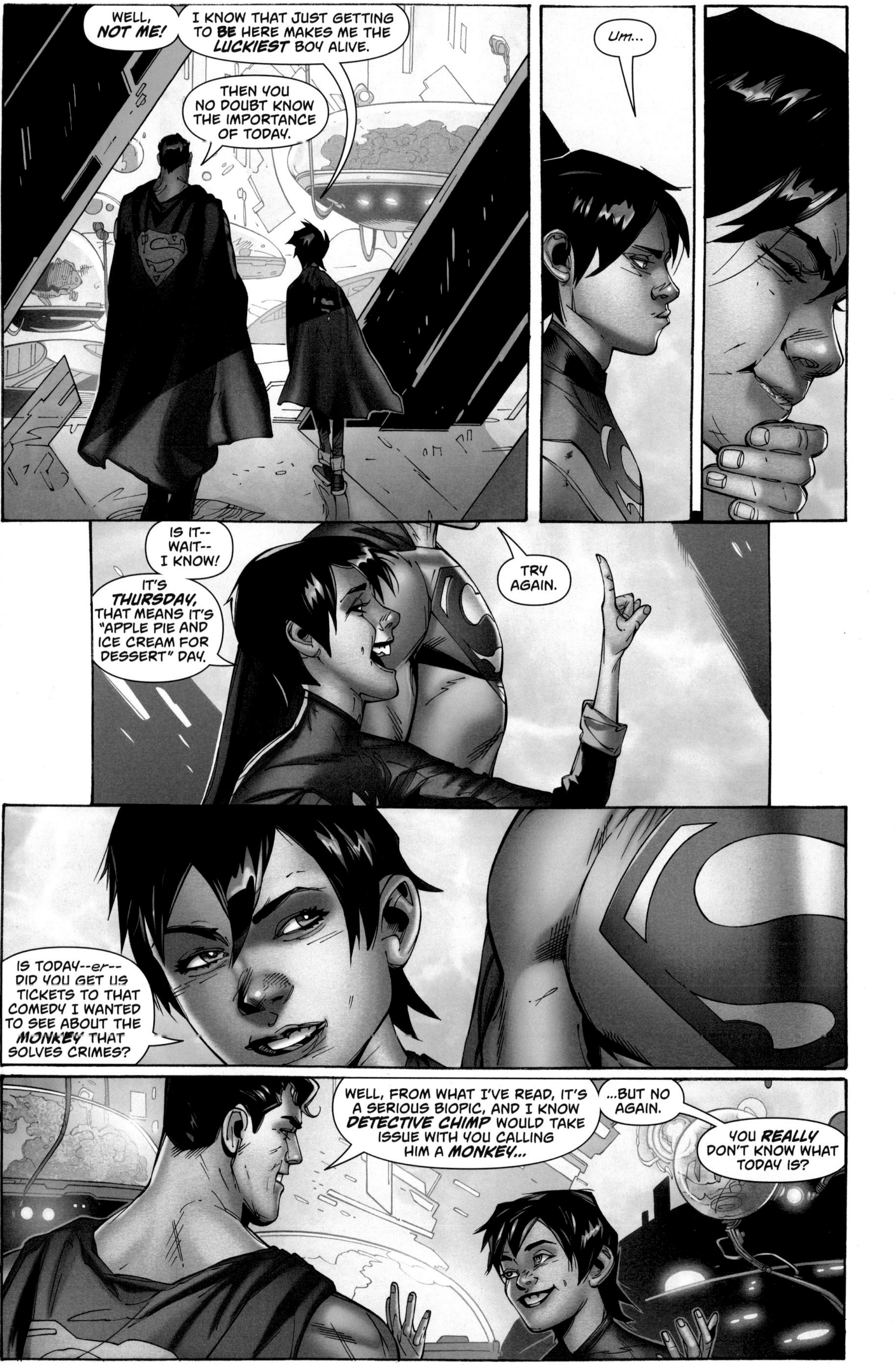

WELL, NOT ME!
I KNOW THAT JUST GETTING TO BE HERE MAKES ME THE LUCKIEST BOY ALIVE.
THEN YOU NO DOUBT KNOW THE IMPORTANCE OF TODAY.
Um...
IS IT-- WAIT-- I KNOW!
IT'S THURSDAY, THAT MEANS IT'S "APPLE PIE AND ICE CREAM FOR DESSERT" DAY.
TRY AGAIN.
IS TODAY--er-- DID YOU GET US TICKETS TO THAT COMEDY I WANTED TO SEE ABOUT THE MONKEY THAT SOLVES CRIMES?
WELL, FROM WHAT I'VE READ, IT'S A SERIOUS BIOPIC, AND I KNOW DETECTIVE CHIMP WOULD TAKE ISSUE WITH YOU CALLING HIM A MONKEY...
...BUT NO AGAIN.
YOU REALLY DON'T KNOW WHAT TODAY IS?

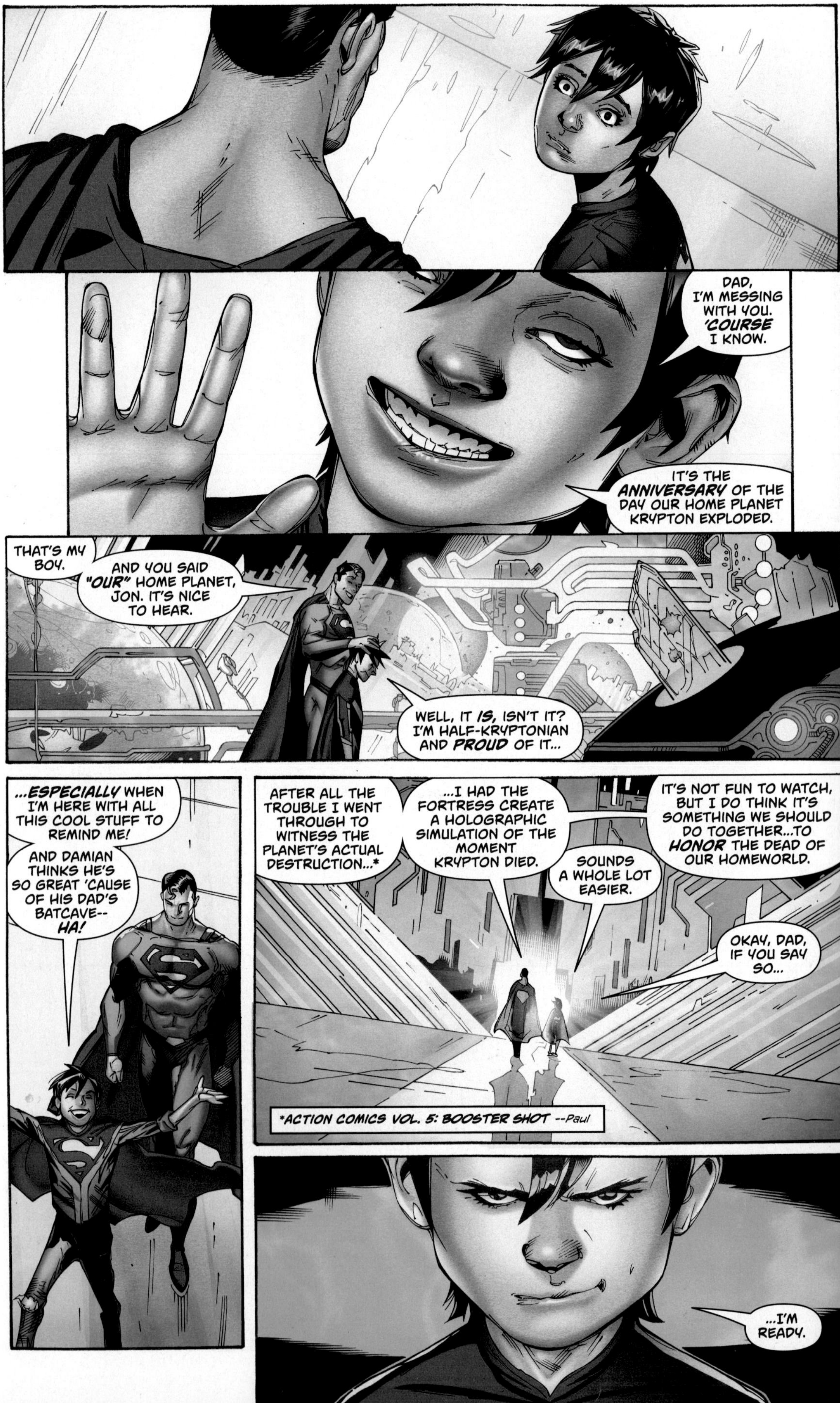

DAD, I'M MESSING WITH YOU. 'COURSE I KNOW.
IT'S THE ANNIVERSARY OF THE DAY OUR HOME PLANET KRYPTON EXPLODED.
THAT'S MY BOY.
AND YOU SAID "OUR" HOME PLANET, JON. IT'S NICE TO HEAR.
WELL, IT IS, ISN'T IT? I'M HALF-KRYPTONIAN AND PROUD OF IT...
...ESPECIALLY WHEN I'M HERE WITH ALL THIS COOL STUFF TO REMIND ME!
AND DAMIAN THINKS HE'S SO GREAT 'CAUSE OF HIS DAD'S BATCAVE--HA!
AFTER ALL THE TROUBLE I WENT THROUGH TO WITNESS THE PLANET'S ACTUAL DESTRUCTION...*
...I HAD THE FORTRESS CREATE A HOLOGRAPHIC SIMULATION OF THE MOMENT KRYPTON DIED.
SOUNDS A WHOLE LOT EASIER.
IT'S NOT FUN TO WATCH, BUT I DO THINK IT'S SOMETHING WE SHOULD DO TOGETHER...TO HONOR THE DEAD OF OUR HOMEWORLD.
OKAY, DAD, IF YOU SAY SO...
*ACTION COMICS VOL. 5: BOOSTER SHOT --Paul
...I'M READY.

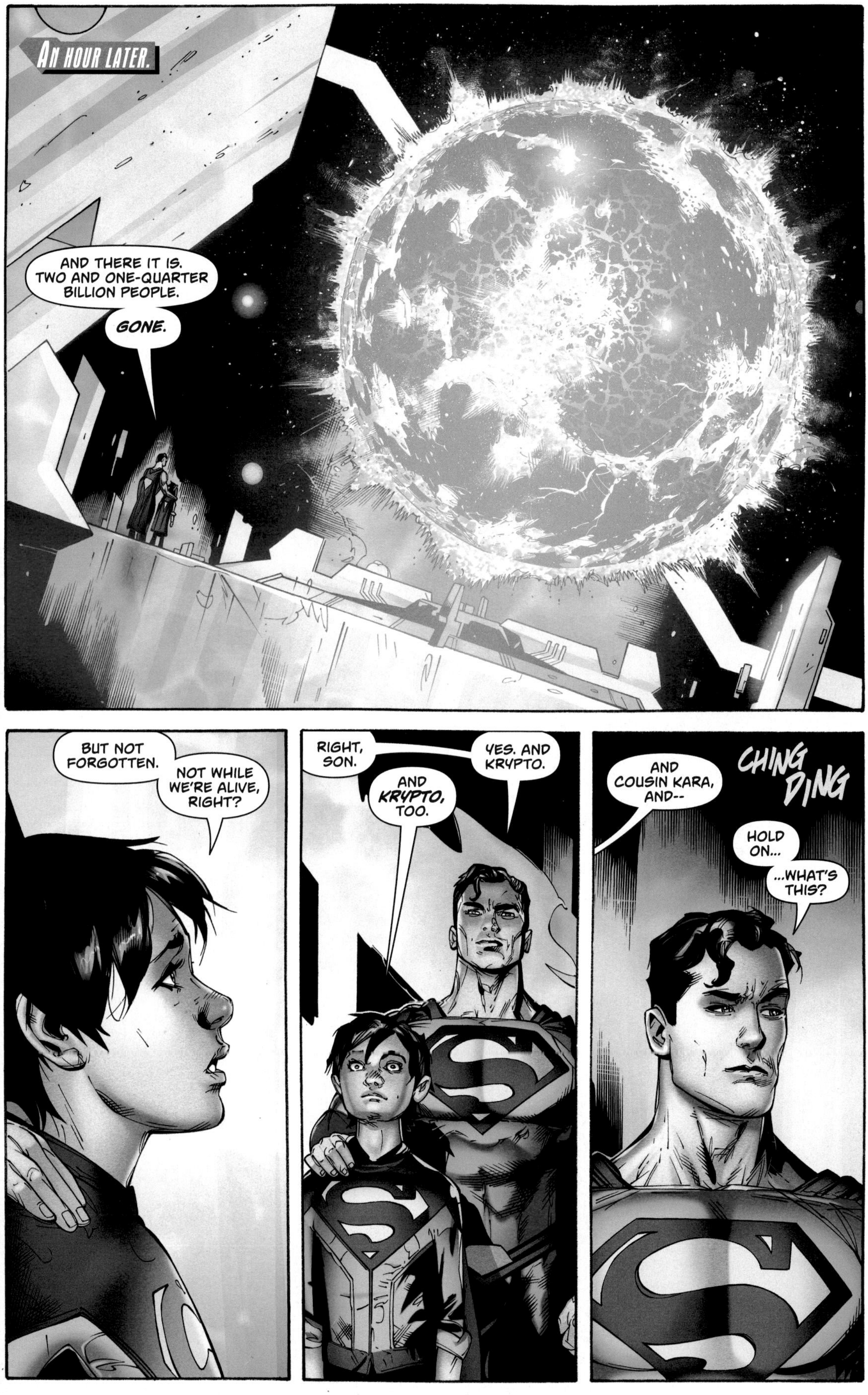
AN HOUR LATER.
AND THERE IT IS. TWO AND ONE-QUARTER BILLION PEOPLE.
GONE.
BUT NOT FORGOTTEN.
NOT WHILE WE'RE ALIVE, RIGHT?
RIGHT, SON.
YES. AND KRYPTO.
AND KRYPTO, TOO.
AND COUSIN KARA, AND--
CHING DING
HOLD ON...
...WHAT'S THIS?

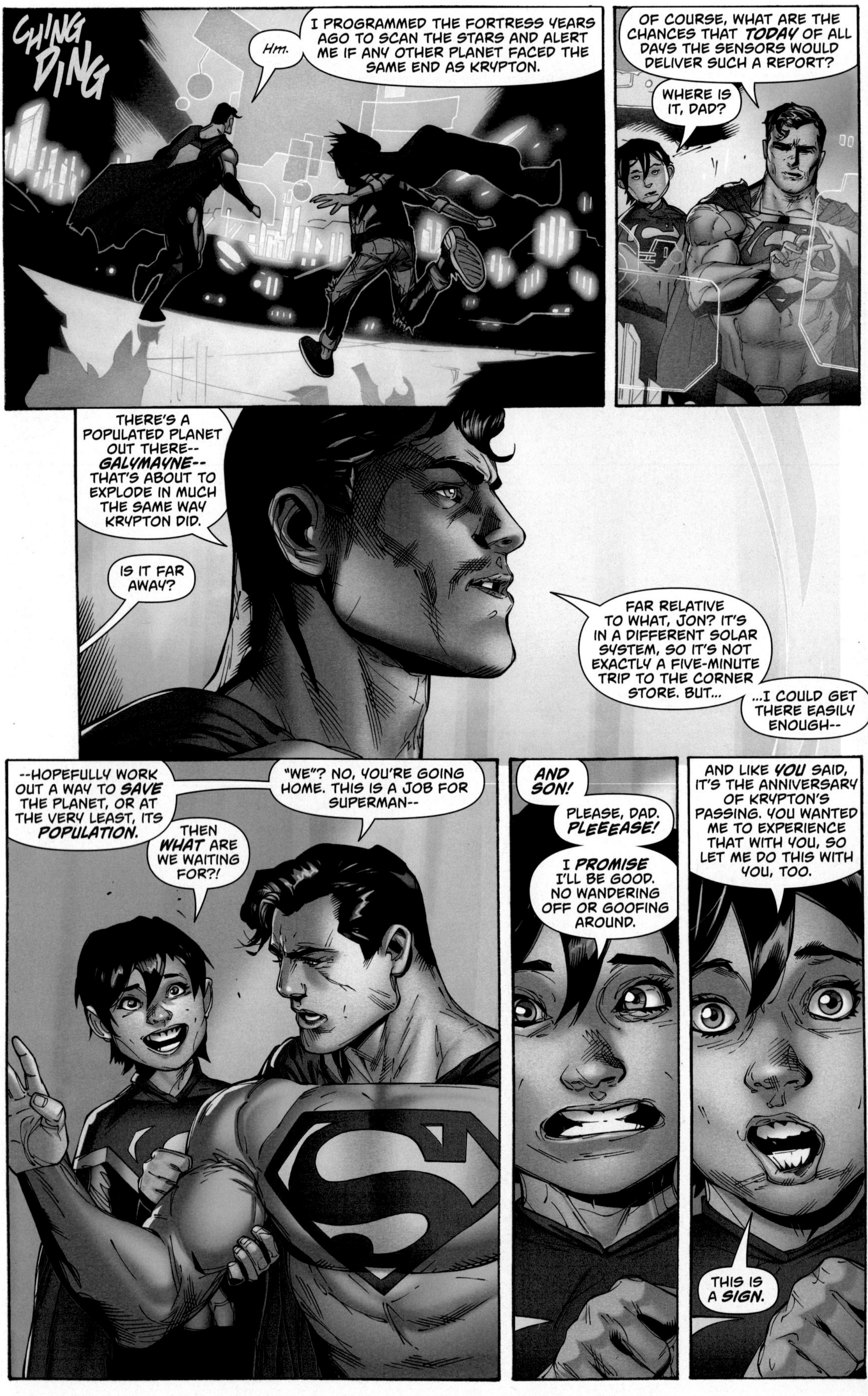
CHING DING
Hm.
I PROGRAMMED THE FORTRESS YEARS AGO TO SCAN THE STARS AND ALERT ME IF ANY OTHER PLANET FACED THE SAME END AS KRYPTON.
OF COURSE, WHAT ARE THE CHANCES THAT TODAY OF ALL DAYS THE SENSORS WOULD DELIVER SUCH A REPORT?
WHERE IS IT, DAD?
THERE'S A POPULATED PLANET OUT THERE-- GALYMAYNE-- THAT'S ABOUT TO EXPLODE IN MUCH THE SAME WAY KRYPTON DID.
IS IT FAR AWAY?
FAR RELATIVE TO WHAT, JON? IT'S IN A DIFFERENT SOLAR SYSTEM, SO IT'S NOT EXACTLY A FIVE-MINUTE TRIP TO THE CORNER STORE. BUT...
...I COULD GET THERE EASILY ENOUGH--
--HOPEFULLY WORK OUT A WAY TO SAVE THE PLANET, OR AT THE VERY LEAST, ITS POPULATION.
THEN WHAT ARE WE WAITING FOR?!
"WE"? NO, YOU'RE GOING HOME. THIS IS A JOB FOR SUPERMAN--
AND SON!
PLEASE, DAD. PLEEEASE!
I PROMISE I'LL BE GOOD. NO WANDERING OFF OR GOOFING AROUND.
AND LIKE YOU SAID, IT'S THE ANNIVERSARY OF KRYPTON'S PASSING. YOU WANTED ME TO EXPERIENCE THAT WITH YOU, SO LET ME DO THIS WITH YOU, TOO.
THIS IS A SIGN.

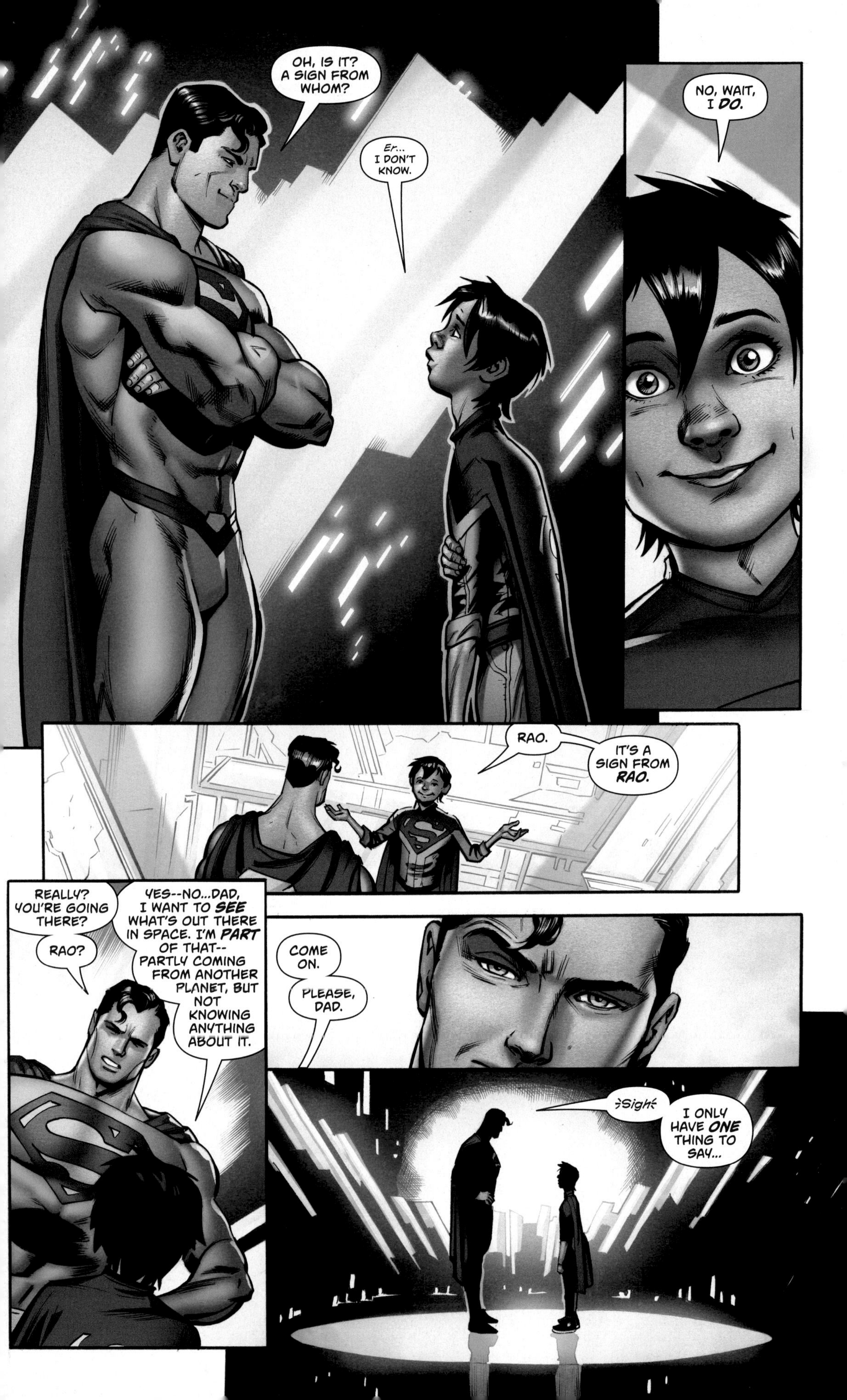
OH, IS IT? A SIGN FROM WHOM?
Er... I DON'T KNOW.
NO, WAIT, I DO.
RAO.
IT'S A SIGN FROM RAO.
REALLY? YOU'RE GOING THERE?
RAO?
YES--NO...DAD, I WANT TO SEE WHAT'S OUT THERE IN SPACE. I'M PART OF THAT--PARTLY COMING FROM ANOTHER PLANET, BUT NOT KNOWING ANYTHING ABOUT IT.
COME ON.
PLEASE, DAD.
Sigh
I ONLY HAVE ONE THING TO SAY...

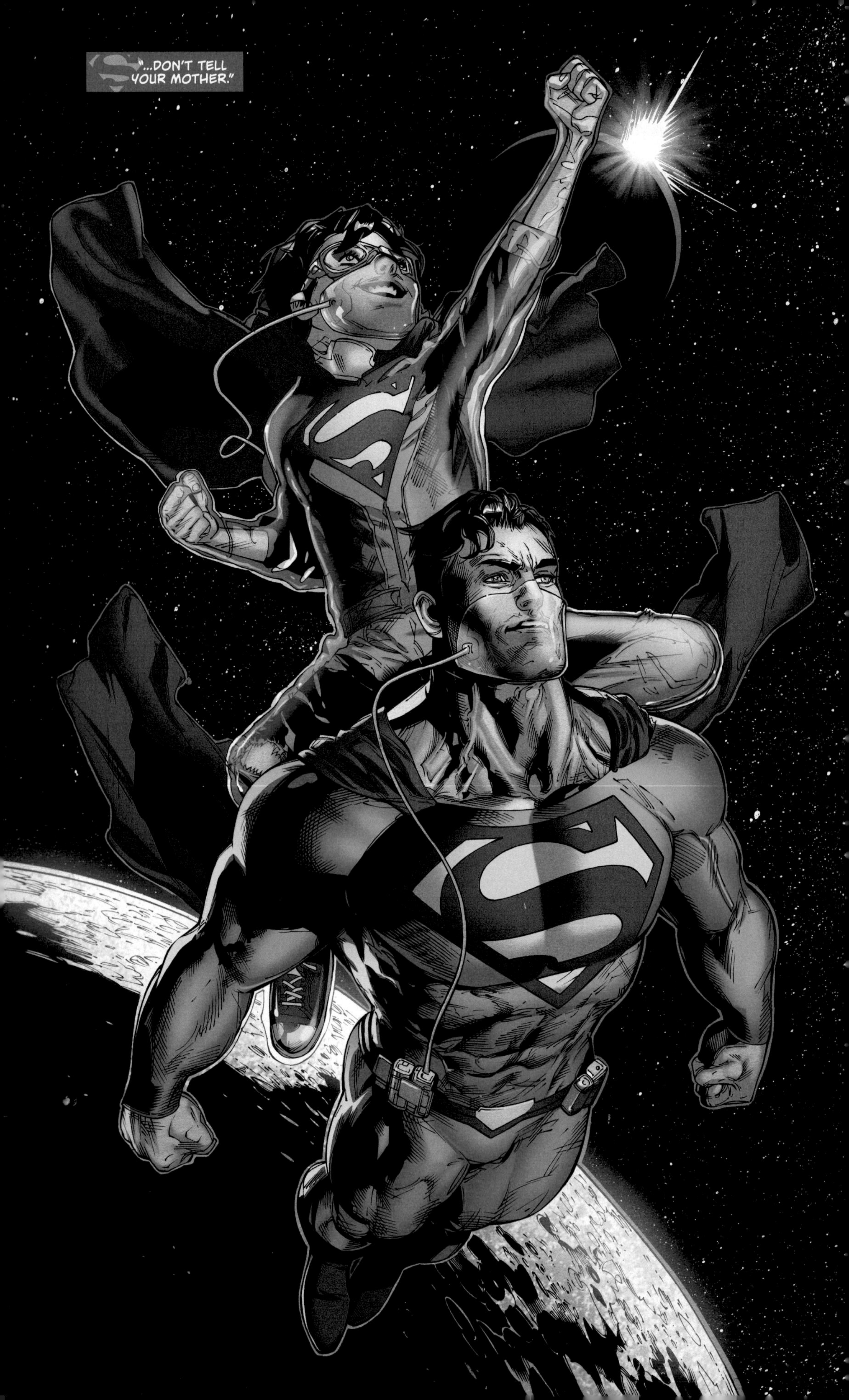
"...DON'T TELL YOUR MOTHER."

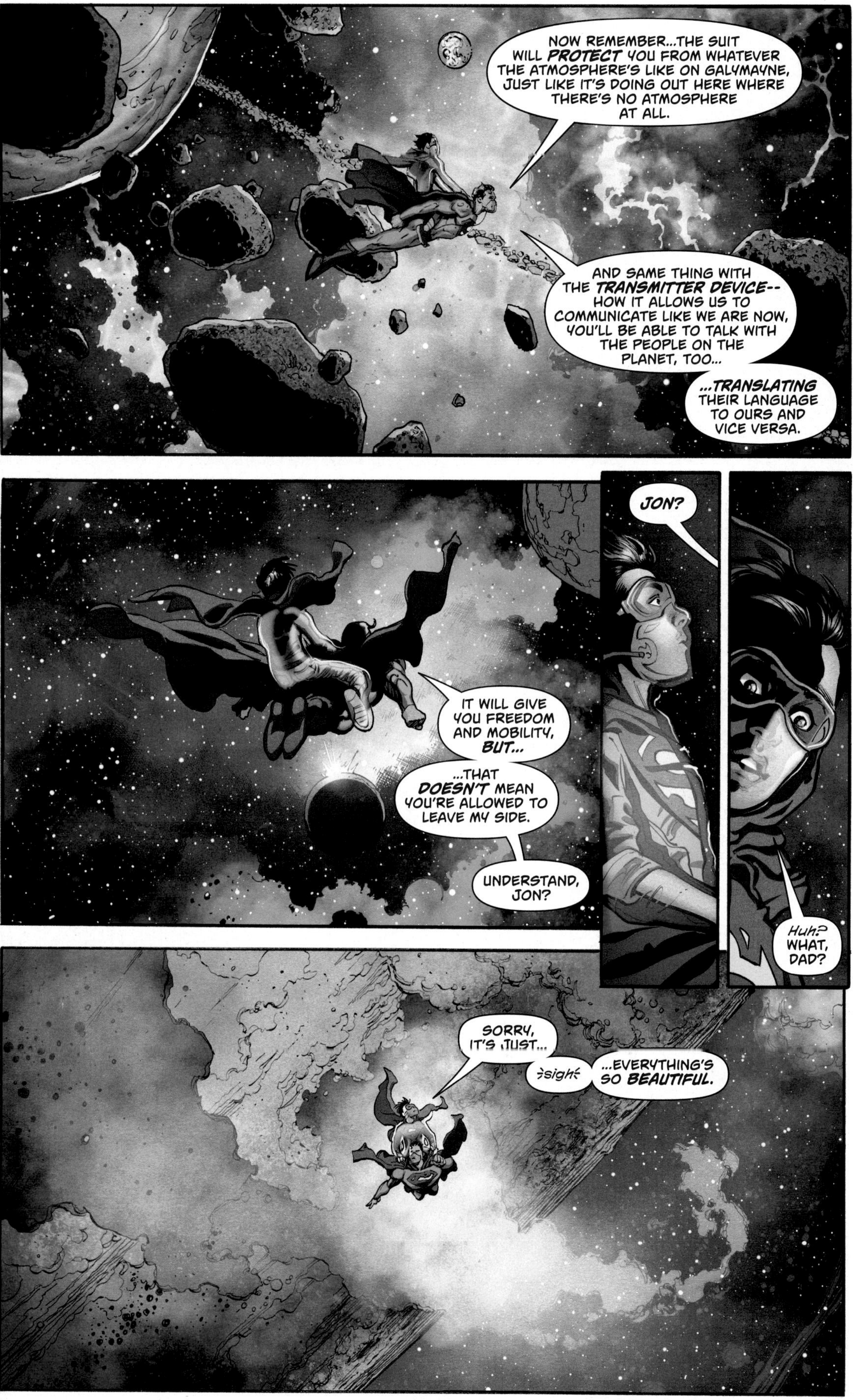
NOW REMEMBER...THE SUIT WILL PROTECT YOU FROM WHATEVER THE ATMOSPHERE'S LIKE ON GALYMAYNE, JUST LIKE IT'S DOING OUT HERE WHERE THERE'S NO ATMOSPHERE AT ALL.
AND SAME THING WITH THE TRANSMITTER DEVICE-- HOW IT ALLOWS US TO COMMUNICATE LIKE WE ARE NOW, YOU'LL BE ABLE TO TALK WITH THE PEOPLE ON THE PLANET, TOO...
...TRANSLATING THEIR LANGUAGE TO OURS AND VICE VERSA.
IT WILL GIVE YOU FREEDOM AND MOBILITY, BUT...
...THAT DOESN'T MEAN YOU'RE ALLOWED TO LEAVE MY SIDE.
UNDERSTAND, JON?
JON?
Huh? WHAT, DAD?
SORRY, IT'S JUST...
>sigh<
...EVERYTHING'S SO BEAUTIFUL.

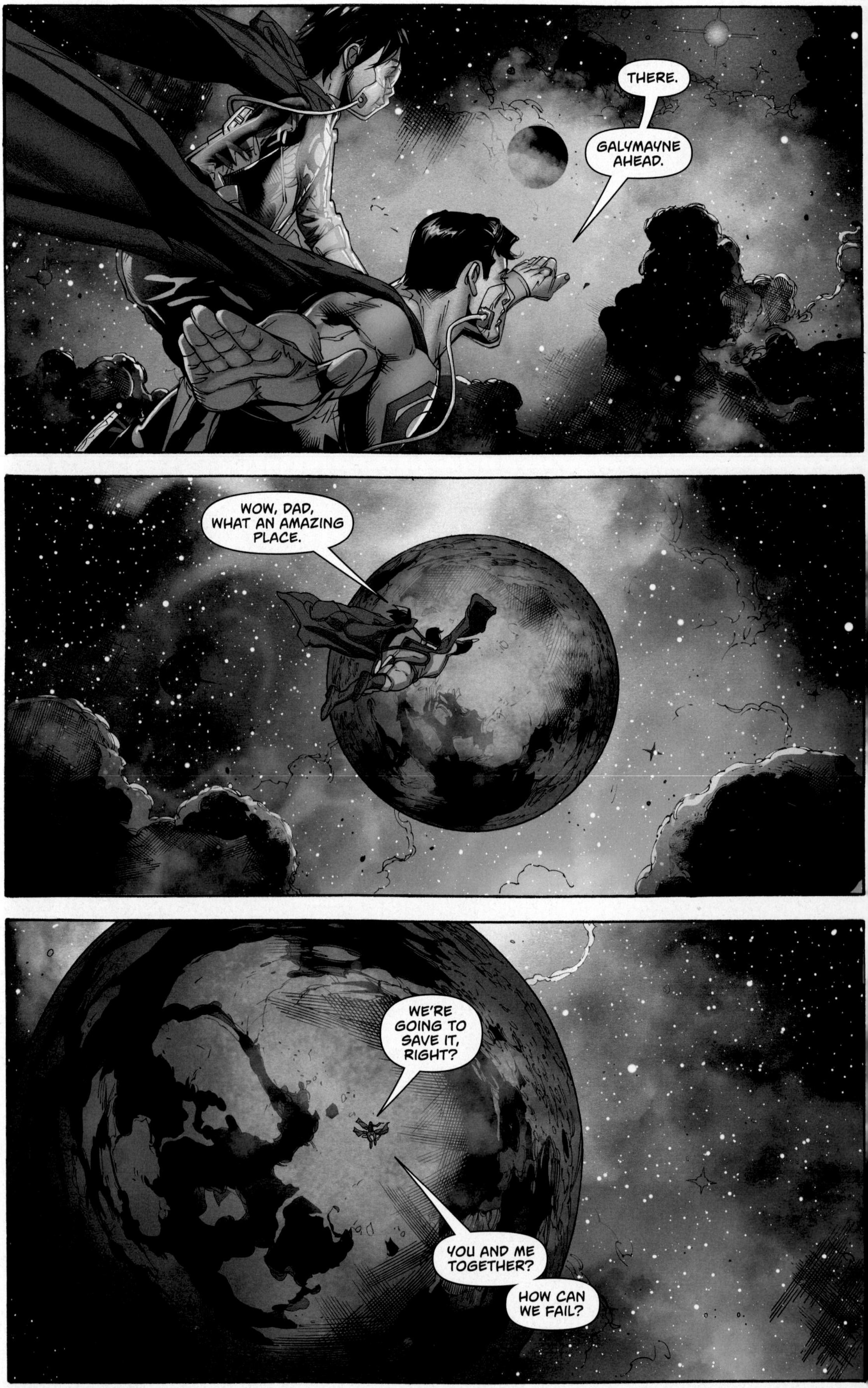
THERE.
GALYMAYNE AHEAD.
WOW, DAD, WHAT AN AMAZING PLACE.
WE'RE GOING TO SAVE IT, RIGHT?
YOU AND ME TOGETHER?
HOW CAN WE FAIL?

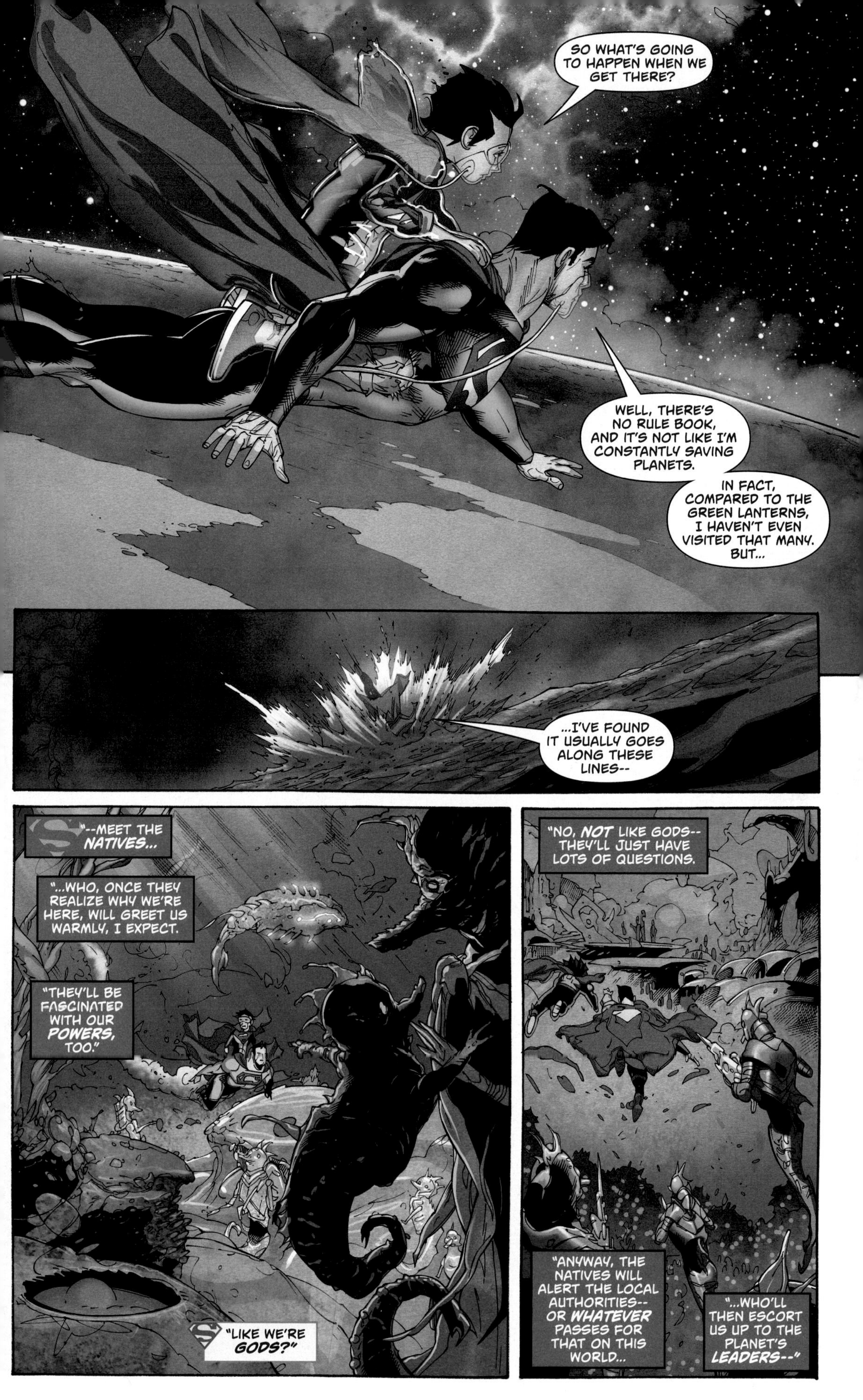
SO WHAT'S GOING TO HAPPEN WHEN WE GET THERE?
WELL, THERE'S NO RULE BOOK, AND IT'S NOT LIKE I'M CONSTANTLY SAVING PLANETS.
IN FACT, COMPARED TO THE GREEN LANTERNS, I HAVEN'T EVEN VISITED THAT MANY. BUT...
...I'VE FOUND IT USUALLY GOES ALONG THESE LINES--
"--MEET THE NATIVES...
"...WHO, ONCE THEY REALIZE WHY WE'RE HERE, WILL GREET US WARMLY, I EXPECT.
"THEY'LL BE FASCINATED WITH OUR POWERS, TOO."
"LIKE WE'RE GODS?"
"NO, NOT LIKE GODS-- THEY'LL JUST HAVE LOTS OF QUESTIONS.
"ANYWAY, THE NATIVES WILL ALERT THE LOCAL AUTHORITIES-- OR WHATEVER PASSES FOR THAT ON THIS WORLD...
"...WHO'LL THEN ESCORT US UP TO THE PLANET'S LEADERS--"

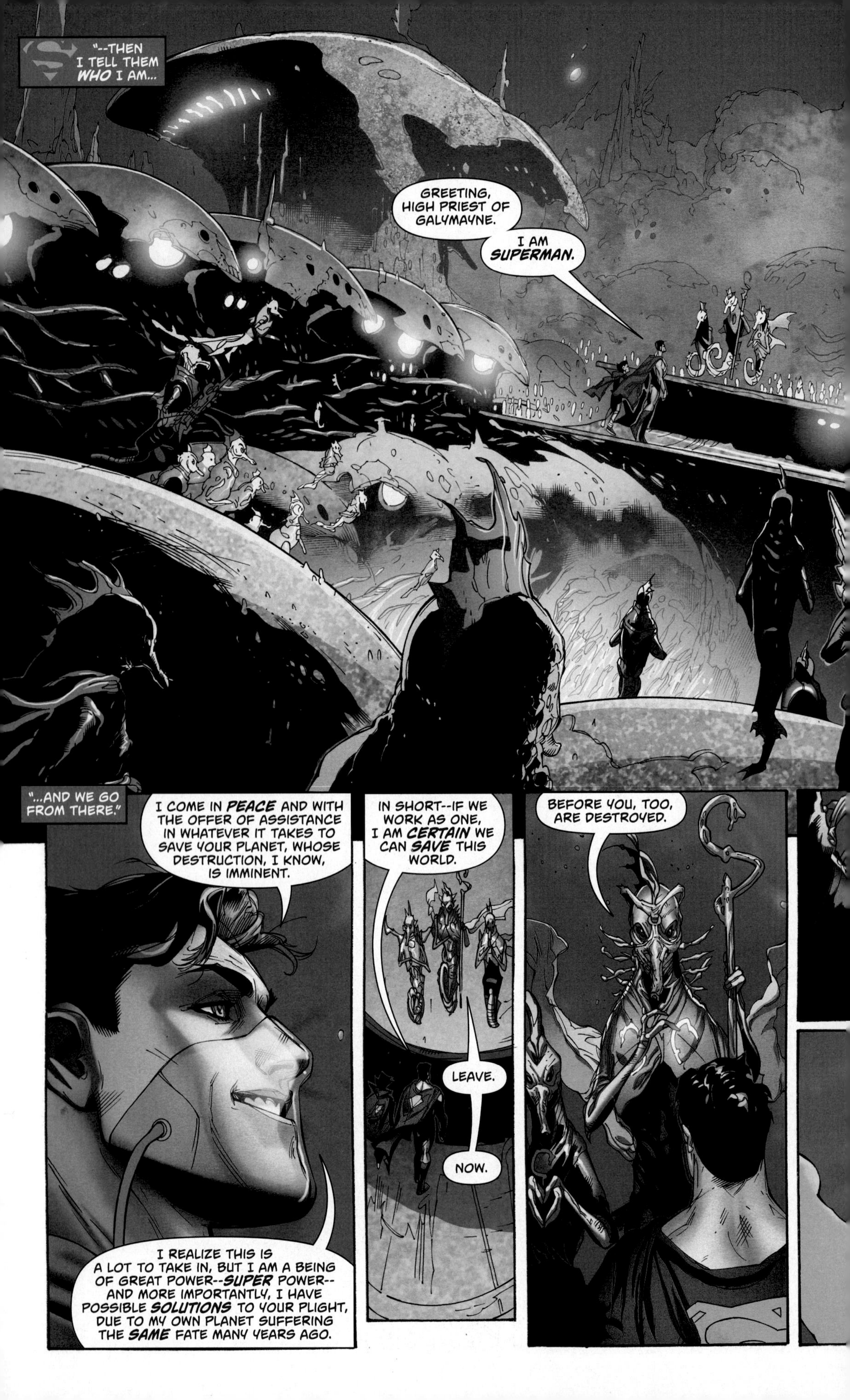
"--THEN I TELL THEM WHO I AM...
GREETING, HIGH PRIEST OF GALYMAYNE.
I AM SUPERMAN.
"...AND WE GO FROM THERE."
I COME IN PEACE AND WITH THE OFFER OF ASSISTANCE IN WHATEVER IT TAKES TO SAVE YOUR PLANET, WHOSE DESTRUCTION, I KNOW, IS IMMINENT.
I REALIZE THIS IS A LOT TO TAKE IN, BUT I AM A BEING OF GREAT POWER--SUPER POWER--AND MORE IMPORTANTLY, I HAVE POSSIBLE SOLUTIONS TO YOUR PLIGHT, DUE TO MY OWN PLANET SUFFERING THE SAME FATE MANY YEARS AGO.
IN SHORT--IF WE WORK AS ONE, I AM CERTAIN WE CAN SAVE THIS WORLD.
LEAVE.
NOW.
BEFORE YOU, TOO, ARE DESTROYED.

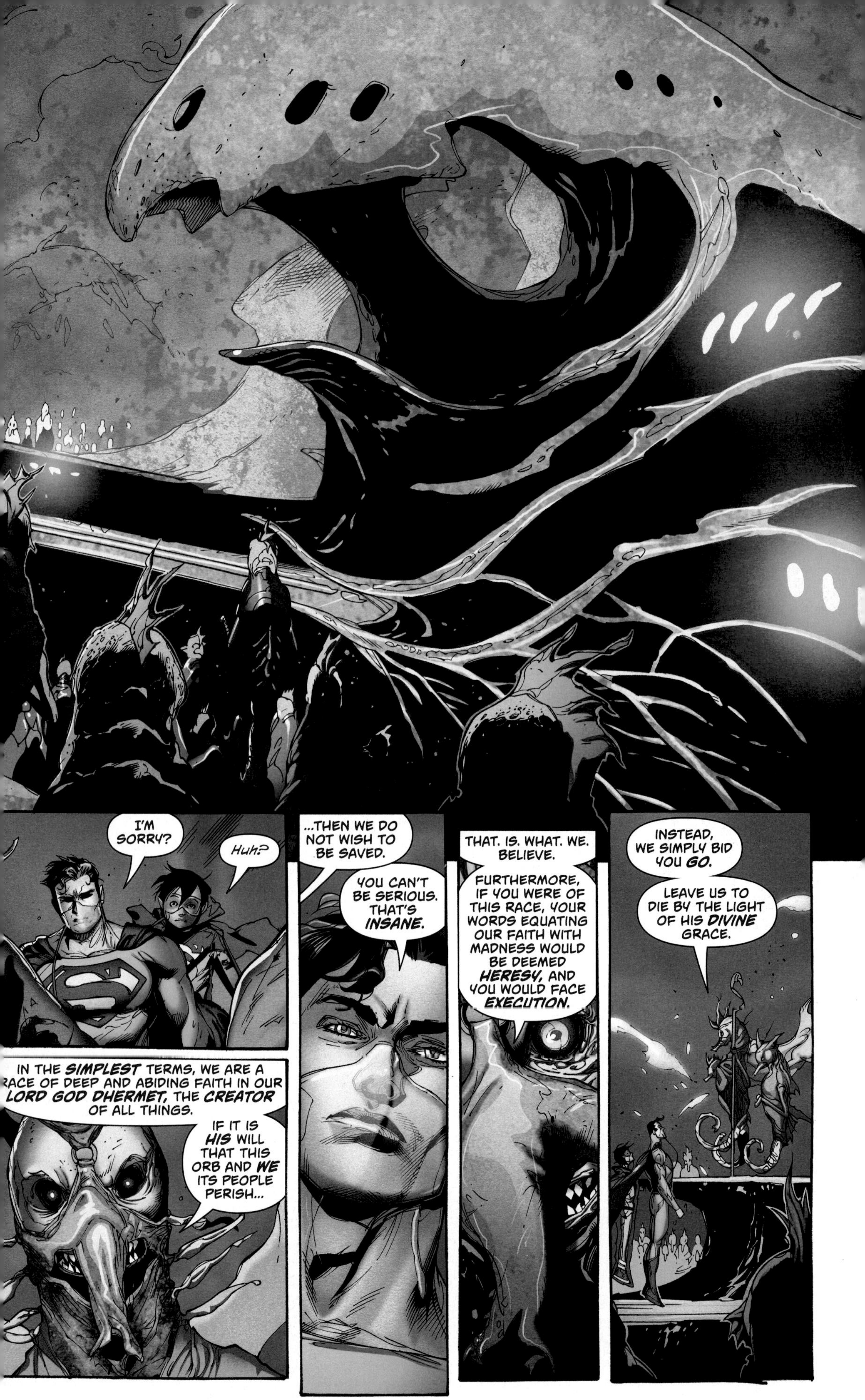

I'M SORRY?
Huh?
IN THE SIMPLEST TERMS, WE ARE A RACE OF DEEP AND ABIDING FAITH IN OUR LORD GOD DHERMET, THE CREATOR OF ALL THINGS.
IF IT IS HIS WILL THAT THIS ORB AND WE ITS PEOPLE PERISH...
...THEN WE DO NOT WISH TO BE SAVED.
YOU CAN'T BE SERIOUS. THAT'S INSANE.
THAT. IS. WHAT. WE. BELIEVE.
FURTHERMORE, IF YOU WERE OF THIS RACE, YOUR WORDS EQUATING OUR FAITH WITH MADNESS WOULD BE DEEMED HERESY, AND YOU WOULD FACE EXECUTION.
INSTEAD, WE SIMPLY BID YOU GO.
LEAVE US TO DIE BY THE LIGHT OF HIS DIVINE GRACE.

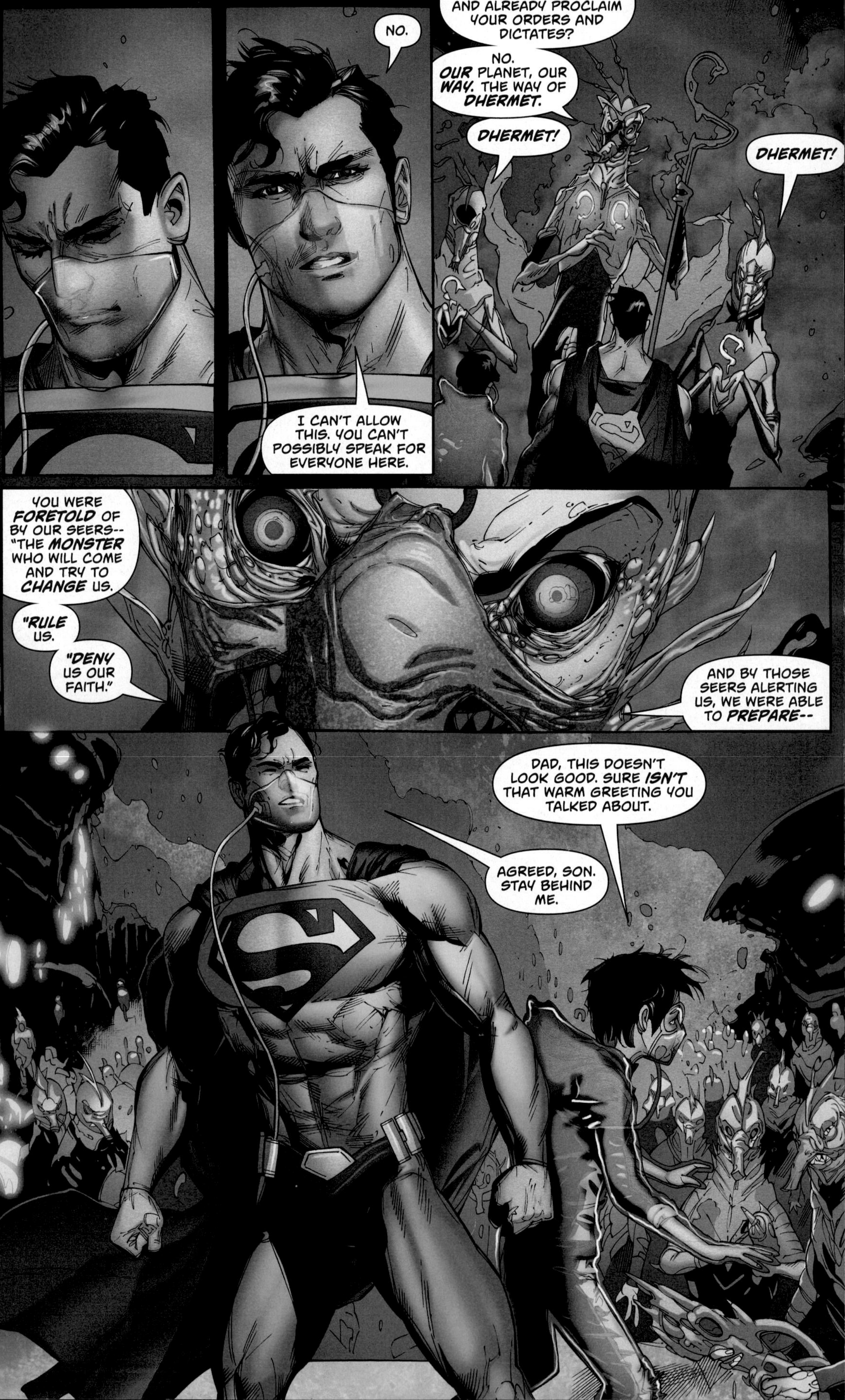
NO.
I CAN'T ALLOW THIS. YOU CAN'T POSSIBLY SPEAK FOR EVERYONE HERE.
OH? YOU VISIT OUR PLANET THIS ONE TIME AND ALREADY PROCLAIM YOUR ORDERS AND DICTATES?
NO. OUR PLANET, OUR WAY. THE WAY OF DHERMET.
DHERMET!
DHERMET!
YOU WERE FORETOLD OF BY OUR SEERS--"THE MONSTER WHO WILL COME AND TRY TO CHANGE US.
"RULE US.
"DENY US OUR FAITH."
AND BY THOSE SEERS ALERTING US, WE WERE ABLE TO PREPARE--
DAD, THIS DOESN'T LOOK GOOD. SURE ISN'T THAT WARM GREETING YOU TALKED ABOUT.
AGREED, SON. STAY BEHIND ME.

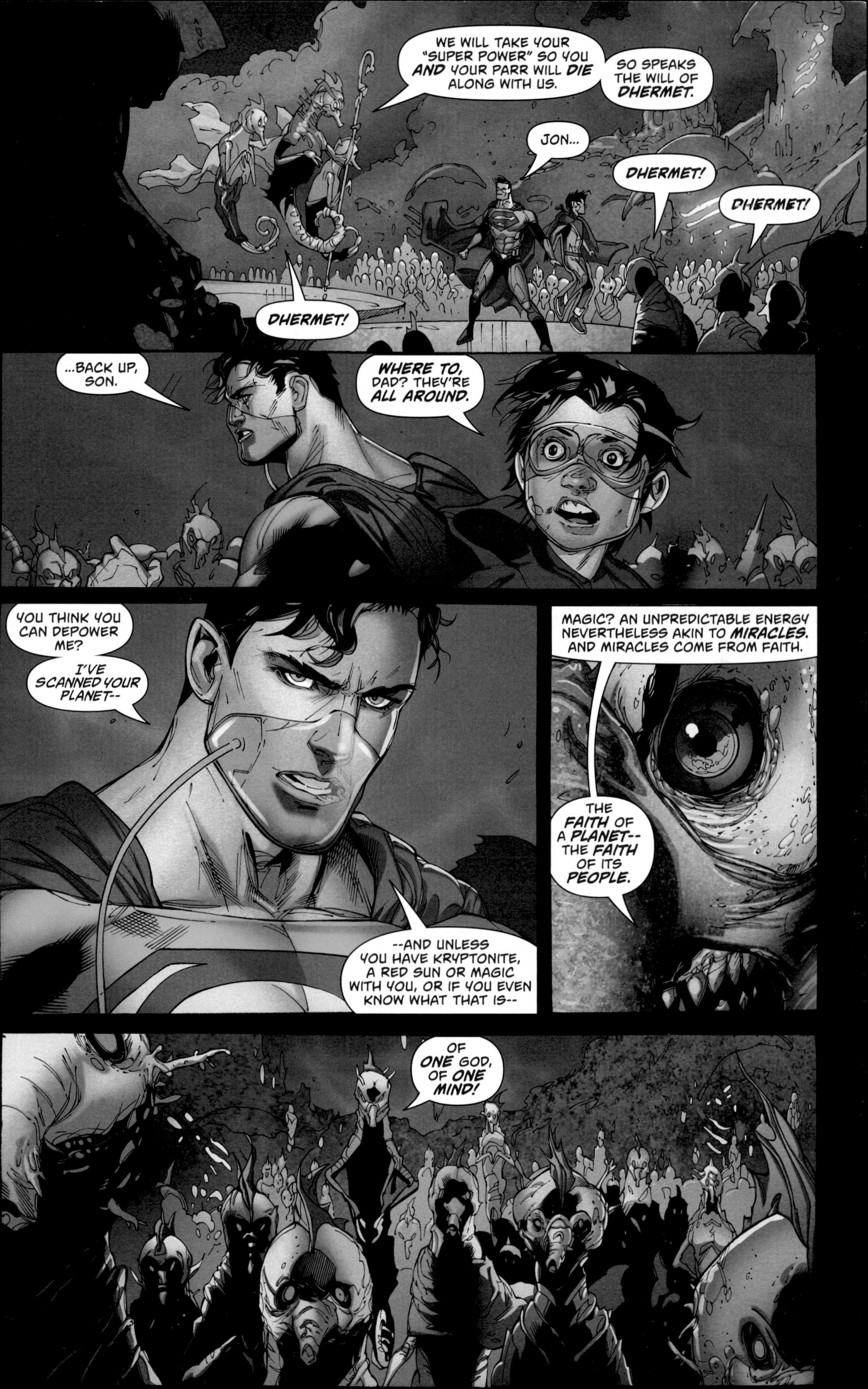
WE WILL TAKE YOUR "SUPER POWER" SO YOU AND YOUR PARR WILL DIE ALONG WITH US.
SO SPEAKS THE WILL OF DHERMET.
JON...
DHERMET!
DHERMET!
DHERMET!
...BACK UP, SON.
WHERE TO, DAD? THEY'RE ALL AROUND.
YOU THINK YOU CAN DEPOWER ME?
I'VE SCANNED YOUR PLANET--
--AND UNLESS YOU HAVE KRYPTONITE, A RED SUN OR MAGIC WITH YOU, OR IF YOU EVEN KNOW WHAT THAT IS--
MAGIC? AN UNPREDICTABLE ENERGY NEVERTHELESS AKIN TO MIRACLES. AND MIRACLES COME FROM FAITH.
THE FAITH OF A PLANET-- THE FAITH OF ITS PEOPLE.
OF ONE GOD, OF ONE MIND!

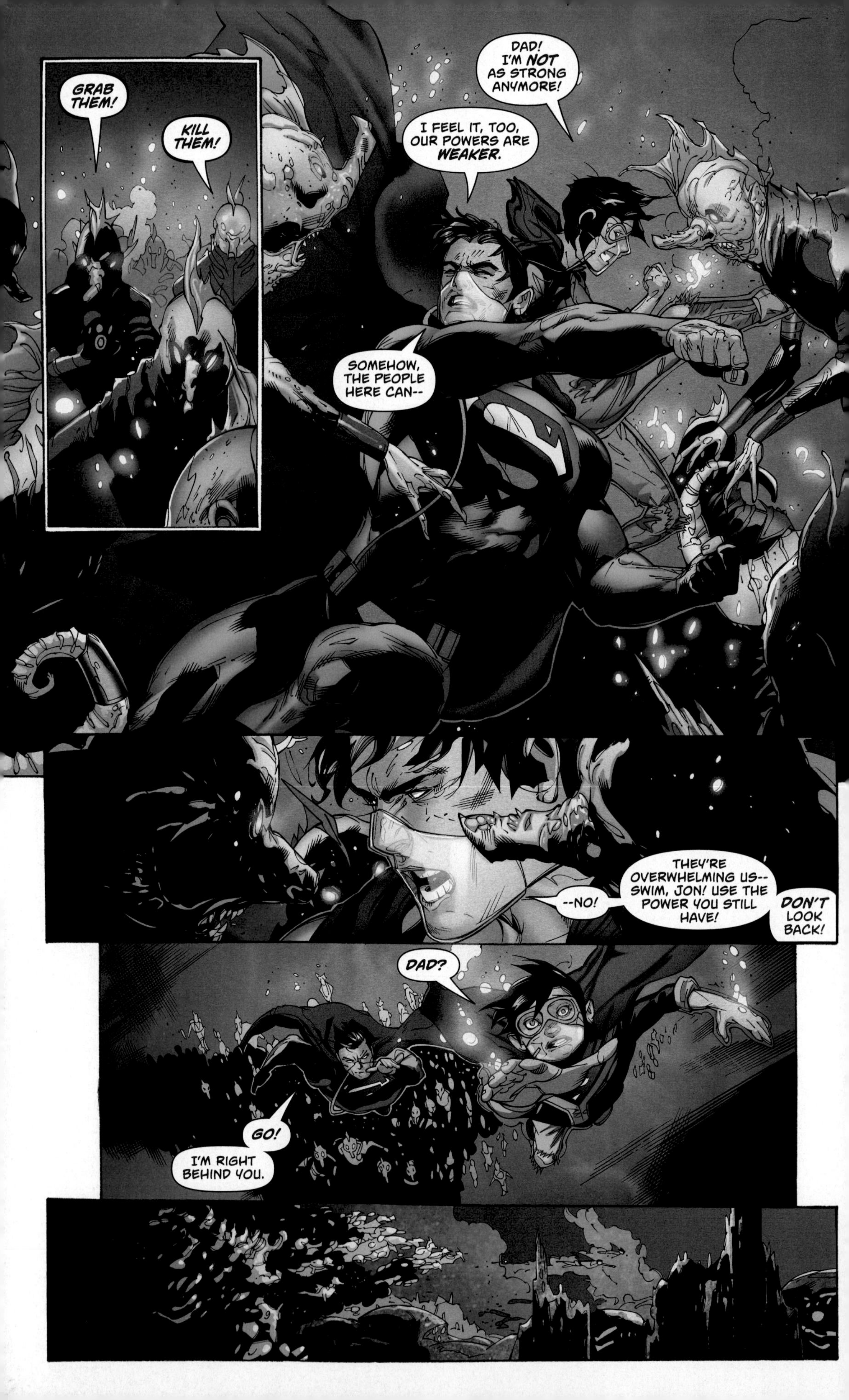
GRAB THEM!
KILL THEM!
DAD! I'M NOT AS STRONG ANYMORE!
I FEEL IT, TOO, OUR POWERS ARE WEAKER.
SOMEHOW, THE PEOPLE HERE CAN--
--NO!
THEY'RE OVERWHELMING US-- SWIM, JON! USE THE POWER YOU STILL HAVE!
DON'T LOOK BACK!
DAD?
GO!
I'M RIGHT BEHIND YOU.

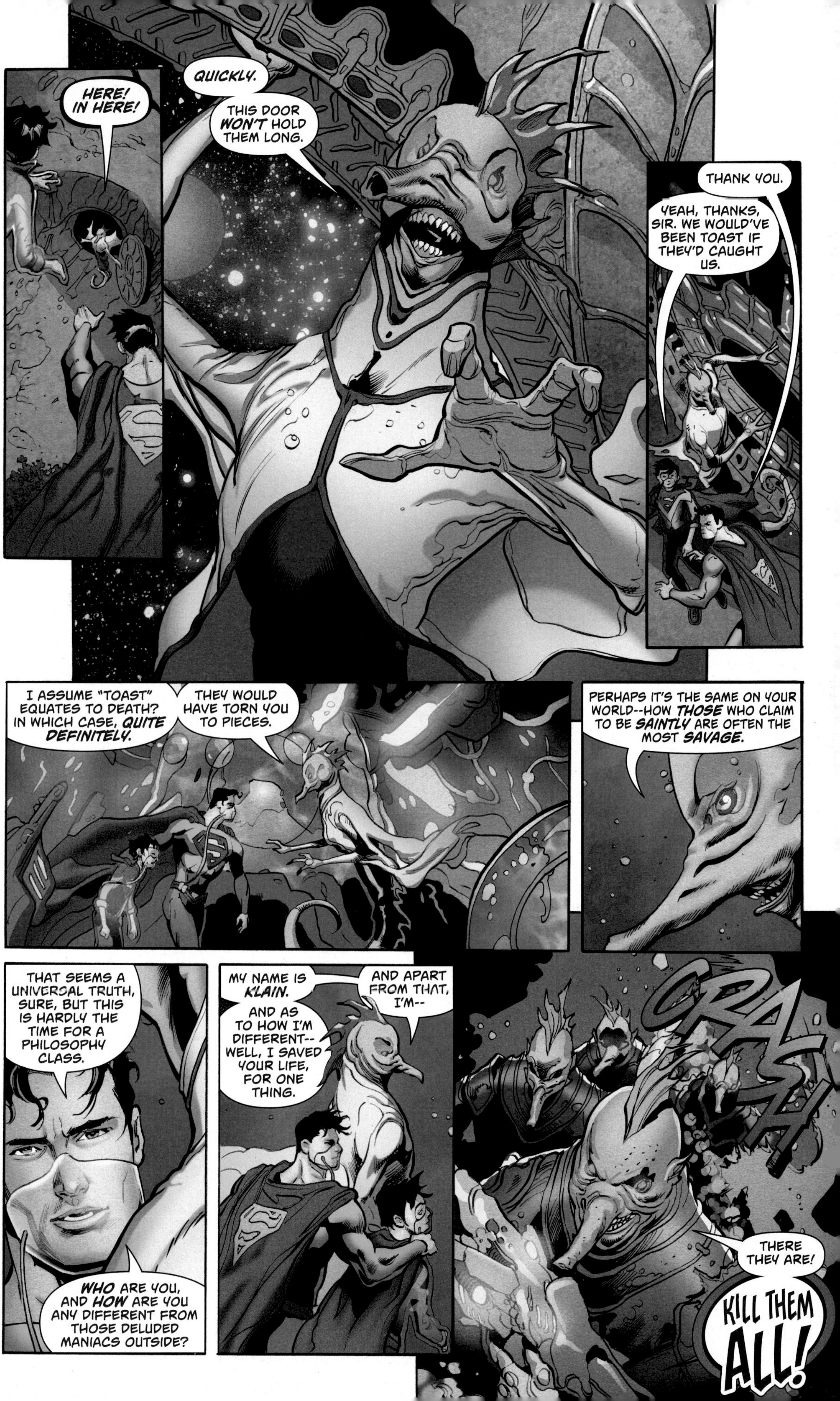
HERE! IN HERE!
QUICKLY.
THIS DOOR WON'T HOLD THEM LONG.
THANK YOU.
YEAH, THANKS, SIR. WE WOULD'VE BEEN TOAST IF THEY'D CAUGHT US.
I ASSUME "TOAST" EQUATES TO DEATH? IN WHICH CASE, QUITE DEFINITELY.
THEY WOULD HAVE TORN YOU TO PIECES.
PERHAPS IT'S THE SAME ON YOUR WORLD--HOW THOSE WHO CLAIM TO BE SAINTLY ARE OFTEN THE MOST SAVAGE.
THAT SEEMS A UNIVERSAL TRUTH, SURE, BUT THIS IS HARDLY THE TIME FOR A PHILOSOPHY CLASS.
WHO ARE YOU, AND HOW ARE YOU ANY DIFFERENT FROM THOSE DELUDED MANIACS OUTSIDE?
MY NAME IS KLAIN.
AND AS TO HOW I'M DIFFERENT--WELL, I SAVED YOUR LIFE, FOR ONE THING.
AND APART FROM THAT, I'M--
CRASH
THERE THEY ARE!
KILL THEM ALL!

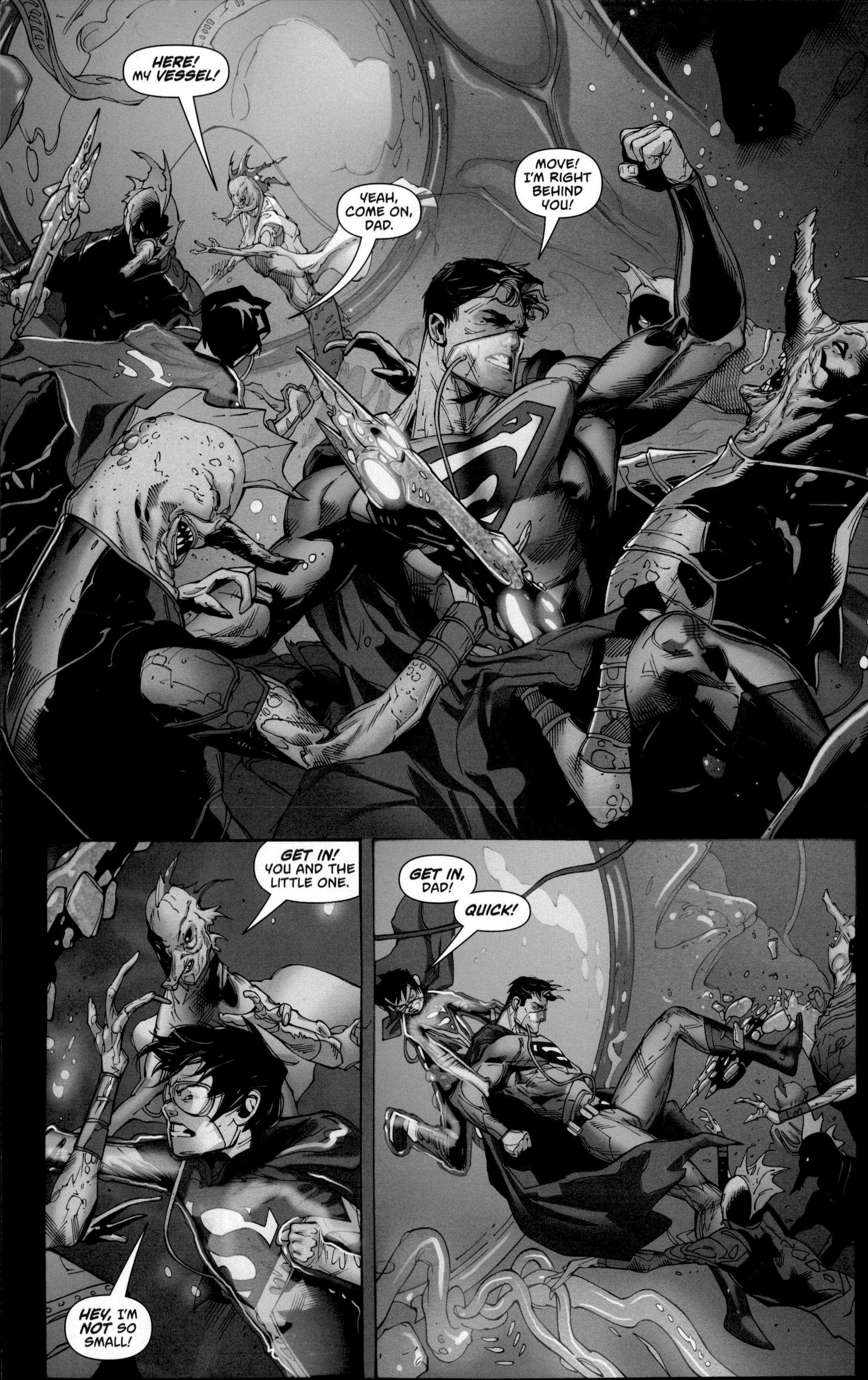
HERE! MY VESSEL!
YEAH, COME ON, DAD.
MOVE! I'M RIGHT BEHIND YOU!
GET IN! YOU AND THE LITTLE ONE.
HEY, I'M NOT SO SMALL!
GET IN, DAD!
QUICK!

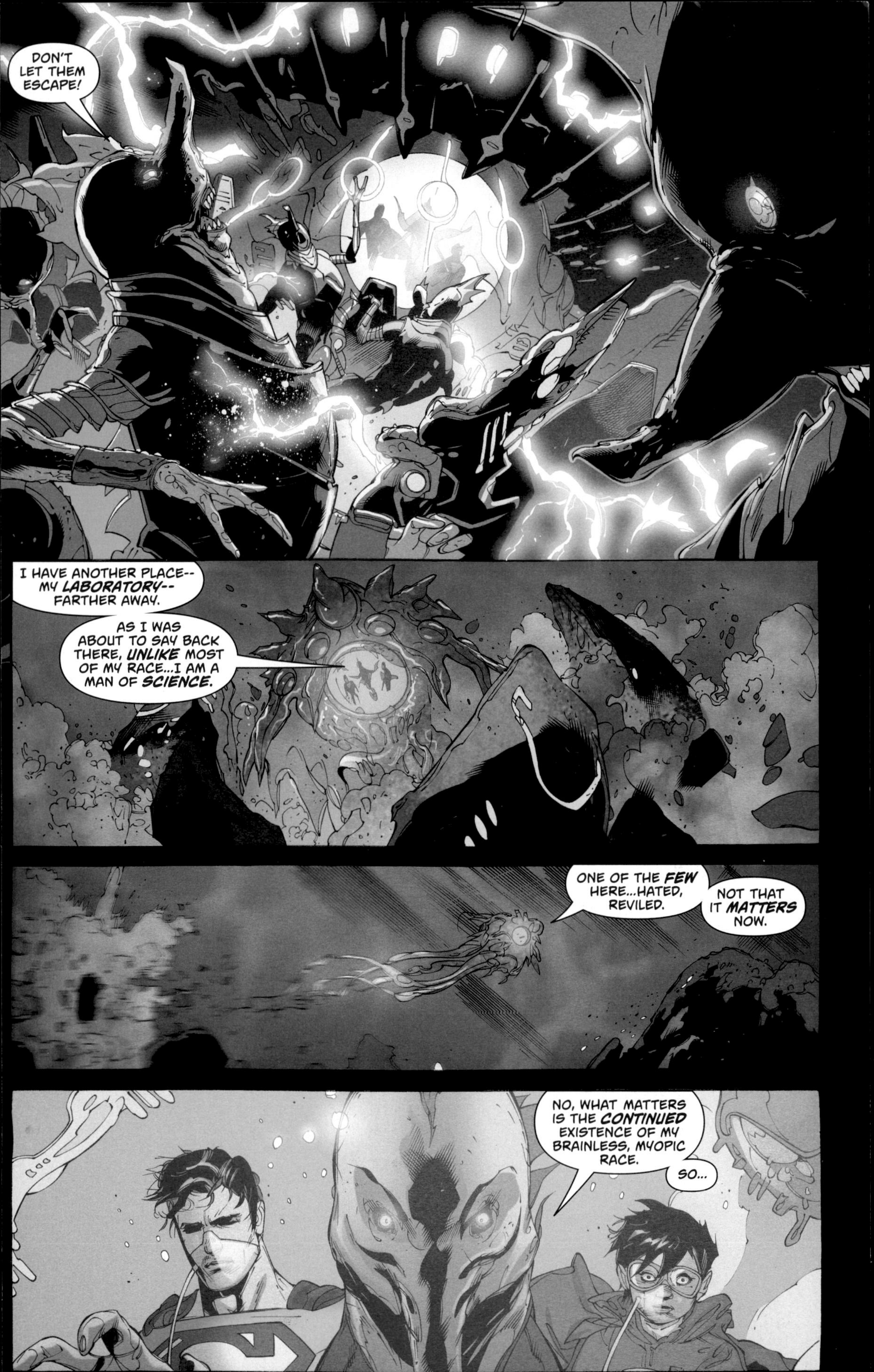
DON'T LET THEM ESCAPE!
I HAVE ANOTHER PLACE-- MY LABORATORY-- FARTHER AWAY.
AS I WAS ABOUT TO SAY BACK THERE, UNLIKE MOST OF MY RACE...I AM A MAN OF SCIENCE.
ONE OF THE FEW HERE...HATED, REVILED.
NOT THAT IT MATTERS NOW.
NO, WHAT MATTERS IS THE CONTINUED EXISTENCE OF MY BRAINLESS, MYOPIC RACE.
SO...

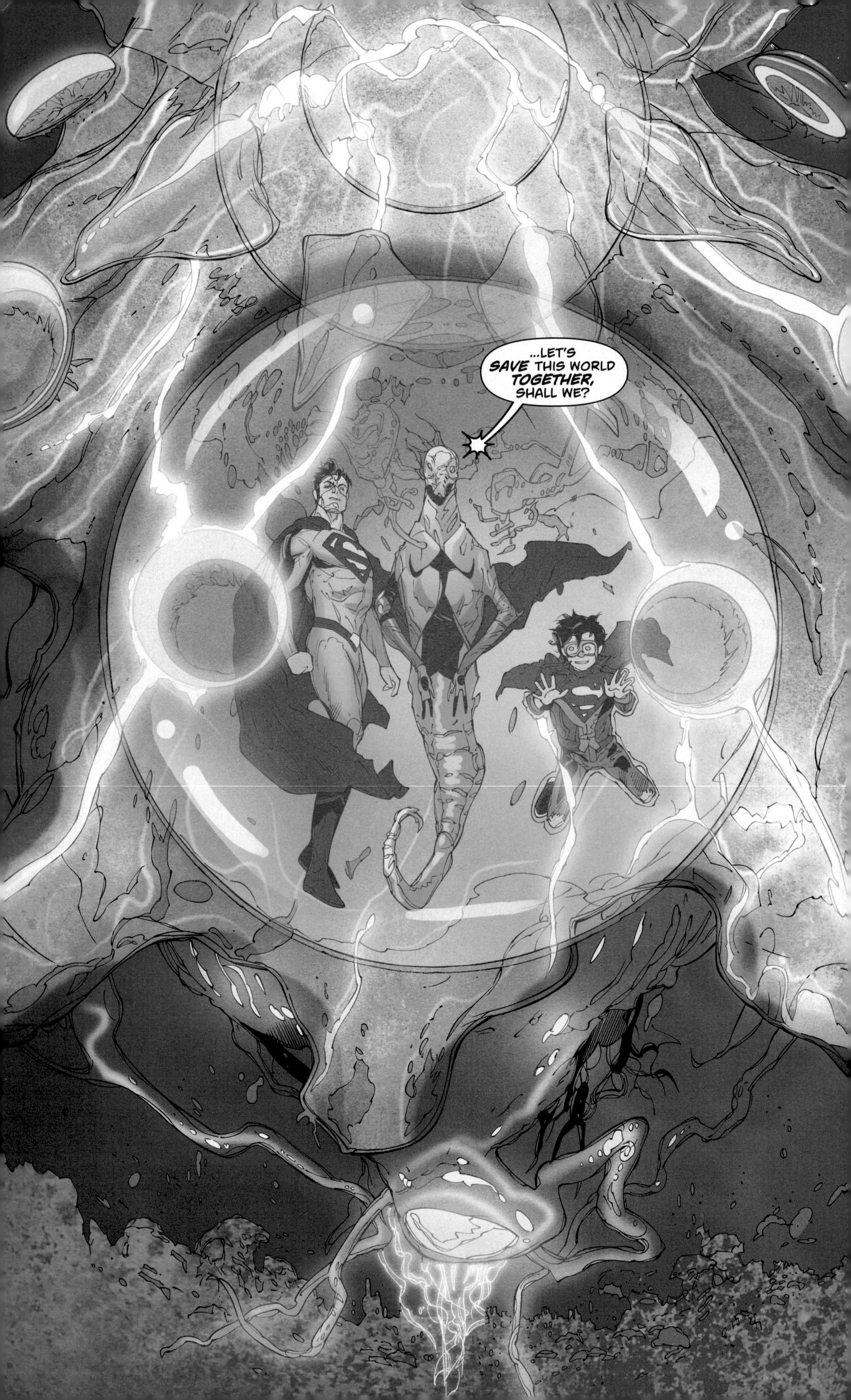
...LET'S SAVE THIS WORLD TOGETHER, SHALL WE?

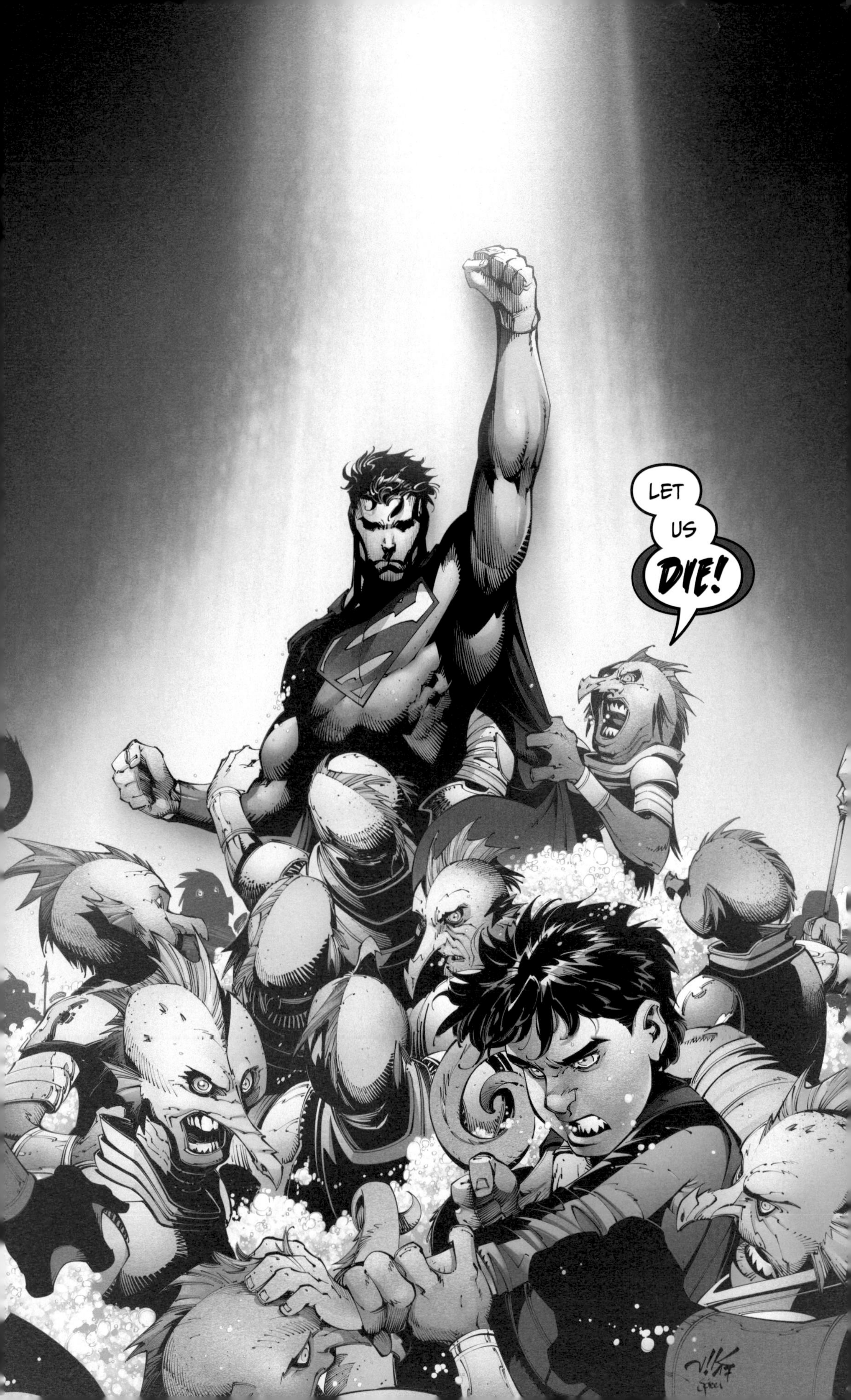
LET US DIE!

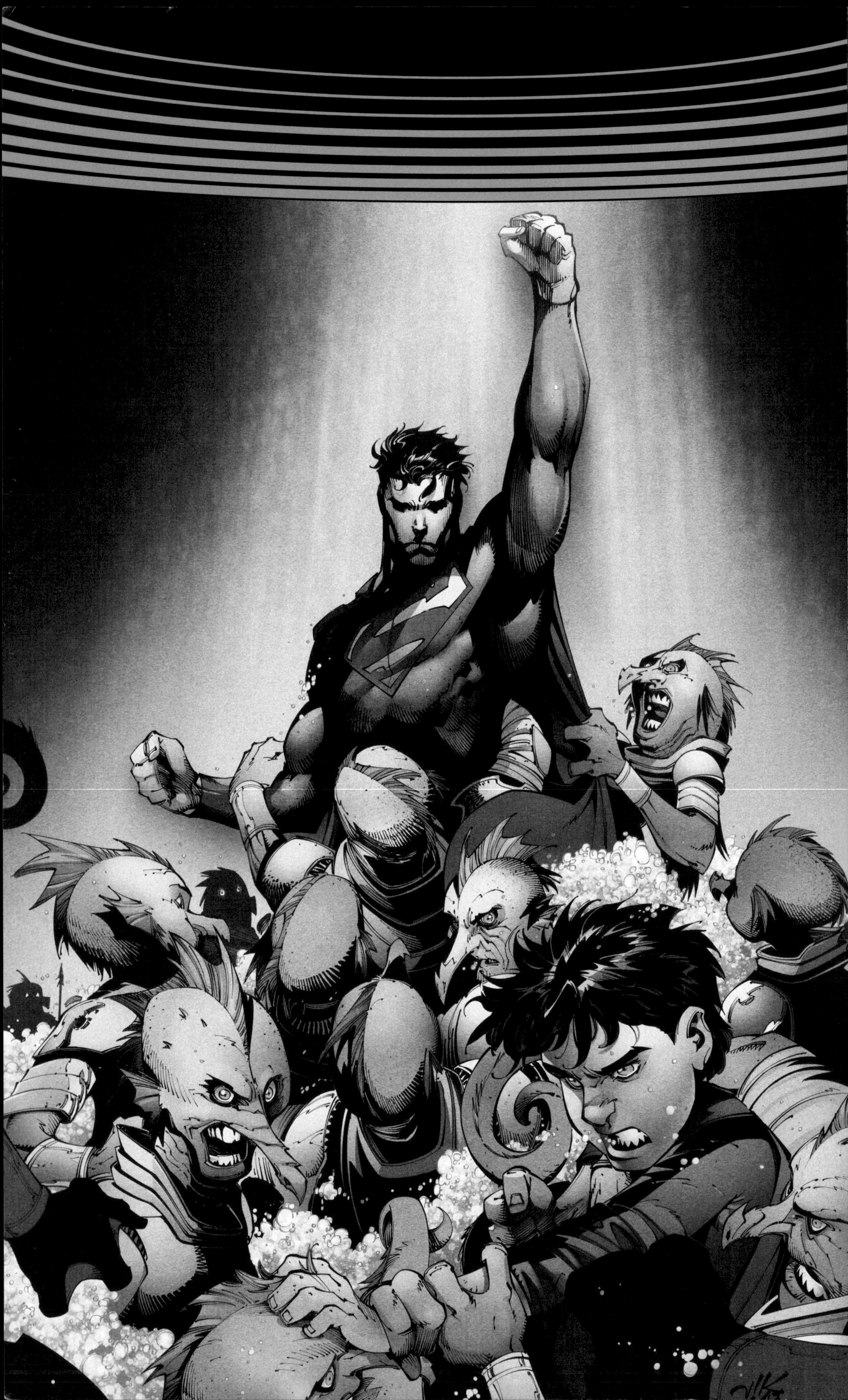

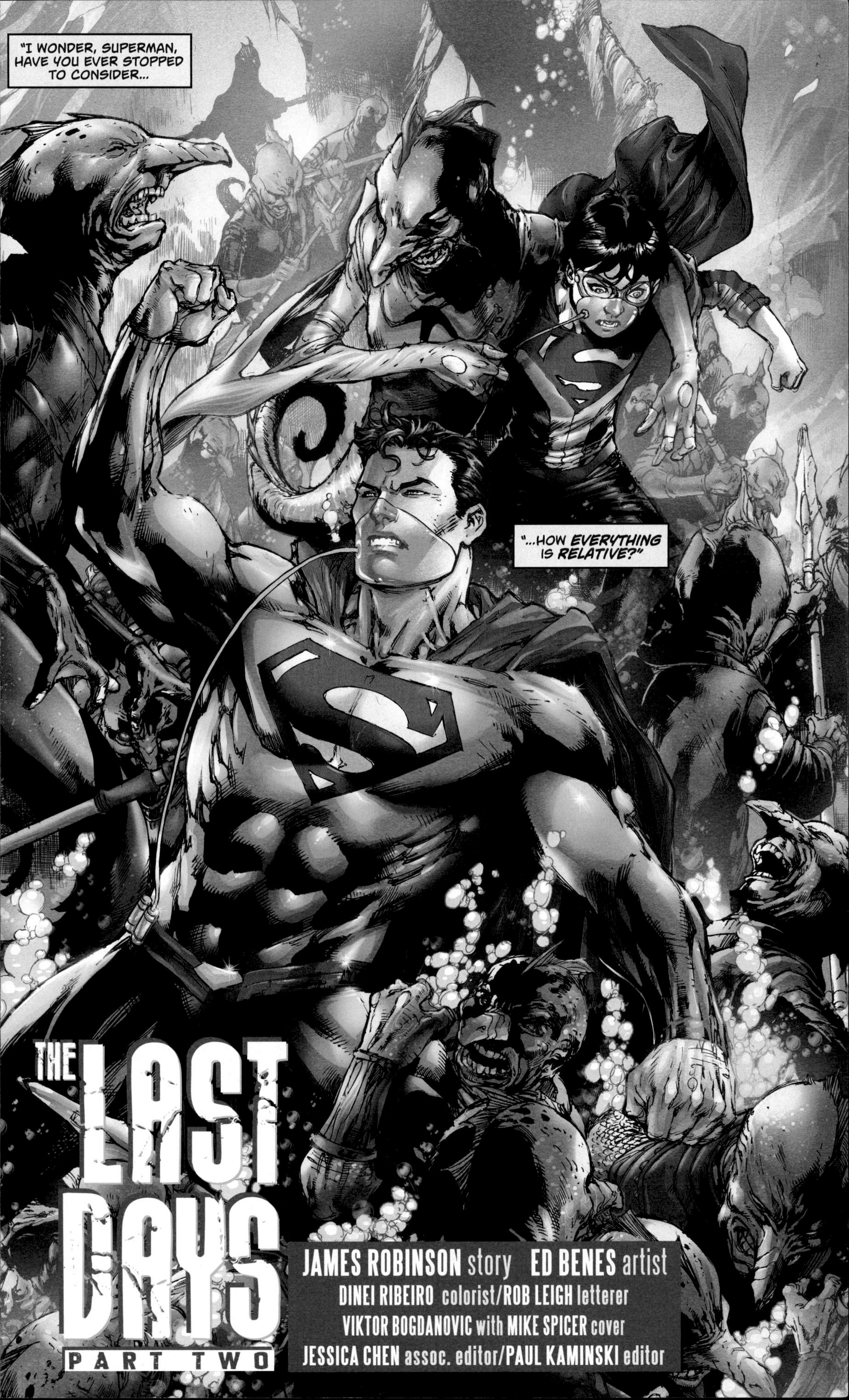
"I WONDER, SUPERMAN, HAVE YOU EVER STOPPED TO CONSIDER...
"...HOW EVERYTHING IS RELATIVE?"
THE LAST DAYS
PART TWO
JAMES ROBINSON story ED BENES artist
DINEI RIBEIRO colorist/ROB LEIGH letterer
VIKTOR BOGDANOVIC with MIKE SPICER cover
JESSICA CHEN assoc. editor/PAUL KAMINSKI editor

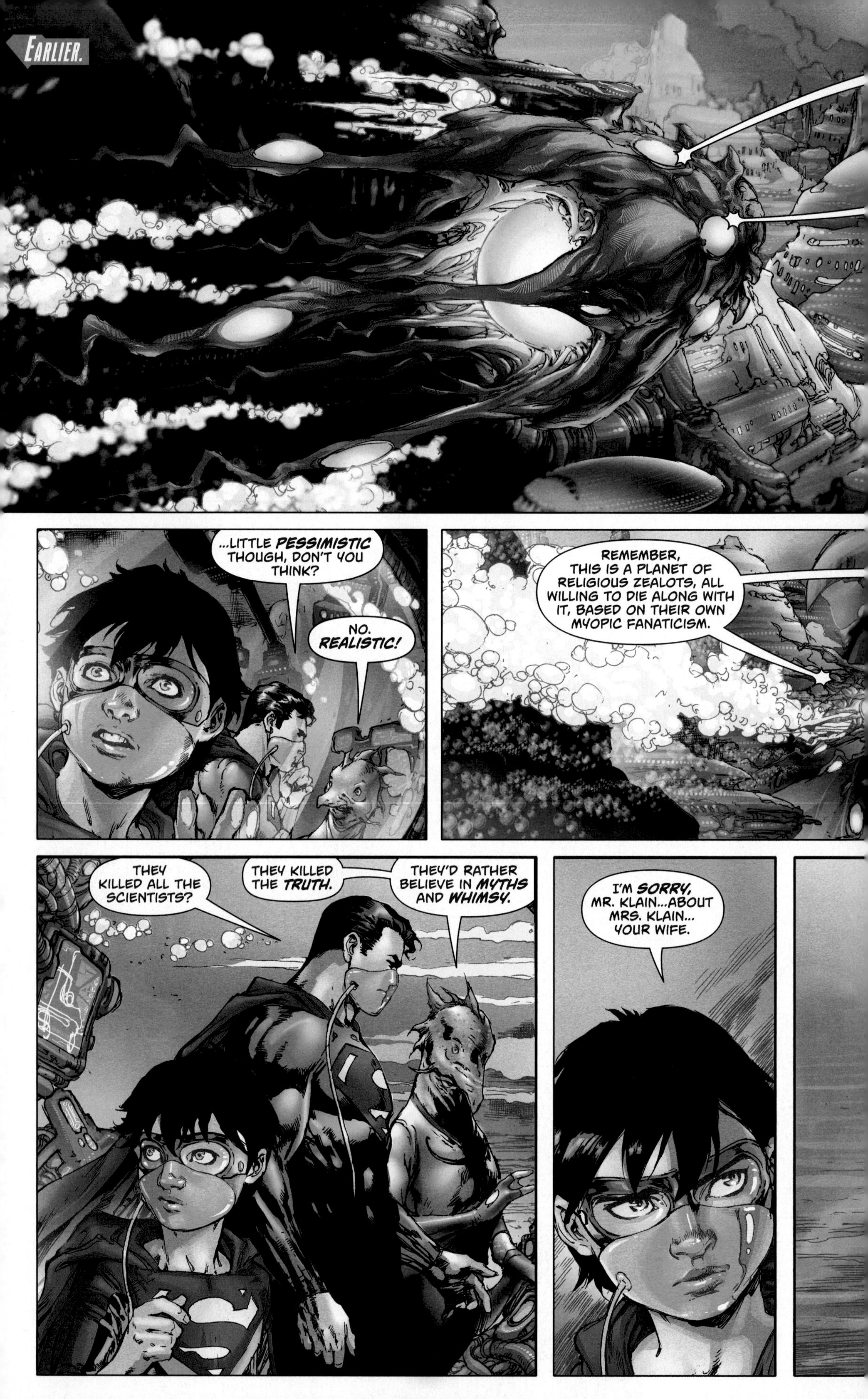
EARLIER.
...LITTLE PESSIMISTIC THOUGH, DON'T YOU THINK?
NO. REALISTIC!
REMEMBER, THIS IS A PLANET OF RELIGIOUS ZEALOTS, ALL WILLING TO DIE ALONG WITH IT, BASED ON THEIR OWN MYOPIC FANATICISM.
THEY KILLED ALL THE SCIENTISTS?
THEY KILLED THE TRUTH.
THEY'D RATHER BELIEVE IN MYTHS AND WHIMSY.
I'M SORRY, MR. KLAIN...ABOUT MRS. KLAIN... YOUR WIFE.

ACTUALLY, YES, KLAIN--IT'S CROSSED MY MIND ONCE OR TWICE.

THEN YOU'LL APPRECIATE THAT I WAS JUST ABOUT TO SAY, "WE'LL BE *SAFE* AT MY HIDDEN LABORATORY UP AHEAD"--

--BUT EVEN AS THE WORDS CAME TO MIND, I REALIZED THE MILITIA OF MY HOMEWORLD, GALYMAYNE, IS NO DOUBT ALREADY *SCOURING* EVERY TRENCH AND REEF ON THE PLANET TO FIND US.

AND THE PLANET'S ABOUT TO *EXPLODE*.

I GET IT-- SAFETY'S RELATIVE. FLEETING...

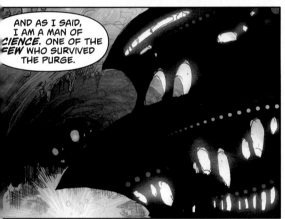

AND AS I SAID, I AM A MAN OF *SCIENCE*. ONE OF THE *FEW* WHO SURVIVED THE PURGE.

MY WIFE... WASN'T SO LUCKY.

THANK YOU, YOUNG MAN. I CAN TELL YOUR FATHER IS A CHAMPION OF GOOD HEART.

YOU HAVE THAT SAME LIGHT IN YOU.

HERE WE ARE.

"HOME."

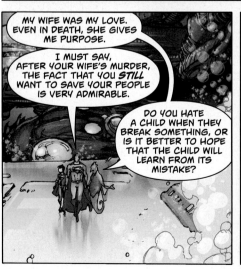

MY WIFE WAS MY LOVE. EVEN IN DEATH, SHE GIVES ME PURPOSE.

I MUST SAY, AFTER YOUR WIFE'S MURDER, THE FACT THAT YOU *STILL* WANT TO SAVE YOUR PEOPLE IS VERY ADMIRABLE.

DO YOU HATE A CHILD WHEN THEY BREAK SOMETHING, OR IS IT BETTER TO HOPE THAT THE CHILD WILL LEARN FROM ITS MISTAKE?

YOU'RE A GOOD MAN, KLAIN.

GOOD? TO *YOU*, PERHAPS.

TO MY PEOPLE, I AM THE EMBODIMENT OF *EVIL*. THEY THINK ME NOT JUST AN UNBELIEVER, BUT ONE WHO WOULD RIP APART THEIR CREDO.

WAIT, EARLIER YOU SAID YOU WANTED TO SAVE THE WORLD. I KNOW SCIENCE ENOUGH TO KNOW THAT ALIEN OR NOT, FROM WHAT I'VE STUDIED OF MY FATHER'S WORK...

...THERE'S *NOTHING* HERE THAT COULD POSSIBLY HELP SAVE THE PLANET.

I *MISSPOKE*. THE PLANET *IS* BEYOND SAVING. TOO FAR *GONE*, TOO *LITTLE* DONE.

IT IS MY *RACE* THAT I WANT TO SURVIVE.

I SEE THE *ROCKET* THERE, BUT UNLESS IT'S A PROTOTYPE, I DON'T SEE HOW YOU CAN SAVE *YOUR PEOPLE*.

YOU NEED A SPACE ARK? I'LL CERTAINLY HELP YOU BUILD IT.

ME, TOO. I'M *STRONG!*

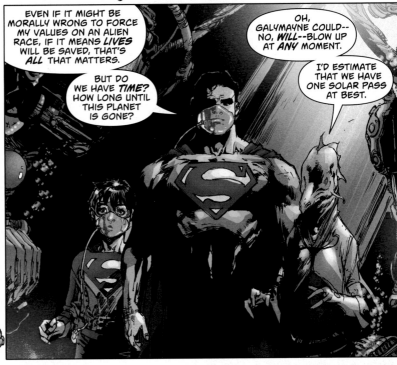

EVEN IF IT MIGHT BE MORALLY WRONG TO FORCE MY VALUES ON AN ALIEN RACE, IF IT MEANS *LIVES* WILL BE SAVED, THAT'S *ALL* THAT MATTERS.

BUT DO WE HAVE *TIME?* HOW LONG UNTIL THIS PLANET IS GONE?

OH, GALYMAYNE COULD-- NO, *WILL*--BLOW UP AT *ANY* MOMENT.

I'D ESTIMATE THAT WE HAVE ONE SOLAR PASS AT BEST.

AS I SAID, NOT ENOUGH HAS BEEN DONE IN THE TIME LEFT.

APART FROM THAT, THE INHABITANTS OF THIS WORLD DON'T *WANT* SALVATION.

AND PERHAPS YOU'RE RIGHT TO SAY YOU SHOULDN'T PUSH DIFFERING VALUES ON THEM.

MY *SPECIES* THOUGH...

...THAT IS A *DIFFERENT* THING.

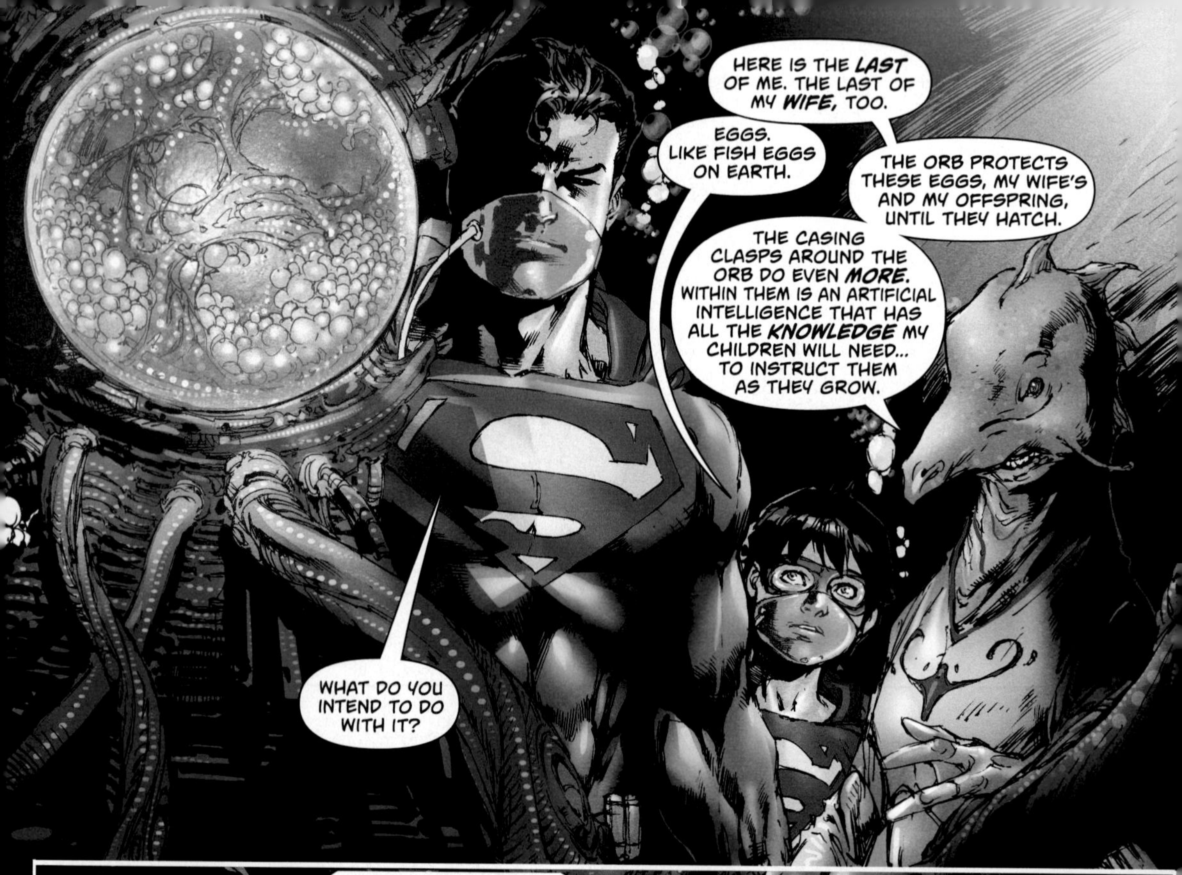
HERE IS THE LAST OF ME. THE LAST OF MY WIFE, TOO.
EGGS. LIKE FISH EGGS ON EARTH.
THE ORB PROTECTS THESE EGGS, MY WIFE'S AND MY OFFSPRING, UNTIL THEY HATCH.
THE CASING CLASPS AROUND THE ORB DO EVEN MORE. WITHIN THEM IS AN ARTIFICIAL INTELLIGENCE THAT HAS ALL THE KNOWLEDGE MY CHILDREN WILL NEED... TO INSTRUCT THEM AS THEY GROW.
WHAT DO YOU INTEND TO DO WITH IT?
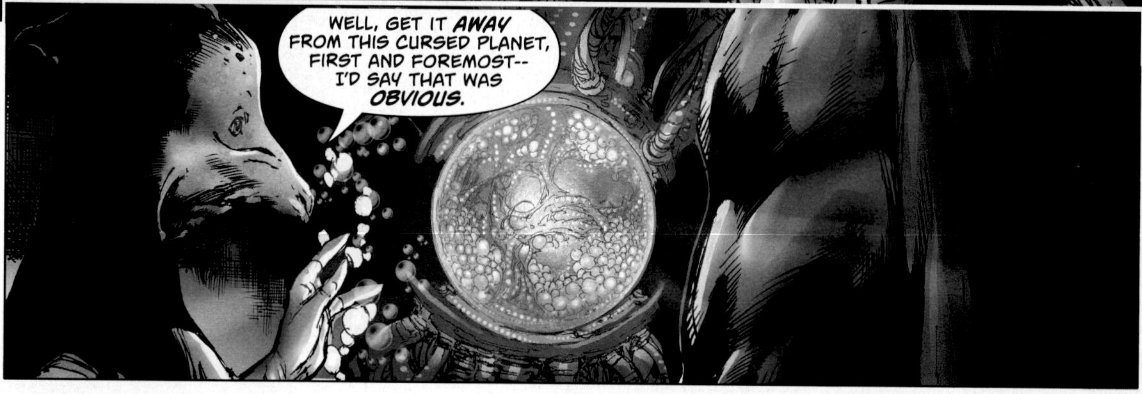
WELL, GET IT AWAY FROM THIS CURSED PLANET, FIRST AND FOREMOST-- I'D SAY THAT WAS OBVIOUS.
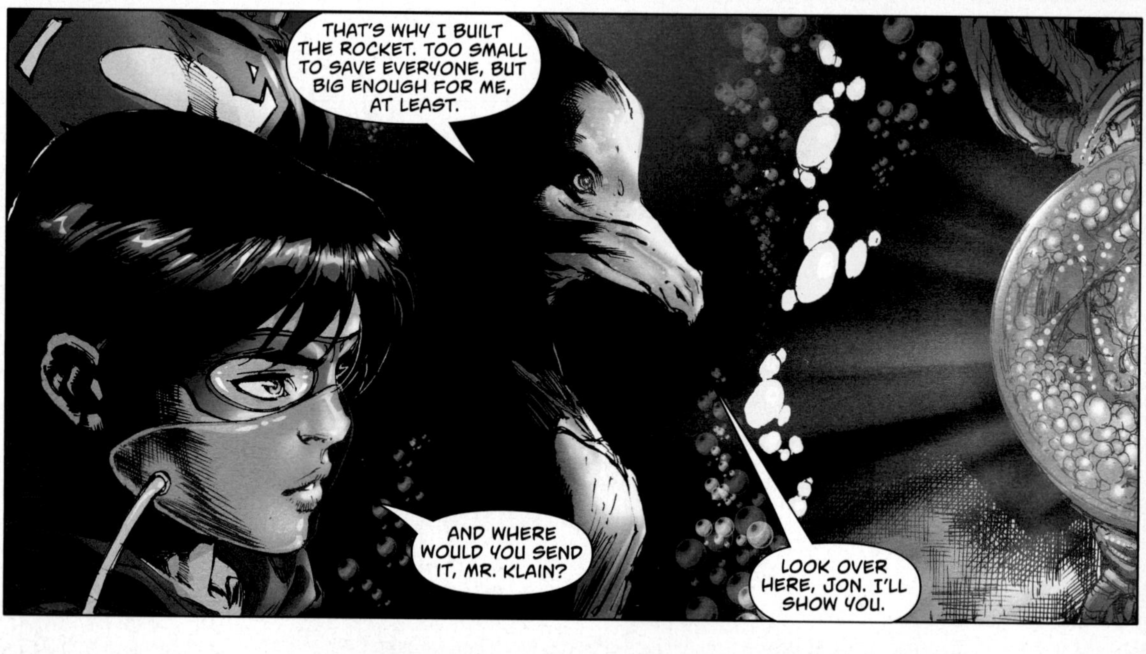
THAT'S WHY I BUILT THE ROCKET. TOO SMALL TO SAVE EVERYONE, BUT BIG ENOUGH FOR ME, AT LEAST.
AND WHERE WOULD YOU SEND IT, MR. KLAIN?
LOOK OVER HERE, JON. I'LL SHOW YOU.

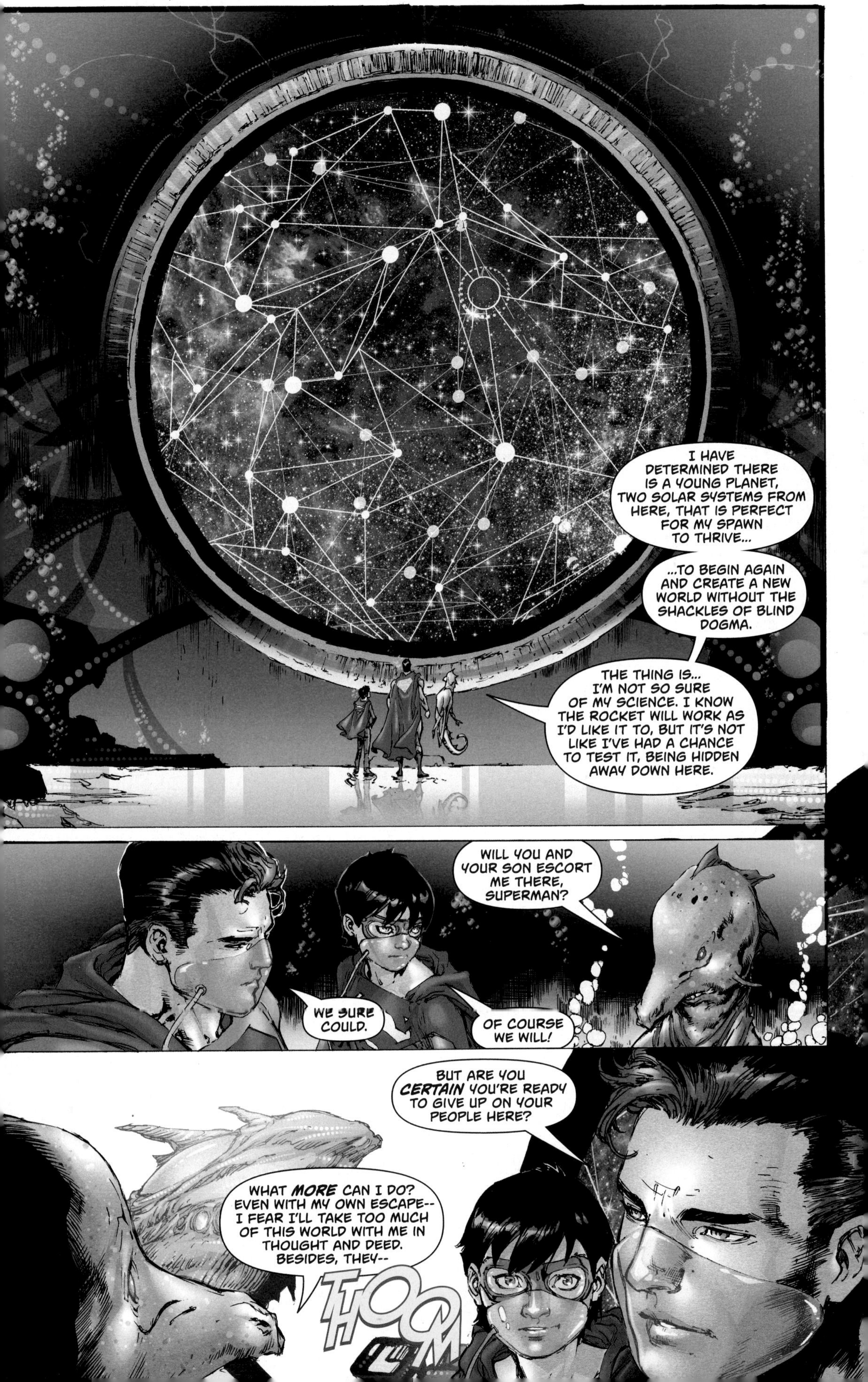
I HAVE DETERMINED THERE IS A YOUNG PLANET, TWO SOLAR SYSTEMS FROM HERE, THAT IS PERFECT FOR MY SPAWN TO THRIVE...
...TO BEGIN AGAIN AND CREATE A NEW WORLD WITHOUT THE SHACKLES OF BLIND DOGMA.
THE THING IS... I'M NOT SO SURE OF MY SCIENCE. I KNOW THE ROCKET WILL WORK AS I'D LIKE IT TO, BUT IT'S NOT LIKE I'VE HAD A CHANCE TO TEST IT, BEING HIDDEN AWAY DOWN HERE.
WILL YOU AND YOUR SON ESCORT ME THERE, SUPERMAN?
WE SURE COULD.
OF COURSE WE WILL!
BUT ARE YOU *CERTAIN* YOU'RE READY TO GIVE UP ON YOUR PEOPLE HERE?
WHAT *MORE* CAN I DO? EVEN WITH MY OWN ESCAPE-- I FEAR I'LL TAKE TOO MUCH OF THIS WORLD WITH ME IN THOUGHT AND DEED. BESIDES, THEY--
THOOOM

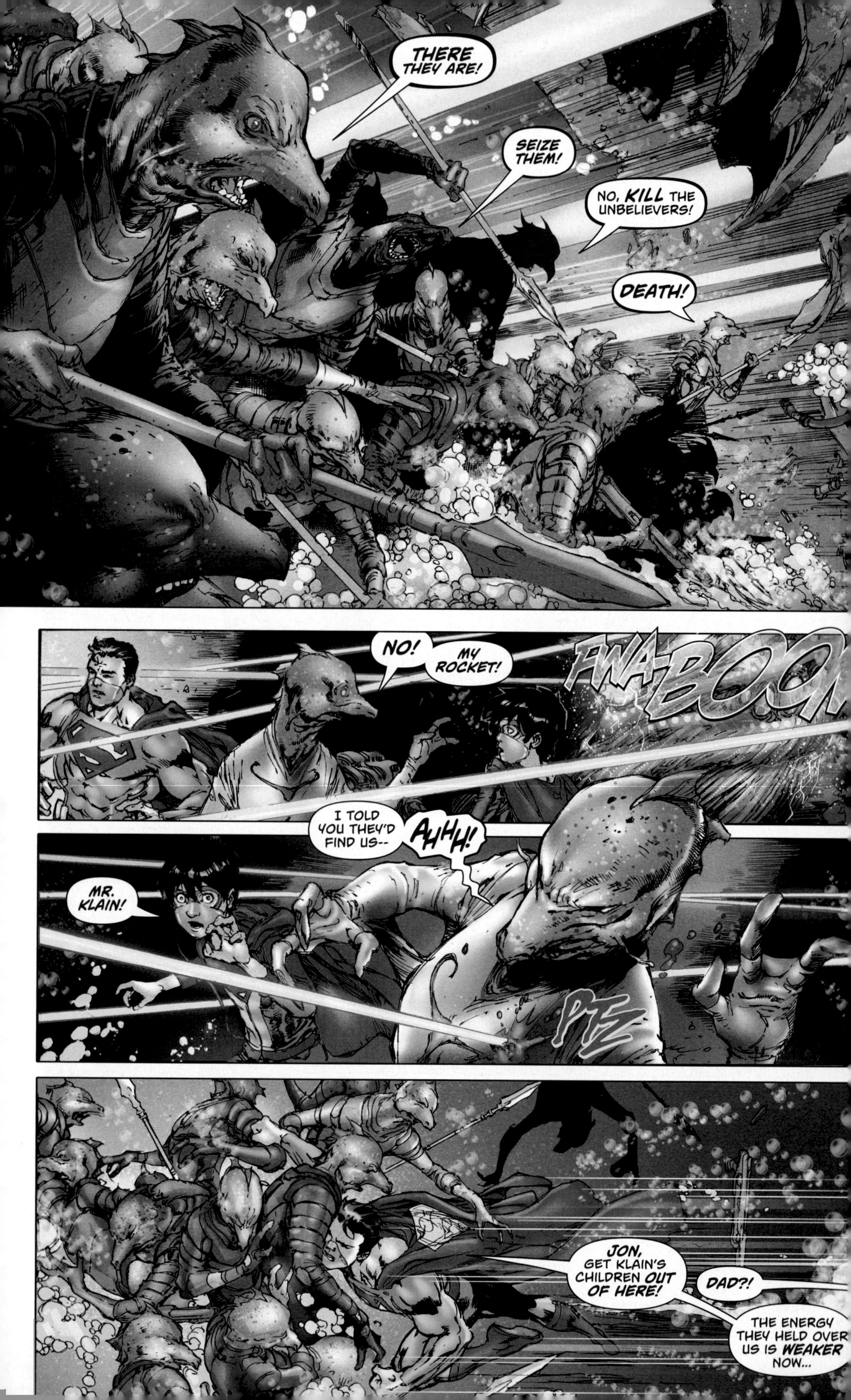
THERE THEY ARE!
SEIZE THEM!
NO, KILL THE UNBELIEVERS!
DEATH!
NO!
MY ROCKET!
FWA-BOOM
I TOLD YOU THEY'D FIND US--
AHHH!
MR. KLAIN!
PTZ
JON, GET KLAIN'S CHILDREN OUT OF HERE!
DAD?!
THE ENERGY THEY HELD OVER US IS WEAKER NOW...

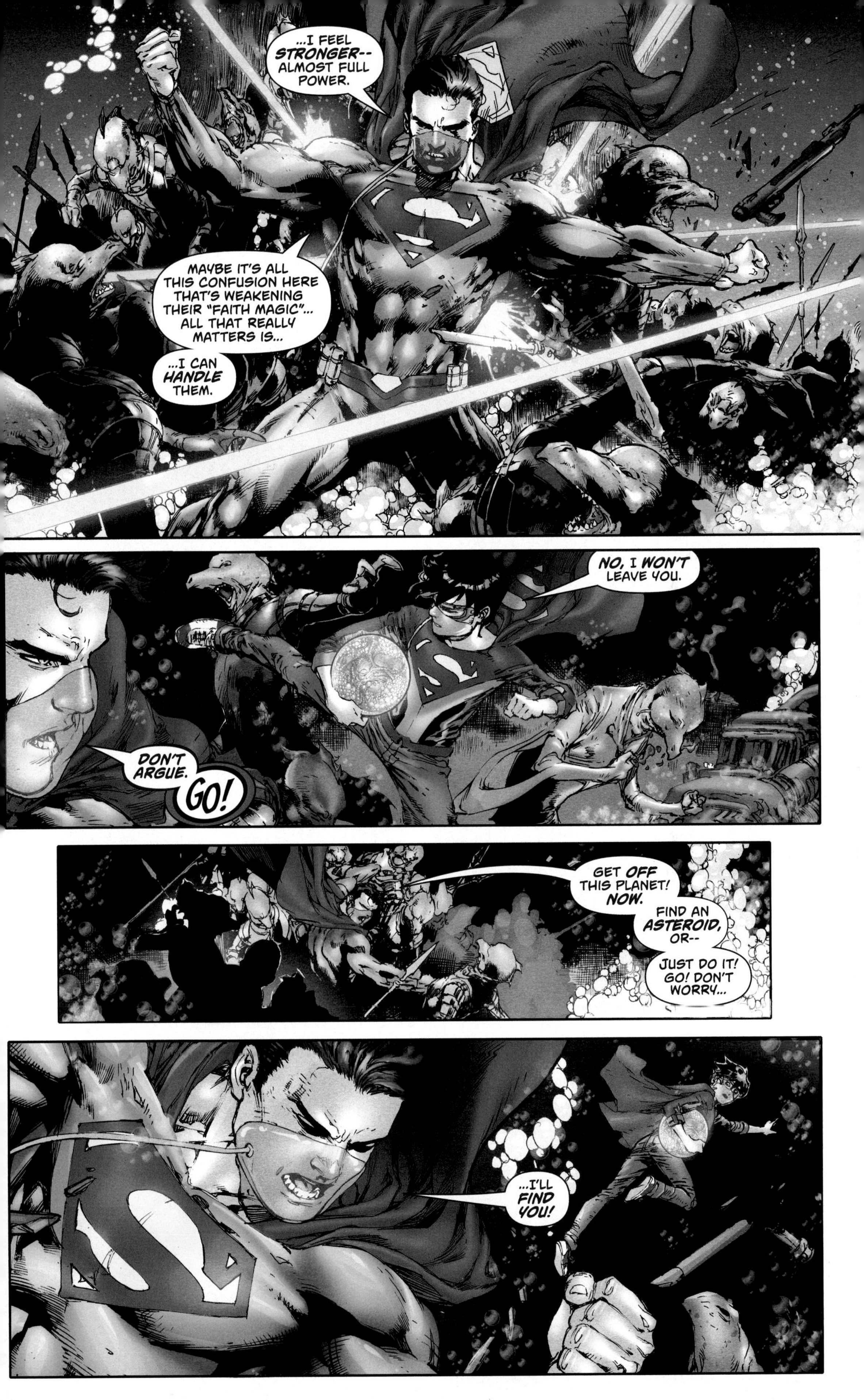
...I FEEL STRONGER-- ALMOST FULL POWER.
MAYBE IT'S ALL THIS CONFUSION HERE THAT'S WEAKENING THEIR "FAITH MAGIC"... ALL THAT REALLY MATTERS IS...
...I CAN HANDLE THEM.
NO, I WON'T LEAVE YOU.
DON'T ARGUE.
GO!
GET OFF THIS PLANET! NOW.
FIND AN ASTEROID, OR--
JUST DO IT! GO! DON'T WORRY...
...I'LL FIND YOU!

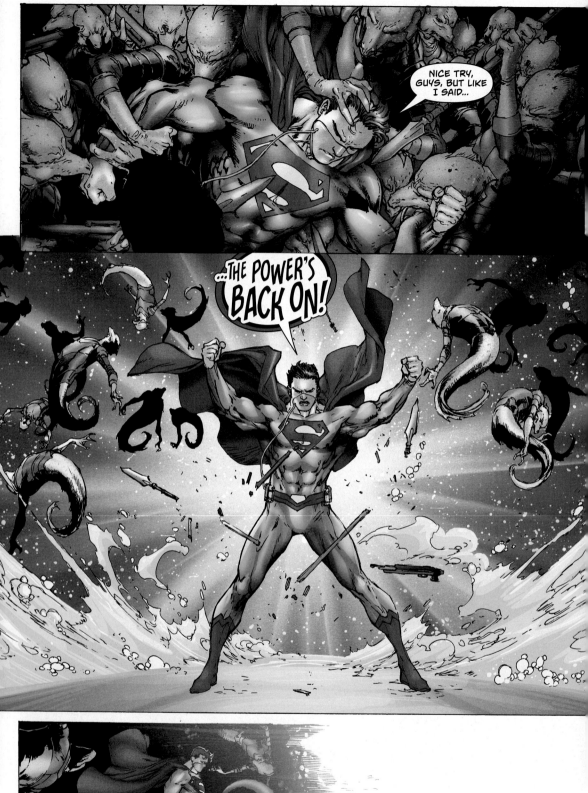

NICE TRY, GUYS, BUT LIKE I SAID...

...THE POWER'S BACK ON!

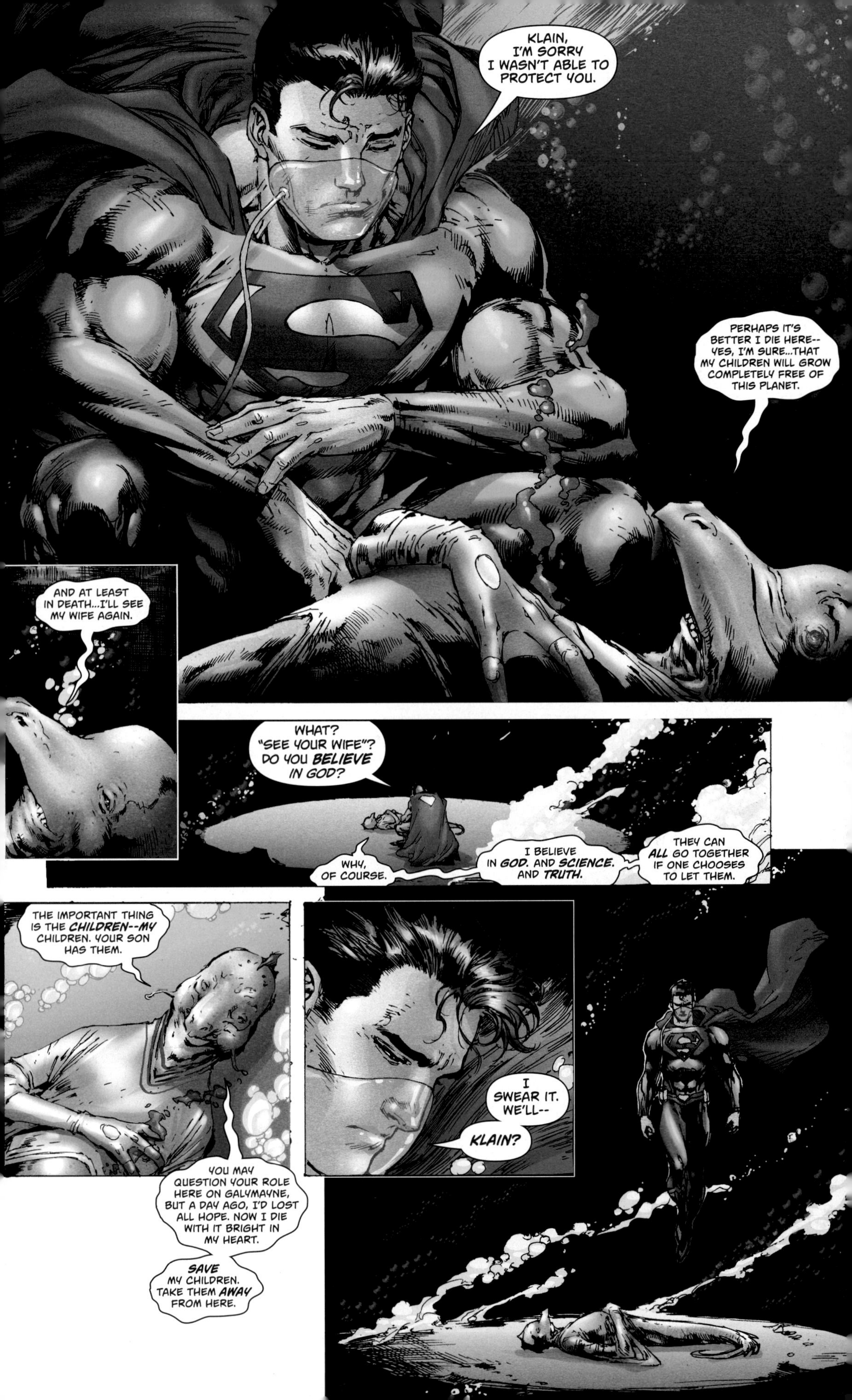
KLAIN, I'M SORRY I WASN'T ABLE TO PROTECT YOU.
PERHAPS IT'S BETTER I DIE HERE-- YES, I'M SURE...THAT MY CHILDREN WILL GROW COMPLETELY FREE OF THIS PLANET.
AND AT LEAST IN DEATH...I'LL SEE MY WIFE AGAIN.
WHAT? "SEE YOUR WIFE"? DO YOU BELIEVE IN GOD?
WHY, OF COURSE.
I BELIEVE IN GOD. AND SCIENCE. AND TRUTH.
THEY CAN ALL GO TOGETHER IF ONE CHOOSES TO LET THEM.
THE IMPORTANT THING IS THE CHILDREN--MY CHILDREN. YOUR SON HAS THEM.
YOU MAY QUESTION YOUR ROLE HERE ON GALYMAYNE, BUT A DAY AGO, I'D LOST ALL HOPE. NOW I DIE WITH IT BRIGHT IN MY HEART.
SAVE MY CHILDREN. TAKE THEM AWAY FROM HERE.
I SWEAR IT. WE'LL--
KLAIN?

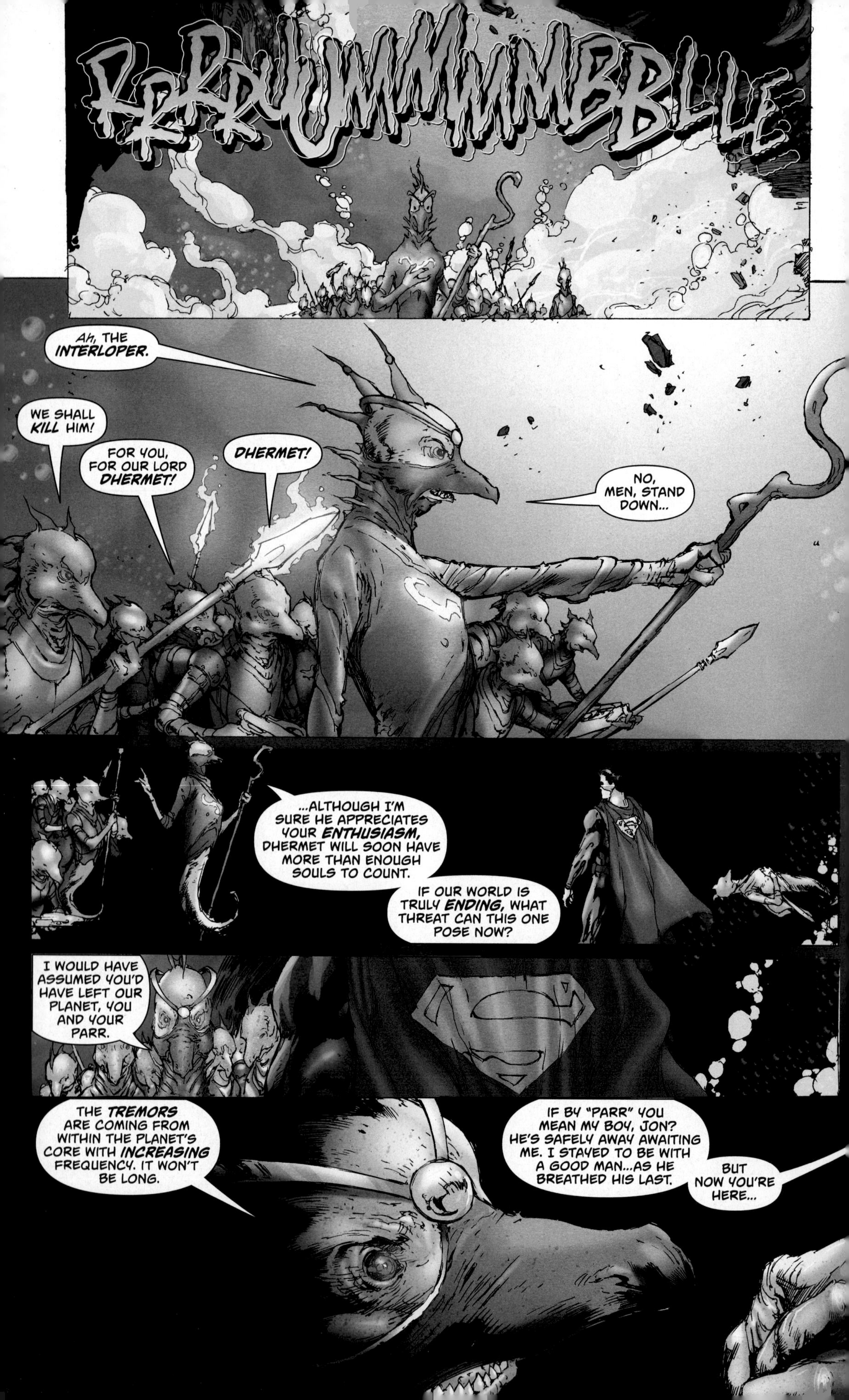
RRRUMMMMMBBLLE
AH, THE INTERLOPER.
WE SHALL KILL HIM!
FOR YOU, FOR OUR LORD DHERMET!
DHERMET!
NO, MEN, STAND DOWN...
...ALTHOUGH I'M SURE HE APPRECIATES YOUR ENTHUSIASM, DHERMET WILL SOON HAVE MORE THAN ENOUGH SOULS TO COUNT.
IF OUR WORLD IS TRULY ENDING, WHAT THREAT CAN THIS ONE POSE NOW?
I WOULD HAVE ASSUMED YOU'D HAVE LEFT OUR PLANET, YOU AND YOUR PARR.
THE TREMORS ARE COMING FROM WITHIN THE PLANET'S CORE WITH INCREASING FREQUENCY. IT WON'T BE LONG.
IF BY "PARR" YOU MEAN MY BOY, JON? HE'S SAFELY AWAY AWAITING ME. I STAYED TO BE WITH A GOOD MAN...AS HE BREATHED HIS LAST.
BUT NOW YOU'RE HERE...

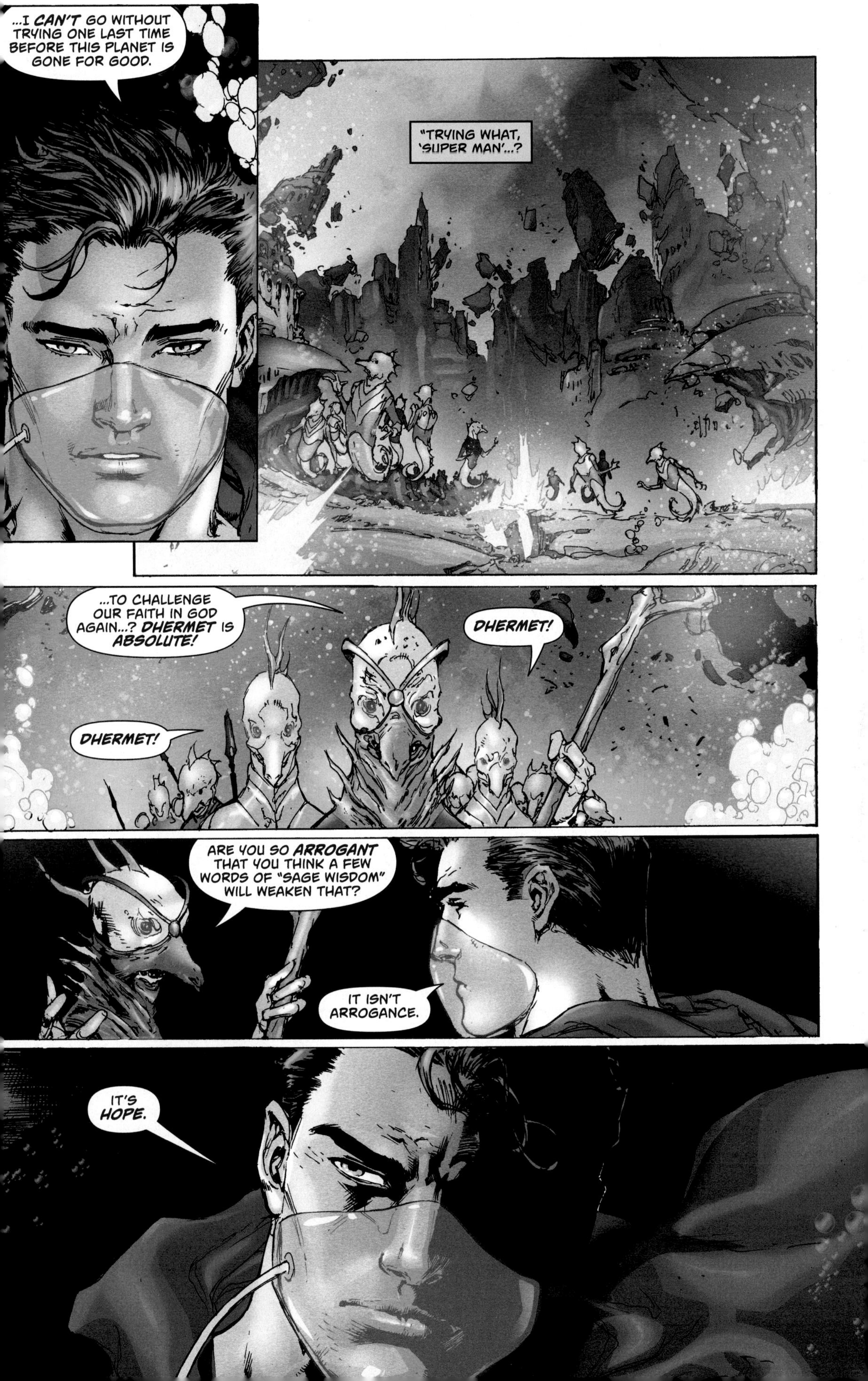
...I CAN'T GO WITHOUT TRYING ONE LAST TIME BEFORE THIS PLANET IS GONE FOR GOOD.
"TRYING WHAT, 'SUPER MAN'...?
...TO CHALLENGE OUR FAITH IN GOD AGAIN...? DHERMET IS ABSOLUTE!
DHERMET!
DHERMET!
ARE YOU SO ARROGANT THAT YOU THINK A FEW WORDS OF "SAGE WISDOM" WILL WEAKEN THAT?
IT ISN'T ARROGANCE.
IT'S HOPE.

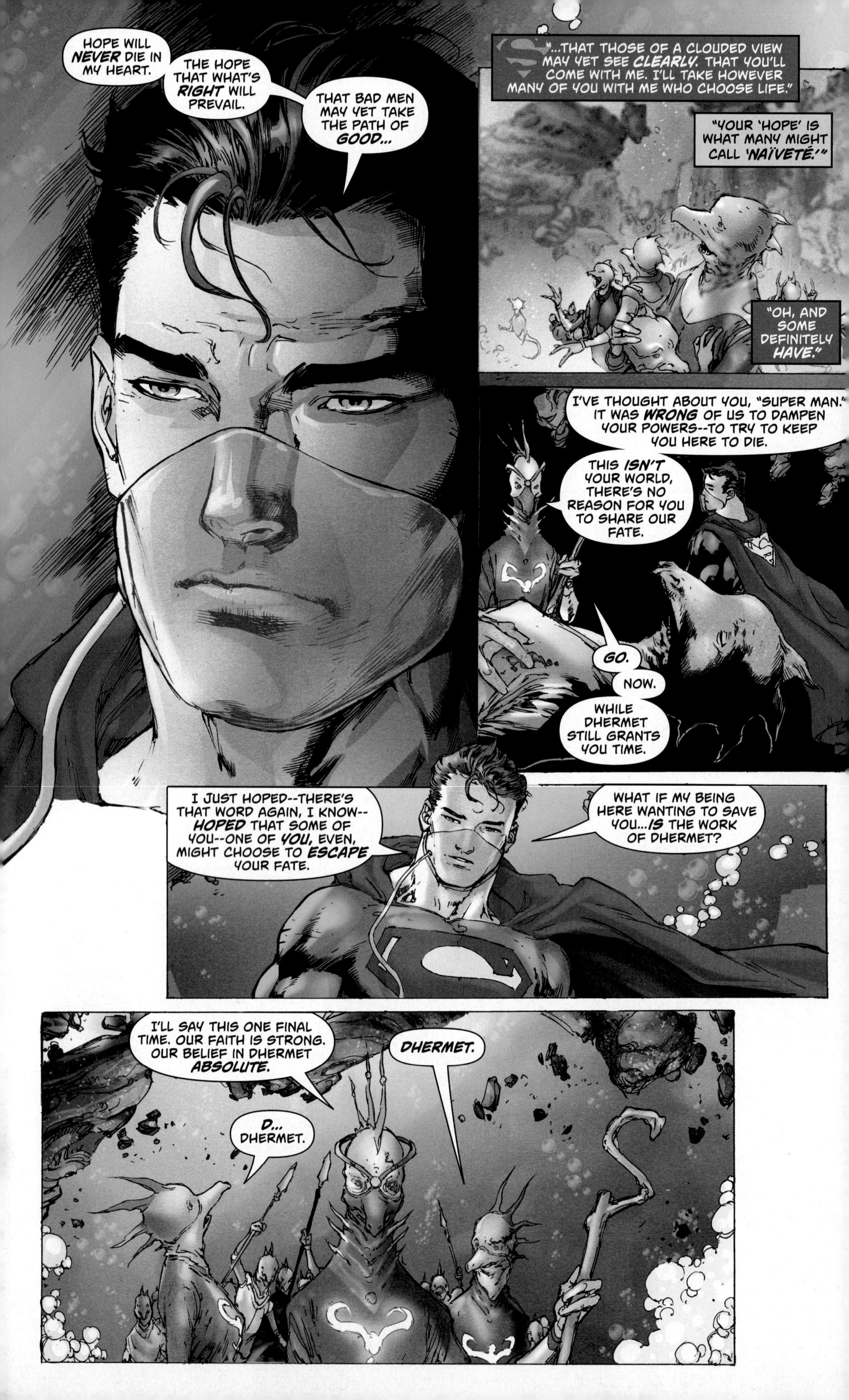
HOPE WILL NEVER DIE IN MY HEART.
THE HOPE THAT WHAT'S RIGHT WILL PREVAIL.
THAT BAD MEN MAY YET TAKE THE PATH OF GOOD...
"...THAT THOSE OF A CLOUDED VIEW MAY YET SEE CLEARLY. THAT YOU'LL COME WITH ME. I'LL TAKE HOWEVER MANY OF YOU WITH ME WHO CHOOSE LIFE."
"YOUR 'HOPE' IS WHAT MANY MIGHT CALL 'NAÏVETÉ.'"
"OH, AND SOME DEFINITELY HAVE."
I'VE THOUGHT ABOUT YOU, "SUPER MAN." IT WAS WRONG OF US TO DAMPEN YOUR POWERS--TO TRY TO KEEP YOU HERE TO DIE.
THIS ISN'T YOUR WORLD, THERE'S NO REASON FOR YOU TO SHARE OUR FATE.
GO.
NOW.
WHILE DHERMET STILL GRANTS YOU TIME.
I JUST HOPED--THERE'S THAT WORD AGAIN, I KNOW--HOPED THAT SOME OF YOU--ONE OF YOU, EVEN, MIGHT CHOOSE TO ESCAPE YOUR FATE.
WHAT IF MY BEING HERE WANTING TO SAVE YOU...IS THE WORK OF DHERMET?
I'LL SAY THIS ONE FINAL TIME. OUR FAITH IS STRONG. OUR BELIEF IN DHERMET ABSOLUTE.
DHERMET.
D... DHERMET.

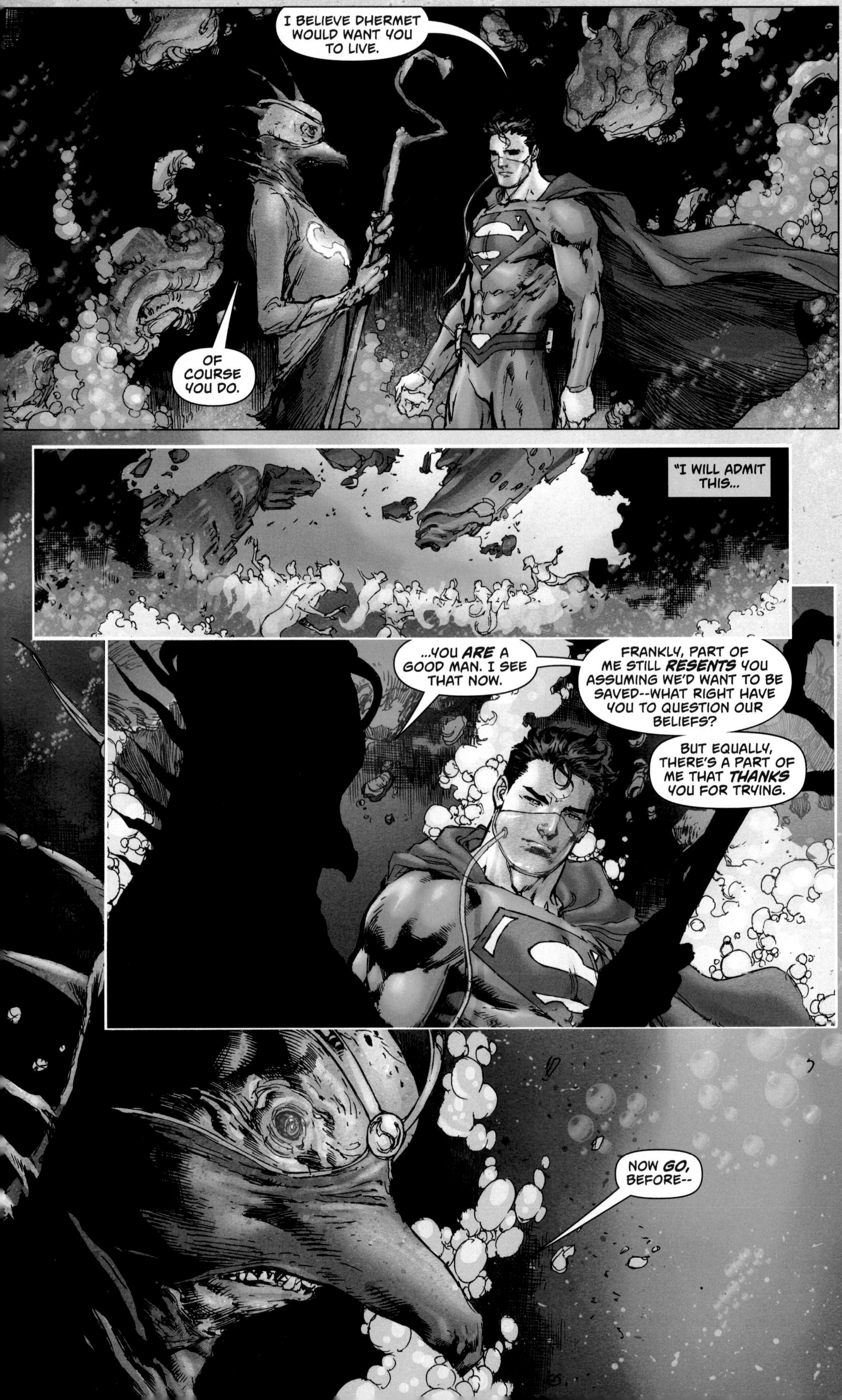
I BELIEVE DHERMET WOULD WANT YOU TO LIVE.
OF COURSE YOU DO.
"I WILL ADMIT THIS...
...YOU ARE A GOOD MAN. I SEE THAT NOW.
FRANKLY, PART OF ME STILL RESENTS YOU ASSUMING WE'D WANT TO BE SAVED--WHAT RIGHT HAVE YOU TO QUESTION OUR BELIEFS?
BUT EQUALLY, THERE'S A PART OF ME THAT THANKS YOU FOR TRYING.
NOW GO, BEFORE--

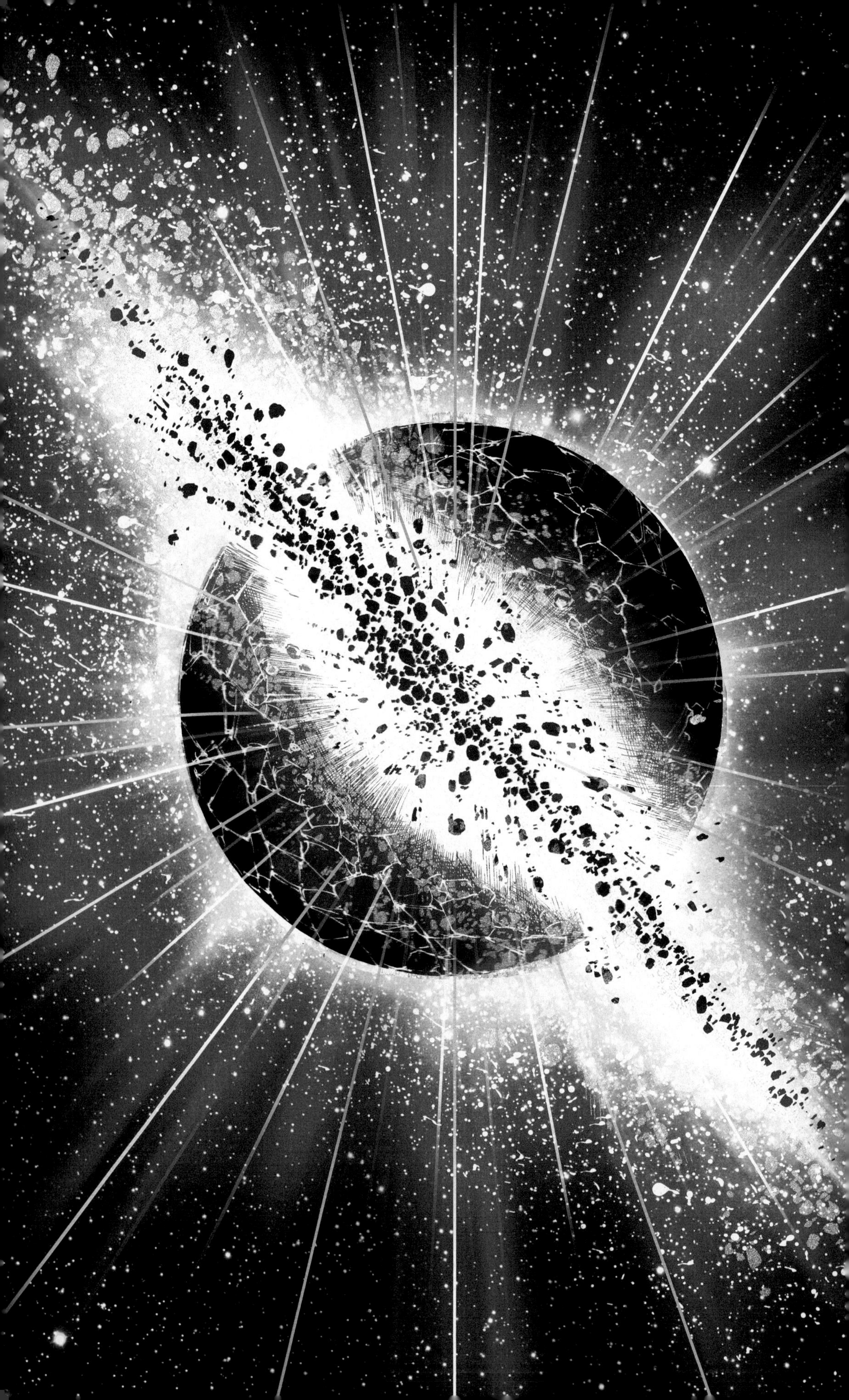

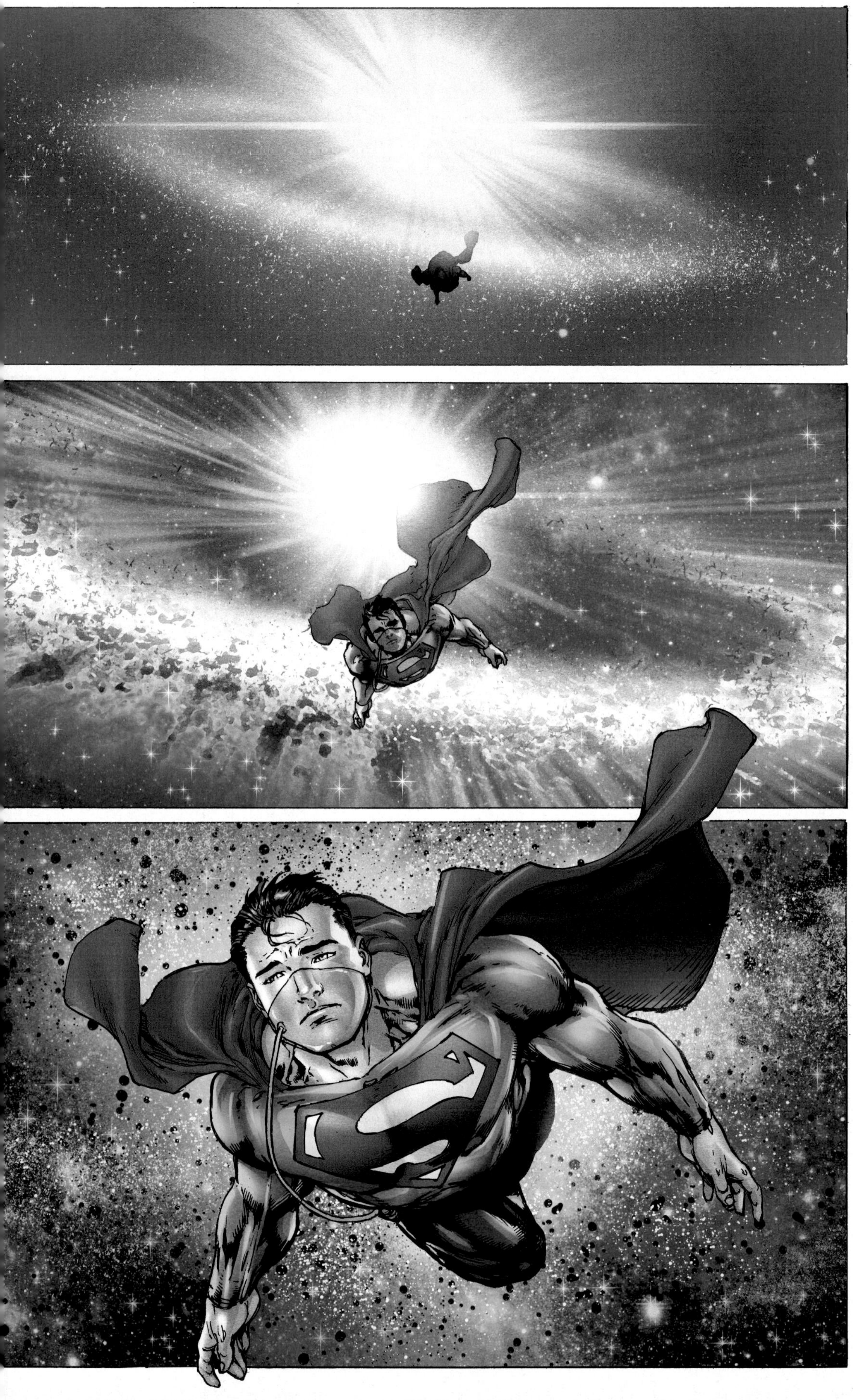

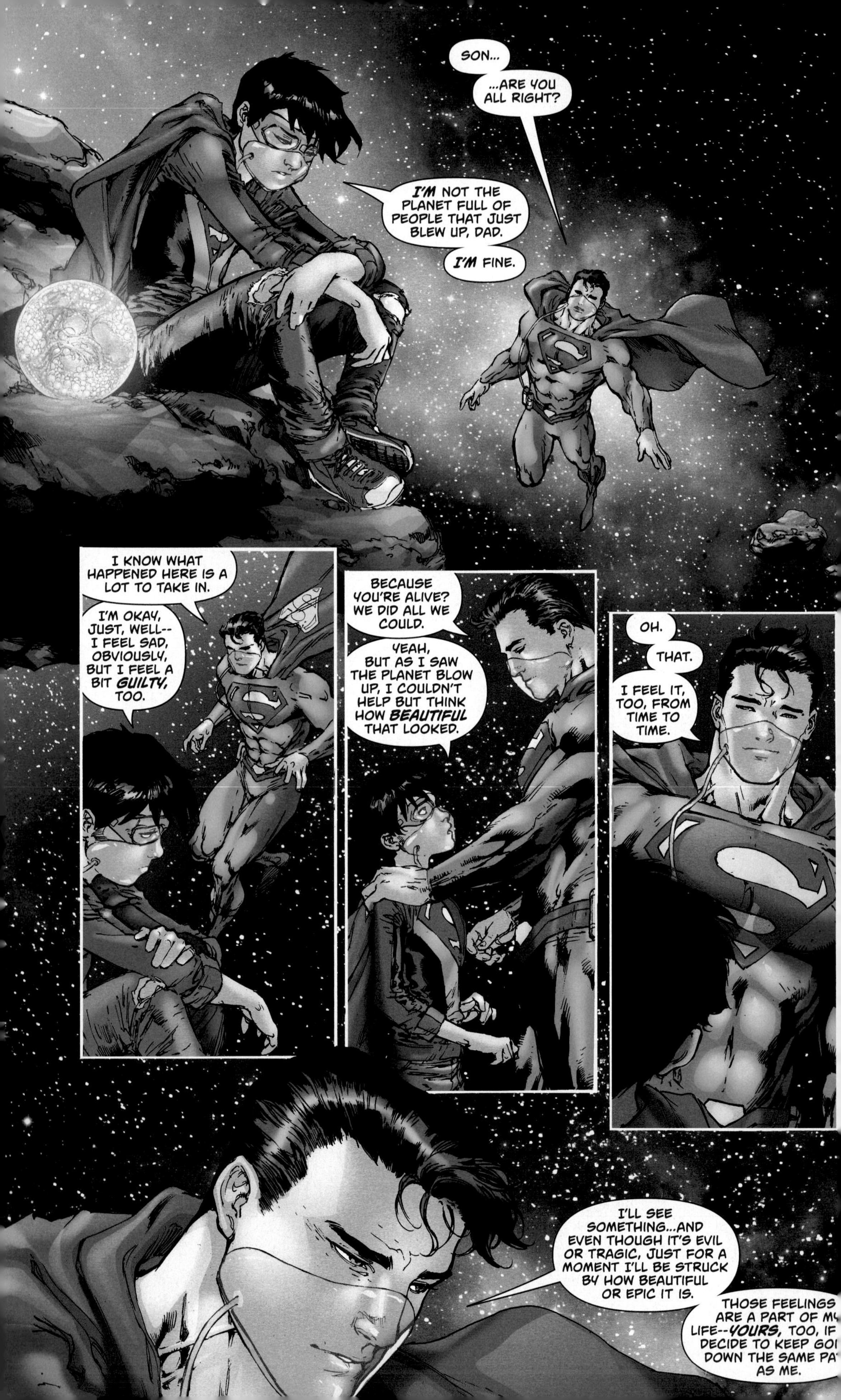
SON...
...ARE YOU ALL RIGHT?
I'M NOT THE PLANET FULL OF PEOPLE THAT JUST BLEW UP, DAD.
I'M FINE.
I KNOW WHAT HAPPENED HERE IS A LOT TO TAKE IN.
I'M OKAY, JUST, WELL-- I FEEL SAD, OBVIOUSLY, BUT I FEEL A BIT GUILTY, TOO.
BECAUSE YOU'RE ALIVE? WE DID ALL WE COULD.
YEAH, BUT AS I SAW THE PLANET BLOW UP, I COULDN'T HELP BUT THINK HOW BEAUTIFUL THAT LOOKED.
OH.
THAT.
I FEEL IT, TOO, FROM TIME TO TIME.
I'LL SEE SOMETHING...AND EVEN THOUGH IT'S EVIL OR TRAGIC, JUST FOR A MOMENT I'LL BE STRUCK BY HOW BEAUTIFUL OR EPIC IT IS.
THOSE FEELINGS ARE A PART OF MY LIFE--YOURS, TOO, IF DECIDE TO KEEP GOI DOWN THE SAME PA AS ME.

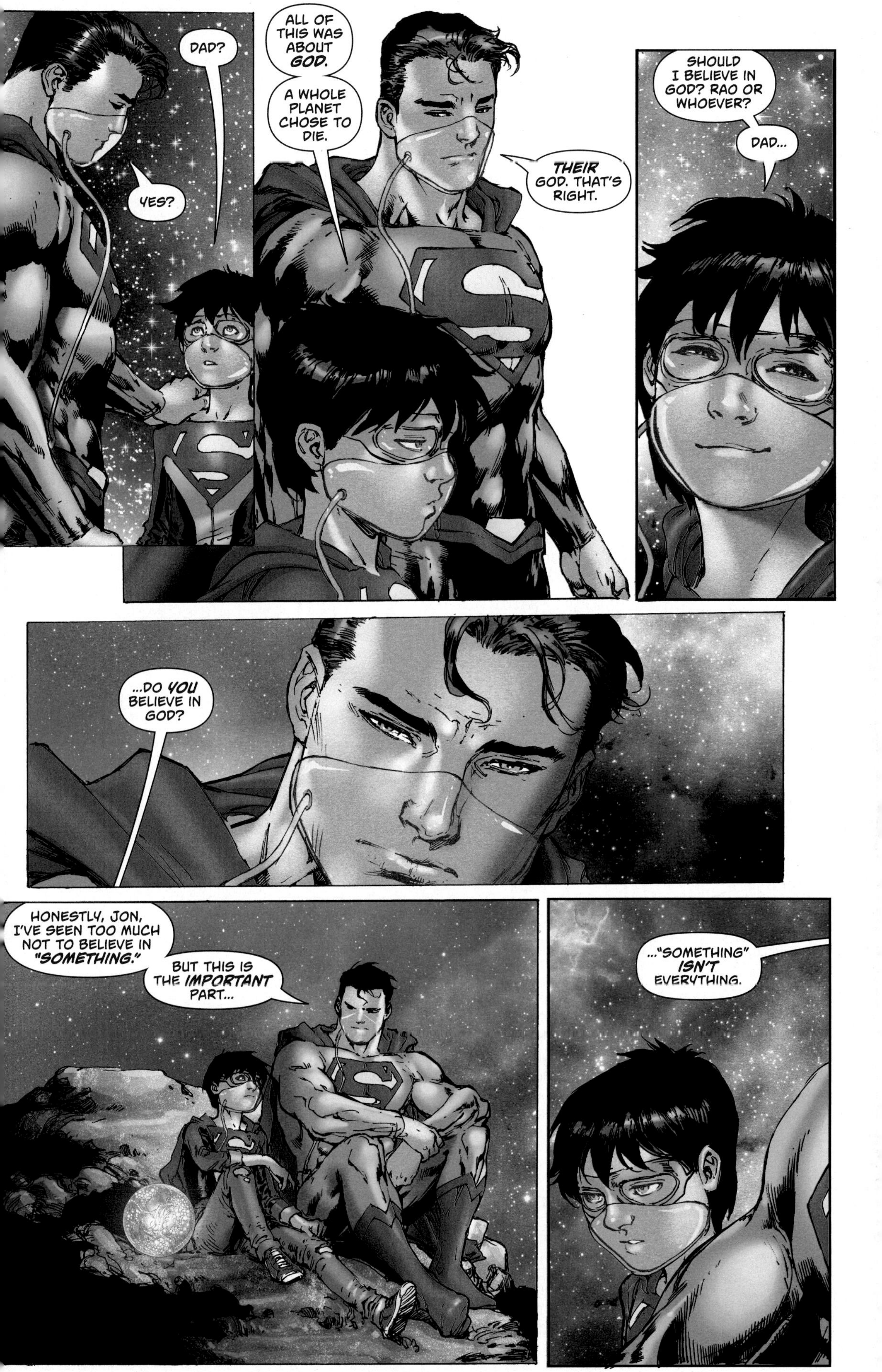
DAD?
YES?
ALL OF THIS WAS ABOUT GOD.
A WHOLE PLANET CHOSE TO DIE.
THEIR GOD. THAT'S RIGHT.
SHOULD I BELIEVE IN GOD? RAO OR WHOEVER?
DAD...
...DO YOU BELIEVE IN GOD?
HONESTLY, JON, I'VE SEEN TOO MUCH NOT TO BELIEVE IN "SOMETHING."
BUT THIS IS THE IMPORTANT PART...
..."SOMETHING" ISN'T EVERYTHING.

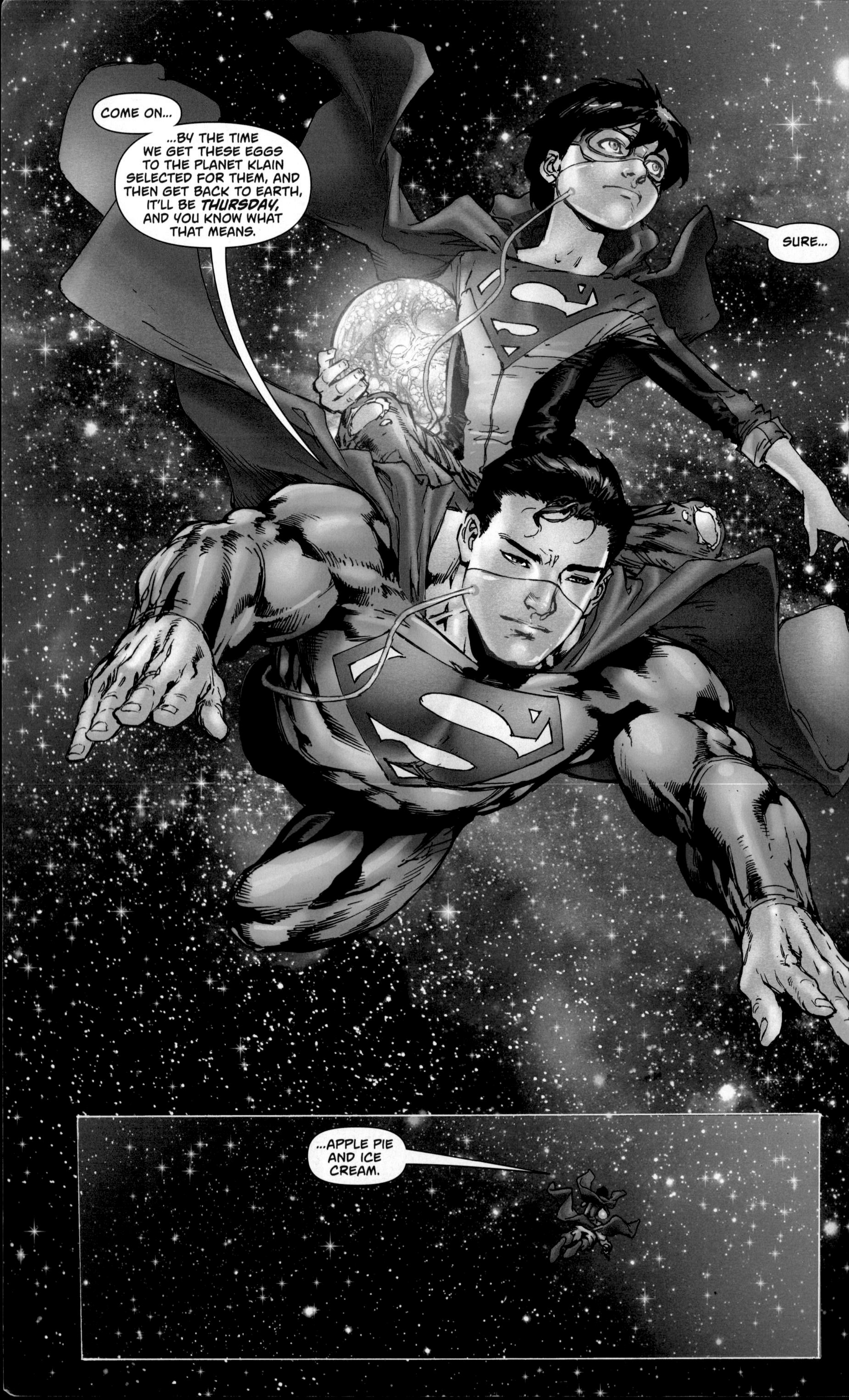
COME ON...
...BY THE TIME WE GET THESE EGGS TO THE PLANET KLAIN SELECTED FOR THEM, AND THEN GET BACK TO EARTH, IT'LL BE *THURSDAY,* AND YOU KNOW WHAT THAT MEANS.
SURE...
...APPLE PIE AND ICE CREAM.

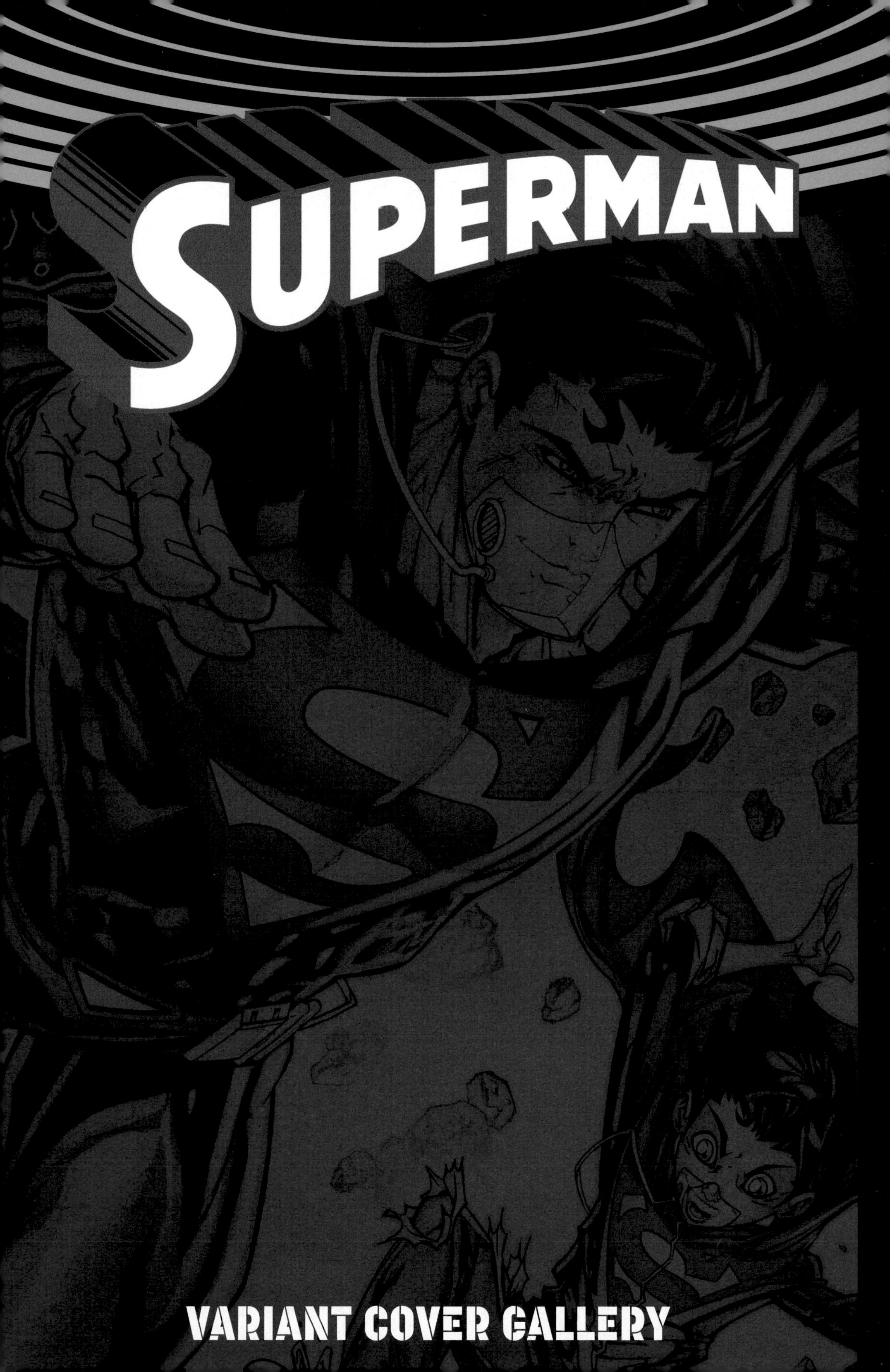
SUPERMAN
VARIANT COVER GALLERY

SUPERMAN #33 variant cover by JONBOY MEYERS

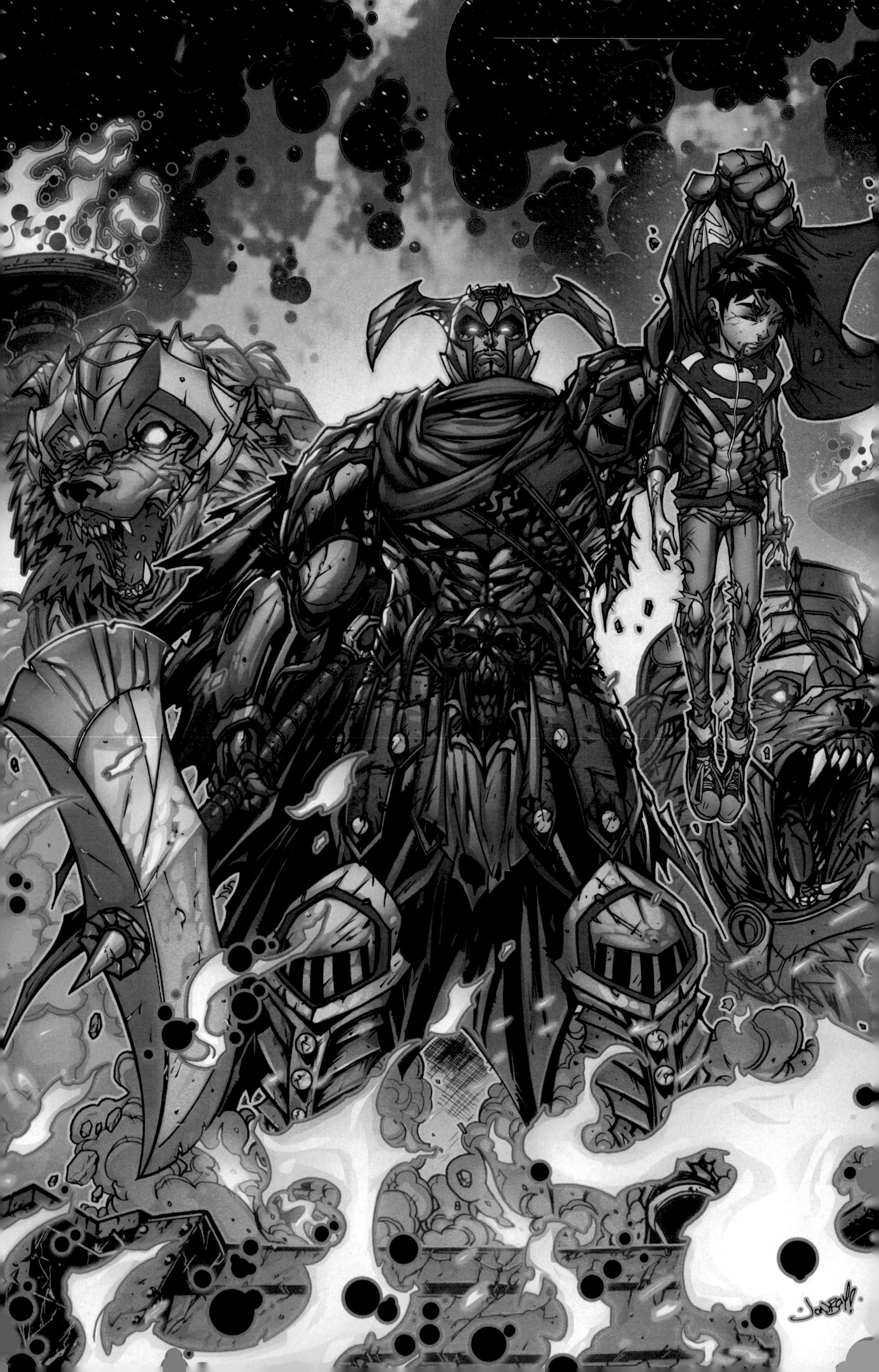
JONBOY!

SUPERMAN #34 variant cover by TONY S. DANIEL & TOMEU MOREY

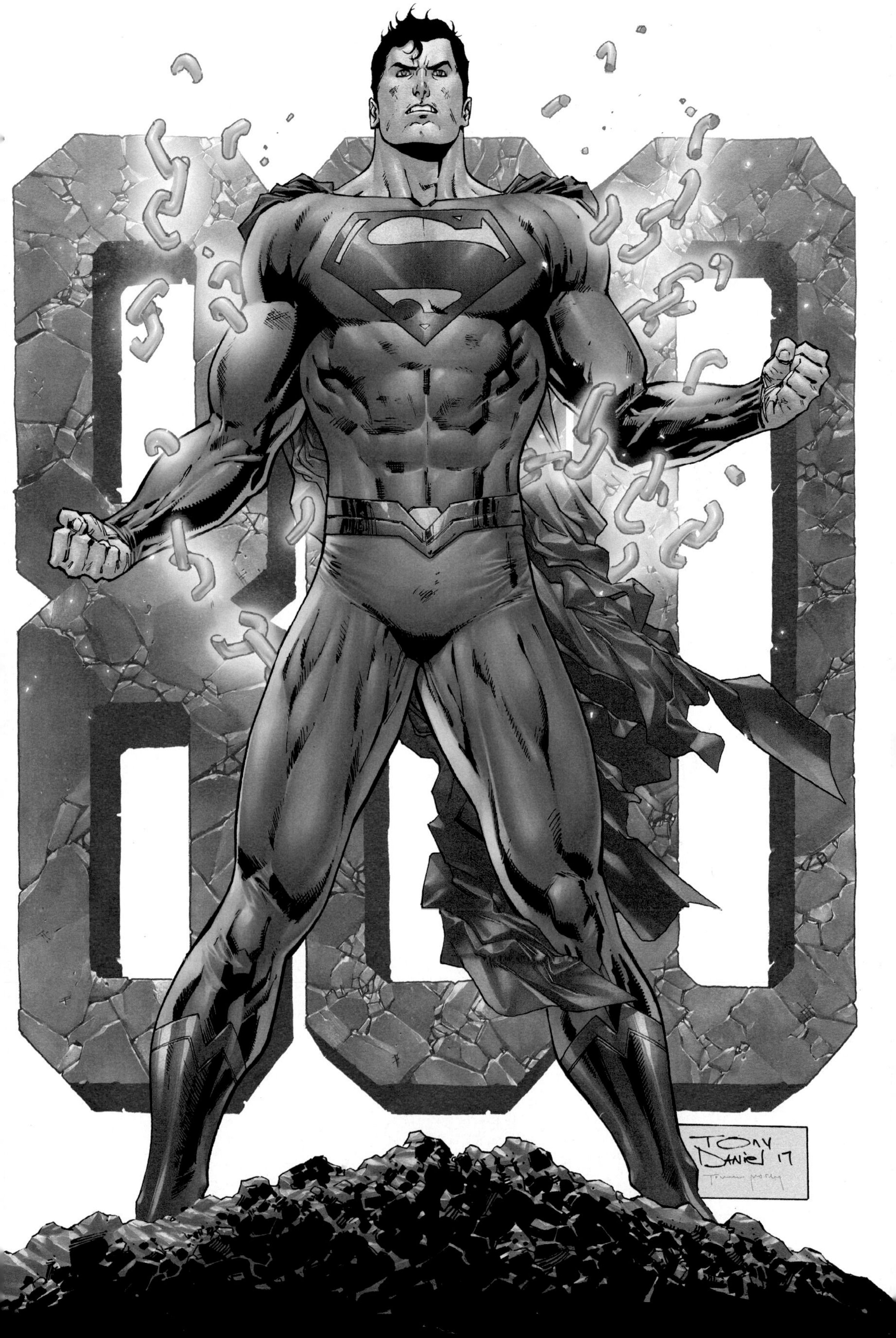
TONY DANIEL 17

SUPERMAN #35 variant cover by RENATO GUEDES

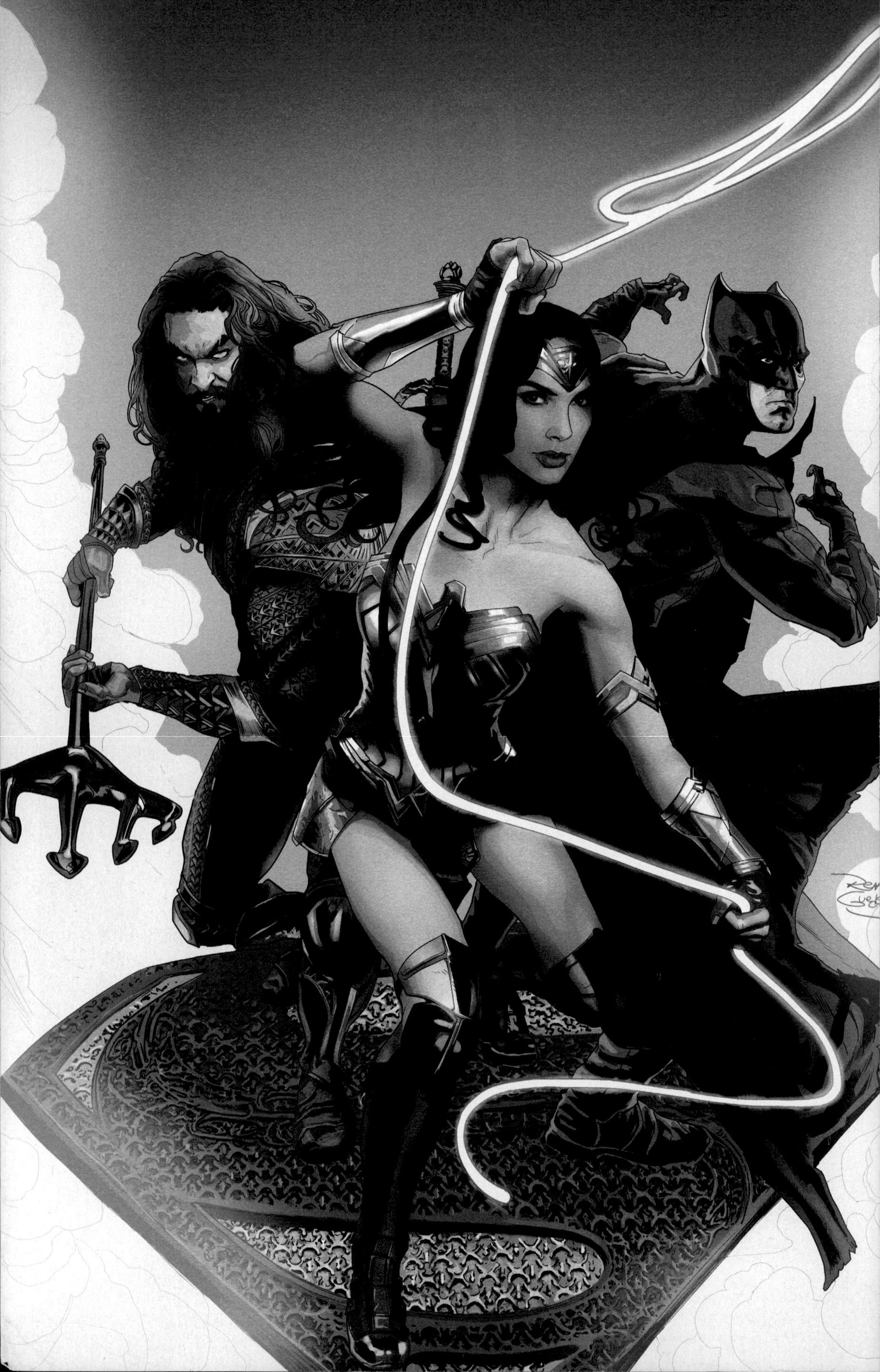

SUPERMAN #36 variant cover by JONBOY MEYERS

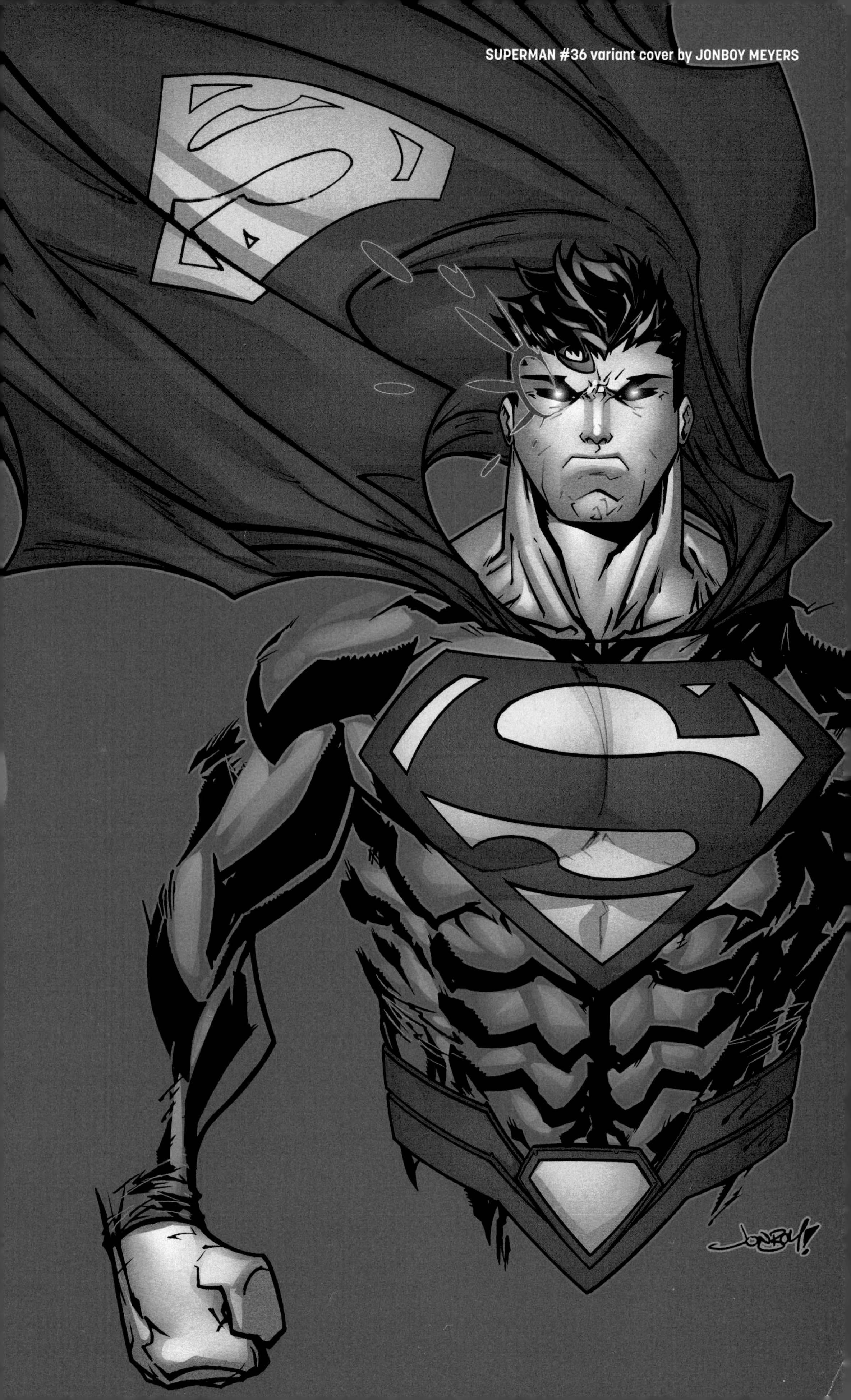
JONBOY!

SUPERMAN #39 variant cover by JONBOY MEYERS

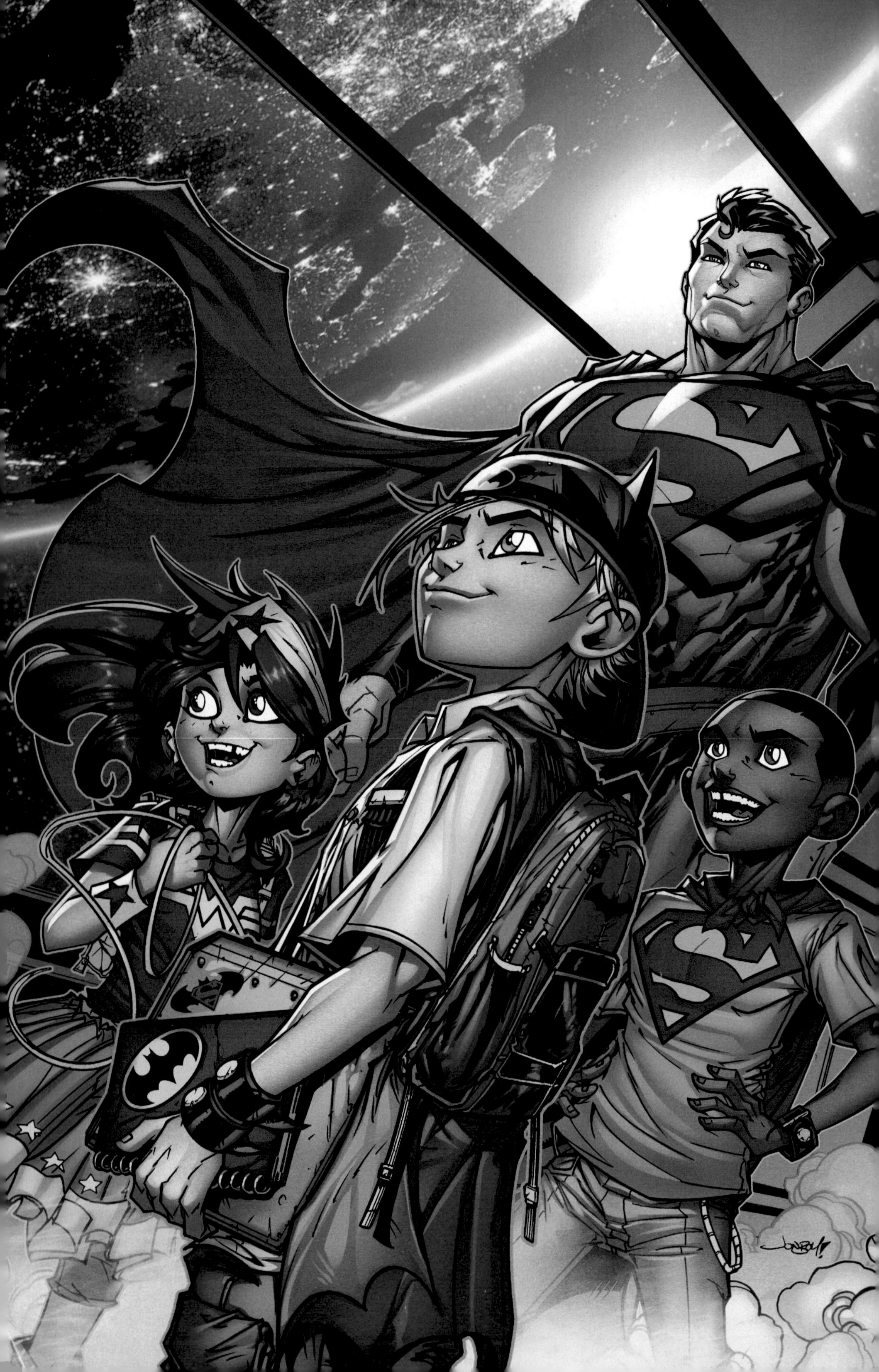
JONBOY!

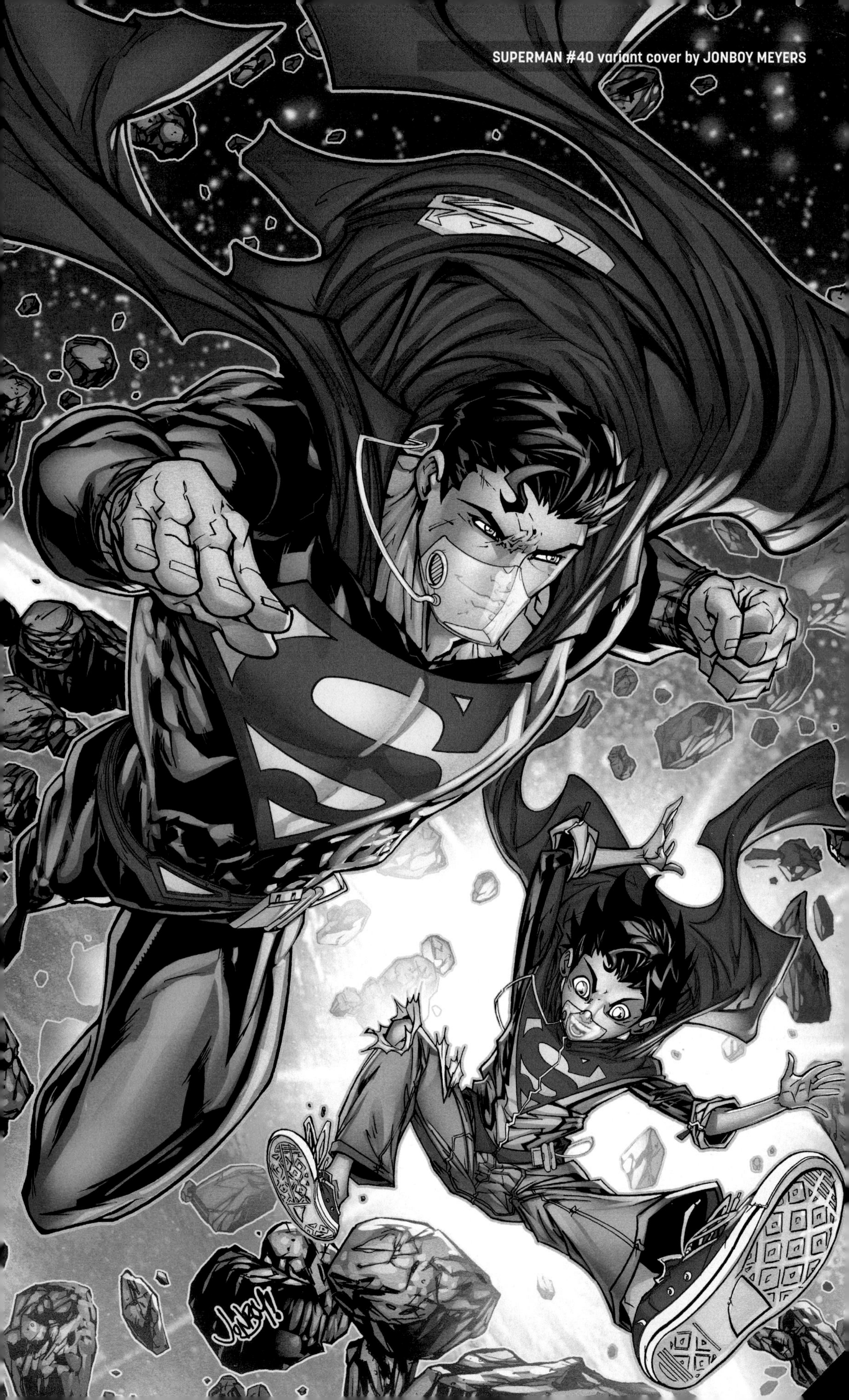

SUPERMAN #40 variant cover by JONBOY MEYERS

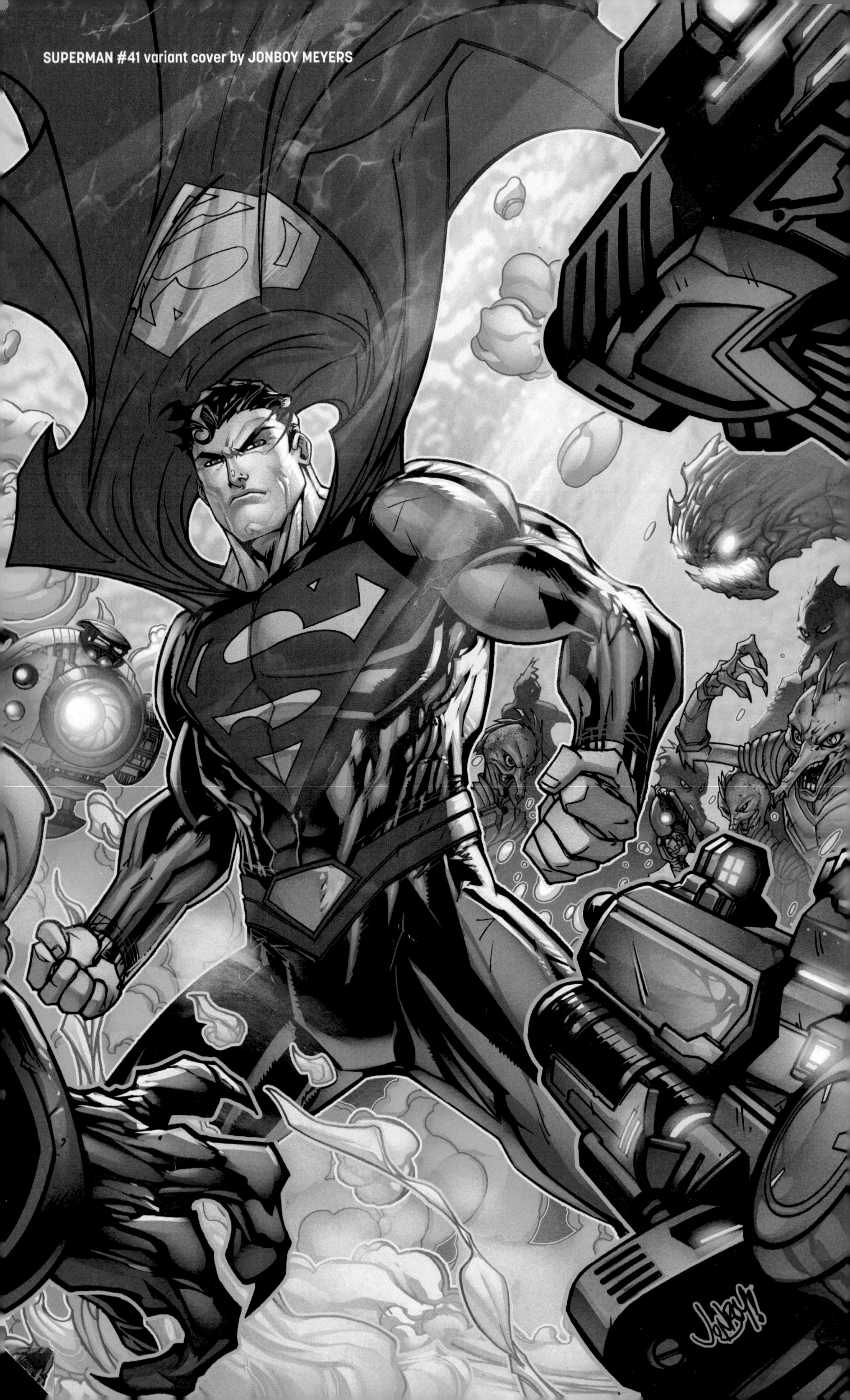
SUPERMAN #41 variant cover by JONBOY MEYERS